Hiking the
California Coastal Trail

Volume Two: Monterey to Mexico

To

the memory of Gary Matson and Winfield Mowder
may these true builders of community and caring not have died in vain,
— B. L.

Coastwalk founders Tom McFarling and Vivian McFarling,
who have provided constant and faithful support for seventeen years now,
— R. N.

Coastwalk board president Emily DeFalla
for her dedicated leadership as we grew through the 1990s,
— R. N.

and

all the people who have fought hard to save the California coast.
— B.L. and R.N.

Hiking the California Coastal Trail

A Guide to Walking the Golden State's Beaches and Bluffs from Border to Border

Volume Two: Monterey to Mexico

Bob Lorentzen and Richard Nichols

Forewords by
Mary Nichols, California Secretary for Resources
and
Peter Douglas, Executive Director, California Coastal Commission

BORED FEET PRESS – MENDOCINO, CALIFORNIA
COASTWALK – SEBASTOPOL, CALIFORNIA
2000

©2000 by Robert S. Lorentzen and Coastwalk.
First Edition, May 2000
Printed in the United States of America
on acid-free 20% recycled paper (100% post-consumer)

Design and composition by Elizabeth Petersen, Fort Bragg, California
Maps by Marsha Mello
Edited by Donna Bettencourt

Co-Published by

Bored Feet Press
Post Office Box 1832
Mendocino, CA 95460
(707)964-6629, (888)336-6199
FAX (707)964-5953
www.boredfeet.com

Coastwalk
1389 Cooper Road
Sebastopol, CA 95472
(707)829-6689, (800)550-6854
www.coastwalk.org/coastwalk

Distributed by Bored Feet Press

Library of Congress Cataloging-in-Publication Data
Lorentzen, Bob, 1949–
    Hiking the California Coastal Trail : a guide to walking the Golden State's beaches and bluffs from border to border / Bob Lorentzen and Richard Nichols : forewords by Mary Nichols and Peter Douglas : [maps by Marsha Mello]. — 1st ed.
        p.   cm.
    Includes bibliographical references and index.
    Contents: v. 2. Monterey to Mexico
    ISBN 0-939431-19-X
    1. Hiking—California—California Coastal Trail—Guidebooks.
    2. Trails—California—California Coastal Trail—Guidebooks.
    3. California Coastal Trail (Calif.)—Guidebooks. I. Nichols, Richard, 1942– . II. Title
GV199.42.C22C235 2000
796.51'09794—DC21

10 9 8 7 6 5 4 3 2 1

Contents

Feature Articles

Foreword

by Mary Nichols
Secretary for Resources, State of California

FROM MONTEREY BAY TO THE RUGGED OUTCROPPINGS OF BIG SUR, from the arroyos of San Luis Obispo to the warm beaches of Orange and San Diego counties, California's central and southern coasts are among the great treasures of the Golden State. All too often, however, visitors to these magnificent vistas speed by them in their cars. They would do well to stop those automobiles, get out, and spend some time on foot along our coast.

The California Coastal Trail allows them to do just that. Recognized by the White House as one of the nation's Millennium Legacy Trails, the Coastal Trail is indeed a wonderful way to experience our famous coastline. It weaves a thread linking historic sites, urban settings, wild shorelines and rolling, open bluffs.

Even brief walks along the Coastal Trail reveal a delightful variety of views—and sounds. One hears the deep bellowing of the Northern elephant seal male long before one sees him at Point Piedras Blancas in San Luis Obispo County. Two-ton bull seals lumber ashore while the smaller females cluster amidst the seawood with their newborn pups.

Sand dunes sprawling for miles along the central coast change shape daily as sand verbena, lupine and sea rocket struggle to take hold, slowly halting the flow of sand between sea and land.

Hearst Castle offers the opportunity to step back into the Roaring Twenties and visit the Xanadu on a hill that newspaper magnate William Randolph Hearst built. This world-renowned building and art collection is visited by thousands each day.

The many lighthouses along the coast hold a fascinating history of strong-willed, independent men and women who chose this solitary and difficult life.

The ocean along the coast can be both gentle and awe-inspiring. Challenging waves lure surfers and windsurfers from all over the world. Watching them from the meandering path along California's shore as they carve the waves is a favorite pastime.

On foot one can enjoy the variety of plants and wildlife. The coreopsis, or giant sunflower, the Monterey cypress, the Santa Lucia fir and the Torrey pine of San Diego are but a few examples of rare and unique plants one sees along the coast. Brown pelicans, cormorants and hawks soar and dive in the skies over the coast. Sea otters frolic in the protected coves of Point Lobos State Reserve. The annual monarch butterfly migration offers a brilliant display of color in groves of trees from Bodega Bay to Santa Barbara.

And then, of course, there is Big Sur, one of the most dramatic landscapes in the world with towering redwoods in deep canyons, cliffs plunging to the crashing surf, and a backdrop of rugged wilderness peaks.

Preserving and protecting California's coast is a central priority for myself and for the entire administration of Governor Gray Davis. With the dedicated help of thousands of hardworking members of the Department of Parks and Recreation, the Department of Fish and Game, the Coastal Conservancy, the Coastal Commission and many other state agencies, the State of California is deeply committed on a daily basis to protecting and preserving all its many treasures. These treasures of our glorious coast belong to all of us.

I applaud Coastwalk's efforts to complete the California Coastal Trail and allow access to the entire length of the coast so that all of us—and certainly future generations—have the opportunity to walk and really appreciate the beauty and the grandeur of California's magnificent coastline.

Sacramento
January 2000

Foreword

by Peter Douglas
Executive Director, California Coastal Commission

THE CALIFORNIA COAST IS MANY THINGS—it sustains a remarkable variety and abundance of life, it fires the imagination, sparks dreams, inspires creative expression, and offers sanctuary for body and soul. It is a place of unmatched natural magnificence, of mystery and power where the drama of beginnings and endings is perpetual. Yet for all its grandeur and potency, it is a fragile environment whose integrity and vitality depend on wise human stewardship.

California's story, accentuated by glory and shame, is inextricably linked to its seacoast where powerful forces collide with unpredictable regularity and spectacular and often terrible consequences. Over time, residents and visitors have forged an enriching and enduring bond with this bountiful and tantalizing reach of geography. Both home and resource, the coast is coveted by many who compete fiercely for a piece of the action and their own brief moment in the sun.

Those who take the time to walk the coast can most closely listen to and hear its stories wrapped around human and natural history. Every cove, beach, stretch of rugged cliffs and mountains, expanse of dunes, forest, scrub and grasslands, and each settlement of people along the way has a storied past whether great or small. Coastwalk is dedicated to exposing people to opportunities to hear and feel these stories, the poetry, the songs, and the passion of the coast.

The coast, like every unique piece of geography on Earth, is never finally saved. It is continually being saved. That is why public understanding and active support for coastal conservation is critical. People have the ability to destroy the coast—we have been fairly adept at that by eliminating nearly all coastal wetlands—but we must recognize the opportunity, indeed the obligation, to protect its natural and human community values through preservation and restoration. As a seasoned observer and participant, I am acutely aware of the power of even one individual committed to doing good works, not to mention the impact of many dedicated to the cause of environmental stewardship for the benefit of current and future generations. There is no better way to expand the cause of coastal conservation than to increase opportunities for people to get to, learn about and experience firsthand the wonders of the coast. By taking the time to go out and be with it, the traveler will learn about the opportunities to conserve this precious resource as well as the potential to do harm.

Coastwalk is a vision whose time is here. Formed by individuals who walk often in nature, the group is committed to the realization of a dream: a continuous coastal trail or series of linked ways making it possible for current and future generations to hike the length of California's coastline from Oregon to Mexico. Although not yet complete, the coastal trail is coming into being and long segments can be traversed by people with a spirit of adventure who are able to walk along the shore. This book is more than a useful guide for those who hike the coastal trail. It is a key to understanding and awareness that the coast is a delicately balanced ecosystem whose future well-being rests in our care.

As you use this guide, remember that the spectacular land- and seascapes you observe, the thriving natural habitats you visit, the physical and visual access you have, the quality of your recreational experience, and the public amenities offered by human communities along the way are all results of a protracted and intense struggle waged by environmentalists to "save the coast." California's world leadership in coastal conservation was brought into being by citizen activism and involvement. In 1972 California voters approved against powerful opposition a citizen's initiative that established our strong and effective coastal protection law. When threatened, as it has been many times, the public has effectively rallied to its defense. More than any environmental program I know, California's coastal protection law is a populist law. We must not take for granted the coast as it exists today. Only public initiative, support and activism are responsible for the coast we know today. Remember too, the greatest accomplishments of coastal conservation are the things you do **not** see—the views **not** spoiled, the public access **not** lost, the wetlands **not** filled, the urban sprawl **not** permitted, the natural landforms **not** destroyed, the agricultural lands **not** converted.

The greatest threat to the coast is public ignorance and apathy. That is why environmental education and public participation in coastal stewardship are so important. This book will help you find your way along the California coast, but more significantly, it will ignite awareness of your opportunity to help protect this marvelous natural heritage with which we are blessed.

San Francisco
December 1, 1997

Imagine a
California Coastal Trail

MAGINE A TRAIL along the entire length of the California coast, a diverse route from border to border that explores beaches, bluffs, headlands, bays and coves, staying as near the shore as possible for 1200 miles. Visualize a route that passes through wilderness areas, towns and cities, climbs over high ridges, and crosses hundreds of streams ranging from seasonal trickles to year-round creeks to major rivers.

Happily the California Coastal Trail (CCT) is no longer all in the mind, but too few people realize the CCT already exists, as diverse a long-distance trail as you'll find anywhere on the planet. The CCT has been being created, designated and built for twenty-two years. Finishing it will take several more years of dedicated work, but other long-distance trails have also taken years to complete. The Pacific Crest Trail has taken twenty-seven years to become almost complete since the first guidebook appeared and it's still not done. The Appalachian Trail took even longer.

Coastwalk and Bored Feet think it's time for the public to learn about the California Coastal Trail. We're working toward that goal along three fronts. First, since 1983 we've been telling people about the CCT, leading them on hikes along it every summer, and working to complete the trail.

Second, we've created and published two comprehensive guidebooks for the CCT. You hold the second volume, covering from Monterey County to the California-Mexico border, in your hands. We published *Volume One: Oregon to Monterey* in 1998.

CALIFORNIA
COASTAL TRAIL

Third, we're working to identify the trail by posting signs along the designated route. While the CCT is identified in many places as the Coastal Trail, and in a few others as Coast Trail, most of it isn't marked on the ground or on maps. In fact, in working to complete the CCT, we've found that this lack of clear identification along the trail is a big obstacle to people knowing about it. The initial project to sign the trail has already begun. We're starting in Del Norte County where the CCT is mostly complete. Coastwalk received a small grant to plan signing the CCT, with the goal of posting signs in selected areas over the next few years. Then we'll mark the trail along the rest of the California coast.

In the meantime, our guidebooks will let you find and follow the California Coastal Trail wherever you choose, for as many or as few miles as the spirit moves you. Be forewarned, though, that hiking the CCT can be contagious.

The Wondrous California Coast

California is both a land of superlatives and a land of extremes. It not only has the largest population and third largest land mass of the fifty states, it also has the longest coast of all the states except Alaska. The California coastline stretches, sprawls and twists for 1200 miles from the rain forest north to the desert south.

The CCT attempts to visit as much of the coast as possible while traversing the length of the Golden State in a reasonably efficient manner. In some places, topography prevents the CCT from passing directly along the shoreline. In other places, private or restricted property keeps the trail from the coastline. The Coastal Trail takes the through route along the coast, walking a fine line between the practical and the ideal. The CCT strives to see as much of the coast as possible without going far out of the way without good reason. In many places where the CCT misses a corner of the California coast, we'll tell you about a side trail you can take for a closer look at that corner by taking the side trail out to a point, down to a pocket beach or to another worthy feature.

State of the Trail

Does this California Coastal Trail run all the way along the coast? The answer is both a resounding yes and a qualified no. Yes, it starts on the beach at the Oregon-California line and ends, also on the beach, at the California-Mexico border. The CCT, however, hasn't yet been completed—it's a work-in-progress. In this book and *Volume One: Oregon to Monterey,* we present the trail as it now exists.

Roughly 62 percent of this current route follows existing trails and beaches. Much of the other 38 percent of today's CCT follows road shoulders on a provisional route that gets you from point A to point B, but isn't in most cases the ideal CCT route. Most of the 20 percent of CCT currently on back roads is reasonably safe to follow. This means that about 82 percent, or around 980 miles of the 1197-mile route (485 miles of the 597 miles in this volume), is currently recommended as reasonably safe and worthwhile to follow. The other 18 percent follows highway shoulders. While you can follow the CCT on these highway miles, we present them here more to point out that these parts of the real California Coastal Trail are missing and need to be created than to suggest you walk them.

Of course, if you feel compelled to follow the entire CCT, you can with extreme caution walk the highway segments. Coastwalk's Whole Hike did so successfully in 1996, and a man ran the entire CCT in 1999. Alternately, until the Coastal Trail is complete, you can bicycle these legs or follow them in a vehicle. If you choose to walk or bike any of the highway portions of the CCT, please follow the safety rules later in this chapter.

Day Hikes or Long-Distance Trek? You Choose

Basically you have three ways you can hike the California Coastal Trail. The first and most popular way is to day hike any portion of the CCT whenever you choose. Even if you only walk a mile or two you can still have a quality experience, a little taste of the Coastal Trail.

On the other extreme, we know that a few people will want to through-hike the CCT, that is to walk continuously along the entire 1200-mile trail. Such an undertaking should not to be considered lightly. Modified types of through-hiking include hiking half the CCT, hiking a set number of miles, whether 50 or 500, walking from Oregon to San Francisco or Monterey to Mexico, or hiking the CCT through the county you live in or your favorite coastal county. Before doing any through-hike, read **Through-Hiking the CCT** in the back of the book.

The third way to hike the CCT is to make it an ongoing project. Hike a section whenever you can and keep a checklist of what you've done, striving each year to cover another span of the trail. Perhaps someday you'll head out to hike that final section, and after it's done, you'll be able to take pride in the fact that you've hiked the entire California Coastal Trail.

The Rules of Road Walking

The most basic rule is "If you don't have to road walk, don't!" but when you do road walk, be careful, and follow these safety rules.

1. Always stay off the road and on sidewalks where available or on the highway shoulder.

2. Always walk with a friend or in a group. This considerably increases your visibility to drivers. Always walk single file. When in a group, the lead walker and the one bringing up the rear should carry a CAUTION or SLOW sign.

3. Always wear bright and/or reflective clothing. Your best bet is to wear bright clothing *and* a day-glo reflective highway vest.

4. When you need to cross the road, do so with extreme caution, always looking twice for traffic in both directions. When a group is crossing, they must cross together. Choose a perceptive and responsible leader and follow their lead.

5. It's usually best to walk facing oncoming traffic (bike in the same direction as traffic). In fact California state law says to walk facing traffic, but in many places where the highway's left shoulder has poor visibility or when no left

shoulder exists, it can be safer to walk along the right shoulder of the road.

6. Always pay attention to oncoming vehicle traffic. Many drivers slow for walkers beside the roadway, but all too many do not. Be aware of what approaching drivers are doing. Be especially careful of speeding vehicles, vehicles passing other vehicles, erratic drivers, wide vehicles and trucks. With the latter two, watch for wide side-view mirrors like many RVs have.

7. Never challenge vehicles for the right-of-way or do anything to unnecessarily distract drivers from their complex multiple tasks. That includes clowning around. If you're grouping up to take photos or observe nearby wildlife, make sure you're well off the roadway and not creating a hazard to traffic.

8. Never road walk at night. It's far too dangerous. Even twilight is a particularly hazardous time to be walking any road shoulder.

How This Guide Works for You

Given the immense and diverse nature of the California Coastal Trail, we've broken the guidebook into two volumes, this one for the southern half of California, Volume One for the northern half. We've divided the CCT into easily accessible sections you can hike whenever you're in the area. Every section has road access to one end or the other and most have vehicle access to both ends. This volume covers 78 CCT sections and 4 Alternate Route sections ranging from 2½ miles to 27¾ miles in one-way length, plus a special Alternate Route Section of 66 miles along the Santa Monica Mountains Backbone Trail.

The book describes the CCT from north to south because the coast generally unfolds better when you're walking south. The north to south orientation also lets the prevailing winds push gently or firmly at your back. Be aware, however, that if you're walking south with a strong wind at your back, you'll likely need to walk into the wind if you're returning to your starting point.

We provide detailed access information at the start of each section. At a glance you can tell the section's length in either miles or kilometers, how to get there, whether it's open only to hikers or also to bicyclists, equestrians or dogs, and what kind of surface the CCT section follows. The access information also tells you whether the section is easy, moderate or strenuous, and what the total elevation gain and loss are to walk it in the direction described. We tell you any cautions specific to that section and whom to call to get more information. The access information also details the section's facilities—water, restrooms, phones, picnic areas—and where to find the nearest campgrounds, lodgings, and hostels.

With one exception, every section's access point is at its northern end, or at least leads to its northern end in the shortest possible fashion. Every section also has a southern access point which, unless we state otherwise, also starts the next section.

We describe every section in enough detail so that you can clearly follow it from our text. Additionally we point out what's special about each section and provide a bit of human or natural history to give you a sense of the place. Our 32 feature articles expand on the cultural and physical aspects of the coast.

We show every CCT section on a map created for this guide. Artist Marsha Mello drew the maps to scale from USGS topographic maps. Instead of showing

Map Legend

A Access – CCT Trail Section

A Alternate Access

——— California Coastal Trail

– – – – Alternate Trail/Access Trail

〜〜〜 Water

ⵔ ⵔ ⵔ ⵔ ⵔ Water Crossing

═══ Road/Highway

• • • • • Side Trail

P Parking Area

⌂ Hostel/Accommodations

▲ Campground/Site

☐ Place of Interest

⟨⟩ Private or Protected Area

o—o Gate

◊ Spring

∧ Summit/Peak

++++++ Railroad Track

∧∧∧ Stairs

Sand

Riprap

Reef

Bridge

the contour lines, we show the features most useful in finding your way along the coast. The map legend at left will help you read the maps. Each map indicates its scale and which way is north. While the maps in the book thoroughly support the text, if you feel naked hiking without topographic maps, by all means invest in the USGS maps and take them on your trip. These would be most useful in the steepest terrain, like Big Sur for example.

Of the 83 CCT sections in this volume, three-fourths are less than 9 miles long and offer good day hikes. Of the remaining 24 sections that are 9 or more miles long, four in Big Sur and one in northern Santa Barbara County offer great backpack trips, although you can day hike portions of these sections from a road at one end or the other. Most of the remaining longer sections include considerable road mileage. We hope to improve these parts of the CCT in coming years by getting them off the road.

Have a Safe Hike

The Ten Commandments for CCT Hikers

1. **Never turn your back on the ocean** when you're in the tidal zone or directly above it. **Oversized rogue waves** can strike the coast at any time. **Watch for them. They have killed people.** They are especially common in winter but can occur in any season. **Changing tides** offer the other big danger when walking near the ocean. When walking the coast, carry a current tide table for the area and know how to read it. Don't let rising tides trap you. **Dangerous undertows and rip currents** can occur anywhere along the California coast and can pull anyone in the water out to sea. The farther north you go in California, the colder

the ocean is. Especially north of Point Conception, the ocean may be icy and unforgiving, unsafe for swimming without a wetsuit except perhaps in summer.

2. **Stay back from cliffs.** Coastal soils and rocks are often unstable. Don't get close to the cliff's edge, and never climb on cliffs unless there is a safe trail.

3. **No trespassing.** Property owners have a right to privacy. Please stay off private property unless there's an easement or a presecriptive right of access.

4. **Wild animals** range from very tiny to large. **Ticks** are the most persistent pest, especially in winter and spring. Deer ticks, the smallest of ticks, may carry Lyme disease, which can be a nasty and persistent problem if a Lyme disease carrying tick attaches to you for 24 hours or more. **Mosquitoes** may be a problem anywhere, and wasps, biting spiders, scorpions, and even rattlesnakes occur in coastal areas. In tidal areas, watch for **jellyfish** washed up on the beach and **sea urchins** in tidepools—both have painful stinging spines. On wild parts of the coast, especially north of Point Conception, you may encounter **bears** or **mountain lions,** always potentially dangerous. Bears are most often a problem when you're in camp, so keep all food and utensils put away when not in use. If you encounter a mountain lion on the trail, don't run. Make eye contact and make yourself appear larger by spreading your arms or raising your hiking stick over your head. Skunks and raccoons can also be a problem, but they're generally not life threatening like the larger animals. The bite of any mammal may transmit deadly rabies.

5. **Watch for poison oak** which grows in many forms on coastal bluffs. Any contact can cause a painful, itching rash. Remember, leaves of three, let it be! In winter, poison oak's bare branches can still give you a rash. **Stinging nettles** can cause serious if temporary skin irritation when touched. Also be careful with **mushrooms** and other plants you don't know since many poisonous species occur in coastal areas.

6. **Crime.** Be sure to lock your vehicle when you park it at a trailhead. Leave valuables out of sight, at home, or take them with you. When camping, try not to leave valuables unattended. There are criminals who prey on campgrounds along the coast.

7. **Stream crossings** or fords can be deadly. Deep or rushing waters can overcome even the strongest, most experienced hikers. Never ford a creek or river if it seems unsafe. Always use a hiking stick or two and proceed carefully when you cross moving streams. If you're wearing a backpack, undo the waist belt before crossing. We try to mention in the specific trail section when a stream ford might be dangerous, but even small creeks can become dangerous after rainstorms. High tides and changing tides can also affect coastal stream crossings. In addition, this book includes a few river and bay crossings where you must either hire a boat to take you across or make a long road detour. Never attempt those crossings without a boat of sufficient size.

8. **Be careful with fire.** Always extinguish campfires until cold to the touch. You generally need a campfire permit (free) to have a fire outside a developed campground. Never start a fire in an unsafe spot. Fires may be banned altogether during the dry season.

9. **Trail safety and courtesy.** Never cut switchbacks. Equestrians always have the right of way on trails, because you can move aside for a horse much more easily than its rider can yield to you. When you yield to horse traffic, always

Please Don't Trash our Coast

Most litter, other than that poorly placed banana peel, is not immediately dangerous to humans. Litter does have serious costs, however. It not only degrades the beauty of the natural environment, it also pollutes the ocean and can be deadly to wildlife. Even something as small as a cigarette butt, the filter of which doesn't break down, can be lethal when eaten by a marine organism or bird. Many people toss their orange peels onto the natural environment, but an orange peel can take years to decompose.

If you think litter is a minor problem, consider that each September about 50,000 volunteers comb the coast for California Coastal Cleanup Day, collecting more than three-quarter million pounds of trash and fifty tons of recyclables. In 1998 they collected 333,876 cigarette butts.

Most of the California coast remains relatively unspoiled. Do your part to keep it that way by not littering. Even better, show your appreciation for Mother Nature by hiking with a trash bag and using it to collect trash you find in otherwise pristine places, even little things like cigarette butts, orange peels, bottle caps and pull tabs.

When we request that nobody trash our coast, we also mean preventing unnecessary development on the the bluff's edge, in fragile dunes, wetlands, and other sensitive habitat. That includes no new offshore oil drilling or seabed mining.

stand as far off the trail as possible and speak in a calm, normal voice to the rider to assure the animal that you are a human being. Bicyclists on trails must yield to hikers and horses and slow to walking speed on blind corners.

10. **Always take responsibility for yourself and your party.** The authors and publishers cannot and will not be responsible for you on the trail. Information contained in this book is correct to the best of the authors' knowledge at press time. Authors and publishers assume no liability for damages. **You must take responsibility for your safety and health while on the trail.** The coast is still a wild place. Safety conditions of trails, beaches and tidepools vary with seasons and tides. Be cautious, heed all warnings and cautions in the book, and always check on local conditions. It is always better to hike with a friend. Know where you can get help in case of emergency.

OTHER THINGS TO REMEMBER WHEN HIKING THE CCT: 1. Always park off roadway facing direction of traffic. 2. Never park blocking a gate or road.

How's the Weather on the Coast?

The climate of the California coast can best be described as Mediterranean, although it varies greatly from north to south. Warm dry summers and temperate wet winters characterize this Mediterranean climate found no where else in the United States. The dry season, generally from May through September, offers the best season for hiking, especially in the north where the rains may linger in spring. On the California coast, dry is a relative term since fog and low clouds also characterize the summers, with more persistent and cooler fog in the north than in the south. The persistence of the marine moisture in the north also moderates the temperatures there with Eureka's average August high temperature of 61 degrees contrasting with San Diego's 77 degrees.

During the rainy season from October through April, the California coast still offers excellent hiking opportunities, especially between storms. You'll find, however, that stream fords and river crossings may be more difficult or even impossible during this wet season, especially after big storms, so plan accordingly. You may also encounter beaches eroded of their sand and swamped by high tides and storm-driven waves. Like the temperatures, the amount of precipitation varies greatly from north to south. Crescent City averages 70 inches of rain annually, while San Francisco gets about 20 inches and San Diego typically only 12 inches. Expect higher precipitation where the coast is backed by mountains, like on the Lost Coast which averages around 100 inches each year, or in Big Sur which gets about 50 inches. Winter temperature variations from north to south are generally less than in summer with Eureka's January average of 47 degrees not that different from San Diego's 55 degrees.

Keep in mind that the California coast typically experiences cycles of drought and flood so that averages may not mean much in a given year. Also, the powerful moderating influence of the ocean limits coastal temperatures to a relatively narrow daily and seasonal range with freezing temperatures in winter and temperatures above 90 degrees in summer uncommon. When the California Coastal Trail meanders as little as two or three miles inland, the ocean's moderating influence is lessened significantly.

Always bring layered clothing when hiking along the California coast so that you can add or subtract layers as the weather and your activity dictates. Shorts and T-shirts may be appropriate in summer, but always have enough layers along so that you won't freeze your buns if a big thick, damp gray fogbank moves in from the ocean. You'll want to add waterproof clothes and boots to the mix when hiking in winter.

Preparing for Your Hikes

You can day hike the California Coastal Trail for a mile or two, you can hike entire sections, or you can walk the whole CCT from Oregon to Mexico. The longer your hike, the more gear you'll want to consider taking. If you're making an extended CCT trek, be sure to read **Through-Hiking the CCT** in the back of the book. Here we'll only discuss what to take if you're day hiking.

ESSENTIALS TO TAKE ON YOUR HIKE:
- Layered clothing: T-shirt, long sleeve shirt, shorts, long pants, sweater, sweatshirt, windbreaker, rain gear
- Sunscreen
- Insect repellent
- Sunglasses
- Small first aid kit, including moleskin for blisters
- Hat with a brim
- Current tide table

HIGHLY RECOMMENDED FOR ALL BUT THE SHORTEST HIKES:
- Water container
- Water filter or purification tablets

- Flashlight or headlamp, extra batteries
- Matches and fire starter
- Pocket knife
- Extra food
- Map and compass
- Watch

ADDITIONAL SUGGESTIONS:
- Spare socks
- Bandanna
- Toilet paper and plastic trowel
- Binoculars
- Camera
- Field guides to wildflowers, birds, trees, seashore life

Monterey County

THIS VAST COUNTY sits smack in the middle of California's 1100-mile coast. With famous destinations like Carmel, Point Lobos, Monterey, Pebble Beach and Big Sur, it's no wonder Monterey County is the most popular tourist destination on California's coast. Monterey's spectacular 144 miles of CCT are second in length only to Humboldt's 148 miles, offering a microcosm of this most diverse trail.

In northern Monterey County, the CCT follows the wild beaches of Monterey Bay where abundant birds thrive in dunes and wetlands rimmed with agricultural lands. Then CCT joins the multi-use Monterey Peninsula Recreation Trail, following it along a busy urban waterfront past two public wharves, Monterey State Historic Park and the superb Monterey Bay Aquarium. In Pacific Grove, CCT visits verdant shoreline public parks, then rounds Point Pinos, the tip of the Monterey Peninsula, to explore the wave swept rocky shore and wondrously white dunes of Asilomar State Beach. The Coastal Trail continues along the dramatic coast west of world famous 17-Mile Drive, then turns inland through the exclusive Del Monte Forest/Pebble Beach resort area, returning to the coast at sparkling Carmel City Beach. After a corner of Carmel, CCT follows Carmel State Beach to reach sublime Point Lobos State Reserve. At Point Lobos the Coastal Trail explores "the greatest meeting of land and water in the world," passing thrilling vistas at most every turn in this superb array of coastal habitats harboring abundant marine and bird life.

Leaving Point Lobos, the CCT has not yet traversed one third of Monterey County's gloriously varied shore. After touring affluent Carmel Highlands, CCT must follow Highway 1's shoulder through Garrapata State Park, Big Sur's northern gateway. Happily Garrapata's staff is creating new trail links, routing much of the Coastal Trail off the narrow highway. CCT hikers know they have reached Big Sur when they see the sweeping Bixby Bridge perched at the rugged mouth of Bixby Creek. CCT turns inland, winding along unpaved Old Coast Road through wild coastal hills and valleys, then returns to the coast dramatically, descending to the mouth of the Big Sur River and exploring the shore, slopes and ridges of Andrew Molera State Park. A short highway leg brings Monterey's CCT to its halfway point around Pfeiffer-Big Sur State Park.

The CCT promptly splits into two distinct routes, one of them offering a dramatic highlight and literal high point for California's Coastal Trail. CCT's Big Sur high route traces the coastal ridge through Ventana Wilderness, passing over the highest peak on California's coast, 5155-foot Cone Peak, on a challenging 43-mile route that's recommended for prepared hikers in spring and fall. CCT's Big Sur low route provides a highway-shoulder alternate if abilities or timing don't fit the high route. When these routes rejoin, 27 miles of coastal Monterey County remain. Heading south, CCT explores an expansive marine terrace unlike any other place in Big Sur, follows Highway 1 past Willow Creek's amazing chasm and the amusing outpost called Gorda, then explores the coastal mountains of Silver Peak Wilderness on another challenging and spectacular high route before returning to the highway to leave Monterey County and Big Sur.

Monterey County's leg of the CCT spans from urban culture to rugged wilderness, from beaches to mountains, and from redwood forests to cactus patches. Included in the bargain are wetlands and dunes, waterfalls and mountain meadows, gentle marine terraces and precipitous shoreline cliffs, historic districts and world famous golf courses, and gentle bay and wild ocean..

SECTION 1
Pajaro River to Moss Landing

DISTANCE: **4⅞ miles (7.8 kilometers).**

OPEN TO: **Hikers. Equestrians allowed on beach August 16 to April 14.**

SURFACE: **Beach, highway shoulder, road shoulder.**

ACCESS POINT: **Zmudowski State Beach.**

HOW TO GET THERE: **On Highway 1, 1.5 miles north of Moss Landing, take Struve Road west, then turn west onto Giberson Road and go about 2 miles to the parking lot for Zmudowski State Beach.**

OTHER ACCESS: **Moss Landing State Beach. In summer when you can ford Pajaro River, Palm Beach on Beach Road north of river in Santa Cruz County has access.**

DIFFICULTY: **Easy.**

ELEVATION GAIN/LOSS: **Negligible.**

CAUTIONS: **If hiking from Palm Beach, you must be able to ford Pajaro River to continue south.**

FURTHER INFORMATION: **Monterey State Parks (831)649-2836**

FACILITIES: **Moss Landing has a few stores and restaurants. Chemical toilets at Zmudowski State Beach and Moss Landing State Beach.**

CAMPGROUNDS: **Sunset State Beach on previous section has 90 sites.**

LODGING: **Watsonville has several choices.**

The extraordinary and complex Monterey coastline begins in the north with a long sandy beach covered in two CCT sections. The fishing boat harbor at Moss Landing, with the adjacent bird-rich Elkhorn Slough to its east, separates the two long beach walks. This sandy and remote area contrasts sharply with the sophisticated urban environment on the scenic and rocky Monterey Peninsula.

From the parking area follow the boardwalk west through the dunes to the sandy beach. This first section of Monterey begins on the quiet, undeveloped Zmudowski State Beach with only farmland and dunes in the area. If you are on a quest to walk every foot of the California coast, walk the beach north from the parking lot for ¾ mile to the mouth of the Pajaro River, then backtrack south to the parking area. Add 1½ miles to the book's mileage if you go to the river.

Walk south along the tideline of this lightly visited broad beach. The sand dunes back up against extensive wetlands with good birding, but the land behind the dunes is privately owned.

Around 1¾ miles you leave Zmudowski State Beach for Moss Landing State Beach. Jetty Road which lies to the east is part of the route of the Coastal Trail. First CCT continues south to the end of the beach at 2¼ miles, marked by the

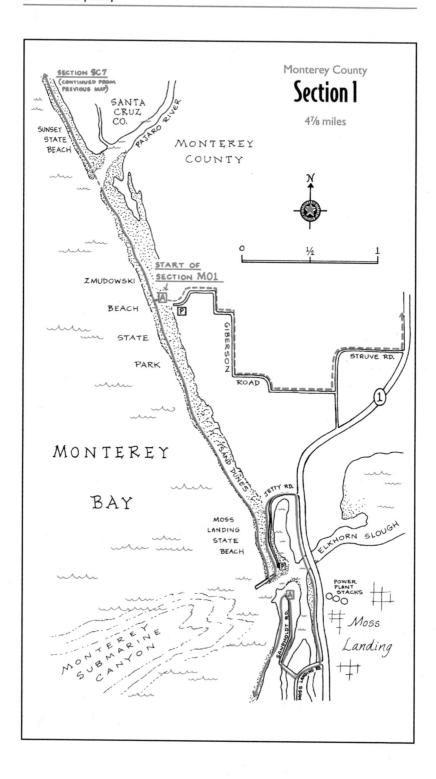

SECTION SC7
(CONTINUED FROM PREVIOUS MAP)

SANTA CRUZ CO.

SUNSET STATE BEACH

PAJARO RIVER

Monterey County
Section 1
4⅞ miles

MONTEREY COUNTY

N

0   ½   1

START OF SECTION M01

ZMUDOWSKI

BEACH

STATE

PARK

GIBERSON

ROAD

STRUVE RD.

1

MONTEREY

BAY

SAND DUNES

JETTY RD.

MOSS LANDING STATE BEACH

ELKHORN SLOUGH

POWER PLANT STACKS

Moss

Landing

MONTEREY SUBMARINE CANYON

SANDHOLDT RD.

MOSS LANDING RD.

The California Coastal Trail Whole Hike of 1996

On National Trails Day, June 1, 1996, six hikers met at the Oregon-California border to begin a hike of nearly 1200 miles along the spectacular, diverse California coast to Mexico. When they completed the trek three months and three weeks later, this remarkable journey became the first group hike of the entire California Coastal Trail. Hundreds of coast lovers joined the six "Whole Hikers" for anywhere from a few miles up to half the CCT. They included Coastwalk organizers, trail activists, housewives, mothers, students, reporters and authors. Donald Murphy, then California State Parks Director, hiked the first eight days. That first day more than 40 supporters came to cheer them on.

Of the six who planned to do the Whole Hike, remarkably all six succeeded. These four women and two men ranged from 44 to 68 years of age, came from all over California and included one Oregonian. Some were lifelong hikers. One described herself as "Not a hiker at all," but that changed by trip's end. The Whole Hike was a life changing journey for virtually everyone involved. This marathon walk forever changed public perception of the California Coastal Trail. This book grew directly from that hike.

Without numerous support people both on and off the trek, the Whole Hikers never would have made it. Most notably the Ford Motor Company provided a grant and two support vans. Volunteer drivers helped shop and cook, meeting the weary hikers at day's end to shuttle them to campground, hostel or community center for the night. One van pulled a trailer with the heavy gear, so hikers could carry only a daypack.

The group walked 1156 miles in the 112-day trek. They averaged a bruising 12.4 miles a day, not counting 16 rest days. Twice the group hiked 20 miles in a day, the longest being 21 miles from Surf to Jalama on the Santa Barbara coast, but the hardest being the 20-mile day from Palomarin at Point Reyes National Seashore up, down and around the rugged Marin Headlands to the Golden Gate Hostel overlooking San Francisco and the Golden Gate Bridge. Their brisk pace covered 15 miles or more on a dozen days.

The most frightening experience? Chest high waves swamped the hikers at a low-tide-only point near remote Cape Mendocino, then the incoming tide trapped them for four hours in a tiny cove. There the drenched, demoralized hikers huddled by a smoky fire and wondered if their luck had run out barely a tenth of the way into their ambitious trek. The plucky group escaped, closer and more determined.

Highlights? Too many to mention, but they included backpacking the Lost Coast through Humboldt and Mendocino counties, crossing the Golden Gate Bridge into San Francisco, rounding Point Conception, and completing the thousandth mile at Santa Monica in Los Angeles County. But the biggest thrill of all was walking up to the Mexico border on the 112th day, each of the Whole Hikers proudly knowing that she or he had completed the Journey of a Lifetime, walking the entire California Coastal Trail.

The event won the Trails for Tomorrow Award from the American Hiking Society, one of ten given, and the Trail Merit Award from the California Trails Conference. In late 1999 California Governor Gray Davis picked the Coastal Trail as California's Millennium Legacy Trail, a national honor.

Also in 1999 a solo runner became the first to run the entire CCT. The 55-year-old Kent Bien finished his run in 81 days. Several others hikers made CCT long distance treks that year, but no one else claimed to have done the whole trail.

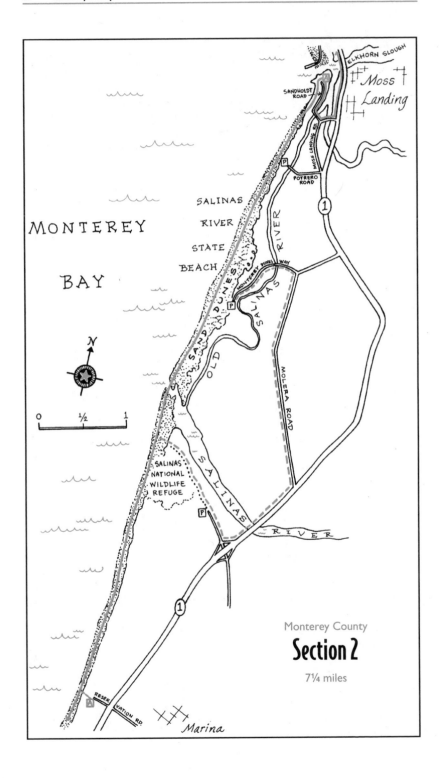

ELKHORN SLOUGH

Moss
Landing

SANDHOLDT
ROAD

MOSS LANDING RD.

POTRERO
ROAD

1

SALINAS

RIVER

STATE

BEACH

MONTEREY

BAY

SALINAS RIVER

MONTEREY DUNES WAY

OLD SALINAS RIVER

N

MOLERA ROAD

0   ½   1

SALINAS

SALINAS
NATIONAL
WILDLIFE
REFUGE

P

RIVER

1

Monterey County
Section 2
7¼ miles

RESERVATION RD.

Marina

jetty at the mouth of Moss Landing Harbor. A half mile offshore begins one of the great canyons on the planet, the Monterey Submarine Canyon, rivaling the Grand Canyon in depth. Find the State Park access road at the jetty and follow it back to the north to 2¾ miles. If you're day hiking you might want to return to the Zmudowski parking lot from here. The Coastal Trail route follows Jetty Road east to Highway 1 at 3 miles. Turn right and walk the highway shoulder south, crossing the bridge over Elkhorn Slough at 3½ miles. The power plant stacks just ahead rise several hundred feet into the air, a landmark all around Monterey Bay.

Continue along the highway shoulder past the power plant. Before 4¼ miles, turn right onto Moss Landing Road which leads into the little port town full of fishing boats, funky buildings, antique stores, and eating establishments. Cross the bridge over the bay. The road turns north and becomes Sandholdt Road. You'll pass marine supply stores, the ocean research facility for the Monterey Bay Aquarium, a deli/fish market, and the fleet of boats docked in the harbor. Complete the walk on the beach at the mouth of the bay at 4⅞ miles.

SUGGESTED ROUND TRIPS & LOOPS: From either Zmudowski or Moss Landing State Beaches, walk out and back on the beach for a serene 4½-mile round trip. Moss Landing State Beach at the end of Jetty Road north of the harbor has a parking fee.

SECTION 2
Moss Landing to Marina State Beach

DISTANCE: 7¼ miles (11.7 kilometers).

OPEN TO: Hikers.

SURFACE: Beach.

ACCESS POINT: Moss Landing.

HOW TO GET THERE: From Highway 1 north of Monterey, turn west on Moss Landing Road, cross the bridge, then take Sandholdt Road to its end at .6 mile.

OTHER ACCESS: Salinas River National Wildlife Refuge.

DIFFICULTY: Moderate.

ELEVATION GAIN/LOSS: Negligible.

CAUTIONS: Salinas River may be unfordable in winter. Soft sand makes this walk more strenuous than a typical beach walk. Watch for big waves on the beach.

FURTHER INFORMATION: Salinas River State Beach (831)649-2836, Marina State Beach (831)384-7695, Salinas River National Wildlife Refuge (510)792-0222.

FACILITIES: Chemical toilets at each end. Water at Marina State Beach.

CAMPGROUNDS: Marina Dunes RV Park (831)384-6914 is near end of section. Sunset State Beach is about 10 miles north.

LODGING: Available in the city of Marina.

This long, quiet, serene and scenic beach walk features extensive dunes, big surf, a national wildlife refuge and soft sand that makes you work harder for each mile. If you like quaint port towns, Moss Landing Harbor merits a look at its cluttered fishing port: fishing and pleasure boats both in their prime and derelict, old buildings, seafood restaurants, and marine supply stores.

Inland from the harbor, Elkhorn Slough covers 2500 acres of salt marsh, mudflats, channels and salt ponds. This tidal embayment provides important habitat for the hundreds of thousands of shorebirds, more than 250 species, that reside or migrate here. It's also a major nursery for myriad sea and land creatures, including the diverse invertebrates that feed the abundant birds. The endangered brown pelican and California clapper rail nest here, and the golden eagle and peregrine falcon are also seen. Consider a side trip to explore Elkhorn Slough either by kayak or canoe or on the more than five miles of trails through the reserve.

Historically the Salinas River emptied into the sea at Moss Landing, four miles north of its present mouth. Then in 1909 locals redirected the river by excavating a channel through the sand dunes where the river meets the ocean today. This decreased flooding and made the rich soil of the old riverbed available for farming. Moss Landing's present entrance and harbor were dredged in 1947 to take advantage of the deep waters of the Monterey Submarine Canyon offshore which keeps the mouth free of sandbars. The sand slides into the deep marine canyon instead of piling up along the shore.

From the south side of the harbor entrance at the end of Sandholt Road, head south along the tideline of the beach. First the southern arm of Moss Landing Harbor lies to the east, then you parallel the Old Salinas River channel. Shorebirds and quiet are the norm here. Not many people make this trek in the soft sand. Beyond one mile you pass the access trail from the end of Potrero Road.

Keep walking south with the dunes above the tideline becoming larger as you go. Around 2⅞ miles another access path runs from the beach to the end of Monterey Dunes Way off Molera Road. At 4 miles you reach the mouth of the Salinas River. The mouth is blocked by a sandbar in summer and may be open or closed in winter, depending on river flow and storms. If the sandbar is in place, or when the river is shallow enough to ford, you can continue south along the beach. Otherwise you must retreat to the last access path and follow the Alternate Route.

South of the river mouth you walk through the Salinas River National Wildlife Refuge, an area of beach, dune and estuary alive with wildlife including endangered terns, snowy plovers, brown pelicans and many other birds. Take care not to disturb the birds here, especially the snowy plover which nests on the dry upper beach and is very hard to see. A 200-foot long derelict barge resting in the surf creates its own unique habitat with barnacles, mussels and seaweed clinging to the hull, and eddies of sand forming inside the hull. Eventually rust, the pounding waves and sand will claim this derelict.

After lunch and wildlife observation, continue the march down the beach. Keep an eye to the ocean for sea otters and gray whales. Around 5 miles, large dunes rise steeply from the beach. As you continue south, you may see hang gliders launching from the dunes ahead.

At 7¼ miles a long boardwalk reaches the beach. This section of CCT ends here, but the next one continues along the beach. If you're not continuing south,

Watch Out for That Wave!

The waves we see dashing against the coast start hundreds of miles offshore. As winds blow across the ocean's surface, they create waves of various sizes. A wave's size depends on wind velocity, duration and the distance the wind blows across the open ocean.

Waves break, showing a churning crest of foam along their leading edge when they become oversteep in deep water or when they enter shallow water. Waves break when they reach a water depth around 125% of their height. So we see endless sets of breakers as we explore the shore, each wave different than the wave preceding it, surf varying greatly from one day to the next, sometimes even within a day.

"Never turn your back on the ocean" is a cardinal rule of the coast because each wave can be so different from the last. The constant attack of waves upon the shore fascinates us with its ever changing motion, but it also holds great danger. This danger increases the closer you get to the water and the larger the waves.

Two kinds of waves hold particular danger, sleeper waves and tsunamis. Sleeper waves, also known as rogue or killer waves, can occur any time although they're infrequent and unpredictable. They are most common on days of particularly big surf, when storms are active far at sea or in winter, but you never know when they'll strike. As the nickname killer implies, they present grave danger, sometimes being twice the size of the prevailing surf. They strike with powerful force, running far up the beach.

Large sleeper waves can sweep shoreline visitors into the sea. These rogues have claimed the lives of many an unwary seaside visitor. When you walk the coast, you must be aware that sleeper waves can strike at any time. Always be ready to retreat up the beach at the first hint of oversize waves. If you get swamped, be ready to abandon your gear or backpack. It's better to lose your possessions than your life.

The second dangerous wave, the tsunami or tidal wave, results from earthquakes, slides or volcanic eruptions at sea. Tsunamis offer extreme and widespread danger. You cannot outrun a tsunami. If you see one from the beach it's probably too late. Unlike sleeper waves, tsunamis are predicted by seismographic readings. Radio and TV stations broadcast tsunami warnings whenever seismological activity indicates they might occur. If you hear such a warning, get away from the coast.

Tsunamis 75 feet high have been seen. Tsunamis travel 400 miles an hour and are hardly visible on the open ocean. As they approach shore they rise up suddenly. The shallow depth of California's continental shelf lessens the chance of 75-foot-high tsunamis, but smaller tsunamis can cause serious damage. The April 1964 Alaska quake launched tsunamis at Crescent City, California. A series of 12-foot waves smashed ashore, running a third of a mile inland, destroying 29 blocks of the business district and causing $27 million in damage. Crescent City was rebuilt, its harbor today protected by 1600 25-ton concrete tetrapods shaped like children's jacks.

Be aware of the dangers of oversize waves wherever you explore California's outer coast.

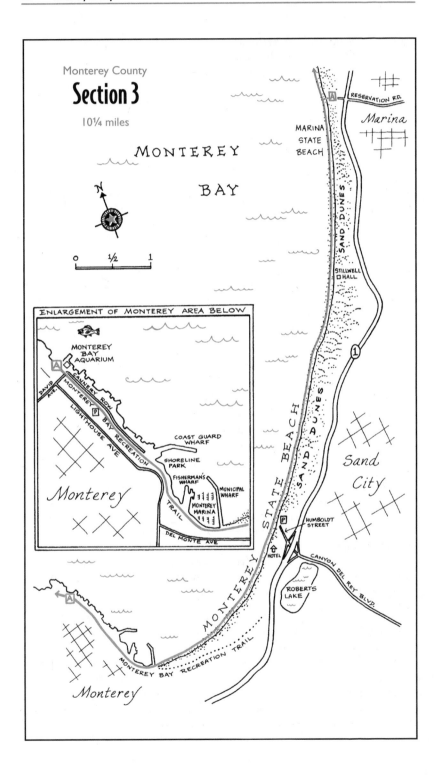

Monterey County
Section 3
10¼ miles

MONTEREY

BAY

N

0   ½   1

ENLARGEMENT OF MONTEREY AREA BELOW

MONTEREY
BAY
AQUARIUM

A

DAVID AVE.

CANNERY ROW

MONTEREY BAY RECREATION

LIGHTHOUSE AVE.

P

COAST GUARD
WHARF

SHORELINE
PARK

FISHERMAN'S
WHARF

MUNICIPAL
WHARF

MONTEREY
MARINA

TRAIL

Monterey

DEL MONTE AVE

A

RESERVATION RD.

Marina

MARINA
STATE
BEACH

SAND DUNES

STILLWELL
HALL

1

MONTEREY STATE BEACH

SAND DUNES

Sand
City

P

HUMBOLDT
STREET

HOTEL

CANYON DEL REY BLVD.

ROBERTS
LAKE

A

MONTEREY BAY RECREATION TRAIL

Monterey

either return the way you came or follow the boardwalk east ⅜ mile to the Marina State Beach main parking lot at the end of Reservation Road.

ALTERNATE ROUTE: When you can't ford the Salinas River, leave the beach at 2⅞ miles to walk Monterey Dunes Way to Molera Road, go south to Highway 1, walk highway shoulder across river, turn right into Salinas River National Wildlife Refuge and follow road and trail to the beach south of the river.

SUGGESTED ROUND TRIPS & LOOPS: A walk around Moss Landing followed by a walk on the beach is a pleasant way to spend the day. Walking the beach to the Salinas River and back is 8 miles. Starting at Marina State Beach and walking to the Salinas River and back is about 7 miles. Also consider a walk along the trails at Elkhorn Slough. Call (831)728-2822 for information.

SECTION 3
Marina State Beach to Monterey Bay Aquarium

DISTANCE: 10¼ miles (16.5 kilometers).

OPEN TO: Hikers. Bicyclists on the Monterey Peninsula Recreation Trail.

SURFACE: Beach, paved trail.

ACCESS POINT: Marina State Beach.

HOW TO GET THERE: Take Reservation Road exit from Highway 1 at the north end of the city of Marina. Drive west to the parking area at the end of Reservation Road.

OTHER ACCESS: Monterey Beach Hotel has public parking and beach access adjacent to it. Anywhere along the Monterey Peninsula Recreation Trail. The waterfront district of Monterey has abundant parking.

DIFfiCULTY: Moderate.

ELEVATION GAIN/LOSS: Negligible.

CAUTIONS: Some of the beach may be impassable at high tide.

FURTHER INFORMATION: Monterey State Beaches, Monterey State Historic Park (831)649-2836, Monterey Bay Aquarium (831)648-4888.

FACILITIES: Marina State Beach has restrooms, water. Monterey has all services.

CAMPGROUNDS: Veterans Memorial County Park is in Monterey. Laguna Seca Recreation Area 7 miles east has 183 sites.

LODGING: Abundant in Monterey area.

The shoreline of Monterey Bay sweeps magnificently along the sandy shore of Marina, Sand City, Seaside, and the great Monterey dunes system, then hooks

Monterey: Center of Mexican California

Juan Cabrillo, a Portuguese captain sailing for Spain, entered Monterey Bay and claimed the area for Spain in 1542, just 50 years after Columbus' maiden voyage to America. In 1602 Sebastian Vizcaino landed at Monterey, naming it for his patron, the count of Monterey. Vizcaino described a fertile land of mild climate with a "noble harbor." By 1770 the Spaniards established northern California's first non-Indian settlement at Monterey.

In 1770 Gaspar de Portola came by land to establish the settlement and a military garrison, or presidio. Though his 1769 expedition came down the Salinas Valley on the way to discovering San Francisco Bay, they missed Monterey Bay because Vizcaino's described ideal harbor did not exist. When Portola's second expedition reached Monterey by land in 1770, Father Junipero Serra soon arrived by ship to establish northern California's first mission. In 1775 the provincial capital of California was moved from Loreto, Baja California to Monterey. Monterey remained the capital for almost 75 years. Juan Bautista de Anza made two overland trips to Monterey, in 1774 and 1776. On the second journey, he brought 247 settlers and 500 cattle to fill out the new town.

As the official seat of government, Monterey was visited by French, English and American ships and emissaries between 1786 and 1796. Still, the town remained isolated, dependent on the two supply ships that arrived from Mexico twice each year. The isolated colonists frequently held fiestas and balls to pass the time. In 1804 Alta California was divided from Baja, with Monterey remaining Alta's capital. When two Argentine ships attacked Monterey in 1818, they easily attacked, sacked and burned the poorly armed settlement, claiming it for the new Argentinian republic, but they left ten days later. Monterey really changed and began to prosper after Mexico won independence from Spain in 1821. Alta California affirmed its allegiance to Mexico in 1822, soon holding its first election and choosing its first native-born governor. Still, only 114 white civilians called Monterey home in 1826. When Richard Henry Dana visited Monterey in 1836, he declared it "decidedly the pleasantest and most civilized looking place in California." That same year, California revolted against Mexican rule, becoming a free state for eight months, with American influence growing, before Mexico reestablished its rule.

In 1842 a U.S. Navy captain, his ship and crew seized Monterey and flew the American flag, believing that the U.S. was at war with Mexico. Two days later they withdrew and apologized, but the Alta California government soon collapsed. Mexico installed two more governments in the next two years, but never really regained control. The United States declared war on Mexico in May 1846 and on July 7 Commodore John Sloat raised the Stars and Stripes over Monterey and declared California a U.S. possession. The war ended within six months.

By the end of 1848, Monterey had a U.S. Post Office. In September 1849 the California state constitutional convention opened in Monterey's Colton Hall. The Spanish influence was still strong, with more than half the 48 delegates speaking only Spanish. The state constitution was ratified on November 13 and the state capital was moved to San Jose. Monterey entered a sleepy period, with a net gain of only 100 residents in the next 50 years. In the 1880s Spanish was still the predominant language spoken at Monterey. In the early 20th century, the sleepy Spanish pueblo finally began to prosper as an American town with distinctive Hispanic influence.

westward to the rocky points of the Monterey Peninsula. This walk offers a great place to stretch out the legs on some very soft sand and observe the Monterey Peninsula as you approach it. The last 1½ miles follows the paved and popular Monterey Peninsula Recreation Trail along Monterey's waterfront full of California history and tourist attractions. This section ends at the splendid Monterey Bay Aquarium where you can experience all the different habitats hiding beneath the ocean's surface as well as some of the onshore habitats you've walked past.

To reach the Coastal Trail from the access point at the main Marina State Beach parking area, walk the boardwalk ⅜ mile to the beach. If the winds are favorable you might be entertained by hang gliders taking off from the deck built for their launching. The Coastal Trail heads north and south along the tideline. As you head south, the beach quickly becomes more quiet and remote as beach strollers turn back and high dunes isolate the area.

Beyond 1⅛ miles you pass the boundary of the former Fort Ord Military Reservation, now providing miles of open space plus places for a new state college and state park. Continue down the beach. At 2½ miles a large wall of riprap drops off the dunes into the surf. It protects the closed enlisted men's club, Stilwell Hall. State Parks now manages the dunes and the beach. Unless the tide is very low, you must carefully climb over the rocks, walk in front of the hall, then find and take the unmarked trail leading south and gently downhill through iceplant to a road. Walk the road to return to the beach around 2⅞ miles.

Continue along the beach through an area once used for war games. Ahead the Monterey Peninsula grows large as you draw near. You finally leave the former fort and reach the badly degraded dunes of Sand City around 5⅜ miles. This whole area has been mined for its fine beach sand.

At 6¾ miles you'll see the tall Monterey Beach Hotel sitting on the dunes to your left. California State Parks has restored the adjacent dunes of Monterey State Beach to illustrate how beautiful the dunes will look after more extensive restoration plans are completed. You can walk on a boardwalk to observe the area. As you continue south, freshwater Roberts Lake sits about ¼ mile inland. A side trail leads from the beach to the lake. Adjacent to the lake at Roberts Avenue, the Monterey Peninsula Recreation Trail reaches its northern terminus. One could follow that paved path all the way to the Monterey Bay Aquarium at this section's end, but for now the Coastal Trail continues along the beach.

As CCT continues down the coast, the beach remains wild but the buildings and bustle of the Monterey area become more prominent. The beach angles southwest then west, aiming for the Monterey Peninsula. As you pass more access ways, you'll find more people enjoying the beach. Finally you walk the narrow strand along the Window on the Bay portion of Monterey State Beach. As the sand ends at 8¾ miles, you come to the Municipal Wharf #2. At the wharf you'll find a popular cafe if you need a lunch break.

After you leave the Municipal Wharf, Monterey State Historic Park nearby on your left features buildings surviving from Monterey's early days. You pass Fisherman's Wharf before 9¼ miles, the Coast Guard Pier around 9⅜ miles, then continue on the busy paved trail for nearly a mile, the last half of it through Cannery Row made famous by John Steinbeck. The sardine canneries closed long ago, but their remnant buildings today house restaurants, bars and abundant gift

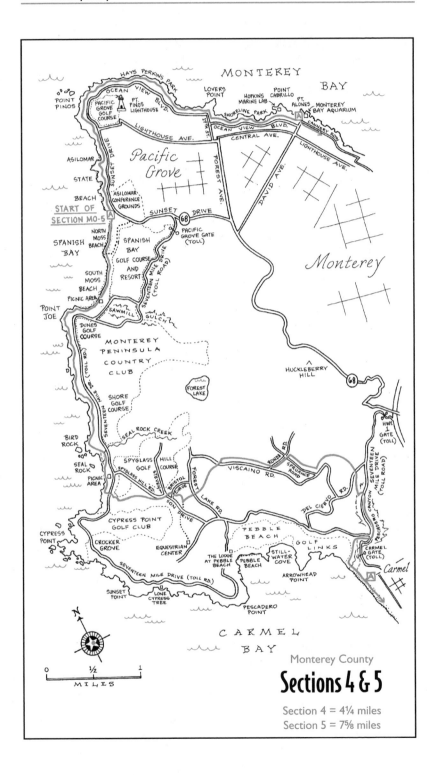

Monterey County

Sections 4 & 5

Section 4 = 4¼ miles
Section 5 = 7⅝ miles

shops of every kind. The paved trail follows the old railroad right-of-way overlooking the waterfront, paralleling the street called Cannery Row downhill on the right.

When you reach David Avenue, you've passed the halfway point on the California Coastal Trail. The Monterey Bay Aquarium is a half block downhill on your right.

SUGGESTED ROUND TRIPS & LOOPS: From Marina State Beach south to Stilwell Hall and back makes a pleasant 5¼-mile round trip on a seldom walked beach. From around the Municipal Wharf in Monterey, walk north for miles on the beach and return, or follow the Monterey Peninsula Recreation Trail to explore the many attractions of the Monterey waterfront. Another nice town walk, the Path of History, branches off the Recreation Trail at Monterey State Historic Park.

SECTION 4
Monterey Bay Aquarium to Asilomar State Beach

DISTANCE: 4¼ miles (6.8 kilometers).

OPEN TO: Hikers on all. Bicyclists on first 1¼ miles of trail, streets paralleling CCT beyond that. Dogs OK on leash, except in Lover's Point Park.

SURFACE: Paved trail, trail, boardwalk.

ACCESS POINT: Monterey Bay Aquarium.

HOW TO GET THERE: Exit Highway 1 at top of hill south of Monterey and north of Carmel onto Highway 68 West. Go 2.8 miles, then go right on David Avenue to its end at Cannery Row.

OTHER ACCESS: Anywhere along route.

DIFFICULTY: Easy.

ELEVATION GAIN/LOSS: 100 feet+/100 feet-.

CAUTIONS: Watch for bicycles on first 1¼ miles. No fee parking near access point is a rare commodity.

FURTHER INFORMATION: Monterey State Parks (831)649-2836, Monterey Bay Aquarium (831)648-4888, Pacific Grove Parks Department (831)372-7965, Asilomar State Beach (831)372-4076.

FACILITIES: None at start. Restrooms, water, phone and picnic tables at Lover's Point Park, picnic tables at Perkins Park.

CAMPGROUNDS: Veteran's Memorial County Park is in Monterey near the Presidio, about 1½ miles southwest. Laguna Seca Recreation Area 7 miles east has 183 sites.

LODGING: Asilomar Conference Center at section's end has 315 rooms. More upscale rooms along route at Green Gables Inn, Martine Inn, Seven Gables Inn, Grand View Inn, Lover's Point Inn and Borg's Ocean View Motel.

This convoluted, remarkably rocky urban shoreline offers a great hike around the dramatic tip of the Monterey Peninsula. You'll likely find this trail section frequented by locals and visitors at its beginning and end portions, but you may find very few walkers along the even more dramatic part around Point Pinos, where you'll see the 1855 lighthouse, the oldest continuously operating beacon on the west coast (open to the public Saturdays and Sundays, 1–4 pm). Of course the wonderful Monterey Bay Aquarium and the shops and historic buildings of Cannery Row offer tempting distractions at the start of this section. The entire hike follows the shore of the Pacific Grove Marine Gardens Fish Reserve where you can observe floating and foraging sea otters, sea kayakers, and spouting whales in season.

Only a short block uphill from the entrance of the Monterey Bay Aquarium, on David Avenue just down from Wave Street you'll find the Monterey Peninsula Recreation Trail, a popular paved multiple-use path that follows the old Southern Pacific Railroad right-of-way through town near the waterfront. You can follow it east almost 4 miles to Roberts Lake in the town of Seaside (CCT's Monterey Section 3 follows the first 1½ miles). This section heads northwest along the waterfront, following the paved level path to the Monterey city limits in only 400 feet. Here you enter the town of Pacific Grove—Butterfly Town, USA. Cyclists and skaters can continue along the 2-lane paved path on the left. Hikers want to follow the gravel track beside it on the right through Shoreline Park.

As you pass Stanford University's Hopkins Marine Lab on the bay side, you can glimpse the rocky coastline where birds perch on offshore rocks. At ¼ mile rocky Point Cabrillo juts seaward, the southernmost of two points named for the Portuguese navigator, the first European to sail the California coast. Continue past a pretty cove and beach where the shore is fenced from public access. It's all marine lab property until a rest bench at ⅜ mile. Contour along the curving path beside a convoluted rocky shore punctuated by picturesque Monterey cypress. At ½ mile lovely little Jacobsen Park perches on a rocky knoll across Ocean View Blvd.

At ⅝ mile the gravel track splits in two. While you can take either path, the right one offers better coastal views as you pass through verdant Berwick Park approaching Lover's Point. After the forks rejoin, enter Lover's Point Park before one mile. Here you can either descend to a beach or contour along the bluffs.

The blufftop path passes a big parking lot. As it meets 17th Street, the Monterey Peninsula Recreation Trail ends as the old railroad right-of-way continues straight onto private property. You want to turn right and follow the sidewalk 300 feet, then veer to the right into Lover's Point Park (no dogs, please) past restrooms and picnic tables, with the rocky point a short side trip directly ahead.

By 1⅛ miles the gravel path resumes, turning northwest between the street and the shore. Follow the narrow path northwest along the shore of Hays-Perkins Park. No bikes are allowed on the path beyond this point. Pass two stairways down to the nearby beach around 1¼ miles. Contour through the park past exotic vegetation including giant dudleyas or hen and chicks.

Pass a parking area and a stairway to a tiny beach at 1½ miles. Your path turns north along the shore until 1¾ miles, then angles northwest and west toward Point Pinos. On reasonably clear days you can look north across the broad mouth of Monterey Bay to Point Santa Cruz 23 miles away, backed by the Santa Cruz Mountains.

Pass tiny, wooded Esplanade Park across the street at 2 miles. Around 2⅛ miles the path becomes indistinct for the first time, but it's still easy to follow this lightly traveled shoreline. You encounter more rest benches and side paths to the ocean's edge, just fewer people. Round a rocky point with vehicle access beyond 2¼ miles. The path improves here as you near Point Pinos.

Your path virtually disappears at a small beach beyond 2⅜ miles, then resumes. Around 2½ miles Crespi Pond and a golf course lie across the road, with the Point Pinos Lighthouse on a knoll beyond them. CCT continues along the shore, circling the point on an inconstant path.

At 2¾ miles an unmarked spur on the right crosses a sandy beach and heads

California Lighthouses

California's rugged 1200-mile coastline has long been renowned for the fury of its hazardous waters and the deception of its offshore reefs and rocks. Only after California entered the United States in 1850 was any effort made to provide navigational aids. In 1854 Alcatraz Island Lighthouse in San Francisco Bay became the Golden State's first, soon followed by Fort Point inside the Golden Gate, Farallon Island 25 miles outside the Gate, and Point Loma near San Diego, four of the original eight west coast lighthouses. By 1900 48 lighthouses guided ships along the California shore.

Today 33 of theses still stand, with 25 operational. The California Coastal Trail passes by or at least comes within view of most of them. In San Mateo County, the CCT passes two lighthouses converted to hostels where you can spend the night.

Only two of the 14 lighthouses on the California coast between Monterey and Mexico allow visitors during specific days and hours. In Pacific Grove on CCT Section Monterey 4, it's easy to stop by and see the 1855-era Point Pinos Lighthouse. The oldest continuously operating light station on the west coast, it allows visitors every Saturday and Sunday from 1 to 4 pm.

You'll need to plan ahead to visit dramatic Point Sur Lightstation. It's west of Highway 1 a few miles north of Andrew Molera State Park and Section Monterey 10, perched 361 feet above the surf on a large volcanic rock. The stone lighthouse, in continuous operation since it was first lit in 1889, opens for guided tours on Saturdays and Sundays year round and on some other days during the busy season. Occasional moonlight tours from April to October make a visit even more dramatic. Call (831)625-4419 for information.

You won't find another lighthouse open to visitors on the California coast from Point Sur south. To the north up the California coast in Marin County you can tour the Point Reyes Lighthouse in the National Seashore on interpretive tours held most days, and the Point Bonita Lighthouse in Golden Gate National Recreation Area on weekend afternoons. In Mendocino County you can visit the Point Arena Lighthouse, open for tours on most days, and the recently restored Point Cabrillo Lighthouse, open for tours during special events. The Crescent City Lighthouse in California's far north opens for tours on days when low tides permit.

northwest to the tip of Point Pinos, ¼ mile round trip. The Coastal Trail turns southwest following the unsheltered Pacific Ocean shore. Your narrow track disappears again at 3 miles. Either walk the beach or the broad gravel shoulder beside the road, then contour beside or through dunes draped with iceplant. Around 3⅛ miles you reach the only house on this section that lies on the ocean side of the road. (The dwelling predated the Coastal Initiative by 25 years.) The property is fenced to dissuade hikers. Either continue along the road shoulder or turn right on a path beside a green barrel that leads into the dunes, then follow the rocky tideline south.

Either way you go, the path improves by 3¼ miles, once again following the bluff's edge above an amazing rocky shoreline. Now you can see Point Joe to the southwest on the next CCT section. You soon follow a boardwalk past a viewing gazebo, then continue on gravel tread alternating with boardwalks, passing many spurs to the rocky then sandy tide zone.

A small sign welcomes you to Asilomar State Beach around 3⅜ miles. Drop to a sandy beach at 3½ miles, returning to the blufftop before 3⅝ miles. After paralleling Sunset Drive briefly, a boardwalk returns you to the shoreline. Continue on a gravel path from 4 miles.

Beyond 4⅛ miles the landscape changes dramatically. Along the shore ahead lie the milelong sands of North Moss Beach backed by the Spanish Bay Golf Course and Resort. Your path soon curves left to end at Sunset Drive. You can either walk the beach or the broad road shoulder south ⅛ mile to section's end. The landmark indicating the end of the section is a pergola across the road that is the start of a boardwalk into the Asilomar Conference Grounds, a state park facility. If you'd like to take a break inside, the boardwalk leads to the public reception area in less than ¼ mile where a large stone fireplace, restrooms and gift shop may be worth a visit.

SUGGESTED ROUND TRIPS & LOOPS: Walk the shoreline northwest to Point Pinos, round the point, then loop back on Lighthouse Avenue through Pacific Grove's shopping district. You can also walk the entire section, take a stroll through the lovely Asilomar Conference Grounds to see the historic architecture, then catch the #1– Lighthouse Avenue bus back to your starting point.

HOW TO IMPROVE CCT HERE: The only notable improvement would be to have a designated path along the middle section from 2⅛ to 3¼ miles.

SECTION 5
Asilomar State Beach to Point Joe to Carmel City Beach

DISTANCE: 7⅝ miles (12.3 kilometers).

OPEN TO: Hikers. Equestrians from Seal Rock Creek Beach south to section's end. Bicyclists can follow 17-Mile Drive's shoulder without paying a fee.

SURFACE: Trail, boardwalk, beach, road shoulder.

ACCESS POINT: Asilomar State Beach.

HOW TO GET THERE: Exit Highway 1 at top of hill south of Monterey and north of Carmel onto Highway 68 West. Go 2.9 miles to Sunset Drive where you follow the highway left. Follow Sunset Drive 1.2 miles to access point opposite the pedestrian boardwalk entrance to Asilomar Conference Grounds.

OTHER ACCESS: Various points along 17-mile Drive (toll charge for vehicles).

DIFFICULTY: Easy.

ELEVATION GAIN/LOSS: 665 feet+/665 feet-. To Seal Rock Picnic Area: 55 feet+/55 feet-.

CAUTIONS: Please stay off adjacent private property and respect privacy of residents. Equestrians have the right of way on horse paths—give them plenty of room to pass. Please respect the quiet required by golfers when you walk past them playing their round.

FURTHER INFORMATION: Asilomar State Beach (831)372-4076, 17-Mile Drive (831)624-3811, Carmel City Beach (831)624-3543.

FACILITIES: Restrooms, water, phone at Asilomar Conference Grounds Reception Area near start, at Bird Rock Overlook and at Carmel City Beach at end.

CAMPGROUNDS: Veteran's Memorial County Park is in Monterey near the Presidio, about 2 miles southeast. Laguna Seca Recreation Area 11 miles east has 183 sites.

LODGING: Asilomar Conference Center at section's start has 315 rooms. Upscale lodgings along route include The Inn at Spanish Bay and The Lodge at Pebble Beach. The Monterey Peninsula has many other choices.

MAP: See page 34.

You've probably heard of the famed 17-Mile Drive that explores the exclusive Pebble Beach/Del Monte Forest corner of the Monterey Peninsula. Billed as "Nature's Drive-Through," you can motor the scenic toll road for a fee. The California Coastal Trail offers a healthier, no-fee and vehicle-free tour of the same environs, reaching one of the trail's affluent highlights. This CCT section traverses the Del Monte Forest lands of the venerable Pebble Beach Company, passing the seven world famous golf courses on Monterey Peninsula's wooded windward side. CCT passes right by the famed Pebble Beach Golf Course and ends at the north end of sparkling Carmel City Beach. Very few people know about this combination of trails that explore shore and forest in this swank resort area, and even fewer people use these paths. Enjoy this unique and lightly traveled leg of the

CCT and marvel that a public trail explores these gorgeous, posh environs. Another choice is bicycling the 17-Mile Drive, also toll free.

The section starts on the beach side of Sunset Drive across the street from the pergola (gateway) marking the west end of the pedestrian boardwalk into the Asilomar Conference Grounds. Follow the path that leads down to the tideline of Asilomar State Beach. Turn left and follow the tideline southwest along the shore of Spanish Bay. (Another choice is to follow the boardwalk of the Spanish Bay Shoreline Pedestrian Trail from Asilomar State Beach until it ends, then continue along the tideline.) You quickly leave the Asilomar grounds and follow the tideline of what has traditionally been called North Moss Beach.

By ⅜ mile you pass a small point marking your passage to South Moss Beach. Continue along an increasingly wild beach that contrasts with the groomed greenery of the Spanish Bay Golf Course not far inland. Pass the Spanish Bay Beach parking lot around ½ mile and continue down the strand. Cross Sawmill Gulch beyond ¾ mile, approaching the end of the beach. The sandy beach ends by one mile where CCT swings northwest, paralleling a rough cobble beach to a point. After rounding a north-facing promontory, the path heads for west-facing Point Joe.

Reach Point Joe around 1⅜ miles. This most exposed point on the entire Monterey Peninsula was named for the Chinese man who lived here in a driftwood shelter in the early 1900s. From the point CCT follows the west shoulder of paved 17-Mile Drive briefly, but it soon picks up a separate path along the bluffs that occasionally returns to the road shoulder. Continue past small promontories around 1¾ miles and 2⅛ miles, then past a small cove around 2⅜ miles where the Shore Course of the Monterey Peninsula Country Club lies across the street. As you continue south, CCT soon parallels the paved access road to a large parking lot at the point overlooking Bird Rock at 2¾ miles. You might make use of the only restroom and drinking fountain directly on this CCT section before its end. In addition to providing nesting sites for gulls and seabirds, barren Bird Rock provides a haul-out for sea lions and harbor seals.

From the Bird Rock Overlook, CCT follows the Nature Trail south from the point. It soon leads to the little-known, little-used fine white sand beach at the mouth of Seal Rock Creek. Where the path forks, you can descend to the beach for the shortest route or continue on the Nature Trail, slightly longer. Seal Rock rises beyond the breakers to the southwest.

Just beyond the beach the Nature Trail ends at a signed equestrian trail. Follow the horse path, marked by green and white posts with a green square, along the bluff's edge. Around 3¼ miles the equestrian trail meets 17-Mile Drive. If you must have a coastal view on the next stretch or want to visit Fanshell Beach, Cypress Point or the Crocker Grove of Monterey cypress to the southwest, you need to follow the road shoulder from here. The Coastal Trail crosses 17-Mile Drive and follows the horse trail inland, climbing southeast on the loose-sand track into the dunes. As you labor up this tough hill (tough because of the loose sand), be sure to turn around and enjoy the grand vistas of the coast you just walked and wooded Cypress Point southwest.

At the top of the dune, the green blazes inexplicably give way to red ones. Follow the red trail as it veers left and soon descends with golf course views, coming to a path marked Del Monte Forest Trail. Make a sharp left turn here and ascend. You're still on the red-marked route, but you see no marker for about 200 feet. You soon come to a road with red markers on both sides. You can see the Spyglass Hill Clubhouse not far north. Walk east across the road, then veer right to follow the blue-marked path south along a ridgetop.

At 4 miles CCT crosses a road called Bristol Curve. Continue on the blue path, marked with orange at intersections, parallel to Stevenson Drive. By 4⅛ miles your path meets Stevenson and an important intersection. The blue path crosses the road to head for the nearby stables. You want to turn left and follow the orange-marked path northeast into forest, then follow it east with the driving range on your right.

Around 4¼ miles your orange trail crosses Forest Lake Road and climbs northeast. You can take a ¾-mile side trip down Forest Lake and Alvarado, turning right to descend 17-Mile Drive to the famous Lodge at Pebble Beach where you might lunch at one of four restaurants or visit the coastal access to Stillwater Cove, down Cypress Drive from the lodge.

CCT ascends northeast on the orange/blue trail, lined with fences here, through forest, crossing quiet roads in an exclusive residential neighborhood. Continue ascending the path until it crests a hill and descends briefly to cross a quiet street. Follow it across a 2-lane street and down through a gully, then rise to another 2-lane road, cross it and continue your ascent.

When you reach a trail junction with a golf tee on your left, turn right to head southeast with the Poppy Hills Course on your left. Contour beside the course to 5⅛ miles, where you meet Ronda Road near a stop sign. Cross Ronda and follow the orange-blazed trail across Spruance Road around 5⅜ miles. Then your path veers right, following orange blazes paralleling Spruance on a gentle descent. After veering away from Spruance your orange path descends to a curving road at 5¾ miles. Stay on its left past a green-marked trail junction, then climb along a fire road that soon turns southeast, then south through the de facto wilderness of Del Monte Forest.

Where the fire road swings left to head east, CCT continues south, descending a narrow path. At a vague junction, head south on the path marked by an orange arrow. Descend to a 2-lane road, cross it and continue downhill on the orange blaze path. While the tread is indistinct, the route is well blazed. Tread improves after another paved road. Descend to a trail junction around 6⅛ miles where you veer right to follow the orange path. Contour above deep, wooded Pescadero Canyon on your left, which divides Del Monte Forest from Carmel.

You soon descend south through the forest with filtered views of the coast ahead. Around 6⅝ miles you drop to a busy 2-lane road, famous 17-Mile Drive. Turn left and follow it 125 feet. Just before a road sign at a Y, descend southwest on an unmarked trail. It comes to 2-lane Carmel Way. You can turn right and descend the road shoulder 400 feet to its crossing of Pecadero Creek. The CCT crosses the road and descends on vague tread. Turn right and follow an old path, in places stone wall-lined, downstream. It passes a private path with a bridge over Pescadero Creek, then continues downstream through a pleasant redwood grove.

About 700 feet before Carmel Way, the path disappears. Pick your way through tall grass to a stone pillar beside Carmel Way around 7⅛ miles. Set in the stone wall facing the road, a brass plaque reads "HORSE TRAIL—REDONDO REAL." Cautiously cross Carmel Way to a gravel road with a stone garage on its right.

This house designed by Frank Lloyd Wright perches above Carmel City Beach.

Follow that road 350 feet to its end at the famous Pebble Beach Golf Course. Then follow a vague path marked by low stakes along the left edge of the course above Pescadero Creek, heading southwest toward the creek's mouth. Please be quiet if golfers are present. Near the mouth of the creek, descend a narrow path to the beach at 7½ miles. Turn left and follow the tideline to section's end at the Carmel City Beach parking lot at the end of Ocean Avenue at 7⅝ miles.

If the trail is flooded near the creek's mouth in winter, continue along the street ¼ mile, passing Carmel Gate where Carmel Way becomes North San Antonio Avenue. Follow it to the stop sign at 4th Avenue. Turn right and walk what looks like a driveway with a metal fence on your right. In 125 feet you'll find a post marked "ACCESS." Follow this path 250 feet to a forks at the top of the beach. The right fork drops to the tideline. Take the left fork south past volleyball posts and a restroom to section's end at the parking lot at Ocean Avenue's end.

ALTERNATE ROUTE: From the dune path junction at 3¼ miles, you can continue along the shoulder of 17-Mile Drive around Cypress and Pescadero points until you reach the brass plaque on Carmel Way at 8¼ miles (ideal for bicyclists).

SUGGESTED ROUND TRIPS & LOOPS: Walk the shoreline to Point Joe or Bird Rock, returning via the Spanish Bay Shoreline Trail. Walk the whole section to Carmel City Beach and catch the #22 bus, asking the driver for a transfer and directions to Asilomar. Explore the scenic Asilomar Conference Center and its architecture.

HOW TO IMPROVE CCT HERE: Build a path on the few portions where you must walk the road shoulder. Clean up the delightful stone wall path on lower Pescadero Creek. Build a designated path down the right of way to the mouth of the creek.

SECTION 6
Carmel City Beach to Point Lobos State Reserve Entrance

DISTANCE: 3½ miles (5.6 kilometers).

OPEN TO: Hikers. Dogs OK off leash on City Beach and on leash on State Beach.

SURFACE: Beach, trail, road shoulder, highway shoulder at end.

ACCESS POINT: Carmel City Beach at Ocean Avenue.

HOW TO GET THERE: Turn west off Highway 1 south of Monterey at Milepost 73.85 onto Ocean Avenue. Go 1.1 miles to its end and park.

OTHER ACCESS: Anywhere along Scenic Road, or on Highway 1 at Mileposts 71.4 and 71.1.

DIFFICULTY: Easy.

ELEVATION GAIN/LOSS: 80 feet+/ 80 feet-.

CAUTIONS: In winter and early spring you may not be able to ford the Carmel River. Please stay off adjacent private property.

FURTHER INFORMATION: Carmel Beach City Park (831)624-3543, Carmel River State Beach (831)624-4909.

FACILITIES: Wheelchair accessible restrooms, water, phone at start, restrooms around ½ mile and at San Jose Creek State Beach.

CAMPGROUNDS: Veteran's Memorial County Park is in Monterey near the Presidio, about 3 miles northeast. Laguna Seca Recreation Area 12 miles east has 183 sites.

LODGING: Asilomar Conference Center at start of previous section has 315 rooms. The Monterey Peninsula has many other choices, with upscale lodging at nearby Lodge at Pebble Beach. Most affordable choices in Carmel include Carmel River Inn and Colonial Terrace Inn, both of which are an easy walk from the CCT.

This hike follows the dramatic shoreline of the posh little seaside town of Carmel. Carmel originally gained fame as an artist's community, an important stop among the bohemian social circles of the early 20th century.

From the access point you can either walk the sparkling white sand beach or take the wooded, paved blufftop path above it. For the path, walk back up Ocean Drive to the first corner. Turn right and walk along Scenic Road. You'll pick up the paved blufftop path ¼ mile from the parking lot. The description follows the beach route.

From the parking lot descend west 300 feet to the tideline. Turn left and walk the tideline south along the fine white sand beach. By ¼ mile a broad stairway on your left descends from the Scenic Road blufftop path. It's the first of eight stairways and a ramp linking the blufftop and the beach.

Continue along the broad beach, enjoying its dramatic setting bracketed by Point Lobos to the south and Pescadero Point to the northwest. Pass a stone stairway beyond ½ mile and continue to the end of the beach before ¾ mile. At low

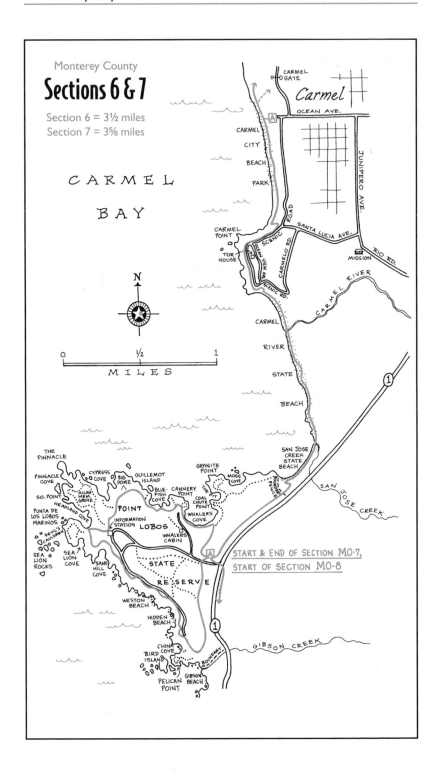

Monterey County
Sections 6 & 7

Section 6 = 3½ miles
Section 7 = 3⅝ miles

CARMEL BAY

CARMEL
Carmel

CARMEL GATE
OCEAN AVE.

CARMEL CITY BEACH PARK

JUNIPERO AVE.

CARMEL POINT

SANTA LUCIA AVE.

SCENIC ROAD

OCEAN VIEW AVE.

CARMELO RD.

SCENIC RD.

TOR HOUSE

RIO RD.

MISSION

CARMEL RIVER

N

CARMEL RIVER STATE BEACH

1

0   ½   1
MILES

THE PINNACLE

SAN JOSE CREEK STATE BEACH

SAN JOSE CREEK

PINNACLE COVE

CYPRESS COVE

BIG DOME

GUILLEMOT ISLAND

GRANITE POINT

MOSS COVE

SO. POINT

ALLAN MEM. GROVE

BLUE-FISH COVE

CANNERY POINT

THE PIT

BOUNDARY FENCE

POINT

HEADLAND COVE

COAL CHUTE POINT

PUNTA DE LOS LOBOS MARINOS

INFORMATION STATION

LOBOS

WHALERS COVE

DEVILS CAULDRON

WHALERS CABIN

SEA LION ROCKS

SEA LION COVE

SAND HILL COVE

STATE

RESERVE

START & END OF SECTION MO-7,
START OF SECTION MO-8

WESTON BEACH

HIDDEN BEACH

1

CHINA COVE

BIRD ISLAND

BOUNDARY

GIBSON CREEK

PELICAN POINT

GIBSON BEACH

tide you might be able to continue over slippery tidal rocks, but not beyond nearby Carmel Point, occupied by a Frank Lloyd Wright-designed house. The Coastal Trail turns southeast to leave the beach by the last stairway. At the top of the stairs, turn right and continue along the ocean-fronting shoulder of Scenic Road. While no developed path exists beyond the stairs, locals and visitors alike walk the road frequently—that's why there's a 15 MPH speed limit. Follow the blufftop as it swings toward Carmel Point with a last look at the beach below.

After you round Carmel Point at one mile, parallel Scenic Road south with open ocean on your right and picturesque homes on the left. The big stone house before Stewart Way is Tor House, the home of poet Robinson Jeffers until he died there in 1961 (tours by reservation on Friday and Saturday, 831-624-1813). Before 1¼ miles both CCT and Scenic Road make a hairpin turn left. Walk another 250 feet along the shoulder to the corner of Ocean View Avenue, then take the stairway on the right that descends to Carmel River State Beach.

Walk the beach down near the tideline and follow it south. The beach becomes increasingly wild on the way to the mouth of the Carmel River, thanks to the Carmel River Nature Preserve to the east. Watch out for large waves along the steep tideline, backed by a dangerous undertow.

When you reach the mouth of the river before 1⅝ miles, you may have an easy ford of the highly seasonal stream, or perhaps the river mouth is closed off by the barrier beach. When the river runs high after winter and spring rains, however, you may need to turn back here. If you need to ford the river, it's best to walk 200 feet inland where the water calms before cascading to the tideline.

Assuming you can reach the south shore of the river, continue south above the tideline. By 1¾ miles you pass some large rocks on the beach. Pick your way past the granitic rocks to return to a sandy beach with scattered rocks by 1⅞ miles. Follow the tideline of this curving beach until you encounter more large rocks before 2¼ miles. Turn left and ascend eleven steps to find a blufftop path. Follow it south, contouring along the bluff's edge for ⅛ mile. Then CCT descends to the beach and follows its graceful curve toward a divine looking church.

Reach the mouth of San Jose Creek, usually an easy ford or a walk across a barrier beach at 2⅜ miles. Beyond the stream, follow the tideline as it swings southwest toward Point Lobos with Highway 1 drawing near on the left. Before you reach the fence at the end of San Jose Creek State Beach, you want to turn left and head for the restrooms, then walk up to Highway 1 at 2¾ miles.

The Coastal Trail turns right and follows the broad highway shoulder southwest for ¾ mile to reach the entrance of Point Lobos State Reserve, start of the next section. From Riley Ranch Road you can follow a pleasant path on the highway's west side that parallels the reserve's fence for the final ⅛ mile to the Reserve entrance.

SUGGESTED ROUND TRIPS & LOOPS: Walk City Beach to its end then return along the Scenic Road path for an easy 1⅝-mile loop. Walk the State Beach from the Scenic Road stairway or the highway end to Carmel River and return.

SECTION 7
Point Lobos State Reserve

DISTANCE: 3⅝ miles of Coastal Trail, 7 miles with all the side trips (5.8 to 11.3 kilometers).

OPEN TO: Hikers.

SURFACE: Trail.

ACCESS POINT: Point Lobos State Reserve Entrance.

HOW TO GET THERE: Drive south on Highway 1 from the Monterey Peninsula. Only 2 miles from the Carmel River bridge, the only entrance to Point Lobos State Reserve is west of the highway at Milepost 70.4. No fee daytime parking on highway shoulder near entrance.

OTHER ACCESS: Drive into Reserve. You can reach the CCT from every parking area.

DIFFICULTY: Easy.

ELEVATION GAIN/LOSS: 390 feet+/390 feet- for CCT. Add 400 feet+/400 feet- for all spurs.

CAUTIONS: Reserve open 9 am to 5 pm, later in summer. Do not disturb natural features. No dogs, stoves, fires or trailers allowed. No motor homes allowed on weekends and holidays, nor Memorial Day through Labor Day. Picnics allowed only in the three picnic areas. Access may be limited on busy days. No charge to walk in.

FURTHER INFORMATION: Point Lobos State Reserve (831)624-4909.

FACILITIES: Restrooms, water, phones, picnic areas at various places in the Reserve.

CAMPGROUNDS: Veteran's Memorial County Park is in Monterey near the Presidio, about 6 miles north. Bottchers Gap Walk-In Camp lies 9 miles up Palo Colorado Road from Garrapata State Park on Section 8 in Los Padres National Forest. For showers and other facilities, try Saddle Mountain Recreation Park up Carmel Valley Road.

LODGING: Asilomar Conference Center at start of Section 5 has 315 rooms. Also see Lodging for Section 6.

MAP: See page 44.

Point Lobos State Reserve may be the jewel of the entire California coast with its diverse habitats packed in a compact 1300 acres, about two square miles, with more than half of it underwater. Landscape painter Francis McComas called it "the greatest meeting of land and water in the world," and no one has quibbled with his description. Here you'll find wooded and grassy wildflower-rich head-lands, rocky and sandy coves and beaches, tidepools, Monterey cypress groves and pine forests, meadows, creeks, granite domes, and offshore rocks of every size. Point Lobos offers one of the richest marine environments anywhere. One reason for this is the presence of submarine Carmel Canyon, 600 feet deep just ⅜ mile from the north shore.

The whole adds up to so much more than all the wonderful parts that Point Lobos State Reserve sometimes seems in danger of being loved to death. Yet the state park system has taken numerous measures in the past 20 years that protect this stellar place from overuse, the most important of which is a limit of 450 visitors allowed into the reserve at one time. On busy days this may mean that people arriving at the entrance as soon as two hours after the 9 am opening time will need to wait until other visitors leave to enter. Other rules and restrictions are listed in our cautions and in the park brochure.

Point Lobos also offers a rich and varied history. Shell middens and mortar holes indicate that the Ohlone people visited here to harvest the rich bounties of both land and sea. The Spaniards settled the Monterey area in the late 18th century, giving Point Lobos its name but otherwise using the land only for grazing livestock. After California became a state, granite was quarried at Point Lobos and shipped to San Francisco for building, including the San Francisco Mint. In 1862 Portuguese whalers set up a shore whaling station, hunting whales from small boats and boiling whale blubber in cauldrons on the beach. Robert Louis Stevenson visited Point Lobos in 1879, using the landscape as inspiration for the setting of *Treasure Island*. After a mining company acquired land here, coal was mined nearby and loaded onto ships anchored in Whalers Cove. They subdivided parts of today's reserve and sold 25-foot-wide lots in "Point Lobos City." From 1897 until 1922 a substantial abalone cannery operated at Whalers Cove, shipping their harvest fresh to California restaurants and canned to Japan.

In 1898 A. M. Allan bought 640 acres from a mining company and began buying up the residential lots. Allan and his wife wanted to save this place rather than exploit it. Visitors began coming to explore the beauty. The Allans' foresight led to a movement to establish Point Lobos as a park. With funds from Save-the-Redwoods League and public support, Point Lobos became part of California's new state park system in 1933.

From Highway 1 at the park entrance, the CCT follows the pedestrian path on the north side of the park entrance road into Point Lobos State Reserve. When you reach the entrance kiosk, continue another 30 feet, then turn right on the Carmelo Meadow Trail. It dips downhill through pine forest with a dense understory. Reach a more open understory by ¼ mile where you can see Whalers Cove and the parking area on its left.

CCT comes to a T junction above the rim of the cove. CCT 's through route turns left here. Consider exploring the side trail on the right, which follows the shore north and east past Coal Chute Point and Granite Point (spur on left beyond ¼ mile), crossing a grassy treeless marine terrace to end after ⅝ mile at a small rocky point overlooking the northeastern boundary of the state reserve, with Monastery Beach of San Jose Creek State Beach beyond a fence.

From the T junction, CCT turns left to follow the rim of Whalers Cove, meeting a paved road at the historic Whalers Cabin, now a museum. Turn right and walk the road north to the parking lot at its end beyond ½ mile, where restrooms are on your left.

From the end of the lot, CCT climbs stairs on the North Shore Trail to top Cannery Point, passing a short view loop on the right. Continue up steps to the next junction where CCT and North Shore Trail go left. (A 75-foot detour along the spur on your right offers a breathtaking vista of nearby Guillemot Island and wooded Big Dome to the west.)

After a short climb, the CCT/North Shore Trail dips toward Bluefish Cove, then ascends and dips again to a junction with the Whalers Cabin Trail on the left. Continue straight on the North Shore Trail, climbing through forest above the shore. After passing the short Guillemot Island spur on the right, contour through open pine forest to meet the Whalers Knoll Trail on the left at ⅞ mile.

CCT continues straight on the North Shore Trail to rise and dip through dense forest along the northwest face of Whalers Knoll, with views across Carmel Bay to Cypress Point and Point Santa Cruz beyond. Beyond a spur on the right before one mile, follow the North Shore Trail through cypress forest to overlook small sparkling Big Dome Cove at 1⅛ miles, then pass another junction with the Whalers Knoll Trail.

CCT descends west on the North Shore Trail, passing above Cypress Cove at

Watch for Whales, Dolphins and Porpoises

The California Coastal Trail provides some of the best whale watching in the state. If you hike the coast between November and May, you'll have excellent chances to see some of the 24,000 California gray whales that swim the west coast each year. If you hike CCT in summer or autumn, you might spot humpback whales, dolphins or porpoises swimming or breeding offshore.

Unlike other whales, grays migrate in sight of land, giving you a great chance to observe their 12,000-mile round trip between Alaska's Bering Sea and Baja California. The gray whales, led by pregnant mothers, first appear off northern California in mid-November, continuing their trek south to Baja into February. They travel about five miles an hour up to twenty hours a day, cruising a mile or two offshore.

Grays return north in March and April. Mothers with young calves (1500 pounds at birth!) dawdle along as late as July. The northern trekkers minimize current drag by swimming just beyond the forming breakers.

California's official marine mammals usually travel in pods of three to eight, although some prefer to cruise solo. An average gray weighs 30 tons and is 40 feet long, with a life span similar to ours. They've been making their annual trek for around five million years. Their ancestors once lived on land, turning to the sea around 30 million years ago.

Humpback whales also migrate off California's coast, but mostly stay far from shore. While spotting humpbacks from land is unpredictable, they come closest to local shores during summer or autumn feeding. Sometimes humpbacks breed along the north coast, a rare sight to see from land. Harbor porpoises, much smaller cetaceans, sometimes visit the California coast in summer.

You're most likely to spot the whale by its spout or blow, the misty exhalation from the blowhole atop its head. Grays and humpbacks blow steam six to 15 feet high. You might hear the "whoosh" of exhalation from a half mile away.

Whales typically blow three to eight times at 10- to 30-second intervals, then take a deep dive, or sound, flipping the fluke (tail) on the way down. A normal dive lasts about four minutes, reaching depths of 120 feet.

Your best whale watching occurs when the ocean is calm before winds and waves pick up, often in the morning. Binoculars enhance viewing, but when whales are there you can see them with the naked eye. For the best viewing from shore, find a point jutting out to sea. If you are visiting the coast during prime whale season, consider taking a whale watching cruise from the nearest harbor.

1¼ miles. You soon pass a short spur on the right that leads to a view of the old Veteran Cypress above Cypress Cove. CCT climbs through dense coastal scrub dominated by poison oak to reach the end of the North Shore Trail by 1⅜ miles. On the right the Cypress Grove Trail makes a shady ⅞-mile loop through the Allan Memorial Cypress Grove, a worthy side trip.

The CCT turns left, quickly reaching a parking lot. Walk south through the lot 200 feet, then veer to the right beside cypress trees on the Sea Lion Point Trail. It soon crosses dense coastal scrub overlooking Headland Cove. Above the cove at 1½ miles you gain a rocky ridge with views north and south. One can continue west to Sea Lion Cove and onto Punta de los Lobos Marinos (source of the park's name), but CCT turns left to climb south above a rocky shore. Follow this Sand Hill Trail to overlook Sand Hill Cove and the rugged shore to the south.

At the next junction, CCT veers right to descend the South Shore Trail past Sand Hill Cove at 1¾ miles. Continue past two spurs to tideline and reach a small parking area at 1⅞ miles. A restroom and picnic area are tucked between forest and meadow to the east. CCT continues south along the narrowing South Shore Trail, gaining open coastal vistas. The light rocks ahead are Pelican Point and Bird Island near the preserve's south boundary with Yankee Point beyond.

Your trail passes another small parking area before 2⅛ miles with a welcome drinking fountain. South Shore Trail/CCT soon returns to the shore and the bluff edge above it, then winds east beside pebbly Weston Beach. The trail winds away from the road and over a small knoll where you see the first trees along the shore since Allan Grove. Wind above a convoluted rocky shoreline with trees crowding the coastal scrub, drawing near Bird Island.

Pass another drinking fountain around 2½ miles and meet a short spur on the right that drops to tiny, sheltered Hidden Beach. Continue down coast on the South Shore Trail, coming to road's end at 2⅝ miles where you'll find a final pleasant picnic area and drinking fountain.

CCT continues south, following the Bird Island Trail over a rocky knoll shrouded in trees and coastal scrub. Reach the junction with the spur to lustrous China Cove and China Beach at 2¾ miles. CCT veers left toward Gibson Beach. In just 150 feet it meets a T junction. CCT goes left to leave the Point Lobos shore, but consider another side trip first. Both China Cove and Gibson Beach are treats, but my favorite is the ⅜-mile loop on the Bird Island Trail, which goes right to head west from the T junction.

From the T junction, CCT heads east. In only 50 feet the Gibson Beach Trail forks right. CCT stays left on the South Plateau Trail, climbing over Vierra's Knoll around 2⅞ miles, then descending north through forest to return to the reserve entrance, the only way out of the park. The trail climbs then dips again to meet the Pine Ridge Trail on the left at 3¼ miles. CCT continues north on South Plateau Trail, rising over another knoll, then dipping to the entrance road and kiosk beyond 3½ miles. Turn right and walk out to Highway 1 and section's end at 3⅝ miles.

ALTERNATE ROUTE: Of course you can skip the loop through Point Lobos State Reserve to save 3⅝ miles, but you would miss a fabulous experience.

SUGGESTED ROUND TRIPS & LOOPS: If you follow the entire loop and take all the side trails, you'll cover about 7 miles and see virtually all the Point Lobos shore.

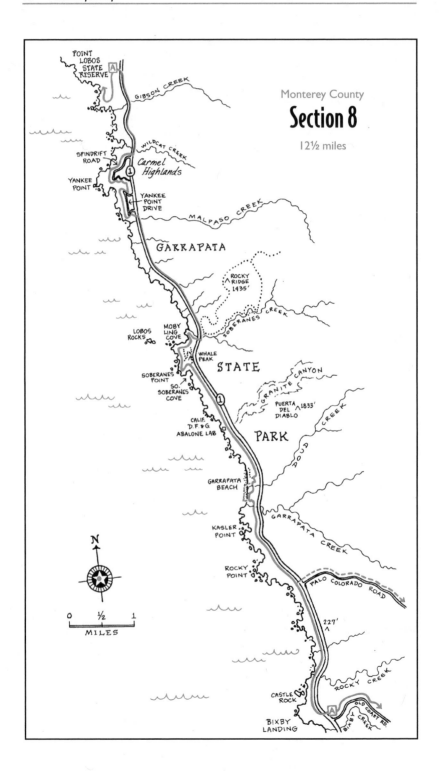

POINT LOBOS STATE RESERVE

GIBSON CREEK

Monterey County

Section 8

12½ miles

WILDCAT CREEK

SPINDRIFT ROAD

Carmel Highlands

YANKEE POINT

YANKEE POINT DRIVE

MALPASO CREEK

GARRAPATA

ROCKY RIDGE 1435'

SOBERANES CREEK

LOBOS ROCKS

MOBY LING COVE

WHALE PEAK

STATE

GRANITE CANYON

SOBERANES POINT

SO. SOBERANES COVE

PUERTA DEL DIABLO 1833'

CALIF. D.F.&G. ABALONE LAB

PARK

DOUD CREEK

GARRAPATA BEACH

GARRAPATA CREEK

KASLER POINT

ROCKY POINT

PALO COLORADO ROAD

N

227'

0 ½ 1
MILES

ROCKY CREEK

CASTLE ROCK

OLD COAST RD

BIXBY LANDING

BIXBY CREEK

SECTION 8
Point Lobos State Reserve Entrance to Bixby Bridge

DISTANCE: 12½ miles (20.1 kilometers).

OPEN TO: Hikers. Bicyclists on highway.

SURFACE: Highway shoulder, secondary road, trail.

ACCESS POINT: Point Lobos State Reserve entrance.

HOW TO GET THERE: Drive south on Highway 1 from the Monterey Peninsula. Only 2 miles from the Carmel River bridge, the only entrance to Point Lobos State Reserve is west of the highway at Milepost 70.4. No fee daytime parking on highway shoulder near entrance.

OTHER ACCESS: Garrapata State Park, especially at gates 7, 8, 10, 18 and 19.

DIFFICULTY: Moderate.

ELEVATION GAIN/LOSS: 1220 feet+/1020 feet-.

CAUTIONS: Wear bright clothing, stay out of roadway and on shoulder if you walk provisional route along the highway where you'll find narrow shoulders in places. Use extreme caution crossing highway. Access point parking allowed only during daylight hours. Vehicles left overnight may be towed. If you walk the tideline of Garrapata State Park, be extremely wary of surf and changing tides. Many rogue waves strike here, and several people have been killed. Most dangerous in winter and at high tide, but rogue waves can occur at any time. Also use caution on steep coastal bluffs.

FURTHER INFORMATION: Garrapata State Park (831)667-2315, (831)624-4909.

FACILITIES: Restrooms and phone near access point inside Reserve. Chemical toilets near Soberanes Point.

CAMPGROUNDS: Bottchers Gap Walk-In Camp lies 8 miles up Palo Colorado Road from Garrapata State Park in Los Padres National Forest. For showers and other facilities, try Saddle Mountain Recreation Park up Carmel Valley Road.

LODGING: The luxury Carmel Highlands Inn is en route. The Carmel River Inn near Section 6 offers the nearest affordable lodging with many other choices on the Monterey Peninsula.

This section marks the passage from the urbane and affluent Monterey Bay area to wild and remote Big Sur. Photographer Ansel Adams lived much of his life in a house above Malpaso Creek, looking south over the dramatic coastal landscape, preserved since 1980 in 3000-acre Garrapata State Park. Adams' black-and-white images of this shoreline have attained near archetypal status as photography's representation of oceanside beauty.

The Coastal Trail is forced to follow the shoulder of busy Highway 1 for most of the section, but progress is being made. The only exceptions to the highway hike are the pleasant walk through Adams' adopted town—the upscale oceanside community of Carmel Highlands—and the invigorating blufftop trails of Garrapata State Park. At press time only two short blufftop paths provide a through route for the CCT at Garrapata, but there will soon be more. The southernmost CCT blufftop link here was constructed in summer 1999, and one or two more blufftop paths are due to be built in spring 2000. We mention the locations of these new CCT links although they were not done as we go to press.

From Point Lobos State Reserve entrance, CCT follows the shoulder of Highway 1 south. After ⅜ mile it crosses Gibson Creek and leaves the reserve, quickly entering the small town of Carmel Highlands. At ¾ mile, CCT and the highway pass the last general store/gas station until Big Sur on Section 10. Continue along the shoulder of the winding highway with occasional coastal views, crossing the historic 1933 Wildcat Canyon bridge at 1⅜ miles.

Watch on your right for Spindrift Road at 1½ miles. CCT turns right to descend along Spindrift. After a short ascent around 1¾ miles, the descent continues with spectacular coastal vistas including a look north to the rugged Point Lobos shore. Ascend Spindrift Road to Highway 1 at 2⅜ miles, then turn right and follow the highway shoulder south ⅛ mile.

Around 2½ miles CCT turns right on Yankee Point Drive. Descend along the quiet residential street with glimpses of the coast until 3¼ miles. Then follow Yankee Point Drive as it climbs toward the highway. Be sure you turn right at the intersection of Yankee Point and Carmel Riviera Drive, following Yankee Point Drive to Highway 1 at 3⅜ miles.

CCT turns right and follows Highway 1's shoulder south, quickly crossing the 1935-vintage Malpaso Creek bridge. Rugged Malpaso Creek marks the start of Big Sur, which extends south 70 miles to San Luis Obispo County. Follow the highway as it contours down coast, crossing another canyon around 3¾ miles, then entering Garrapata State Park at 4⅛ miles, with the park on both sides of the highway.

Cross another canyon at 4¼ miles and pass the first shoreline access for the park, a path through the fence west of the highway, marked "1." Typical of access paths in this mostly narrow coastal state park, that path descends to tideline but has no access up and down the coast. This point is more notable for your first clear view south to the high promontory of Point Sur.

Continue down the coast on narrowing highway shoulders. CCT and Highway 1 cross a landfill over another canyon at 4⅝ miles. By 4⅞ miles the road widens, providing adequate shoulders once again. Climb over a rise, then descend to cross two more canyons around 5⅛ miles.

After following the highway shoulder over another rise, dip down past coastal access gate 7 at Milepost 65.9. The spur trail descends west to overlook Soberanes Creek Beach, created when recent El Niño storm waves piled tons of sand on a previously submerged rocky tideline. Eventually the CCT will likely leave the highway at gate 7, but to do so now requires a difficult ford of Soberanes Creek.

Follow the shoulder south over a landfill crossing of Soberanes Creek at 5½ miles. Immediately beyond the creek you have a choice. The shortest route follows the highway another ⅛ mile to gate 8. For a longer blufftop route, CCT turns right just south of the creek and descends a narrow path west following the bank of the creek to the point southwest of the creek's mouth at 5⅝ miles, where

Sea Otters

While sea otters fascinate, even enchant people with their cute faces and amusing antics, they are a remarkable and extremely specialized aquatic animal. Southern sea otters inhabit the giant kelp forests growing just offshore along the California coast, while two other sea otter subspecies live in the kelp beds of southern Alaska and northeastern Asia. Scientists estimate that these otters once numbered between 150,000 and 300,000 animals, but commercial hunting of sea otters for their wonderful fur during the 18th and 19th centuries nearly drove them to extinction.

Around 1900 only 1,000 or 2,000 sea otters had survived. In California the southern sea otter was believed extinct. Then in 1915, scientists found an isolated colony of about 50 otters in Bixby Creek Cove on the Big Sur coast. They managed to keep their find a secret until after the coast highway opened through Big Sur. In 1938 the public became aware of the remnant population, and people's fascination with sea otters has been growing ever since. All of today's estimated 1,500 to 2,000 California sea otters descended from those 50 individuals. The northern populations have rebounded more quickly to around 150,000 animals.

California's sea otters range from Año Nuevo in San Mateo County to Avila Beach in San Luis Obispo County, with the highest concentration between Santa Cruz and southern Big Sur. They are considered "threatened" under the Endangered Species Act and are a "fully protected mammal" under California law.

Adult sea otters are about four feet long and weigh between 40 and 80 pounds. They use their webbed hind feet as flippers for swimming, but use their unwebbed short front paws for feeding and grooming. In fact otters use stones as tools, prying shellfish loose from underwater rocks, then breaking the shells while floating on their backs on the surface. Otters spend much of their time grooming because their dense fur is invaluable, both for buoyancy and warmth. Unlike all other marine mammals, otters have little blubber to insulate them from chilly ocean temperatures. Because of this an otter must consume about 25 percent of its body weight each day, 2½ tons of food each year. The sea otter's thick fur is the densest animal fur on earth, with up to a million hairs per square inch.

The sea otter is the second smallest of the marine mammals, also the slowest swimmer and least streamlined member of that group. Sea otters were also the last group of marine mammals to leave land for the ocean. Scientists believe their ancestors turned to the sea five to seven million years ago, gradually adapting to ocean life. Sea otters are one of the largest members of the mustelid family, which also includes river otters, weasels, skunks, minks and badgers. Sea otters usually swim belly-up on their backs while river otters, which are no more than half as large and will sometimes enter the ocean, swim belly down.

Spotting sea otters can be tricky because the kelp floats of the kelp beds they favor resemble otter heads, but by observing carefully, especially with binoculars, you'll eventually pick out the often light colored head of the sea otter along with the upturned belly and outstretched forepaws. They'll frequently entertain you with their antics, preening, yawning, rolling or even cracking open a shellfish dinner with a rock held in their agile paws. If you should find a dead, sick or wounded otter on shore, never touch the animal but immediately notify the California Department of Fish and Game.

spurs descend to fishing access. CCT turns south to contour along the bluff edge. In about 250 feet it meets a spur that drops south to the rocky shore of Moby Ling Cove, a.k.a. North Soberanes Cove. CCT heads east briefly, then angles southeast toward a cypress grove. Before the grove it meets the well beaten path from nearby gate 8 on your left.

Veer right and follow the trail south into the cypress grove at 5⅞ miles where you'll find an outhouse. CCT leads out of the grove to a junction with an overgrown trail on the left at 6 miles. That spur leads to the top of nearby Whale Peak, but CCT continues straight, passing another spur on the right in about 200 feet. The through trail soon climbs steps to overlook a keyhole cove on your right. Continue along the path heading toward the point on the ocean side of Whale Peak.

Around 6⅛ miles the trail forks again, this time with both choices being through trails. You can take the right fork for a closer look at the shore around the northern point that faces Lobos Rocks offshore, but the CCT contours straight across the headlands covered with coastal scrub vegetation. In 450 feet the lower path rejoins the CCT. By 6¼ miles the ocean churns directly below. Descend toward Soberanes Point, the southernmost of the two nearby points. As you descend, the high rise of Point Sur appears to the south.

Reach Soberanes Point beyond 6⅜ miles where you pass a metal bench mark placed in 1875 and side trails to the tideline. CCT turns east to follow the winding bluff edge toward the highway. It soon turns north heading for Whale Peak.

By 6⅝ miles you reach a fork where the spur on the right heads to a nearby outhouse. The spur once continued southeast to Highway 1, but is now blocked by a fence. CCT heads north from the junction, climbing quickly to a junction beside gate 10. CCT turns right to return to the highway shoulder, but consider exploring the spur on the left which offers a ⅛-mile side trip to the summit of Whale Peak for excellent vistas. From the gate 10 junction, day hikers want to follow the northbound path over the east flank of Whale Peak, then descend to the junction south of the cypress grove where they turn right to retrace their steps to their starting point.

From gate 10, the Coastal Trail follows the highway shoulder south, contouring across a steep slope. From here south Garrapata State Park lies only west of the highway. Pass gate 11 around 7⅜ miles. Eventually another CCT blufftop path will run south from gate 11 to gate 12 just before Department of Fish and Game's Abalone Research Station west of the highway, but until it's built, CCT follows the shoulder, dipping across an unnamed canyon and passing a two-pronged promontory extending into the Pacific, then continuing above a steep, convoluted and rocky coast.

CCT and highway cross the big arched bridge over rugged Granite Canyon at 7¾ miles. The terrain gets even steeper and the road shoulders get narrower as you climb then contour across the base of Portuguese Ridge, which has a 1833-foot peak called Puerta del Diablo only 1⅛ miles from tideline. You're directly below it when you cross the deep canyon at 8 miles. Another new stretch of CCT to be constructed in 2000 begins at gate 17, extending south to return to the highway shoulder before the canyon at 8½ miles.

The coastal terrace soon becomes less steep and extends farther west of the highway. After crossing the deep unnamed canyon at 8½ miles, the highway descends toward Doud Creek, coming to gate 18 just north of it at 8¾ miles.

Turn right and walk through the gate, following the trail that descends west 100 feet to a junction at 8⅞ miles. The trail on the right angles northwest to soon end at the bluff's edge. Take the left fork and descend southwest by two switchbacks to a junction where the spur on the right makes a loop with the first spur. CCT stays left, soon dropping by a stairway (not yet built at press time) to Doud Creek and a third fork.

The fork on the right descends the canyon about 200 feet to Garrapata Beach. In summer, unless it's high tide the beach route makes a pleasant CCT alternate route, returning by the stairway near the south end of the beach. In early winter the beach may be inaccessible at Doud Creek due to a seasonal lagoon that forms at the canyon's mouth. Until the lagoon breaks through the barrier beach, it may be as deep as chest high. Garrapata Beach is not recommended at high tides or during storm surf because of the powerful surf and undertow.

At Doud Creek the main CCT route turns left, following the creek upstream briefly to a ford. (By spring 2000 two sturdy bridges should replace the fords here, one for each fork of the trail.) Follow the trail as it climbs to the bluff, where you should watch for poison oak, then out to bluff's edge and a sweeping vista at 9 miles. The golden strand of Garrapata Beach stretches below, with Soberanes Point to the north and the houses on Kasler Point to the south.

CCT contours south along the bluff edge, soon meandering inland around a gully. By 9⅛ miles you reach a junction where the spur on the right descends to a stairway to the south end of Garrapata Beach, also where the beach alternate returns to the main trail. CCT veers left and climbs to the highway at gate 19.

CCT turns right and follows the highway shoulder south. At 9¼ miles it passes private driveways on the west and east. Then the shoulders narrow abruptly as highway and CCT cross the Garrapata Creek bridge, leaving

Garrapata's rugged cliffs take the ocean's raging force.

Garrapata State Park. CCT continues south along the highway shoulder, with private residences west of the highway. After passing a sparkling cove with a privately owned coast at 9½ miles, follow the shoulder over Kasler Point, where the coast and hills once again turn unremittingly steep. After passing above another inlet around 9⅝ miles, climb over Rocky Point, which has a restaurant perched dramatically on its south slope west of the highway. Descend to the intersection with Palo Colorado Road (access to northern Ventana Wilderness—8 miles) on the left at 10½ miles. Follow the highway across Palo Colorado Canyon and past Notleys Landing, site of a lumber mill around 1900. Ascend to a summit at 11⅜ miles, 227 feet above the crashing Pacific below. Follow the highway as it descends across a no-name canyon, then Rocky Creek at 12 miles in deep Las Piedras Canyon.

Climb a hill over the flank of Division Knoll with Castle Rock and Bixby Landing along the sheer coast on your right. When you see the Bixby Bridge ahead, you're approaching section's end. The section ends at 12½ miles at the north approach to the famous Bixby Bridge. Section 9 turns left to follow Old Coast Road, finally getting the CCT off Highway 1 for a long stretch.

ALTERNATE ROUTE: For a particularly rugged alternate CCT Big Sur high route, head up narrow, winding and paved Palo Colorado Road 8 miles to Bottchers Gap Campground and Trailhead, walk the dirt road south to Pico Blanco Boy Scout Camp at 11 miles, follow Little Sur Trail to 13.9 miles, then go left on Mt. Manuel Trail which ends at Pfeiffer-Big Sur State Park at 26 miles.

SUGGESTED ROUND TRIPS & LOOPS: The Soberanes Point/Whale Peak Loop offers several choice day hikes ranging from 1⅛ to 2⅜ miles. Across the highway from gate 8, the Rocky Ridge/Soberanes Canyon Loop offers a longer hike with dramatic vistas up and down the coast. You can extend that basic 4½-mile loop with a steep ascent of Peak 1977, which adds 1⅜ miles round trip and even better views. Or avoid most of the climbing and simply take a 3-mile round trip hike up Soberanes Creek canyon, enjoying the transition from chaparral and prickly pear cactus to redwood forest, with a short pretty loop through the forest along the creek before the trail turns north to climb steeply to the ridge.

HOW TO IMPROVE CCT HERE: Develop more blufftop trails through Garrapata.

SECTION 9
Old Coast Road, Bixby Bridge to Andrew Molera State Park

DISTANCE: 10¾ miles (17.3 kilometers).

OPEN TO: Hikers, bicyclists.

SURFACE: Dirt road.

ACCESS POINT: North end of Bixby Bridge on Highway 1.

HOW TO GET THERE: Drive south on Highway 1 from the Monterey Peninsula. In 13.1 miles from Carmel River bridge, turn left at Milepost 59.15 onto unpaved Old Coast Road and park.

OTHER ACCESS: Anywhere along route.

DIFFICULTY: Strenuous.

ELEVATION GAIN/LOSS: 2110 feet+/2340 feet-.

CAUTIONS: Watch and listen for traffic. Stay off adjacent private property. Road may be impassable to vehicles after wet weather. No camping allowed along Old Coast Road.

FURTHER INFORMATION: Monterey County Road Department (831)755-4925.

FACILITIES: None except at Molera State Park at south end, which has chemical toilets, water, phone.

CAMPGROUNDS: Molera Walk-In Camp is at south end. Car camping available along Highway 1 south of Molera at three private campgrounds and Pfeiffer-Big Sur State Park.

LODGING: None on route. See Lodging for Sections 6, 8 and 10.

Big Sur remained a coastal wilderness after most of the California coast had been settled, its steep and rugged terrain throwing up barriers to all kinds of travel. The native Esselen people left their harsh native lands to settle near the Catholic missions in the 18th century. While a few solitude loving settlers arrived before 1870, a small community only finally developed in the Big Sur River Valley in the 1870s. By 1900 landings for ships had been built at Palo Colorado Canyon and Bixby Creek in the north and at Partington Cove and the mouth of Big Sur River in central Big Sur. In that year Big Sur residents built a road south from Malpaso Creek to Bixby's, but only a rugged pack trail continued south. By 1910 one could take a ten-hour stage ride from Monterey to the new Pfeiffer's Resort, which operated on the site now occupied by Big Sur Lodge. That stage followed what's now called Old Coast Road, the CCT route today.

Only in 1919 did work begin on surveying a highway along the Big Sur coast between Carmel and San Simeon. Local residents, hardened by their wilderness lifestyle, scoffed, claiming the road would only be built as Hearst's personal driveway. Construction began in 1921 only to be put on hold by a skeptical governor from 1923 to 1927. When building resumed, convict crews provided the labor. In

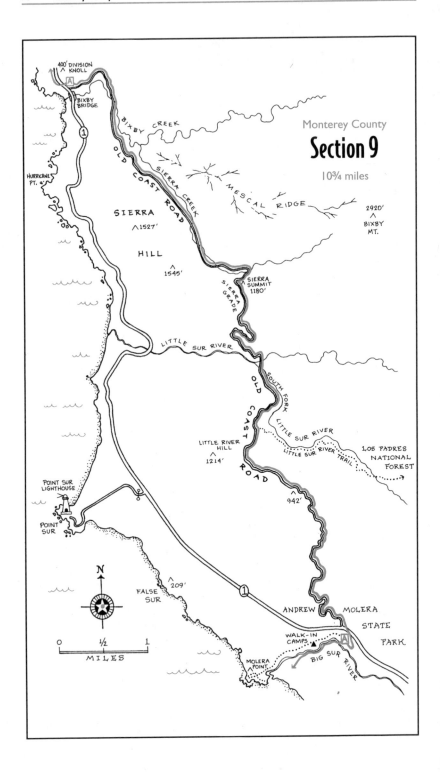

Monterey County

Section 9

10¾ miles

1934 a rough road finally opened, but creek crossings were steep and chancy in the several spots where bridges hadn't yet been built. Finally in 1937 this dramatic leg of Highway 1 officially opened.

In the meantime the bridge over Bixby Creek had opened in 1932. Called Rainbow Bridge at the time, it was then the longest concrete arch bridge in the west. We call it Bixby Bridge today. It's still the longest bridge in Big Sur and one of the most dramatic spans in the world with its setting at the precipitous meeting of land and sea. Completion of the bridge made the inland route up Bixby and Sierra Creeks a side road except when the new coast route was closed by slides or washouts. The bridge gained further fame in the 1950s when Beat writer Jack Kerouac wrote about his stay in Lawrence Ferlinghetti's cabin beneath the bridge.

Today Old Coast Road offers a steep route almost entirely through private property, but one that provides a pleasant and remote track, a preferable alternative to walking the narrow shoulders of the busy highway. Old Coast Road presents steep hills, rewarding vistas and intimate contact with lush stream corridors, most notably the beautiful crossing at the Little Sur River. South of the river, the road offers access to the Little Sur Trail, a route into the Ventana Wilderness. The last time we took Old Coast Road, we saw the local sheriff taking a nap at the grandest vista point and only four cars in the 10½ miles.

The California Coastal Trail follows the dirt track of Old Coast Road, ascending a hill with great views on the right into rugged Bixby Creek Canyon where the road soon leads. Be sure to look behind you for awesome vistas of the gracefully arched Bixby Bridge. Pause when you reach the summit at ⅜ mile to absorb the route's only views north along the coast.

Follow Coast Road on a winding steep descent, crossing Bixby Creek before one mile. Ascend along the west wall of the canyon where redwoods grow from the steep rocky slope. After a brief descent around 1⅝ miles, your gradual climb resumes. By 2⅛ miles you're ascending along Sierra Creek, an alder-lined fork of Bixby Creek that lies 50 feet below the road on your left. Beyond 2½ miles your ascending road quickly crosses the creek five times. From 3 miles redwood groves offer some shade. After passing a lovely grove across the creek on the right at 3⅜ miles, the ascent turns moderate. Leave the canyon by a hairpin turn to the right at 3¾ miles, beginning a steep climb with expanding coastal views.

Reach Sierra Summit by 4 miles after gaining 1100 feet in a 3-mile ascent. Ocean vistas there range from northwest to south. Pass a sign informing you that the private lands of El Sur Ranch line the road for the next 6 miles. Make a winding descent across steep chaparral slopes with scattered cypress and yuccas and views of 3710-foot Pico Blanco southeast. According to Ohlone legend, this dramatic peak was where Coyote brought civilization to people.

Descend past a spring on the left around 5¼ miles, then through a stand of Bishop pines followed by redwoods. Reach the Little Sur River at the confluence of its main and south forks at 5¾ miles, crossing it on a Bailey Bridge in a gorgeous spot beneath large pines, redwoods, alders and maples. You quickly cross the South Fork on another Bailey Bridge, then begin a steep ascent.

After a tight hairpin turn around 6¼ miles, watch for a wide spot in the road, one of the few places several cars might park on Old Coast Road. East of the road here is the unmarked start of the Little Sur Trail which descends to ford the South

Fork Little Sur River, entering Ventana Wilderness and Los Padres National Forest in about one mile. That trail then climbs over the flank of Pico Blanco and ends in 6⅛ miles at the Mt. Manuel Trail, which leads north to Bottchers Gap and south to Pfeiffer-Big Sur State Park.

CCT continues along Old Coast Road, climbing through oak woodlands. By 7¼ miles you gain views of Pico Blanco to the east and the canyons of the Little Sur River. As you approach the road's third summit (942 feet) before 8 miles, magnificent views open to the southwest of the coastal marine terrace and ocean.

A winding descent drops through oak woodlands with periodic coastal vistas. By 8½ miles you're back among redwoods. The road contours from 8¾ to 9¼ miles with vistas of Molera Point and the mouth of the Big Sur River. As you re-

How Big Sur Almost Became a National Park and Why It Didn't

In autumn 1977 Gary Koeppel, a Big Sur gallery owner, learned that some affluent Monterey Peninsula residents led by Ansel Adams wanted to make Big Sur a national park. What irked Koeppel and the Big Sur residents he told was that the park advocates had held secret meetings with county, state and federal officials. An informal poll found 98% of Big Sur people opposed the park idea, so Koeppel vowed to stop federalization by whatever means necessary.

Ironically, Adams and Koeppel and most Sur residents shared the goal of protecting Big Sur. They simply differed radically about how to do it. When park proponents started the Big Sur Foundation in spring 1978, Koeppel countered by starting the monthly Big Sur Gazette to communicate among the locals. The state attorney general soon called the paper "inaccurate and highly inflammatory," but locals loved it.

In early 1979 the California Coastal Commission directed the county board of supervisors to develop a Big Sur Local Coastal Plan (LCP). Big Sur residents enthusiastically participated in the hearings to draft the LCP, seeing it as the local control alternative to becoming a national park. Adams and his group ignored the LCP, pressuring Washington instead. In November, Adams presented President Carter with a confidential memo about preserving Big

Sur. In January 1980 evidence was revealed that Adam's Big Sur Foundation had been lobbying the Senate Energy Committee about placing Big Sur under federal ownership. That month Senator Alan Cranston (D-CA) tacked an amendment on an omnibus parks bill that would allow Los Padres National Forest to expand by any amount of land. When the powerful senator asked Senator S. I. Hayakawa (R-CA) to support the amendment, however, Hayakawa called Big Sur residents instead. Cranston's office was flooded with 2000 telegrams and phone calls urging that he drop the amendment. Cranston did so, but later quietly introduced a new bill virtually the same.

Tactics shifted. In February the Wilderness Society, now led by Adams' former business manager, announced a plan to make Big Sur "the first national scenic area." The only difference between this plan and Adams' original was that Big Sur would be under the Department of Agriculture rather than the Department of the Interior. Cranston introduced another bill to "save" Big Sur under the Wilderness Society plan, complete with a $100 million appropriation to start buying Big Sur land. When Cranston scheduled a day of hearings on the bill in Washington, Big Sur residents had to journey 3000 miles to argue their case. Several Sur residents

sume a steady descent, the magnificent view expands to include Point Sur and its historic lighthouse, then more of the Big Sur River Canyon.

The road drops into Molera State Park around 10¼ miles, passing a trail on the right that leads nowhere. Continue down the road to its end at Highway 1 at 10½ miles. Be very careful and watchful of speeding cars as you cross the highway and descend the signed paved road into the heart of Molera State Park. Turn right at 10¾ miles and walk past the entrance kiosk, coming to section's end in the main Molera parking lot.

ALTERNATE ROUTE: A CCT Big Sur High Route could ascend Palo Colorado Road from Garrapata State Park to Bottchers Gap, then follow the Mt. Manuel Trail past Pico

Big Sur – continued

stayed a week, breaking into teams and visiting as many senators as they could. At a pivotal meeting with Cranston, they expressed their concerns, but it became clear that Cranston not only hadn't written the bill, he didn't know it's content. When they got to the meeting with the next senator, they were told the meeting had been canceled after Senator Cranston's office called. In fact the Cranston staff had called every senator connected with the bill to say the group's objections had been resolved. The Big Sur resident-lobbyists had to call and reset the rest of the week's appointments, then call every senator they'd already met with to repeat their concerns. The bill died in the Senate for lack of support.

Meanwhile the Big Sur park idea was taken up by Philip Burton (D-CA), powerful head of the House parks subcommittee, so action shifted to the House. Burton told Monterey County congressman Leon Panetta (D-CA), "Either you do it or I'll do it." In June Panetta introduced his own bill with several concessions to local control. Panetta saw the Big Sur park as an important local issue and attempted "the best solution I could come up with." Resistance in Big Sur continued at the same fevered pace. Panetta held hearings in Monterey where both supporters and opponents of the bill presented compelling arguments. When Burton's committee held another day of hearings in Washington, much of the testimony opposed the bill, but Burton pushed hard and got the House to pass the bill by a two-thirds majority.

Cranston pledged to guide the bill through the Senate, but the election year recess loomed just two days away. The Big Sur park advocates decided to gamble all for their original goal. Cranston got Senator Bumpers (D-AR) to make six amendments that removed all local control from the Big Sur park. When the Senate neared adjournment without the committee voting on Big Sur, Phil Burton tried a last ditch technical maneuver, attaching the Big Sur bill to a minor noncontroversial bill bound to pass. Why pass the bill through the House when it had already passed it? Because the Senate had already approved the non-controversial bill (without the Big Sur attachment), it would likely be rushed through for approval without anyone noticing that the Big Sur park was attached.

It nearly worked, but fortunately for Big Sur residents Senator Hayakawa's staff had placed a "hold" on any legislation concerning Big Sur. Thus the Senate minority leader was required to inform Hayakawa that the bill was back in the Senate. The bill was shelved for the next session of Congress. Five weeks later Ronald Reagan was elected president and when Congress reconvened, both Democrats and Republicans agreed to pass only noncontroversial legislation. Obviously the Big Sur park bill didn't qualify. It was never introduced again.

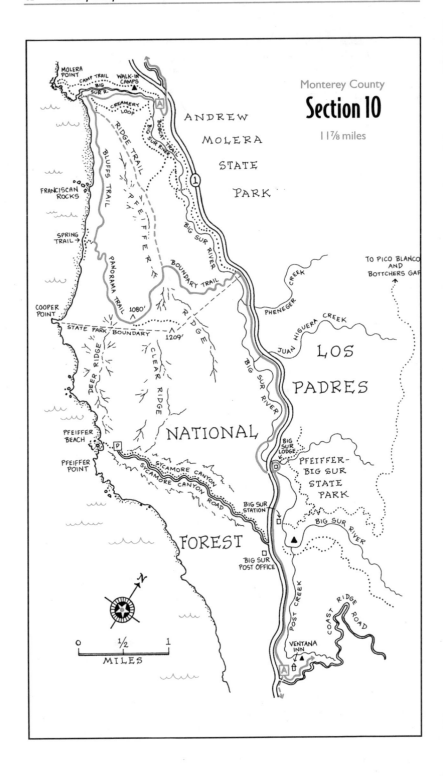

Monterey County
Section 10
11⅞ miles

Blanco Boy Scout Camp. In summer or early autumn, when you're certain you can safely ford the Little Sur River, you could turn right and descend the Little Sur Trail to Old Coast Road. Otherwise, one could continue on the Mt. Manuel Trail to Pfeiffer-Big Sur State Park, finding the way from there to Ventana Inn and the start of Section 11.

SUGGESTED ROUND TRIPS & LOOPS: The highlights of this steep and winding dirt-road route are the views from the three summits, with the first one only ⅜ mile from the highway, a brisk but short climb from Bixby Bridge. Whether or not you walk the entire road, consider a side trip on the Little Sur Trail down to the ford or up from there to the Geer Homestead site at 2¾ miles.

SECTION 10
Andrew Molera State Park to Ventana Inn at Highway 1

DISTANCE: 11⅞ miles (19.1 kilometers).

OPEN TO: Hikers. Bicyclists on first 2¼ miles of trail and paved road portion.

SURFACE: Trail, highway shoulder.

ACCESS POINT: Andrew Molera State Park.

HOW TO GET THERE: From the Monterey Peninsula, drive south on Highway 1. In 21 miles from the Carmel River Bridge, turn west off Highway 1 at Milepost 51.2 into Molera State Park. Descend .25 mile, turn right and pass entrance kiosk, then park.

OTHER ACCESS: North end of South Boundary Trail, anywhere along highway portion.

DIFFICULTY: Easy for first 2⅝ miles and final 5 miles, moderate to strenuous from 2⅝ miles to 6¾ miles.

ELEVATION GAIN/LOSS: 2450 feet+/1130 feet-.

CAUTIONS: Trail may be inaccessible in winter and spring when river runs high–do not ford river when unsafe. Marauding raccoons can cause trouble at Molera Walk-In Camps—keep all food in car when not actively cooking. Use extreme caution walking the shoulder of busy highway leg.

FURTHER INFORMATION: Molera State Park (831)667-2315, Big Sur Station (State Park & USFS) (831)667-2315.

FACILITIES: Chemical toilets, water, phone at access point. Picnic tables, restrooms, phones at or near Big Sur Lodge. Small store with deli, post office, phones on highway portion.

CAMPGROUNDS: Molera State Park Walk-in Camps near start are delightful and inexpensive. Pfeiffer-Big Sur State Park has 218 car camping units, while three private campgrounds offer alternatives just up the highway. Private Ventana Inn's Campground at section's end is for tenters only.

LODGING: Big Sur Cabins, Glen Oaks Motel and Ripplewood Resort on highway portion and Big Sur Lodge are the most economical choices in area. Post Ranch Inn and Ventana Inn at section's end are luxury resorts.

Andrew Molera State Park, spanning the lower reaches of the Big Sur River to its mouth, occupies the northern heart of the Big Sur coast. The gentle terrain around the river's mouth belies the steep, rugged coast that winds south all the way into northern San Luis Obispo County. From the river mouth, the Bluffs Trail offers a pleasant, easy trek. Then the Panorama Trail requires an invigorating ascent, gaining the ridgetop to reveal the dramatic sweep of rugged coast to the south. Since private property lies between the ridge and the coast south, CCT follows the Ridge Trail north, then the South Boundary Trail east to descend to Highway 1. After 2 miles along the highway shoulder, trails through Pfeiffer-Big Sur State Park offer a pleasant respite. The section concludes by ascending the highway shoulder south briefly to section's end at the Ventana Inn turnoff. That's the start of the 43-mile backpack that follows or the Alternate Route's 26⅜ miles of highway shoulder walking.

Two trails leave the Molera parking lot heading for the beach. From the parking lot's north end, the Camp Trail leads to a fine walk-in campground in ¼ mile, continuing to the beach at 1⅛ miles. That route requires fording the lagoon at the river mouth just before the beach unless the summer bridge is in place. From the parking lot's west side, the Creamery Trail, marked "BEACH—1.0 MILE," is preferable unless the river, only 75 feet from the lot, runs too high to safely ford. From about May to November a temporary bridge crosses the river at that spot. The Creamery Trail contours to a junction in 300 feet. Turn right on the trail signed "BEACH." It contours through riparian woodland around ⅛ mile, then continues downstream with the river hidden in dense vegetation on your right. Pass a large cottonwood around ¼ mile and contour west across a grassy flood plain.

By ¾ mile you can see the Big Sur River on the right. You quickly reach a junction with the Ridge Trail. Veer right and pass the river bank, then contour west on a sandy path. At ⅞ mile the rock outcrop on your left marks the base of Pfeiffer Ridge.

In only 200 feet the beach lies straight ahead as you meet a junction with the Bluffs Trail on the left. The CCT turns left here, but consider a side trip 150 feet to the magnificent driftwood strewn beach. At low tide you can walk the beach south, but it takes a very low tide to continue to the bottom end of the Spring Trail 1¾ miles south.

CCT follow the Bluffs Trail as it quickly ascends to 50 feet elevation, then contours along the bluff edge with grand views south along the shoreline to rocky Cooper Point and west to nearby Molera Point with Point Sur rising beyond it. To the east Pico Blanco and the rugged Santa Lucia Range rise steeply.

Around 1⅛ miles the Bluffs Trail passes two unmarked left forks that connect with the Ridge Trail visible to the east. (You can also return to the parking lot that way, taking the next left fork.) CCT continues along the Bluffs Trail on a gentle ascent, angling away from the bluff edge.

At an unmarked fork before 1¼ miles, veer right for the Bluffs Trail and CCT, returning to bluff's edge and following it down the coast. By 1⅜ miles your trail climbs gradually, again angling away from the brushy bluff edge. The Franciscan

Rocks stand in the surf zone below.

Meet a deep eroded gully beyond 1½ miles. The trail turns east to merge with the upper path and wind through the gully, crossing its seasonal creek at 1⅝ miles. Return to the bluff, then dip through a second gully at 1¾ miles. Wind above a third gully at 2 miles, then dip and rise to a fourth. Contour along the blufftop, with no bikes allowed beyond 2¼ miles. Dip and rise, then cross an up-lifted dune around 2⅜ miles.

Descend through coastal scrub into the biggest gully yet. The trail climbs above the arroyo, then contours across the bluff to a junction around 2⅝ miles. The Bluffs Trail ends here. CCT continues as the Panorama Trail on the left. On the right the Spring Trail makes a winding ⅛-mile descent to the beach at the mouth of the next big gulch, which has a year-round creek. From the beach at low tides when the surf is not too big, you can walk a mile to Cooper Point. People have scrambled over rocks there and beyond to Pfeiffer Beach, but that extremely rugged, exposed route is not recommended.

CCT follows the Panorama Trail down through the deep, unnamed gulch, then climbs along the steepening bluff. You soon turn east on a steep, winding ascent of a scrub-covered slope. Climb past a thicket of young redwoods on the left around 3 miles. Ascend to a view south to Cooper Point at 3⅛ miles, then to a view north to the tip of Pico Blanco.

Gain the ridgetop at 3¼ miles where a welcome contour offers a break. After dipping through a small gully, resume climbing moderately along a brushy ridge. After another glimpse of Cooper Point before 3½ miles, it disappears behind the brushy ridge to your south. Your ascent eases through a brush-choked gully, then turns moderate again through grasslands with a view north to Molera Point and Point Sur. Resume a steady ascent through coastal scrub with abundant California fuchsia.

At 4 miles you gain a hilltop beside the fence marking the park's south boundary. Suddenly the panorama expands to include the rugged Big Sur coast to the south with the Santa Lucia Range behind it. Rounded Pfeiffer Point lies below on the coast with Sycamore Canyon in front of it, but private property lies in between. After a break to savor the view, continue up the Panorama Trail along the south boundary. Gain the section's summit at 4¼ miles, marked by a junction and a rest bench. While the Panorama Trail climbs quickly to top one more hill, the CCT turns left and descends the Ridge Trail. Enjoy the views north as you descend chaparral-cloaked slopes, but also watch for bikes which are allowed on this broad, well-graded track.

By 4½ miles you leave the brushy slopes for a mixed woodland of coast live oaks, chinquapins, pines and redwoods with a lush understory. Contour through the forest past an eight-foot-diameter redwood, then descend gently through a grove of corkscrew redwoods as the Big Sur River canyon appears on your right. From 4⅞ miles, the trail drops fitfully through grasslands with scattered brush and glimpses of the coast.

Make a right turn on the South Boundary Trail at 5 miles. Follow this broad track over a rise, then down through grasslands on a winding, fitful roller-coaster descent to a gate around 5¾ miles. Leave the broad track there, turning left to descend steadily on a narrow path through mixed forest. After a seasonal creek at 6 miles, descend a grassy ridge to 6⅜ miles, then wind down through forest to the canyon floor beyond 6½ miles.

When you reach a marked junction, turn left and head down canyon beneath sycamore trees. Where the trail meets the river around 6¾ miles, the summer bridge may be in place for an easy crossing. If not, a wet ford is required—not advisable during high water. The trail quickly ends at Highway 1. Day hikers can veer left just before the road and follow the River Trail back to the parking area.

CCT turns right and follows the highway shoulder upriver, crossing Pheneger Creek and Juan Higuera Creek, then passing three private campgrounds in the 2 miles before entering Pfeiffer-Big Sur State Park. At 9 miles CCT leaves the highway, turning right onto a fire road behind a green gate. It swings south through forest to cross a seasonal bridge over the Big Sur River. Stay to the left as you contour past two group camps. Beyond 9⅛ miles you pass a water faucet beside a campfire center. Climb a short hill to a junction, then turn left and ascend the Buzzards Roost Trail for ⅛ mile to the next junction. Turn left and descend past redwoods, then follow the trail upriver.

At 9½ miles, turn left and follow the trail under the highway bridge, then the park road's bridge. By 9⅝ miles you reach another seasonal footbridge. Cross the river on it, or climb to the park road if the bridge is missing. Where the trail forks beyond the river, take the path on the left to cross the park road and come to the Big Sur Lodge (store, cafe, lodging). Walk to the right around the lodge and out to Highway 1. Turn left and follow the highway shoulder uphill past Big Sur Station (information, campfire permits) at 10⅛ miles. Continue up the shoulder, passing Sycamore Canyon Road west of the highway at 10¾ miles and the small commercial center of Big Sur just beyond, at 11⅞ miles reaching the turnoff on the left for Ventana Inn where this section ends.

ALTERNATE ROUTE: If the fords/seasonal bridges are impassable in winter or spring, the only alternative is to follow the highway to Ventana Inn.

SUGGESTED ROUND TRIPS & LOOPS: A pleasant, easy 2-mile loop follows the CCT to the beach, returning via the Camp Trail—a river ford may be required. For a 7⅛-mile loop, continue along the Ridge Trail beyond the South Boundary Trail, returning via Hidden Trail and River Trail. For a 9¼-mile loop, follow the River Trail downstream from the bottom of the South Boundary Trail. Another option is to explore the many fine trails in Pfeiffer-Big Sur State Park, especially the Pfeiffer Falls, Oak Grove, and Valley View trails.

HOW TO IMPROVE CCT HERE: Build a permanent bridge over the Big Sur River from the Molera parking lot. Acquire a trail easement between the Panorama Trail and Pfeiffer Beach.

SECTION 11
Ventana Inn at Highway 1 to Upper Bee Camp Junction, Ventana Wilderness

DISTANCE: 18¾ miles, plus ½-mile side trip to Cold Spring Camp and ¼-mile side trip to Bee Camp (30.2 + .8 + .4 kilometers).

OPEN TO: Hikers, dogs, equestrians.

SURFACE: Dirt road, trail.

ACCESS POINT: Ventana Inn turnoff from Highway 1 at Post's, Big Sur.

HOW TO GET THERE: Turn east off Highway 1 at Milepost 44.3, .1 mile north of the top of the hill, .6 mile south of the Big Sur post office. Take the right fork toward Ventana Inn (Ventana Campground on left fork) to day-use parking .15 mile from the highway.

OTHER ACCESS: None.

DIFFICULTY: Strenuous.

ELEVATION GAIN/LOSS: 3300 feet+/810 feet- to Upper Bee Camp Trail Junction.

CAUTIONS: Wildfires burned area around Bee Camp in October 1999, call before going for updates and closure information. In summer this route can be very hot and black flies a problem—start early or take highway route. Winter weather can be very cold and snow is not uncommon; spring and autumn are best. Please stay off adjacent private property. Yield to vehicles on road portion. Campfire permits required during fire season, May to October. Trail traverses remote, isolated country with no services and extremely limited water sources. Watch for rattlesnakes, ticks and poison oak. Bear bag your food. Always purify drinking water in wilderness. Day-use parking means just that. If planning a hike with an overnight, contact the Ventana Inn to make arrangements to leave your car there, or park in the wide turnout on highway .1 mile north of turnoff.

FURTHER INFORMATION: Monterey Ranger District, Los Padres National Forest (831)385-5434, Ventana Inn (800)628-6500, (831)667-2331.

FACILITIES: None until Cold Spring Camp unless you camp or lodge at the Ventana Inn. Cold Spring Camp has water, stock trough, table and stove.

CAMPGROUNDS: Near section's start, Ventana Inn has a pleasant campground for tenters only (831-667-2688) with showers. Camping en route at Cold Spring Camp (10 miles) and Upper Bee Camp (19 miles).

LODGING: The neighborhood inns, Ventana and Post Ranch, both start around $200/ night. For more affordable rates, look south to historic Deetjen's Big Sur Inn or north to Ripplewood Resort, Big Sur Cabins, Big Sur Lodge or Glen Oaks Motel.

This historic route originated in the 1920s, predating Highway 1 as a north-south route through Big Sur. That, and the tendency of Highway 1 to be closed by storm damage during many winters, has kept the substantial portions of this route that cross private property open to hikers and equestrians over the years. Much of the route probably follows ancient Indian paths. Historically the original through

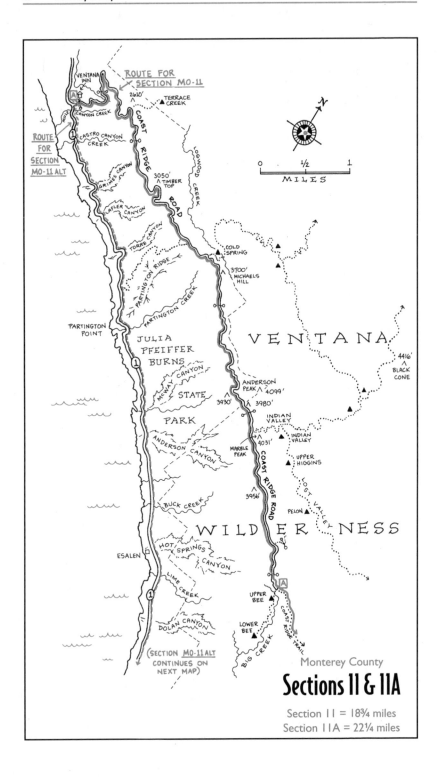

ROUTE FOR
SECTION MO-11

VENTANA INN

2610'

TERRACE CREEK

CANYON CREEK

COAST RIDGE ROAD

ROUTE FOR SECTION MO-11 ALT

CASTRO CANYON CREEK

LOGWOOD CREEK

GRIMES CANYON

3050' TIMBER TOP

LAFLER CANYON

TORRE CANYON

PARTINGTON RIDGE

COLD SPRING

3700' MICHAELS HILL

PARTINGTON CREEK

PARTINGTON POINT

JULIA PFEIFFER BURNS

V E N T A N A

4416' BLACK CONE

MCWAY CANYON

STATE

PARK

ANDERSON PEAK 4099'

3930'

3980'

INDIAN VALLEY

ANDERSON CANYON

MARBLE PEAK

4031'

INDIAN VALLEY

UPPER HIGGINS

COAST RIDGE ROAD

3956'

BUCK CREEK

LOST VALLEY

PELON

W I L D E R   N E S S

ESALEN

HOT SPRINGS CANYON

LIME CREEK

UPPER BEE

DOLAN CANYON

LOWER BEE

COAST RIDGE TRAIL

BIG CREEK

(SECTION MO-11 ALT
CONTINUES ON
NEXT MAP)

N

0   ½   1
M I L E S

Monterey County

Sections 11 & 11A

Section 11 = 18¾ miles
Section 11A = 22¼ miles

road descended back to the coast via the spur road at 14⅝ miles, but in the 1950s the Forest Service and local property owners constructed the road to its present terminus around 18½ miles, with the route continuing south from there much as today's trail does. All the apparent road portions south of that point were actually constructed as fire roads or fire breaks during specific fires.

Planning your trek is critical here since all the campsites and reliable water sources have long hikes of 9 or 10 miles between them. The old road offers a steady moderate ascent to 4 miles, then a gradual ascent followed by some pleasant contours along a view-studded ridge. You may see no trespassing signs along this route, but they refer to vehicles and bicycles, not to hikers or equestrians.

WILDFIRE UPDATE: Large fires once again burned Ventana Wilderness in October 1999. Crews used Coast Ridge near Bee Camp as fire line. Fire damage and control measures have affected trail, but extent of damage will not be known until after publication. Before you go, call Monterey Ranger District for more information and to make sure trail is open.

This high-route section officially starts where the Ventana Inn's road leaves the highway just north of Post's. Walk briefly down paved Ventana Road to the fork, veer right and climb past the day-use parking and on up the road past the Inn's scenic overlook. Where the road forks and the pavement swings left, Coast Ridge Road continues straight to a locked gate at ¼ mile. This is the official start of Coast Ridge Road, but we'll continue the mileage count we started upon leaving the highway.

Walk past the gate and savor a view down coast that includes Cone Peak on your route with Cape San Martin 28 miles away on the coast beyond it. Continue up the gravel road with the Ventana Inn on your left. By ½ mile you leave behind the Ventana Inn, and for the time being, the coastal views. Follow the road as it ascends along the wooded north face of a ridge. Make a big bend right by ¾ mile and continue a steady moderate ascent.

From one mile you climb through deep woods along Post Creek on your left. Cross it at 1⅛ miles and continue a winding gradual ascent. Pass some yuccas by 1¼ miles and glimpse the ocean to the west. Soon a 30-foot waterfall tumbles on your right where a tiny creek crosses the road. The falls drop over a rock formation that looks like a stalagmite sans cave. In fact it's formed by limestone in the creek that precipitates out during the low flow of dry season.

Leave the woods for a sunny slope by 1⅜ miles, with many yuccas on the right and ocean vistas on the left. Cross a gully and pass the second locked gate at 1½ miles, continuing a steady ascent. Gain your first view of Point Sur by 1¾ miles, but far better vistas unfold at the hairpin turn just before 2 miles, marked by an immense buckeye tree beyond a fence. There you look straight down the Big Sur River's fault valley and out to Point Sur. To the right stands Mount Manuel with Pico Blanco peeking over its left shoulder. From north to northeast beyond the deep river canyon rise the impressive craggy summits of Ventana Double Cone (4853'), Ventana Cone (4727') and South Ventana Cone (4965').

Coast Ridge Road ascends to a saddle at 2¼ miles with a view into the heart of the Ventana Wilderness, then continues a moderate climb across dry slopes, passing a private track on the left at 2⅝ miles. Then your road climbs through two gullies where shade offers relief on warm days. Beyond 3 miles a winding ascent crosses several more gullies that provide little shade.

As you round a broad bend to the left at 3½ miles, enjoy your last best vista north. Then the road/CCT ascends northeast following the ridgetop. The Ventana view returns with even more peaks visible, including Black Cone (4416') to the east-southeast, as you gain the first summit at 4 miles. Contour to a saddle, then to the Terrace Creek Trail junction near a residence at 4⅛ miles, elevation 2590 feet. The signed Terrace Creek Trail on the left descends 1250 feet in only 1⅝ miles to Terrace Creek Camp just above the junction with Pine Ridge Trail.

CCT continues along Coast Ridge Road, ascending gradually east into Los Padres National Forest through open grasslands to gain a ridgetop, then following the ridge south past several private roads and homes. Around 4¾ miles your views suddenly shift toward timbered country to the southeast. Descend south to a saddle at 5 miles, then follow the ridge to the third locked gate at 5¼ miles with a filtered view down Castro Canyon to the coast.

Follow Coast Ridge Road as it mostly follows the ridgetop, undulating through grasslands and chaparral offering views, but now with stands of oaks, bay laurels and madrones providing some shade. Enjoy grand coastal views on a moderate ascent from 5¾ to 6¼ miles. After a brief descent, pass an ascending spur road on the right at 6⅜ miles. Coast Ridge Road bends left to round the summit called Timber Top, graced by ponderosa pines. Upon reaching its north side at 6⅞ miles (3050'), enjoy the wilderness vista north.

The road dips slightly, then climbs gently to round another view-rich summit before 7⅝ miles. Cross shady, north-facing slopes to reach a saddle beyond 8¼ miles with more pines and an ocean view south down Torre Canyon. As you continue along the ridge, the views soon switch to north over the wilderness again. Gain the crest for a short contour to the probably unmarked junction with the historic DeAngulo Trail on the right at a saddle around 8⅞ miles, a difficult and steep route down Partington Ridge. (A better, more maintained link with the DeAngulo Trail heads west from Coast Ridge Road at a saddle at 9 1/16 miles.)

Continue along Coast Ridge Road as it climbs east along the ridgetop, then traverses north slopes before regaining the crest and meeting the newer DeAngulo spur at a saddle with an awesome view south down the coast, with Cone Peak flanked by its sister Twin Peak on the right. Follow the road along the flanks of the ridge, passing another ocean-view saddle at 9⅜ miles. Continue to a saddle without a view where you meet the Cold Spring Road at 9½ miles, 3430 feet.

While CCT continues along Coast Ridge Road, you'll probably need to detour east down Cold Spring Road ½ mile to Cold Spring Camp (3260'), where ample water in a big green tank, a stove and table sit beneath trees near the end of the spur road, offering filtered views. The road ends just beyond a flat clearing with a stock tank and table, but the Big Sur Trail continues into the wilderness, heading 4½ miles to Rainbow Camp on South Fork Big Sur River.

After a night's sleep, return to Coast Ridge Road and turn left to follow its least traveled leg. Climb east along a wooded north slope. By 10¾ miles you contour along wooded north- and east-facing slopes of Michaels Hill with wilderness views, including the first vistas of broad Junipero Serra Peak 14 miles across the wilderness. Also known by the native name Pimkolam, at 5862 feet it's the highest point in the Santa Lucia Range. At 11⅛ miles you regain the crest at a saddle with your fourth locked gate, then pass a ridgetop cabin. An easy descent offers ocean views until the saddle at 11⅜ miles.

Coast Ridge Road ascends moderately along the ridgetop, then to the right of it. After a spur road on the left at 12 miles, contour east through ponderosa pine forest, nearing the wilderness boundary. As the road bends south briefly around 12½ miles, gain your first view of 4099-foot Anderson Peak with Cone Peak beyond, both ahead on your route. By 13 miles (the final milepost along the route) you descend toward a saddle, then ascend steeply to Anderson Peak's southwest ridge at 13½ miles (3930 feet) after passing a paved gated spur to an Air Force Tracking Station atop the peak. At this ridge, pause to appreciate the best coastal view this side of Cone Peak, with great views of Ventana Double Cone and Cone Peak as well.

Coast Ridge Road turns east on a short steep descent along Anderson Peak's south slope, finally entering Ventana Wilderness, though no sign indicates this accomplishment. Ironically homes still lie ahead and the road is maintained. Your road contours through a graceful, tall Ponderosa pine forest along the ridgetop. Pass a 3980-foot summit at 14 miles, then descend to the fifth locked gate at 14¼ miles, marked "MARBLE PEAK RANCH, 1885." Continue dropping toward brushy Marble Peak to 14½ miles, then contour past trail signs, passing the north fork of Marble Peak Trail just beyond. Resume your descent, passing a private road on the right at 14⅝ miles. The left fork, Coast Ridge Road, heads southeast soon climbing to views. Ascend across chaparral slopes with views down Anderson Canyon to pass below the peak's southeast corner. From there you can see the south, maintained fork of Marble Peak Trail descending to meet your road. From the junction at 15 miles, it drops east to Indian Valley and the Lost Valley Trail.

CCT follows Coast Ridge Road, contouring southeast along the ridgetop through an immense glade to 15½ miles. Climb fitfully on the ridgetop through chaparral slopes, then dip to a saddle at 16 miles. After a short ridgetop contour, make a longer descent to a wooded saddle before 16⅝ miles where a spur road descends south to a large house. After a brief ascent, descend across chaparral-draped slopes with unlimited vistas. Pass a saddle with a turnaround and a gated spur on the left at 17⅜ miles. Another brief climb leads to a long descent south with views west into rugged Hot Springs Canyon, followed by a climb to the last residential spur at 18⅛ miles. In 250 feet the road has a turnaround and the sixth locked gate.

The brush-crowded, seldom traveled road continues less than a mile before disintegrating to a trail. After contouring ½ mile beyond the locked gate, look for a hard-to-spot junction with the Upper Bee Camp Trail on the right at 18¾ miles (3400 feet), about 400 feet beyond a saddle. This section ends here, with Section 12 continuing along Coast Ridge Trail. All but superhumans will want to descend to Upper Bee Camp for water and a night's rest.

If it's not signed, the Bee Camp spur Trail can be easy to miss. Look for an old jeep trail descending southeast in the brush along a spur ridge. After a few steps the tread becomes obvious and turns moderately steep. This continues ¼ mile to the base of a dry gully. Then walk 120 feet downstream to the base of a second gully and Bee Camp hidden behind a large fallen oak at 19 miles (3190 feet), where you might have to wrestle blackberry vines and poison oak for enough level room to pitch two tents. Water flows most of the year in the adjacent stream, the headwaters of North Fork Big Creek. If it's not flowing, head downstream to

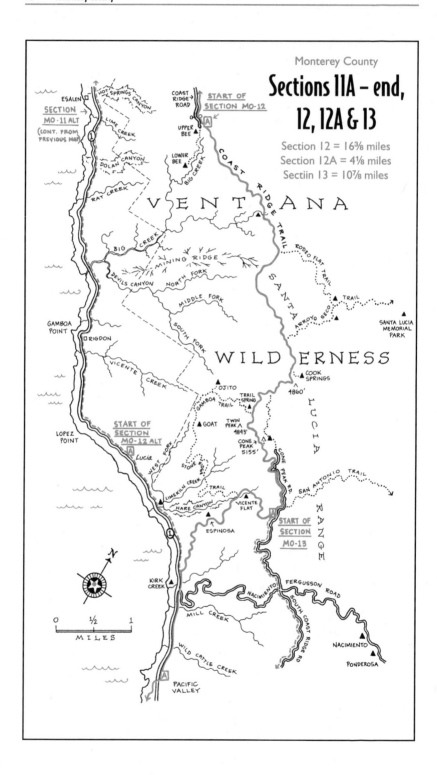

Monterey County

Sections 11A – end, 12, 12A & 13

Section 12 = 16⅜ miles
Section 12A = 4⅛ miles
Sectiin 13 = 10⅞ miles

find several small pools. The trail to Lower Bee Camp shown on the Ventana Wilderness map no longer exists, although the level camp still exists on the west side of the creek about a mile downstream. If Bee Camp is too crowded or overgrown, you can filter water there and carry it up to a dry camp astride the trail on the ridgetop, just west of the vague spur junction.

ALTERNATE ROUTE: See Highway Route, Monterey Section 11Alt and 12Alt.

SUGGESTED ROUND TRIPS & LOOPS: You can make a rewarding full-day or overnight loop of 11¼ miles, up Coast Ridge Road, then returning via Terrace Creek and Pine Ridge trails to Big Sur Station where a short shuttle is required to return to Ventana Inn.

SECTION 12
Upper Bee Camp Junction to Cone Peak, Ventana Wilderness, to upper Vicente Flat Trailhead, Cone Peak Road

DISTANCE: 16⅜ miles, plus recommended ⅝-mile side trip to top of Cone Peak (26.4 kilometers + 1 km).

OPEN TO: Hikers, dogs, equestrians.

SURFACE: Trail, dirt road, firebreaks.

ACCESS POINT: Upper Bee Camp junction.

HOW TO GET THERE: Hike in from Ventana Inn or Cone Peak Trailhead. No vehicle access to north end.

OTHER ACCESS: Cone Peak Road at Cone Peak Trailhead.

DIFFICULTY: Strenuous.

ELEVATION GAIN/LOSS: 3765 feet+/3975 feet-. Add 355 feet+/355 feet- to summit Cone Peak.

CAUTIONS: Wildfires burned area around Bee Camp in October 1999, call before going for updates and closure information. Spring and autumn are best. In summer this route can be very hot and black flies a problem—start early each day or take highway route. Winter weather can be very cold and snow is not uncommon. Campfire permits required during fire season, May to October. Trail crosses remote, isolated country with no services and extremely limited water sources. Watch for rattlesnakes, ticks and poison oak.

FURTHER INFORMATION: Los Padres National Forest, Monterey District (831)385-5434.

FACILITIES: None.

CAMPGROUNDS: Trail camps at Bee Camp and Trail Spring Camp. Car camping at Kirk Creek Campground (developed) on Highway 1 or at primitive Redwood Springs Camp on Cone Peak Road 3.5 miles south of section's south end.

Coast Ridge Road traverses this immense glade on Marble Peak Ranch.

LODGING: Nearest lodging on Highway 1 at Lucia north of Kirk Creek or Gorda to south.

The Big Sur high route continues through Ventana Wilderness on this remote section, the steepest in Volume Two. Here you'll explore spectacularly beautiful country as well as experience some challenging routefinding and steep terrain. The highlight of the entire Big Sur high route must be reaching the top of Cone Peak, the highest point on the entire California coast. We hope you find better weather than we did when we summited. Although the previous day had been crystal clear, a front moved in on the morning we left Trail Spring Camp for the summit, placing us in clouds with no view whatsoever when we topped the peak. Consider that you can also day hike to the summit from Cone Peak Trailhead. For more about the high route, be sure to read Monterey Sections 11 and 13.

WILDFIRE UPDATE: Large fires once again burned Ventana Wilderness in October 1999. Crews used Coast Ridge near Bee Camp as fire line. Fire damage and control measures have affected trail, but extent of damage will not be known until after publication. Before you go, call Monterey Ranger District for more information and to make sure trail is open.

From Upper Bee Camp junction (3400 feet elevation), follow Coast Ridge Trail east and southeast as it undulates along the ridgetop on a rocky firebreak. At 7/8 mile it drops to a saddle (3460 feet) where a trail once descended south and west to Lower Bee Camp. Heavy brush has obscured all signs of that spur. Coast Ridge Trail climbs east-southeast up a brushy corridor, gaining the ridgetop at a very large saddle at 1⅛ miles (3593 feet), then ascends by a winding road choked with chaparral and occasionally difficult to follow to a third saddle at 1¾ miles. From there it undulates along the ridge to reach a junction with the steep Lost Valley Connector Trail beyond 2⅜ miles at a grassy saddle with a few Santa Lucia firs, a rare tree. The spur descends north just west of a spur ridge.

Follow Coast Ridge Trail climbing east along the ridgetop. It ascends to a top around 2¾ miles, dips then contours east, regaining the ridgetop around 3 miles. Climb southeast west of the ridgetop, passing a seasonal seep in the trail at 3½ miles, usually a trickling but reliable water source in wet season. Climb southeast through a gully then across brushy slopes with conglomerate rock, once an ancient river bed, around 3¾ miles. The ascent ends and your track dips to a saddle before 4¼ miles (4330 feet). Your firebreak ridgetop trail quickly climbs east to a high point with an awesome panoramic vista spanning from ocean to the east side of the wilderness.

Descend along the ridge to another saddle before 4½ miles where the trail may be confusing. Here a berm or tank trap blocks the ridgetop firebreak rising straight ahead, and the Coast Ridge Trail turns right. If you mistakenly continue straight (we did!), you'll climb an increasingly steep hill, and when you struggle to a summit, you'll suddenly find yourself on the unmarked Rodeo Flats Trail. At the saddle with the berm across the ridgetop, Coast Ridge Trail turns right and dips slightly to cross a small gully with a seasonal stream marked by a roomy volunteer camp before the ford, then climbs south steeply with more views, coming to the signed Rodeo Flats Trail junction (4485 feet) at a broad saddle at 4⅞ miles.

From the junction, Coast Ridge Trail climbs southeast along a firebreak on the ridgetop, descends slightly to a smaller saddle at 5⅛ miles, then climbs steeply south on the ridgetop. But in only 400 feet, veer left on a trail overgrown with chaparral at the junction and ignore the rest of the southbound ridgetop firebreak. Your trail contours, then climbs gradually to traverse the eastern slope of a ridge. The trail, crowded by brush, soon becomes more of a road, then enters a severely burned area where yerba santa and brush continue to impede progress. Continue south, regaining the ridgetop at 6 miles and dipping to an ocean-view saddle at 6⅛ miles, 4490 feet.

Follow the rocky, intermittently brushy road southeast past fire-scarred tanoaks and along the north side of the ridge to a long saddle at 6⅝ miles. Head east on the broad ridgetop track to 7⅛ miles, then ascend moderately on road through more fire damage offering extensive ocean vistas. Traverse a southwest-facing slope to a saddle at 7⅜ miles, then cross the ridgetop and traverse a shady northeast-facing slope to a wooded saddle at 7⅝ miles. A short climb takes you across southwest-facing slopes with more views down Devils Canyon to the sea. Then a short, steep descent leads to the Arroyo Seco Trail junction at a saddle at 8⅛ miles.

Coast Ridge Trail ascends southeast on the road, passing two more saddles by 8⅜ miles. Climb the road through a stately stand of sugar pines, passing a steeply ascending spur on your right at 8⅝ miles. Beyond 8¾ miles sandstone boulders beside the trail offer a fine view northeast to Junipero Serra Peak. The track turns southwest, then south along an open sandstone ridge to cross burned slopes littered with sandstone boulders. Then follow the crest to the Cook Springs Camp Trail junction beyond 9¼ miles, marked by a fallen sugar pine giant.

Coast Ridge Trail climbs south, then west across an ascending ridge. At the ridgetop and a junction with the old Carrizo Trail, the Coast Ridge Route reaches its high point, 4860 feet. Here the road is replaced by a trail that arcs southwest with the first great view south to nearby Cone Peak. Pass burnt snags on fire-ravaged slopes, then head west and south to a marble saddle atop the Coast Ridge at

9⅞ miles. After you pass a spur ridge on your right, be sure to look back for a view of the rugged cliffs of the spur and main ridges. Ocean vistas also excel as you reach the Gamboa Trail junction before 10¼ miles.

Here you really have two choices. The Coast Ridge Trail continues on the left, ascending toward Cone Peak but then contouring east of the ridge before dropping to the end of Cone Peak Road at 11¾ miles without a chance to gain the peak's summit. (You could still take Cone Peak Trail from the next trailhead down the road.) If you take that route, you then need to walk down Cone Peak Road for 2⅞ miles to the Vicente Flat Trail. We prefer the more strenuous, but much more scenic coastal vista route described below.

Veer right on the Gamboa Trail and make a moderate descent southwest through woodlands. After crossing a ridge beyond 11⅛ miles, the trail dips through a brushy gully and angles south, coming to Trail Spring Camp at 11⅝ miles, elevation 3800 feet. This viewless camp nestles a few feet below the junc-

Our National Forests and the New User Fees

If you use federally managed public lands, be warned! The United States government now has a program "to test the public's willingness to pay for outdoor recreation." In October 1996 the feds implemented the Fee Demonstration Program and began charging the public for various types of recreation on selected federal lands, collecting fees that were never charged before. For example, if you park or even drive along any of the many back roads in Los Padres National Forest, the Forest Service expects you to buy a Forest Adventure Pass. They exempted users of Highway 1 from paying the fees (they could charge Coast Highway users where the road passes through the national forest), but expected everyone else to pay, whether sightseeing, exploring, camping, picnicking or parking at a trailhead for a day hike or overnight trip.

The Fee Demonstration Program is a five-year pilot program allowing administrators of our national forests to charge us for using our national forests. So far the fees have been implemented in various ways in eleven of California's eighteen national forests. Fees were established in the most popular national forests first, with many of the least popular still not charging. Some national forests charge for entry,

some only for trailhead parking, and others for climbing, boating, picnicking, or other uses. In 1998 the new fees collected amounted to less than $20 million nationwide, far less than 1% of the forest service budget.

Thousands of individual national forest users, hundreds of environmental groups, and many state, county and city governments have protested the new fees. The California state legislature passed a resolution in 1998 asking Congress to repeal the Fee Demonstration Program for the four most popular southern California forests, while numerous cities and counties have also officially opposed the fees.

Opponents cite several reasons for their resistance to the fees. Foremost is the fact that the public has traditionally had free access to our national forests, unlike most national parks where admission is charged. Fee opponents ask why users should be charged for visiting lands owned by the taxpayers. Other activists ask how the national forests can charge for use when they haven't clearly posted the boundaries of the fee areas. Many fee opponents see the fees as a sign of encroaching commercialism on our federal lands. For example, will car dealers soon offer a free Forest Adventure Pass to buyers of four-wheel-

tion with the Cone Peak Trail in a narrow sloping gully beneath maples, bay laurels and madrones. You can usually find water in the adjacent broad, rocky wash. If not you'll need to descend cross-country down the wash as much as ⅜ mile. CCT ascends the Cone Peak Trail, marked by a sign near the camp. If you don't want or are unable to climb the peak, an alternate route follows the Gamboa and Stone Ridge Trails to Vicente Flat Camp, rejoining the described CCT route there. It's slightly longer but less than half the elevation gain.

The Cone Peak Trail ascends steeply southwest, then southeast up a rocky wash. Beyond 11⅞ miles the trail, much in need of maintenance at press time (many fallen trees, including large ones you must climb over), switchbacks right, crossing the rocky wash you've been following. Climb steeply south, then switchback left beyond 12 miles and ascend east and southeast. After a switchback to the right around 12¼ miles, the ascent eases. Switchback left before 12⅜ miles and ascend steeply southeast. Switchback right around 12½ miles and

Our National Forests – continued

drive vehicles, then advertise that Los Padres National Forest is proudly sponsored by Jeep dealers? The forest service claimed that the public has no right to protest the fees, but in 1999 a California judge ruled that the public has that right.

The Clinton Administration proposed scrapping the Fee Demonstration Program and making the fees permanent in the fiscal year 2000 budget, but Congress decided to let the program run to its September 2001 expiration date. In defense of the fees the forest service cites: the strain on national forest resources in populated areas, the shortage of staff to manage public lands, and Congressional cutbacks of recreation funding. They also point out that unlike previous fee programs, which went into the general fund, 95% of the new fees are returned to the national forest where they were collected. But returning 95% of Forest Adventure Pass money to Los Padres National Forest falls far short of guaranteeing wise stewardship of the national forest.

The 1.7 million-acre Los Padres is a prime example of whether the fee program will actually benefit the land rather than just the agency. Most of the Los Padres budget goes to administrative costs, while much of the rest must go into fight-

ing the seasonal wildfires that ravage its remote and rugged terrain. Residents and visitors claim that national forest staff seldom visit most of the vast national forest, with even fewer staff visits to the more than 400,000 acres of designated wilderness in Los Padres. In the 14 days I spent in the Los Padres researching this book, I never once saw a national forest staffer outside the office. When I visited an office on a week day to purchase a Forest Adventure Pass, it was closed. Wilderness trails are poorly maintained (if at all), and trails, boundaries and campsites desperately lack signing, making for hazardous hiking. Los Padres National Forest currently charges people to visit the least visited and least accessible portions of the forest, but charges only an overnight parking fee at Big Sur Station where 85% of visitors to Ventana Wilderness start their trips. Forest Service campgrounds and offices in the Big Sur region are staffed by employees of a company under contract, not by government employees. If Los Padres National Forest were to charge $1 for each visitor who drives Highway 1 through the national forest, they would collect $3-4 million a year, far more than they are currently collecting from Forest Adventure Passes.

climb through open mixed conifer/live oak forest. Promptly switchback left in 200 feet, then again at a steep rocky wash before 12⅝ miles. Ascend steeply with two more short switchbacks, coming to the ridgetop junction with the Cone Peak spur around 12¾ miles.

We strongly recommend you drop your pack here and treat yourself to an ascent of Cone Peak, the highest point on the California coast at 5155 feet, for the best view in Ventana Wilderness and one of the best on the entire coast. The spur trail gains the summit a little more than ¼ mile from the junction.

Return to the trail fork, pick up your pack and descend the Cone Peak Trail. It drops generally south by several switchbacks to 13⅜ miles, then makes a long sidehill descent north and east. Descend generally southeast by 13⅞ miles, passing through a large burn area from 14⅛ miles. Your trail turns south, reaching a burned ridgetop saddle beyond 14¼ miles, where it turns east on a winding descent to Cone Peak Road Trailhead, elevation 3720 feet, beyond 14¾ miles.

Turn right and descend Cone Peak Road for 1⅝ miles to the Upper Vicente Flat Trailhead (3190 feet) marked by a wilderness boundary sign on the right side of the road at the south end of a saddle with a small dry camp nearby at 16⅜ miles. While the main route of the CCT descends Vicente Flat Trail to return to the coast, see the discussion of several other high-route options in Alternate Routes below.

ALTERNATE ROUTES: For a route that does not require backpacking, see the highway route of Monterey Sections 11A and 12A.

Backpackers have several choices to extend the main Big Sur High Route on an arduous ridge route that avoids the CCT's highway walking through southern Big Sur. Maps, compass, routefinding ability and good planning are all essentials if you continue south on the High Route.

Instead of leaving Cone Peak Road to descend Vicente Flat Trail, follow the road south. That dirt track continues more or less along Coast Ridge for 26 more miles, with five more trail or trail/road routes offering return to the coast. We describe their distances from upper Vicente Flat Trailhead. At 4.1 miles Coast Ridge Road crosses Nacimiento Road. The unmarked Mill Creek Trailhead lies below on the right just beyond the intersection. A fire road behind a yellow gate descends to the coast in about 8 miles, though the bottom end is so overgrown that it's better to follow Nacimiento Road for the last ¾ mile to the coast. Continuing along Coast Ridge Road, you reach Road 23S14 on the right at 12.7 miles. For a 10¼-mile route to the coast, that road descends to Willow Creek Trail, which ends with a 2⅜-mile hike on Willow Creek Road required to reach Highway 1. Otherwise continue on Coast Ridge Road to 20.5 miles, where you can descend Willow Creek Road, turn left and drop to Alder Creek Camp, then follow the Buckeye Trail to rejoin CCT at Upper Cruickshank Camp on Monterey Section 15. Or continue along Coast Ridge Road to 25.5 miles, turn right and descend 4¼ miles on Cruickshank Trail to join Section 15 just above Upper Cruickshank Camp. A final choice continues on Coast Ridge Road to 26 miles and descends Salmon Creek Trail for 5¾ miles to meet Section 15 on Highway 1 just south of Salmon Creek. If you hike any of these, be careful, follow your progress on good maps, and carry enough food and water to reach your goal.

SUGGESTED ROUND TRIPS & LOOPS: If you don't backpack, you can still visit Cone Peak, the highlight of this route, by the following round trip or loop day hike. Call the forest service before you go to be sure the road is open. Turn east off Highway 1 just south of Kirk Creek onto Nacimiento Road. Drive 7.2 miles, turn left on Central Coast Ridge Road (aka Cone Peak Road) and go 5.3 miles to Cone Peak Trailhead. Ascend the Cone Peak Trail (and CCT) for 2 miles to a fork, then turn right and climb steeply to the summit, reaching the lookout tower there just beyond 2¼ miles to enjoy the panoramic view of Big Sur and the coast, quite possibly the best coastal vista in California. You can return the same way, 4⅝ miles round trip. Or take this rugged 7⅞-mile loop: when you return to the fork, turn right and descend Cone Peak Trail to Trail Spring Camp, then turn right and ascend the Gamboa Trail to the ridge and the junction with the Coast Ridge Trail. Turn right and follow Coast Ridge Trail up the ridge and across the peak's east face until the trail ends at the end of Cone Peak Road. Walk down the road 1¼ miles to Cone Peak Trailhead to finish the loop.

HOW TO IMPROVE CCT HERE: Provide better signage and trail maintenance along Coast Ridge Trail.

SECTION 13
Upper Vicente Flat Trailhead, Cone Peak Road, to Pacific Valley, Highway 1

DISTANCE: 10⅞ miles (17.5 kilometers).

OPEN TO: Hikers. Dogs and equestrians in wilderness, bicyclists on highway.

SURFACE: Trail, highway shoulder.

ACCESS POINT: Upper Vicente Flat Trailhead on Coast Ridge/Cone Peak Road.

HOW TO GET THERE: Drive Highway 1 to southern Big Sur. Just south of the Kirk Creek bridge at Milepost 18.9, turn east on Nacimiento-Fergusson Road and drive 7.2 steep winding miles, then turn left on South Coast Ridge Road also known as Cone Peak Road and go 4.1 miles to the unmarked upper Vicente Flat Trailhead at a saddle with a wide spot in the road. Trail climbs southwest from south side of saddle and a small dry camp is just north.

OTHER ACCESS: Kirk Creek Campground or the lower Vicente Flat Trailhead across the highway, anywhere south on highway for three miles to Pacific Valley.

DIFFICULTY: Strenuous for trail portion, easy for highway leg.

ELEVATION GAIN/LOSS: 690 feet+/3720 feet-. Trail portion: 450 feet+/3440 feet-.

CAUTIONS: Cone Peak Road may be closed to vehicles during periods of bad weather or extreme fire danger. Call first. If you park on Cone Peak Road, the Forest Service currently requires that you have a "Forest Adventure Pass," available for purchase at Los Padres National Forest offices. Wildfires burned area around Vicente Flat in October 1999, call before going for updates and closure information.

FURTHER INFORMATION: Los Padres National Forest, Monterey Ranger District (831)385-5434.

FACILITIES: None until Kirk Creek Campground which has restrooms and water. Phone, restrooms, picnic tables and water at Sand Dollar Beach parking area on next section.

CAMPGROUNDS: Trail camps at Vicente Flat Camp and Espinosa Camp. Car camping at Kirk Creek Campground (developed, no showers) and Limekiln State Park (2 miles north, developed, showers) on Highway I and at Redwood Springs Camp (primitive) .6 mile up Cone Peak Road.

LODGING: Nearest lodging on Highway I at Lucia north of Kirk Creek or Gorda to south.

MAP: See page 72.

This southern leg of CCT's Big Sur high route returns to the Ventana Wilderness to descend into Hare Canyon, passing through a wonderful redwood grove around Vicente Flat, then contours across steep slopes before descending to Highway 1 opposite Kirk Creek Campground. While the Forest Service's Ventana Wilderness map shows it as the Kirk Creek Trail, that's really a misnomer since the trail never touches Kirk Creek nor enters its canyon. We still recommend that map for its updating of the outdated USGS topographic maps.

Sadly, once you reach the Coast Highway, CCT is forced to follow the highway shoulder south for this section's final 3 miles. Be forewarned that services are no longer available at Pacific Valley. The nearest services to Kirk Creek Campground are 2 miles north at Limekiln State Park, which has a very small and limited store, and almost 10 miles south at Gorda, where the store is small but crammed with goods. Gorda has a good restaurant, gas station and lodging as well.

WILDFIRE UPDATE: Large fires once again burned Ventana Wilderness in October 1999 including Vicente Flat area and along Stone Ridge and Gamboa Trails. Fire damage may have affected trail, but extent of damage will not be known until after publication. Before you go, call Monterey Ranger District for more information and to make sure trail is open.

The access point and upper trailhead is not specifically identified, but can be distinguished by a plastic "WILDERNESS BOUNDARY" sign and a wooden bulletin board.

From the Upper Vicente Flat Trailhead (3190 feet) on the west side of the road, follow the Vicente Flat Trail on a short ascent southwest to a ridgetop, then climb it south to a saddle beyond ⅛ mile. Drop past charred snags to contour to a nearly invisible junction beyond ⅜ mile. The historic and overgrown Girard Trail which went southwest from here is no longer visible or maintained, so veer right and descend the Vicente Flat Trail by twelve short switchbacks. Beyond ⅝ mile the trail descends steeply northwest with views across steep and deep Hare Creek Canyon to towering Cone Peak, passing Coulter pines amidst hardwoods.

Your steep drop ends at a ridge at 1⅛ miles. Descend moderately across a steep slope by five switchbacks to meet Hare Creek beneath redwoods at 1½ miles. Descend along the creek, fording it around 1¾ miles. After angling away from the stream briefly, the trail drops to a second ford before 2 miles. Your trail descends southwest along Hare Creek, crossing it seven more times before 2⅜ miles. Follow the stream south from the last ford, crossing a seasonal side stream from the north.

Reach Vicente Flat Camp at 2⅜ miles, passing upper sites beneath redwoods near the creek to enter a spacious meadow at 2½ miles with more camps. From the clearing, take the trail on the right for 400 feet to the junction with the Stone Ridge Trail, which ascends west. CCT veers left on the Vicente Flat Trail, dropping south to cross many forked Hare Creek on a fallen redwood log identifiable by its scuffed bark.

After a last campsite, the trail climbs moderately south up a ridge. When your trail turns southwest beyond 2¾ miles, contour above steep cliffs in Hare Canyon, coming to a surprising ocean view at 2⅞ miles. Your trail contours through several gullies before topping out at 1860 feet beyond

Looking back at Cone Peak from the Vicente Flat Trail.

3⅝ miles. Cross a grassy ridge with another ocean view, contour southeast to cross another gully, then climb to a redwood-lined stream, the last reliable water source before Highway 1. In the next ¼ mile, you round a ridge and dip through a small gully to reach Espinosa Camp (1700 feet) perched on a small ridge before 4⅜ miles.

CCT crosses a redwood-lined gully, then descends gently west and southwest, gaining a ridge with a panoramic vista around 4⅞ miles. You look north to Cone Peak and its sister Twin Peak (4843') and up and down a large chunk of coast. You can see the tread of the historic Girard Trail dropping west down the ridge. That unmaintained trail becomes overgrown and obscure as it drops into lower Hare Canyon to end in Limekiln Canyon.

Follow the lower Vicente Flat Trail as it makes a steady, well graded descent south with abundant coastal views interspersed with mixed forest. Leave forests and the wilderness behind around 6⅜ miles to crest a ridge (1000') with the last expansive coastal view. Descend south through grasslands and chaparral, then switch back toward the highway. If you've traversed the wilderness route of the last three sections, when the switchbacks end around 7⅜ miles and you look straight down on nearby Highway 1, allow yourself the flood of mixed emotions usually brought on by completing a remote 43-mile backpack. On the one hand, you feel strange to be returning to the world of cars and crowds. On the other hand, you want to know where to find the nearest hot shower and/or cold beer or ice cream. You can shower if you pay to camp at Limekiln Redwoods 2 miles north. Prepared, refrigerated treats might be found at the campground's tiny store, or farther north at Lucia Lodge, but to the south not until Gorda.

Reach the lower Vicente Flat Trailhead on Highway 1 at 7⅞ miles. Kirk Creek Campground across the road has pleasant blufftop sites with flush toilets and cold running water but no showers. The campground has two trails providing coastal access to a narrow beach, the southern one at the mouth of Kirk Creek. At low tide the two trails link for a ⅞-mile loop.

From lower Vicente Flat Trailhead, the CCT turns left to follow the highway shoulder south, crossing the Kirk Creek bridge and the west end of Nacimiento-Fergusson Road. Climb over a rise, then descend to the Mill Creek bridge. Before the bridge, a spur road on the right at 8⅜ miles descends to Mill Creek Picnic Area and a short coastal access path to a sandy beach just north and the rocky mouth of Mill Creek to the south.

CCT continues along Highway 1, climbing over a rise before dropping to cross the Wild Cattle Creek bridge at 9½ miles. Ascend the highway to another high point at 10⅝ miles. Here the land between the road and the coastline, which has been steep, brushy and rocky to this point, fans out into a broad marine terrace covered with grasslands and only isolated brush. However, brush and a fence here hamper access to the terrace west of the highway. Walk the shoulder to 10⅞ miles where a hiker's ladder crosses the fence from a broad turnout west of the highway, just south of Milepost 16.0. This is the start of Section 14.

ALTERNATE ROUTE: See Alternate Routes for Section 12.

SUGGESTED ROUND TRIPS & LOOPS: It's a steep but mostly easy hike down to Vicente Flat Camp but a very steep climb back out. For a challenging, view-rich loop, turn north at Vicente Flat Camp and follow the Stone Ridge Trail and the Gamboa Trail to Trail Spring Camp, then follow the CCT along Cone Peak Trail and Cone Peak Road to return to the upper Vicente Flat Trailhead, a loop of 15½ miles, not including the ⅝-mile side trip up Cone Peak. The hike up from Highway 1 to Espinosa Camp at 3½ miles and on to Vicente Flat around 5⅜ miles offers a generally more maintained trail with better grades.

HOW TO IMPROVE CCT HERE: Develop a route off highway from Kirk Creek to Pacific Valley.

SECTION 11A (Alternate)
Ventana Inn to Lucia via Highway 1 Shoulder

DISTANCE: 22¼ miles (35.8 kilometers).

OPEN TO: Hikers, bicyclists.

SURFACE: Highway shoulder.

ACCESS POINT: Ventana Inn turnoff on Highway 1.

HOW TO GET THERE: On Highway 1 only .6 mile south of the Big Sur post office, the turnoff to Ventana Inn is east of the highway at Milepost 44.3. Section starts there, with day-use parking at Ventana Inn (lot .15 miles up inn road) or dirt turnouts north or south along highway.

OTHER ACCESS: Anywhere along route.

DIFFICULTY: Moderate.

ELEVATION GAIN/LOSS: 1430 feet+/2050 feet-.

CAUTIONS: Narrow shoulders! Use extreme caution if you road walk this narrow, winding and busy section of highway. Wear bright clothes, walk in a group and walk single file. Midweek is best time to do this road walk.

FACILITIES: Julia Pfeiffer Burns State Park along the route has restrooms, water, phone and picnic tables.

CAMPGROUNDS: Ventana Campground is near start or try Pfeiffer-Big Sur State Park not far to the north. Julia Pfeiffer Burns State Park en route has two walk-in/environmental camps, but reservations can only be made in advance, 1-800-444-7275.

LODGING: The local inns, Ventana and Post Ranch, both start around $200/night. For more affordable rates, look south to historic Deetjen's Big Sur Inn and Lucia or north to Big Sur Lodge, Ripplewood Resort, Big Sur Cabins or Glen Oaks Motel.

MAP: See pages 68 and 72.

The same rugged terrain that makes Big Sur a spectacular and unique place to visit also makes the choices for a route for the California Coastal Trail extremely limited. This Big Sur road walk offers a classic example of places where walking south on the highway's left shoulder facing traffic can be hazardous. Still, while the Big Sur high route in the previous three sections offers a far more pristine choice than this much driven highway route, the High Route is not advisable in winter or high summer or at any time by people without backpacking and wilderness experience.

The terrain and vistas you'll see on this section are truly wonderful and dramatic. Just be sure you don't take your mind off the often unrelenting, sometimes unsafe parade of vehicle traffic. Of course this is true whether you walk, cycle or drive this spectacular road. As you travel the route, you might ponder the arduous eighteen-year process involved in its construction, including nine years of pick-and-shovel prison-gang hard labor, tons of explosives, and years of innovative bridge design and construction.

Follow the highway shoulder as it climbs south to a summit before ⅛ mile, where you gain a breathtaking view of the coastline to the south. Then make a long, winding descent, passing several Big Sur landmarks. Before ¾ mile on the right, fabled Nepenthe offers food, drink and inspiring views from its perch high above the Pacific. Wind down past the Henry Miller Memorial Library on your left at one mile, then past the atmospheric Deetjen's Big Sur Inn astride Castro Canyon before 1½ miles. After almost a mile of gradual climbing, your winding asphalt ribbon resumes descending, passing a turnout with a coastal view before 2¾ miles. Another short ascent to 3⅛ miles gives way to another descent past two turnouts with grand views. The turnout near Milepost 41 looks down on an amazing sea lion haul-out on a rocky beach far below.

From 3⅞ miles, ascend, contour, then climb again to 4⅝ miles. Descend to cross the bridge over Torre Canyon at 4⅞ miles, ascend to 5¼ miles, then contour to 5¾ miles before making a longer descent to meet the Partington Cove Trail on your right just before Partington Creek at 6⅞ miles. The side trail on your right drops ¼ mile to a junction and outhouse. If you turn right at the junction, then take the left fork at the second junction in 100 feet, the trail ducks through a 120-foot-long tunnel to reach Partington Cove, a former doghole port and great spot to watch sea otters and sunsets. The right fork at the second junction leads to a tiny beach at the mouth of Partington Creek. The Tan Bark Trail east of the highway climbs 1800 feet in 3¼ miles to the Tin House and grand views. (If the Ewoldsen Trail has been reopened to Tin House, you can take these upper trails for a 6⅜-mile alternate to walking the road, 4¼ miles longer than the road route.)

Continuing along the highway shoulder, follow the road as it climbs to a vista point at 7¾ miles. The Fire Road Trail climbs north from there, reaching the Tin House in 2¼ miles. CCT descends gradually along the highway to 8¾ miles, then moderately to Julia Pfeiffer Burns State Park at 9 miles. Consider a short side trip here of ¾ mile to see the McWay Creek waterfall as it plunges to surf line on a pristine beach. To find it, walk east on the park road for ⅛ mile where you'll find restrooms and a pay phone (a picnic area lies a bit farther up the canyon), then turn right and follow the Waterfall Trail under the highway to the viewpoint.

CCT follows the highway south, descending gradually to cross the bridge over Anderson Canyon at 9½ miles. A short climb leads to a long contour above the rugged shoreline, then dips to cross the Burns Creek bridge at 10½ miles, where the Ventana Wilderness boundary is less than ½ mile upstream. Contour then climb gradually along the road's edge to cross the Buck Creek bridge at 11⅛ miles. The ascent continues briefly, then you descend to the Hot Springs Canyon bridge at 12⅛ miles.

Ascend along the highway, passing the turnoff to famed Esalen Institute on the ocean side, then climbing through a corner of the John Little State Reserve which preserves the coast around Lime Creek, which you cross on the bridge at 12⅝ miles. You soon descend along the narrow highway, dipping to the Dolan Creek bridge at 13¾ miles, then contouring to 14 miles, before descending again to 14⅝ miles to cross the Rat Creek bridge.

Follow Highway 1 as it climbs slightly to 15 miles, descends gradually to 16⅛ miles, then climbs briefly before dropping to the graceful double arch of the Big Creek bridge at 16⅞ miles. Big Creek's immense and stark landscape, also known as Devils Canyon, presents the biggest chasm Highway 1 has crossed since the Bixby Bridge. Much of the surrounding landscape is protected in the Landels-Big Creek Reserve managed by the University of California, with visitation only by occasional guided hikes. The Ventana Wilderness lies about 1½ miles upstream.

Climb the highway shoulder down coast, passing a vista point around 17¾ miles, then continuing a gradual rise to 18⅝ miles. Before 18¼ miles watch on the left for the WPA-era Rigdon Drinking Fountain in a small canyon. There a massive picnic table offers a welcome rest for the weary foot traveler, but alas no working fountain. Nearby stone steps lead to three gnarled old redwoods and a trail that dips under a fence to the creek, the fountain perhaps shrouded in the dense undergrowth.

Descend the twisting highway through the steep, rocky terrain around Gamboa Point, dropping to the Vicente Creek bridge at 19⅜ miles. The highway climbs to 20⅜ miles, then dips to 21⅛ miles where it rounds Lopez Point, only to ascend steeply to 21⅝ miles. Descend briefly to pass the highway sign for Lucia at

22 miles, then contour to section's end at the Lucia Cafe & Cabins at 22¼ miles.

ALTERNATE ROUTE: See Sections 11, 12 and 13 for preferred high route, a strenuous and seasonal alternative to the highway shoulder walk.

SUGGESTED ROUND TRIPS & LOOPS: Take the pleasant ⅝-mile round trip hike to Partington Cove. Explore the upland trails of Julia Pfeiffer Burns State Park. You can make a pleasant shuttle or loop by taking the Tan Bark Trail from Partington Cove to the Tin House, then descending the Fire Road Trail for a 5⅝-mile hike and a .8 mile car shuttle. Or descend from Tin House on the Ewoldsen Trail for a 6⅜-mile hike with a 2.1 mile shuttle.

HOW TO IMPROVE CCT HERE: Develop a coastal route off the highway.

SECTION 12A
Lucia to Kirk Creek Campground

DISTANCE: 4⅛ miles (6.6 kilometers).

OPEN TO: Hikers, bicyclists.

SURFACE: Highway shoulder.

ACCESS POINT: Lucia.

HOW TO GET THERE: Lucia is a tiny cafe/motel on Highway 1 in central Big Sur at Milepost 22.8, about 23 miles south of the Big Sur post office.

OTHER ACCESS: Anywhere along section.

DIFFICULTY: Moderate.

ELEVATION GAIN/LOSS: 350 feet+/510 feet-.

CAUTIONS: Narrow shoulders! Use extreme caution if you road walk this narrow, winding and busy section of highway. Wear bright clothes, walk in a group and walk single file. Midweek is best time to do this road walk.

FURTHER INFORMATION: Los Padres National Forest, Monterey Ranger District (831)385-5434.

FACILITIES: Cafe at Lucia. Water and restrooms at Limekiln and Kirk Creek.

CAMPGROUNDS: Limekiln State Campground is en route, with several units, showers and a very small store. Kirk Creek Campground at section's end has no showers.

LODGING: Lucia has rooms for rent. Next rooms to south are at Gorda.

MAP: See page 72.

The road shoulder walk through the grand terrain of the immense Big Sur country continues on this short section, where the highway route and the wilderness high route rejoin at the Vicente Flat Trailhead across from Kirk Creek Campground. Even then the highway walking doesn't end. It continues for 3½ miles to Pacific Valley where a broad marine terrace provides a delightful 3⅝-mile respite from the pavement. Typically you'll have to contend with somewhat less vehicle traffic in southern Big Sur than you encountered in central Big Sur, but you never want to let your defenses down or let your mind wander far from the task of staying out of harm's way when walking this scenic highway where drivers may be distracted, frustrated or downright crazy.

Follow the highway shoulder down the coast, ascending east out of Lucia with views south to Cape San Martin 10½ miles away. Climb across a gulch at ⅜ mile and reach the first summit at ½ mile. You soon descend, crossing another gulch at ¾ mile, then dropping across an immense slide from 1⅛ to 1⅜ miles. Continue your road shoulder descent, rounding a steep and narrow rocky point around 1¾ miles.

Cross the bridge over Limekiln Creek at 2 miles, coming to the access road to Limekiln State Park on the left at 2⅛ miles. Limekiln has no through trails (the old Girard Trail that once climbed to Vicente Flat on Section 13 has become a bushwhacker's delight), but does offer 40 pleasant if somewhat crowded campsites with showers. It also has a pleasant side trail (one mile round trip) up the wooded creek of Limekiln Canyon to the rusting hulks of old metal kilns in a peaceful spot. Or take an easy ¼-mile round trip stroll to a small beach.

CCT's road route continues, making a gentle ascent for the next 1½ miles. Enter Los Padres National Forest by 2½ miles and cross a creek before 2¾ miles, reaching the summit at 3⅝ miles. Descend gradually across the steep coastal bluffs, coming to the lower Vicente Flat or Kirk Creek Trailhead on the left at 4⅛ miles. The wilderness boundary lies a few feet up the trail. The CCT Big Sur high route rejoins the highway route here. Across the highway is Kirk Creek Campground. Section 14 begins at Pacific Valley 3½ miles down the coast on Highway 1. For a description of the 3½ miles between here and there, see the last two paragraphs of the route description for Section 13.

ALTERNATE ROUTE: See Monterey Sections 11, 12 and 13 for the preferred high route, a strenuous, seasonal alternative to the highway.

SUGGESTED ROUND TRIPS & LOOPS: Walk the trail to the limekilns at Limekiln State Park, one mile round trip, and stroll down to the beach at the mouth of the canyon. You can visit an even more secluded beach via two trails that leave from the north and south ends of Kirk Creek Campground. At low tide they offer a ⅞-mile loop. Best of all, if also most challenging, ascend the Vicente Flat Trail, part of the Big Sur high route, for heart-stopping vistas up and down the Big Sur coast. The latter hike can be as long or short as you like, but for a good workout, hike the 3½ miles to Espinosa Camp, perched on a small ridge beyond a small redwood grove, have a picnic lunch and return the way you came.

HOW TO IMPROVE CCT HERE: Develop a coastal route off the highway.

SECTION 14
Pacific Valley to Cruickshank Trailhead

DISTANCE: 10¼ miles, with 3⅝ miles of blufftop trail (16.5 & 5.8 kilometers).

OPEN TO: Hikers, dogs. Bicyclists on road portion.

SURFACE: Trail, highway shoulder.

ACCESS POINT: Pacific Valley.

HOW TO GET THERE: Park in turnout on west side of Highway 1 at north end of Pacific Valley at Milepost 16.0, 6 miles north of Gorda.

OTHER ACCESS: Several hikers ladders south along highway, Sand Dollar Beach (fee charged), Jade Cove Access and anywhere south along highway portion.

DIFFICULTY: Easy.

ELEVATION GAIN/LOSS: 980 feet+/790 feet-. 290 feet+/210 feet- for trail portion.

CAUTIONS: Watch for poison oak. Watch for rogue waves near tideline. Use extreme caution when walking highway shoulder.

FURTHER INFORMATION: Los Padres National Forest, Monterey Ranger District (831)385-5434.

FACILITIES: Sand Dollar Picnic Area has phone, tables, fire pits and wheelchair-accessible chemical toilets. Gorda has phone, cafe, store, gas and lending library.

CAMPGROUNDS: Car camping at Plaskett Creek Campground east of Highway 1 along this section and at Kirk Creek and Limekiln Campgrounds to north.

LODGING: Extremely limited in southern Big Sur, Gorda has three cabins with views but they're not inexpensive. Lucia Lodge to the north and Ragged Point Inn to south are the only other choices.

West of Highway 1 between Pacific Valley and Jade Cove, a broad coastal marine terrace slopes gently to the shore, providing room for a unique leg of the CCT through Big Sur. The only other place in Big Sur with such gentle terrain along the shore is north of the mouth of the Big Sur River where the terrace is private property. Happily the Pacific Valley terrace is U. S. Forest Service land, and the CCT leaves the highway here to ramble along the ocean bluffs, leaving the roar of highway traffic for the rumble of surf. The convoluted shoreline, dotted with the ancient shell middens of long-gone native seafood harvesters, faces a jumble of offshore rocks that punctuate the coast's beauty. On clear days you'll find long views up and down the rugged coast. When winds are right, you may see hang gliders landing on the terrace. Between two jutting promontories north of Plaskett Creek, the terrace narrows above the graceful sweep of Sand Dollar Beach, a sandy crescent perhaps worth a side trip. Beyond the crossing of Plaskett Creek, the terrace broadens again until CCT crosses the access trail to Jade Cove, which descends to rocky coves popular with rock hunters, worth a detour at a low tide. Soon after that, CCT must return to the highway for another substantial

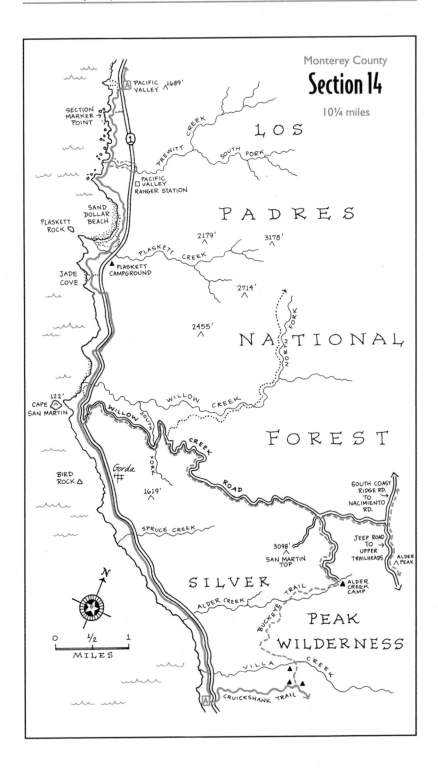

Monterey County
Section 14
10¼ miles

PACIFIC VALLEY 1689'

SECTION MARKER POINT

PREWITT CREEK

SOUTH FORK

LOS

PACIFIC VALLEY RANGER STATION

PADRES

SAND DOLLAR BEACH

PLASKETT ROCK

PLASKETT CREEK

2179' 3178'

PLASKETT CAMPGROUND

JADE COVE

2714'

2455'

NATIONAL

NORTH FORK

WILLOW CREEK

CAPE SAN MARTIN 122'

WILLOW SOUTH

FOREST

CREEK

FORK

BIRD ROCK

Gorda

1619'

ROAD

SOUTH COAST RIDGE RD. TO NACIMIENTO RD.

SPRUCE CREEK

JEEP ROAD TO UPPER TRAILHEADS

ALDER PEAK

3098' SAN MARTIN TOP

ALDER CREEK CAMP

N

SILVER

BUCKEYE TRAIL

ALDER CREEK

PEAK

0 ½ 1

WILDERNESS

MILES

VILLA CREEK

CRUICKSHANK TRAIL

road walk relieved only by the colorful southern Big Sur commercial center called Gorda, the only place with gas, food and lodging for miles.

Climb over the hiker's ladder and walk west 75 feet to where the trail splits into three, with the CCT on the left. The middle path dead-ends on the bluff in 250 feet. The track on the right heads north, then west to drop to a gravel beach north of the rocky point in ¼ mile.

Take the left fork on a gentle descent south paralleling the highway. Before ⅛ mile you contour above the head of two gullies, pass the "PACIFIC VALLEY" sign on the highway, then dip through a third gully. Continue past another hiker ladder to a fork.

Take the right fork to descend southwest to a fork near the bluff's edge at ¼ mile. Veer left on a path that fades as it nears the point in 250 feet, then follow the bluff edge south. Pick up a vague track that contours above the rocky tideline. Follow it past the head of a gully above a small beach at ⅜ mile, then on to merge with a more distinct path from a third hiker ladder in 300 feet.

Contour south with offshore and onshore rocks ahead, passing east of a rock outcrop before ½ mile. Dip through a gully and return to the marine terrace to pass east of another sandstone outcrop. An easy scramble to the top provides a good view of the trail and the broken rocky coast to the south.

Contour south-southeast across the headlands, returning to the bluff edge at ⅝ mile. Continue along the convoluted bluff edge, sometimes trackless. Before ¾ mile you meet a vague track descending from another hiker ladder on the highway. Pass east of a broad rock outcrop (watch for poison oak!) and head south across the headlands.

You soon want to veer right on the path out to a grassy point, coming to a yellow section marker at ⅞ mile. Follow the trail as it continues along the bluff edge, dipping through several tiny gullies. You reach another bench marker at one mile. Then CCT angles southwest to a rocky point at 1⅛ miles where you overlook a small sandy crescent beach.

Follow the bluff edge above the strand, meandering east around a gully, then back west, coming to a fence at 1¼ miles. Cross it on a hiker ladder 50 feet toward the highway, then head southwest to the lip of Prewitt Creek's canyon. Find the path winding down to the creek at 1⅜ miles. It's usually an easy ford—if you can't ford it you must head east to the highway. Across the creek a path winds up the canyon's south wall to the bluff. However, you might first want to walk 100 feet downstream to the creek mouth and a spectacular, rocky low-tide beach. (When the tide is low you might walk the beach south.)

After climbing back to the blufftop, cross another hiker ladder and follow the bluff edge south, passing above arched rocks on the beach below. Cross the head of a gulch at 1⅝ miles, then follow the trail west-southwest heading for the point. As you near the point, the trail turns south to climb over the rocky point near the bluff edge. By 1¾ miles the broad arc of Sand Dollar Beach comes into view to the southeast. You can also see Pfeiffer Point 28 miles up the coast.

Your trail turns east following the low ridgetop. This soon leads across a seemingly misplaced dune. Continue generally southeast following the coastline toward Highway 1, passing a spur on the left that heads east to the Pacific Valley Ranger Station beyond the highway. The route turns brushy before the rock out-

Hikers pause to enjoy the views from the Pacific Valley Headlands.

crop at 1⅞ miles, but pick your way to grasslands for easy walking. Pass to the left of more rock outcrops around 2¼ miles, ignoring the fork on the right.

Climb gradually southeast toward another hiker ladder beside the highway at 2 5/16 miles. Just 125 feet before the ladder, veer right on the track that heads south through a gate to dip and rise through a deep gully and pass a big rock outcrop between you and the coast, its east face shrouded in bay laurel. Dip through another arroyo on this cow path-CCT, then contour across a narrow headland at 2½ miles, heading south toward tall trees.

At 2⅝ miles a hiker ladder just ahead on the left leads to the Sand Dollar Picnic Area and Beach parking lot beneath the trees. A well-graded spur trail on your right descends west to Sand Dollar Beach, the largest strand in Big Sur, ¼ mile round trip.

CCT continues south or southwest across open headlands. Choose either of the two paths that will soon rejoin. The left and shortest trail crosses a broad path (heads west to point) from the south hiker ladder by the parking lot and descends toward Plaskett Creek at 2¾ miles. When the track forks again, take the right fork to a generally easy ford of the rocky stream beneath alders 100 feet below the highway.

Return to the marine terrace at 2⅞ miles and contour south with views west to the chaparral-draped point and Plaskett Rock, the big sea stack offshore. Look north for a grand view up the coast and up the deep canyons of Prewitt and Plaskett creeks. Your trail dips through a gully, then forks. Take the middle of three paths southwest.

At 3 miles you cross a distinct trail from the hiker ladder beside the highway 200 feet east. Continue southwest across several more spurs heading for the shore. Gain vistas south to rugged Cape San Martin and the immense sea stack off that point by 3⅛ miles. Contouring south, you pass west of a rock outcrop and return to the bluff's edge. Merging with another bluff edge path, your trail suddenly turns distinct, with the surf churning 150 feet below.

Cross the Jade Cove Trail at 3¼ miles where it drops to a tideline access stairway. The rocky beach below is best at low tide. Continue along the bluff edge track to a fork before 3⅜ miles. Veer right to follow the bluff's edge, rounding a point with views across the ocean to Cape San Martin. Then your trail turns east-southeast on a gradual ascent toward the highway. You may need to veer due east when brush chokes the path, but by 3½ miles head southeast toward a house with a palm tree east of the highway.

CCT returns to Highway 1 at 3⅝ miles at Milepost 13.06. Walk the road's shoulder south up a gentle hill, crossing a brushy gulch and passing a large eucalyptus grove on the right. The climb ends at a vista point. Descend around the nearby point, passing a spur on the right beyond 4¼ miles. Its overgrown tread descends west and south before dead-ending on the bluff. Continue down the highway to cross the bridge over deep, wide and rugged Willow Creek Canyon at 4⅞ miles. For a closer look at the stark landscape from sea level, turn right on a spur road beyond the bridge to descend to Willow Creek Picnic Area and a rocky beach with a view of Gorda Rock offshore.

CCT continues along Highway 1, ascending over Cape San Martin and up to a junction with Willow Creek Road at 5½ miles. That steep and winding dirt road, also known as Los Burros Road, climbs east along a ridge for 6.3 miles to end at South Coast Ridge Road, elevation 3470 feet. Along the way it meets the Willow Creek Trail on the left at 2.4 miles and the Alder Camp Road on the right at 4.7 miles, which descends 1.4 miles to the camp and the northern Buckeye Trailhead.

Climb south along the highway to a summit around 6⅜ miles, then coast down to the mini-metropolis of Gorda at 6½ miles, where a small store and a good restaurant offer the only provisions along 25 miles of southern Big Sur. Follow the highway shoulder southeast, ascending almost to 6⅞ miles, then gently down to 7⅛ miles before another brief climb to 7⅜ miles.

Descend steadily along the highway to 8¾ miles, where you're only 30 feet above the breakers with sheer slide-torn cliffs east of the road. Ascend gradually beneath more cliffs to the Villa Creek bridge at 9⅝ miles, then steeply to section's end at Milepost 6.5 at 10¼ miles, where the Cruickshank Trailhead east of the highway marks the start of Section 15.

ALTERNATE ROUTE: You could stay on the highway from Pacific Valley to Jade Cove, but you'd miss a wonderful gentle headland route. One could ascend Willow Creek Road, then drop to Alder Camp to follow the Buckeye Trail south to Upper Cruickshank Camp on Section 15, but that would add several miles, wilderness route finding, and much elevation gain and loss. Also see the Alternate Route for Section 12 for the southern Big Sur high route.

SUGGESTED ROUND TRIPS & LOOPS: Follow the described route to Sand Dollar Beach or Jade Cove, then return the way you came or across the upper marine terrace or along the highway.

HOW TO IMPROVE CCT HERE: Develop a CCT route off highway south from Milepost 13.

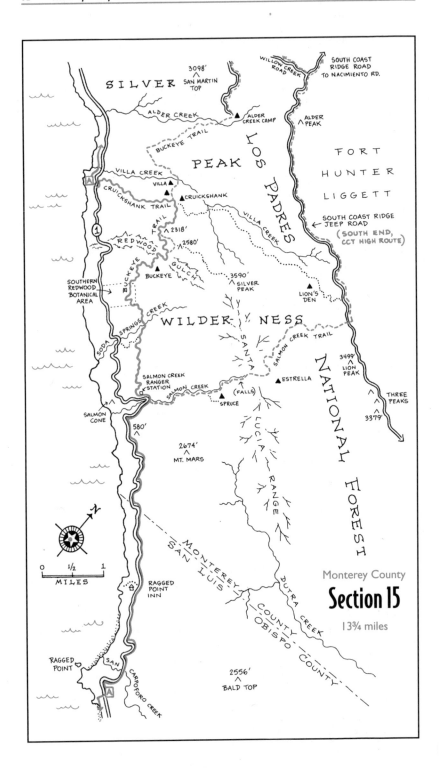

SILVER

3098'
∧
SAN MARTIN
TOP

WILLOW CREEK
ROAD

SOUTH COAST
RIDGE ROAD
TO NACIMIENTO RD.

ALDER CREEK

ALDER
CREEK CAMP

ALDER
PEAK

BUCKEYE TRAIL

PEAK

LOS PADRES

FORT
HUNTER
LIGGETT

VILLA CREEK

VILLA ▲

CRUICKSHANK TRAIL

▲ CRUICKSHANK

SOUTH COAST RIDGE
JEEP ROAD
← (SOUTH END,
CCT HIGH ROUTE)

VILLA CREEK

1

REDWOOD

∧ 2318'

∧ 2580'

BUCKEYE

GULCH

3590'
∧
SILVER
PEAK

LION'S
DEN

SOUTHERN
REDWOOD
BOTANICAL
AREA

BUCKEYE ▲

SODA SPRINGS CREEK

WILDER-NESS

SANTA

SALMON CREEK TRAIL

NATIONAL FOREST

3499'
∧
LION
PEAK

SALMON CREEK
RANGER
STATION

SALMON CREEK

(FALLS)

ESTRELLA ▲

SPRUCE

∧
3379'

THREE
PEAKS

SALMON
CONE

580'
∧

2674'
∧
MT. MARS

LUCIA RANGE

N

0   ½   1
MILES

RAGGED
POINT
INN

MONTEREY
SAN LUIS

DUTRA CREEK

Monterey County

Section 15

13¾ miles

COUNTY

OBISPO COUNTY

RAGGED
POINT

SAN CARPOFORO CREEK

2556'
∧
BALD TOP

A

SECTION 15
Cruickshank & Buckeye Trails, Silver Creek Wilderness, to Salmon Creek to Ragged Point

DISTANCE: 13¾ miles, with 7⅞ miles on Cruickshank and Buckeye Trails (22.1 & 12.7 kms).

OPEN TO: Hikers. Dogs, horses allowed in Silver Peak Wilderness. Bicyclists on highway.

SURFACE: Trail, highway shoulder.

ACCESS POINT: Cruickshank Trailhead.

HOW TO GET THERE: Park on east side of Highway 1 south of Gorda at Milepost 6.5.

OTHER ACCESS: Soda Springs Trailhead, Alder Creek Camp off Willow Creek Road, Salmon Creek Ranger Station or anywhere south from there on highway.

DIFFICULTY: Moderate.

ELEVATION GAIN/LOSS: 3150 feet+/3300 feet- total. 2450 feet+/2160 feet- for trail portion, 2190 feet+/350 feet- to Buckeye Camp.

CAUTIONS: Watch for poison oak and ticks on trail, carry long pants for brush. Always purify water in the wilderness. First mile can be hot on a summer afternoon. Trail from 3 to 4 miles is brushy and hard to follow. We urge you travel with a friend, carry map and compass, pay close attention there and leave time for route finding.

FURTHER INFORMATION: Los Padres National Forest, Monterey District (831)385-5434.

FACILITIES: None at access point or anywhere along trail (except water at camps, which needs to be purified) or highway until Ragged Point Inn, which has phones and gas, food and lodging.

CAMPGROUNDS: Trail camps at Lower and Upper Cruickshank Camps, Buckeye Camp. Car camping to north at Plaskett Creek on Section 14, south at San Simeon State Park at end of San Luis Obispo Section 3.

LODGING: Ragged Point Inn en route in northern San Luis Obispo County has 19 moderately priced rooms. Other lodging available at Gorda on previous section.

You'll find several features that approach both heaven and hell if you walk most or all of this section. Happily the 14,500-acre Silver Peak Wilderness was established in 1992, and the section's first 7⅞ miles follow the Cruickshank and Buckeye trails to explore many highlights of this steep and rugged wilderness. Despite an elevation gain exceeding 2000 feet, most of the trail is well graded, leading to grand vistas of southern Big Sur and the coast south to Santa Barbara County. The immediate scenery is also lovely and dramatic. The real drawback of this wilderness hike consists of a one-mile segment from 3 to 4 miles where the trail is brushy and difficult to follow. We explicitly describe that part of the hike, offering a cross-country route bypassing the worst bushwhacking between 3½ and 4 miles. We urge you to travel with a friend, carry map and compass and pay close attention there. Cruickshank and Buckeye trails are still recommended over walking the winding highway. Several of the CCT Whole Hikers of 1996 considered Buckeye Trail a highlight of their trek despite the difficulties. All camps along the trail offer pleasant sites and water, especially the big meadow at Buckeye Camp.

After CCT leaves the wilderness at the abandoned Salmon Creek Ranger Station, it's once again forced onto the narrow, twisting shoulders of Highway 1. If you walk the road leg, we wish you clear weather for the astounding views as you descend into San Luis Obispo County and out of the Big Sur.

Ascend northeast on the Cruickshank Trail on excellent tread across brushy slopes. After a notice board, climb moderately by switchbacks. Beyond the eighth switchback around ½ mile, a short spur on the left leads to a rocky outcrop with a vista of the rugged coast. You soon cross a ridge and turn north on a steady ascent.

After gaining a second ridgetop at ¾ mile, contour through high brush on the ridge's north face with views up Villa Creek Canyon. After passing the first small redwoods around 1⅛ miles, the high chaparral yields to a stately live oak woodland with an open understory. Descend briefly to 1¼ miles, traversing a steep gulch with four-foot-diameter redwoods, then climb gradually through mixed forest. After a gulch, a short steep climb leads to an ocean view.

The tread gets rougher as you ascend fitfully up canyon, the vegetation a jumble of hardwoods, brush and conifers including ponderosa pines. Beyond 1¾ miles, contour across a dry rocky slope with a Pacific view, then through shady mixed forest.

Cross a seasonal stream on a redwood plank, then another stream to reach pleasant Lower Cruickshank Camp with a table and grill beneath redwoods before 2 miles. Ascend gradually to a junction before 2¼ miles. The north end of the Buckeye Trail forks left to descend ⅝ mile to Villa Creek, where Villa Creek Camp lies just downstream, then contours and climbs to end at Alder Creek Camp, 2¾ miles from the junction.

CCT turns right on the combined Buckeye and Cruickshank Trails, passing rustic Upper Cruickshank Camp and climbing southeast into rolling grasslands. After passing a fenced stock enclosure, you reach the upper junction. Cruickshank Trail forks left, climbing past its namesake homestead site and on up to Lions Den Camp and South Coast Ridge Road in 4¼ miles.

The Coastal Trail forks right to climb southeast, then south on the Buckeye Trail. It contours from 2⅜ to 2½ miles, then resumes a moderate ascent on vague tread sorely in need of maintenance. (It gets much worse beyond the ridgetop!) Orange plastic flagging helps to mark the route. Ascend a ridge to 2¾ miles, then veer to the right up a dark gully. After leaving the gully at 2⅞ miles, ascend steeply west with grand canyon and ocean vistas.

Contour briefly from 3 miles, then ascend rough tread across steep slopes to a ridgetop. Take a minute here to absorb the fine view and orient yourself, especially if you'll return this way, since Buckeye Trail's vague tread tangles with a mix of volunteer and animal paths around the ridgetop. To the north beyond Villa Creek you can see Alder Creek Canyon and San Martin Top (3098') beyond.

Buckeye Trail turns east, dropping left of the ridgetop briefly only to switch back up to and along it on nearly invisible tread. Pass an encouraging sign facing the other direction at 3¼ miles that proclaims "TRAIL AHEAD OPEN." Although the vague track may appear to drop to the right of the ridgetop, it truly ascends along it, passing yuccas and gaining views south to Redwood Gulch. As you ascend for 1000 feet beyond the sign, watch for the spot where Buckeye Trail leaves the ridgetop, a nearly level saddle just east of a ridgetop knob (2318'). Just south of a charred oak snag there, Buckeye Trail and CCT head southeast on a gradual descent. The route is heavily choked with fragrant sage, so we recommend long pants for the next ¾ mile.

Be aware that where Buckeye Trail leaves the ridgetop, a volunteer trail continues up the ridge. On my first hike here I found myself 300 feet above and ¼ mile beyond the actual ridge-leaving spot before I knew I'd left Buckeye Trail. I believe the ridgetop trail actually continues east to Silver Peak (3590'). This trail in fact offers a steeper but less brush-choked and only ⅛ mile longer route. To take it, continue up the ridge to a 2580-foot saddle at 3¾ miles, then descend the spur ridge south that ends at the confluence of two forks of Redwood Gulch. After only a little brush and by angling slightly west of the ridgetop, I dropped right onto the Buckeye Trail a few feet before it traverses wooded Redwood Gulch.

The brushy main trail descends southeast from the ridgetop, winding through two steep gullies, then crossing a southwest-descending ridgetop. Continue descending gradually southeast to pass above a large live oak. The descent increases across a brush-choked gully and steep slopes. Around 3⅝ miles, cross another gully beneath live oaks, then contours east briefly on the roughest, brushiest gully crossing of all. The vague tread contours southeast, then south.

Look south-southeast from here to see large Buckeye Meadow at your elevation, but it's a rough ½-mile hike, especially the next ¼ mile. The view includes Redwood Gulch and much ocean. Continue south past a large live oak and Coulter pines, then east across a steep slope past more pines to cross the top of a gully. Descend southeast through heavy sage with at least two parallel tracks around 3¾ miles. Descend steeply, then contour across a large gully. Make a wind-ing descent through two more gullies, crossing the last beneath a live oak at 3⅞ miles. Continue south-southeast across a west-facing slope past two young Coulter pines.

Buckeye Trail improves as it bends left around the base of a ridge (the spur ridge where cross-country route rejoins trail), then descends east across a gulch beneath oak woodlands. Follow rough but distinct tread that climbs south briefly, then drops into the main channel of Redwood Gulch, fording its stream where tall lilies grow beneath sycamores at 4 miles. Ascend south, then west, then south again, entering the meadow at 4⅛ miles. Stay right at a fork, watching on your right for the pleasant but inconspicuous lower camp beneath oaks at the meadow's west edge. Continue up the sloping meadow between two large black oaks, the east one with a blaze, then through a broken fence to a fork at 4¼ miles.

The main trail angles right to cross a small stream. The left fork quickly leads to the main Buckeye Camp with a table beneath an immense bay tree. While this camp was much in need of repair and cleanup on my April 1999 visit, it sits in a fine grassy clearing rimmed by trees and with a filtered ocean view and a stock enclosure nearby.

Buckeye Trail/CCT head southwest from the fork, winding up to top a hill at 4⅜ miles. Dip through a gully, then contour to a ridgetop at 4½ miles. On the clearest days you can glimpse the coast far to the south, but you must wait until the ridge at 5 miles to see the northern San Luis Obispo coast. The trail descends gradually south from the ridge, then mostly contours for a mile as it dips through several small stream courses. You lose about 200 feet in elevation in the next ¾ mile. While a spring supposedly lies left of the trail at 5¼ miles, I couldn't find it.

Descend steeply, then contour across the top of the Southern Redwood Botanical Area which spans from here to Highway 1. Cross many more small to medium seasonal creeks, then descend to cross two adjacent canyons around 6⅛ miles. You'll likely find water in the second canyon unless it's the heart of the dry season. Buckeye Trail/CCT mostly contours to 6½ miles with Pacific views, winding through more canyons on a steep slope. Beyond a ridge, descend steadily across dry slopes to ford Soda Springs Creek beyond 6¾ miles, where a refreshing 30-foot waterfall splashes above you. Descend to the Soda Springs Trail junction around 7 miles, then pass through a stock fence, closing the gate behind you.

Contour through chaparral and grasslands with unlimited coastal views south to 7¼ miles. Then dip past rock outcrops and ascend briefly to 7½ miles. Descend Buckeye Trail down a brushy drainage. At 7⅝ miles pause to enjoy your only view of Salmon Creek Falls. Then descend steeply on eroded, brush- and poison oak-crowded tread, dropping by switchbacks to leave Silver Peak Wilderness at Salmon Creek Ranger Station (abandoned) on Highway 1 at 7⅞ miles.

The CCT is forced to follow scenic but busy Coast Highway 1 south. From the ranger station, turn left and descend along the shoulder to cross Salmon Creek at 8 miles. South of the creek Salmon Creek Trail returns to the wilderness, climbing to Salmon Creek Falls. Follow the highway as it climbs steeply, leaving the national forest at 8¾ miles. The ascent leads to a big south-facing bend around 9⅛ miles with a grand view down coast to Point Buchon beyond Morro Bay and on clear days to Point Arguello 90 miles away in Santa Barbara County.

A winding gradual descent takes you to the San Luis Obispo County line at 10¼ miles where another fine view encompasses the nearer landmarks of Ragged Point, this section's destination, and wooded San Simeon Point beyond. Ascend the shoulder to 10½ miles, then descend moderately to 11⅛ miles. Contour to 11½ miles, then descend to the commercial oasis of the Ragged Point Inn at 11¾ miles. With the most services since Gorda, it also has a public path down past a waterfall to a small sandy beach and rocky shore, but no access up or down coast.

Follow the highway south with the rugged Big Sur terrain falling behind you. After a nearly level mile, descend steadily to San Carpoforo Creek at 13¼ miles. Where the highway crosses the broad deep valley only 20 feet above sea level, you can see the breakers ⅜ mile west. It's signed "NO TRESPASSING" however, and even if you walk to the beach, it takes serious scrambling on steep slopes to get over Ragged Point ⅜ mile south. Ascend the highway west to a wide turnout at 13¾ miles, marked Milepost 70.8. It has an obvious path heading west, with no sign limiting access, but all forks end in thick chaparral. Walk the highway 250 feet south to a smaller turnout on the west shoulder, this section's end.

ALTERNATE ROUTE: One can walk the twisting Highway 1 shoulder of the wilderness.

SUGGESTED ROUND TRIPS & LOOPS: Hike the first 2 to 4 miles, returning the same way. Hike north from Salmon Creek Station or Soda Springs Trailhead to Buckeye Camp and return, 6¾ miles round trip.

HOW TO IMPROVE CCT HERE: Improve the trail north of Buckeye Camp. Develop a route off highway from Salmon Creek south.

San Luis Obispo County

T The treasures of this rural county's spectacular, diverse shoreline
remain largely undiscovered by the outside world. This moun-
tain-rimmed, largely agricultural coast is characterized by two
large crescent bays, Estero Bay and San Luis Obispo Bay, a pristine
smaller bay, San Simeon, and Morro Bay, an inner bay that's really an estuary. Between the outer bays, eleven named points, four of them major,
punctuate the shore. Three other major features contribute to the distinctive rural character of this coast: the 77,000-acre Hearst Ranch in the
north, Pacific Gas & Electric's (PG&E's) large Diablo Canyon/Pecho coast
property in the center, and the vast Nipomo Dunes in the south.

The Coastal Trail takes 102 miles (including the final 3½ miles of the
previous chapter) to traverse San Luis Obispo County's 96-mile shoreline.
In the far north, the CCT follows twisting Highway 1 above the steep,

rocky coast of southern Big Sur. The coastal landscape changes dramatically at San Carpoforo Canyon, where the Hearst Ranch begins. To the south a rolling marine terrace wedges between the Santa Lucia Range and the shore. The gentle landscape looks inviting, but coastal access on the Hearst Ranch is limited and obscure, currently allowed as a "revocable right to pass." We describe access to and along the coast there via trails used by coast lovers over many years, doing so with the stipulation that such access is revocable at any time. If you visit the wild, remote Hearst Ranch coast, please respect the land by staying on described paths and not camping, not building fires and not smoking.

Where the Hearst Ranch ends south of San Simeon, CCT follows the shore to the pleasant town of Cambria. Then private land forces the Coastal Trail along Highway 1 almost to Cayucos. West of that friendly little town, the Estero Bay acquisition has recently preserved the coast. At Cayucos, the CCT gains a long beach at the base of steep hills, following it to landmark Morro Rock. CCT traverses the harbor district of Morro Bay, another amiable town. A boat shuttle takes CCT across Morro Bay to the sand spit forming its west shore, CCT's first boat ride since Marin.

Then CCT follows the dramatic shore of Montaña de Oro State Park for ten miles, first along the bird-rich sand spit, then below rising bluffs, through dunes and finally along a spectacular convoluted rocky shore backed by the San Luis Range. The CCT currently doubles back on a 20-mile road detour to continue down coast when it reaches Montaña de Oro's southern boundary and the locked north gate of PG&E's Pecho coast property. They own the next 13 miles of shoreline, with their Diablo Canyon nuclear power plant smack in the middle of it. To their credit, PG&E has opened 3¾ miles of superb trail at their property's south end to free guided hikes requiring advance reservations. We urge them to eventually provide access to the entire Pecho coast.

South of the Pecho Coast, the Coastal Trail follows the shores of San Luis Bay into Santa Barbara County. It mostly follows a residential shore until the vast sweep of Pismo Beach, most popular beach since Carmel. Pismo Beach rapidly leads into the vast dune complex occupying the southern San Luis Obispo coast. Sadly the beach south of Pismo is open to motor vehicles for 5¼ miles, a foolish use of a delicate ecosystem. From Oso Flaco Dunes south, walkers regain exclusive use of the sandy shore. Hikers who visit that remote beach usually have little company other than shore birds, pounding waves and drifting sand.

SECTION 1
Ragged Point to Piedras Blancas

DISTANCE: 6¼ miles (10.1 kilometers).

OPEN TO: Hikers. Dogs OK on leash. Bicyclists on road portion.

SURFACE: Trail, beach, highway shoulder.

ACCESS POINT: Highway 1 east of Ragged Point.

HOW TO GET THERE: Drive Highway 1 north from Cambria or south from Monterey or Big Sur to San Luis Obispo County Milepost 70.75 where a small turnout west of the highway is just east of unmarked Ragged Point (not to be confused with the Ragged Point Inn 2 miles north). The indistinct dirt turnout is across the highway from a 20-foot-tall pine, .55 mile south of the San Carpoforo Creek bridge.

OTHER ACCESS: Near Breaker Point south of Arroyo Hondo, Arroyo de los Chinos at Milepost 68.2, Arroyo de la Cruz at Milepost 66.9, the Hearst Gate at Milepost 66.55, or anywhere south from there on highway.

DIFFICULTY: Moderate.

ELEVATION GAIN/LOSS: 400 feet+/430 feet-.

CAUTIONS: Walking the beach at this section's north end should be timed to coincide with a low tide. Watch for rogue waves when walking beach and poison oak on the bluffs. Stay out of roadway and walk single file when walking highway shoulder. Please stay on established access paths and off the rest of the Hearst Ranch.

FURTHER INFORMATION: None.

FACILITIES: None except small store and cafe just south of Piedras Blancas Motel.

CAMPGROUNDS: San Simeon State Park on Section 3 has 202 sites, the 132 sites in the San Simeon Creek unit with hot showers.

HOSTEL: Morro Bay Home Hostel, (805)772-9005, is in Morro Bay 40 miles south.

LODGING: Piedras Blancas Motel has reasonable rates. Ragged Point Inn 2 miles north of access point has rooms at moderate rates. Other lodgings to south in San Simeon and Cambria.

Access to the shoreline here in far northern San Luis Obispo County is limited and obscure. I spent half a day exploring west from the wide turnout at the top of the hill .2 mile north of this access point. A maze of volunteer paths there meanders through pine forests only to lead to a brush-choked headland. I managed to get down to the beach north of Ragged Point by heading west for ¼ mile, then descending a rough, steep path north, but once I reached the beach, the shoreline west and south was impassable and the shoreline north was only passable for ⅛ mile, ⅝ mile at minus tides. The Whole Hikers managed to follow a blufftop path southeast through the pine forest, then bushwhack to bluff's edge and scramble down to the rocky beach, but when I tried to retrace their route in 1999, I got tangled in a huge poison oak thicket. The route described below gets you down

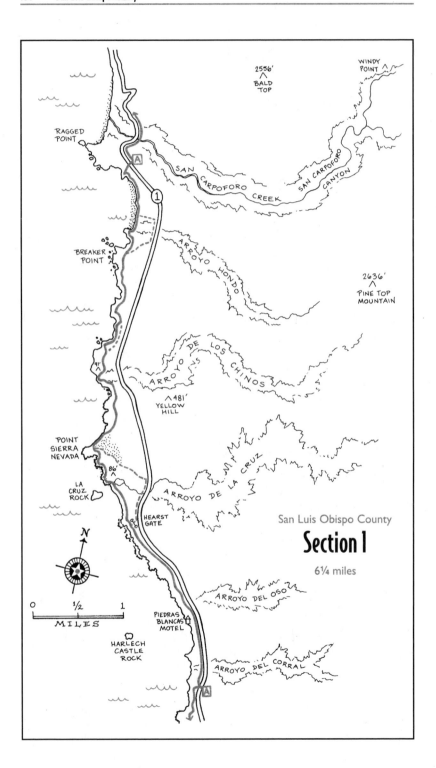

San Luis Obispo County

Section 1

6¼ miles

to virtually the same spot without such difficulty.

A word about access and topography here: Looking south from San Carpoforo Creek (San Carpojo in local lingo), the mountains crowding the southern Big Sur Coast immediately north suddenly draw back from the shore, providing a broad rolling marine terrace. The vast 77,000-acre Hearst Ranch occupies most of this terrace. While the Hearsts have owned the ranch since the 1860s, locals and travelers, mostly surfers, divers and fishermen, have found and used paths to the tideline at several spots, mostly along creeks and arroyos. We ask that you stay off the bulk of the Hearst Ranch, but we believe that the coastal access paths used by avid coast lovers over the past 130 years provide reasonable shoreline access in an area where access is extremely limited. At press time, the Hearst Corporation generally allows this access by granting a "revocable right to pass" at those locations. Technically, that means they can withdraw that right to pass at any time and ask you to leave. Please respect the private property by staying on the established paths we suggest to reach the tideline and to follow the shoreline up and down the coast. In some places it is necessary to pass along the blufftop to get from one beach to the next. Please observe the following if you walk on the Hearst Ranch: no camping, no fires or smoking, keep dogs leashed.

Descend southwest on the vague path just north of the small turnout, watching for low strands of barbed wire only fifteen feet from the road and poison oak beyond. About 450 feet from the highway, take the left fork and head south. It descends to a sea stack attached to the bluff at ⅛ mile. Descend the path east from the outcrop's shoulder on a short rough descent to the tideline of a rocky beach just east of the small south-pointing promontory.

Walk the tideline south with some rock scrambling required in the first 250 feet followed by easy walking on a gravelly beach. Follow the shore of this pristine cove littered with picturesque rocks offshore. Around ½ mile an obvious escape path climbs east to the highway. Unless you prefer the difficult low-tide route described below that continues along the beach to almost one mile, turn left and follow the escape path to the highway at Milepost 69.97, follow the shoulder south across Arroyo Hondo, then head southwest across the blufftop toward Breaker Point.

The tidal route follows the tideline south past a small dune at ⅝ mile, then passes deep Arroyo Hondo, choked with brush and poison oak. Follow the tideline past a point beyond ¾ mile marked by a rounded 50-foot sea stack at its western tip. A short rock scramble leads to the neck of another small point at ⅞ mile. Walk the tideline south 200 feet to the north rim of the next small cove. Unless it's high tide, the beach continues ⅛ mile to the base of a high point, but you need to find a safe place to scramble up to the blufftop to continue south.

The first of three rugged, strenuous choices heads east from the north rim of the cove, a steep scramble up an eroded cliff. The second choice lies 330 feet south, also a rough scramble. I took the third choice 200 feet beyond that where, at one mile, a rough volunteer path climbs steeply southeast up the face of an eroded slide. About 200 feet from the tideline, it meets a nylon rope anchored on the blufftop above. The rope provides hand-hold help to climb the final ten near-vertical feet to the blufftop. The rough, crumbly path beneath the rope is made more challenging by the steep slope below, not a place for people afraid of heights or carrying a heavy backpack.

Whether you choose one of the three rough scramble paths or leave the beach before Arroyo Hondo, once you get onto the blufftop, the walking improves greatly. Follow the bluff edge south, then head southwest on a gentle descent across a sloping blufftop, passing east of two 40-foot-high promontories, the second of which is Breaker Point at 1⅛ miles. When you return to the bluff edge in 200 feet, follow it south. By 1¼ miles turn southeast then south to follow the bluff edge, passing through gentle grasslands with scattered coastal scrub.

Before 1⅜ miles, you meet a 20-foot-deep arroyo in view of a ranch house east of the highway. Take the overgrown path just inland from its mouth, crossing the gulch just below a small deep pool. Though coastal access lies about 30 feet west, return to the blufftop by an easy short scramble. Follow the bluff edge south, making another easy gully crossing in 450 feet. Continue south, crossing two more small gullies near their heads, then crossing a larger one at 1½ miles. All three offer easy traverses.

Contour southeast along the bluff edge to 1⅝ miles, then continue south crossing several more small gullies, all easy. Pass a small point at 1⅞ miles with great views up and down the coast. Harbor seals haul out on the offshore rocks. The faint bluff-edge track quickly passes another small point, then turns east toward the highway. Continue east to round the top of a gully at 2 miles, then turn south to cross a deeper gully and follow the blufftop down coast.

CCT reaches a double gully before 2⅛ miles. Here the CCT descends the gully to the tidal zone. (If the tide is above +3.0 feet, you must cut inland to follow the blufftop south near the highway.) If you can walk the rocky coast south, at 2¼ miles you pass a gulch beyond a fragment of wooden fence, nearing the highway. Continue along the shore beyond the next point to a low point at 2⅜ miles where it's an easy scramble twenty feet up a rocky slope to the blufftop.

Walk the blufftop south, passing east of the high edge of the unnamed point north of Arroyo de los Chinos. Head south toward a low wind-topped pine, passing it at 2⅝ miles. Soon the coast south comes into view, the sandy face of low and long Point Sierra Nevada lying across a shallow cove, with a sphinx-like rock peeking over its left flank.

Continue south to meet deep Arroyo de los Chinos before 2¾ miles. The best path into it lies about 50 feet east of the sheer bluff edge. Take the distinct path there that descends southeast into the arroyo, encountering some poison oak in the coastal chaparral. When you reach the creek, follow it west to its mouth and a pleasant beach guarded by offshore tidal rocks. Cross the creek and climb back onto the bluff via the steep short path at the south side of the mouth of the arroyo. Geraniums grow wild here. An escape/access path heads east to the nearby highway, but CCT turns south following the bluff's edge. After a small point before 2⅞ miles, follow the bluff edge as it cuts inland, then turns south by 3 miles.

Around 3⅛ miles the CCT meets another eroded arroyo. Veer inland 150 feet to find an easy crossing, then follow a cow path south-southwest across the blufftop. When this track bends left, veer right to head south, aiming for the long sandy beach north of Point Sierra Nevada. You'll find an easy descent to the beach at 3⅜ miles.

Walk the tideline southwest toward the rocky point. Just before you reach the rocks at the end of the beach, turn left at 3⅝ miles to head southeast and ascend to the crest of the dunes. Here you must make a choice. At tides below +3.0 feet you can follow the main route of the Coastal Trail, which makes the short descent to the next beach and follows its tideline down the coast with long views of Piedras Blancas Lighthouse and the sphinx-like Harlech Castle Rock near it.

If the tide is high, you need to wait for a lower tide or head east through the dunes for ¼ mile, then head southeast toward the highway visible across the grassy field. The high tide route reaches the highway north of Arroyo de la Cruz around 4¼ miles, then follows the shoulder south across the arroyo and up a hill to meet the northernmost gate on the Hearst Ranch at 4⅝ miles.

The tidal route reaches the low-tide-only-passable point at 4 miles, then comes to the creek and marsh at the mouth of Arroyo de la Cruz in just 200 feet. A creek ford is necessary to continue south from here. In winter and spring you'll probably need shorts and bare feet or sandals, while in midsummer or later, it may be a dry crossing. The easiest ford is generally near the mouth where the creek empties into the ocean, but watch for rocks on the uneven bottom. Don't ford when it's at flood stage like it was during my February 1999 visit. In that case, return to the Point Sierra Nevada dunes and take the Alternate Route east.

Beyond the mouth of Arroyo de la Cruz, CCT follows the tideline of the sandy beach to 4⅜ miles, then ascends the low bluff to follow a bluff edge track. By 4⅝ miles you can see the Hearst Gate not far to the east with the highway just beyond. This is where the two routes rejoin. Continue down the coast along the narrowing blufftop. Not far beyond 4¾ miles the bluff edge and the highway shoulder become one. Stay west of the highway because by 5⅛ miles you'll find a narrow blufftop strip to walk, though it tapers back to the highway shoulder again by 5⅜ miles.

Walk the shoulder south, crossing Arroyo del Oso at 5½ miles and passing Piedras Blancas Motel at 5⅝ miles. Continue along the shoulder with intriguing Harlech Castle Rock directly offshore. After you cross Arroyo del Corral at 6⅛ miles, look for the turnout on the road's west shoulder at Milepost 64.7, just before 6¼ miles, where this section ends.

ALTERNATE ROUTE: Follow Highway 1.

SUGGESTED ROUND TRIPS & LOOPS: From the Hearst Gate at Milepost 66.55, walk the bluff edge and the beach north to the mouth of Arroyo de la Cruz and return, 1¼ miles round trip. Take the volunteer path south of Arroyo de los Chinos at Milepost 68.2 to the beach and follow the CCT north or south.

HOW TO IMPROVE CCT HERE: Acquire a non-revocable easement for the CCT across the Hearst Ranch west of Highway 1. Better yet, purchase the Hearst Ranch and turn it into San Simeon National Seashore.

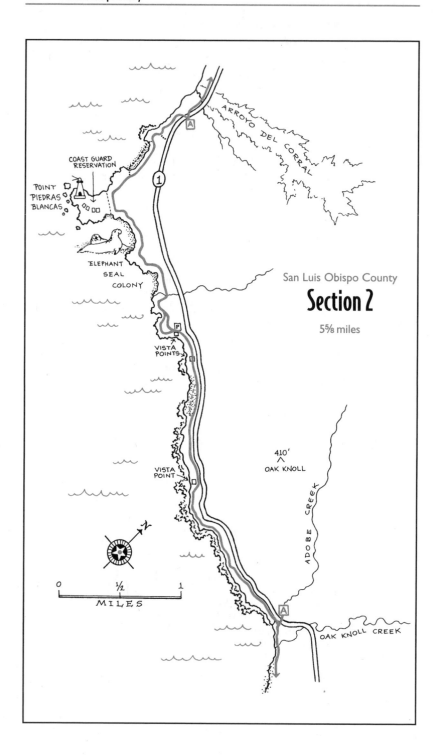

SECTION 2
Piedras Blancas to Adobe Creek

DISTANCE: 5⅝ miles (9.1 kilometers).

OPEN TO: Hikers. Bicyclists on road portion.

SURFACE: Trail, beach, highway shoulder.

ACCESS POINT: North of Point Piedras Blancas.

HOW TO GET THERE: On west side of Highway 1 at Milepost 64.7, 13 miles north of Cambria, park in the small turnout with room for three or four cars.

OTHER ACCESS: Three vista points west of the highway south of Point Piedras Blancas.

DIFFICULTY: Easy.

ELEVATION GAIN/LOSS: 110 feet+/150 feet-.

CAUTIONS: Stay off beaches when elephant seals are on them, usually October through April, sometimes year round. Never get closer than 50 feet to an elephant seal.

FURTHER INFORMATION: None.

FACILITIES: Cafe, small store and gas station beside motel .5 mile north of access point.

CAMPGROUNDS: San Simeon State Park on Section 4 has 202 sites, the 132 sites in the San Simeon Creek unit with access to hot showers.

HOSTEL: Morro Bay Home Hostel, (805)772-9005, is in Morro Bay 30 miles south.

LODGING: Piedras Blancas Motel just north has reasonable rates. Other lodgings are south in San Simeon and Cambria.

The turnout south of Arroyo del Corral offers the first access to the blufftops not signed no trespassing since north of the motel. Surfers and fishermen regularly park here and climb over the fence to reach the shore. The bluffs here are part of the vast 77,000-acre Hearst Ranch, while the bluffs west of Highway 1 a bit south are held by the U. S. Government, managed jointly by the Coast Guard and the Fish and Wildlife Service. At press time, the Hearst Corporation generally allows access at the turnout by granting a "revocable right to pass" there. Please stay on established paths and respect the private property by observing the following: no camping, no dogs, no fires or smoking. It's important that you stay off the beaches along this section whenever elephant seals are on them, generally October through April but possible year round. Never approach closer than 50 feet to an elephant seal. Not only are the huge awkward mammals dangerous and territorial, intrusions may disrupt their breeding and child-rearing.

The explorer Juan Cabrillo named the Piedras Blancas (white rocks) on his 1542 voyage up the California coast upon seeing their guano-coated surfaces. The Salinan tribe then had winter/spring camps in this area so they could harvest the abundant fish and shellfish. In summer and autumn they would move their camps inland to gather berries, seeds and acorns. Even after the Salinans moved north to the San Antonio Mission, they regularly sent runners 30 miles to the coast to collect seafood and bring it back. In 1864 a lookout was built at Point Piedras Blancas to alert whalers at nearby San Simeon when their potential prey was approaching. In 1874 the lighthouse was built on the same spot. The top of the light station looks incomplete because its Fresnel lens and iron lanternhouse were removed in 1949 and replaced with an automated beacon. There is no public access to the lighthouse or coast guard reservation, but the Coastal Trail follows a gentle route along its eastern boundary.

From the north end of the turnout, carefully climb over the barbed wire fence at the wooden crossbar and walk west to the bluff's edge. Turn left and follow the iceplant-covered bluff edge south. Beyond ⅛ mile the bluff is only a narrow strip west of the highway. At ¼ mile, pass a second turnout offering an alternate access and continue down coast, passing a side trail in 200 feet that drops to a pocket beach on your right.

Before ⅜ mile you want to veer right, crossing the top of a small gully to head southwest to return to the bluff edge. Follow it out to a small point, then head south around a covelet to cross the neck of another point. Regaining the bluff edge at ½ mile, follow it southeast toward a black water tank at ⅝ mile. You'll pass spur trails down to the beach which you can follow in summer. Stay off the beach, however, if elephant seals are there.

The bluff edge track passes a fenced pump house beyond the water tank, then crosses a small gully. Contour south through the dunes, passing the end of the beach at ⅞ mile. Continue across the iceplant-covered blufftop on a path heading toward the sphinx-like offshore rock. Follow the path as it ascends a shallow swale until the track swings left beyond one mile. Contour south from there toward the cluster of lighthouse buildings. There's no real path here—just walk over the iceplant.

Beyond 1⅛ miles you reach a small hill above the coast guard reservation fence, now occupied by a U.S. Fish and Wildlife Service group studying marine mammals. Point Buchon, backed by the San Luis Range, comes into view far to the south-southeast. Head for it, staying left of the fence but right of the vegetated sand hills. Cross the lighthouse access road at 1¼ miles and continue along the fence, descending. As you reach the bluff's edge south of Point Piedras Blancas, a small cove behind the fence on your right generally has the first significant herd of elephant seals in season. Turn left and follow the bluff edge northeast.

At 1⅜ miles you overlook one of the elephant seals' favorite beaches where the seals may be seen year round. Continue northeast along the bluff, then contour east through dunes above the beach. Where you must cross a sand gully around 1½ miles, make sure you do so well above all the seals, then follow the sandy bluff southeast above the beach.

You need to head inland around 1 9/16 miles to avoid a cove of the beach. By 1¾ miles you can follow the dunes southeast, generally contouring to the end of the beach at 1⅞ miles. Contour around a sandy point, then follow the sandy bluff edge east above a rocky tidal zone. Soon Hearst Castle appears on a hilltop ahead.

By 2 miles you follow the bluff edge above another beach favored by elephant seals as a haul out. Dip through small gullies to approach the highway. At 2⅛ miles you pass just south of a highway sign reading "VISTA POINT ½ MILE." You need to parallel the highway briefly to continue down coast. Stay near it to around 2¼ miles. Where you pass the last gully on your right, veer right to parallel above the beach. A series of small grassy points here provide great seal viewing in season.

The Elephant Seals of Piedras Blancas

Largest of the world's seals, the elephant seal's name derives from the male's huge size, up to 22 feet long and three tons in weight, and long drooping nose, or proboscis. The females weigh up to 2000 pounds and grow to 12 feet long.

By 1868 the scientific community thought the northern elephant seal was extinct, wiped out by sealers. Their range had been from the Pacific coast of Baja all the way to the Gulf of Alaska. In 1892 a small remnant colony of between 20 and 100 elephant seals was found on Guadalupe Island off Baja California. In 1922 the Mexican government protected the colony. The U.S. government followed suit a few years later when the seals reappeared in southern California waters.

In an astounding reversal, the northern elephant seal now numbers around 160,000. About two thirds of the population breed at the Channel Islands, but healthy breeding colonies have established themselves in several places on the mainland including Piedras Blancas in northern San Luis Obispo County, Año Nuevo State Reserve and Point Reyes National Seashore. They first returned to the mainland California coast at Año Nuevo Point in San Mateo County in 1975.

Elephant seals first returned to Piedras Blancas in 1990. Since then the Piedras Blancas elephant seals have established the fastest growing new colony scientists have ever seen. The first two pups were born here in 1992, with 300 born in 1994, 600 in 1995, and 1900 born in 1999 to a colony of 4000 adults.

The seals come to Piedras Blancas to pup and then breed in the winter months from December to March. In December the males arrive, fighting for dominance over groups of females, or harems. The bulls have fierce and bloody battles with the strongest winning the harem. When the bulls aren't breeding or fighting, they loll about conserving their energy. The females arrive in January to give birth to 65 to 75 pound pups conceived the previous year. The new pups can get lost in the stormy ocean conditions and ferocious male disputes. Mother and pup find each other with distinctive vocalizations. Feeding on rich mother's milk, pups are weaned within a month, growing to between 250 and 500 pounds. By mid-March the mothers mate and leave. The weaners remain, learning to fend for themselves, then head to sea by the end of April. In spring thousands of juveniles return to the beaches, coming to rest and molt. They shed their skins, then grow new ones. After the adolescents move on, the females come to molt in early summer followed by the adult males in late summer.

For much of the rest of the year, elephant seals live alone in the open ocean, spending as much as 98 percent of their time underwater. They dive as deep as 5000 feet, staying down for up to two hours to feed on rays, skates, small sharks and squid. They add the blubber they'll live on for the three months they don't feed during breeding.

It's easy to witness the winter breeding season and spring/summer molting season at Piedras Blancas. Volunteer docents in blue jackets answer questions and direct you to safe seal watching sites from the two vista point parking lots just south of Point Piedras Blancas on most days of the year.

After you cross a gully, the path left of some high dunes provides the best route. Cross a creek at 2⅜ miles, then head southwest to return to coastal and lighthouse vistas. You quickly meet a hard packed path. Turn left and follow it through more dunes, then contouring along the bluff's edge. After crossing an arroyo around 2½ miles, you reach a fork in the path. Though the high route on the left is about 200 feet shorter, the right fork follows the bluff above the rocky shoreline. Both paths soon approach a vista point parking lot.

Climb over the metal gate to reach the lot at 2⅞ miles, then cross the lot on its ocean side. Beyond the lot, follow the bluff edge path to the next vista point at 3⅛ miles, walk that lot to its end, then continue along the bluff edge. In elephant seal season, a barricade at 3⅜ miles forces you to either turn back or hop the fence on your left. The CCT hops the fence and continues along the road shoulder in seal season, while from May through September if seals are absent, you can continue along the narrow bluff edge west of the highway above another elephant seal beach.

From 4⅛ to 4¼ miles, the only route follows the highway shoulder. Then the CCT leaves the road to pass through another vista point lot. Continue along the bluff edge, passing two promontories at 4½ and 4¾ miles. The easy bluff edge walking continues to a gulch around 5⅛ miles. After scrambling through that eroded zone, contour along the narrow bluff edge between the ocean and the highway.

At 5½ miles you reach a prominent point where the blufftop on the ocean side of the highway ends, giving way to a rocky tidal zone, then a sandy beach. At low tide you can pick your way along the tidal zone, but otherwise you need to turn inland to the highway, turn right and walk the shoulder briefly across Adobe Creek. You quickly reach a wide turnout at 5⅝ miles, the start of San Luis Obispo Section 3.

ALTERNATE ROUTE: Stay on highway shoulder.

SUGGESTED ROUND TRIPS & LOOPS: The headlands around Point Piedras Blancas offer excellent easy hiking whether you start from the north or from the vista point at Milepost 62.7. You can walk the bluff edge, then loop back across the headlands nearer the road, although in winter and spring you'll want to avoid the marshy areas south of the lighthouse road.

HOW TO IMPROVE CCT HERE: Acquire a non-revocable easement for the CCT across the Hearst Ranch west of Highway 1. Better yet, purchase the Hearst Ranch and turn it into San Simeon National Seashore.

SECTION 3
Adobe Creek to Pico Avenue Access, San Simeon Acres

DISTANCE: 6⅜ miles (10.3 kilometers).

OPEN TO: Hikers. Dogs OK on leash. Bicyclists on road portion.

SURFACE: Beach, trail, highway shoulder.

ACCESS POINT: Adobe Creek.

HOW TO GET THERE: Park in the wide turnout with the green gate on the ocean side of Highway 1 at Milepost 60.0, 1.8 miles north of northernmost of two San Simeon Village turnoffs.

OTHER ACCESS: W.R. Hearst State Beach, anywhere along the highway between the two San Simeons, San Simeon village and San Simeon Acres.

DIFFICULTY: Easy.

ELEVATION GAIN/LOSS: 230 feet+/250 feet-. Beach/trail portion: 140 feet+/180 feet-.

CAUTIONS: Please respect the Hearst Ranch property—no fires, firearms, camping or smoking, and stay on established paths.

FURTHER INFORMATION: W.R. Hearst State Beach (805)927-2020.

FACILITIES: None except at W.R. Hearst State Beach: picnic tables, water, restrooms.

CAMPGROUNDS: San Simeon State Park on next section has 202 sites, but only the 132 sites in the San Simeon Creek unit have access to hot showers.

HOSTEL: Morro Bay Home Hostel (805)772-9005 is in the town of Morro Bay 25 miles south.

LODGING: San Simeon Acres at section's end and Cambria 4 miles south have many choices.

The vast 77,000-acre Hearst Ranch occupies almost all the coastal land and adjacent marine terrace here. While the Hearsts have owned the ranch since the 1860s, locals and travelers, mostly surfers, divers and fisherpeople, have found and used paths to the tideline at several spots, mostly along creeks and arroyos. We ask that you stay off the bulk of the Hearst Ranch, but we believe that the coastal access paths that have been used by avid coast lovers over the past 130 years provide reasonable access to the shoreline in an area where access is extremely limited. At press time, the Hearst Corporation allows this access by granting a "revocable right to pass" at those locations. Please stay on the established paths and respect the private property by observing the following: no camping, no fires or smoking, keep dogs leashed.

Most of this section follows a scenic and diverse shoreline, passing through cypress and pine forest planted by the Hearsts on San Simeon Point to round the gracefully curving shore at sheltered San Simeon Bay. After passing the historic village of San Simeon and W. R. Hearst State Beach, where you leave the trees,

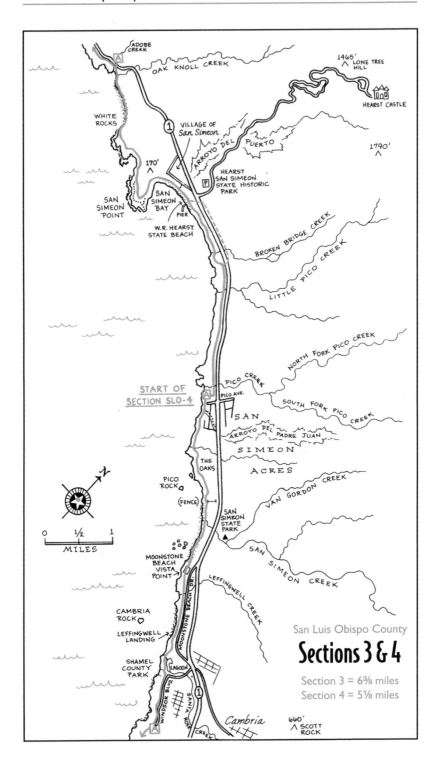

ADOBE CREEK

OAK KNOLL CREEK

1465' LONE TREE HILL

HEARST CASTLE

WHITE ROCKS

VILLAGE OF San Simeon

ARROYO DEL PUERTO

1790'

170'

HEARST SAN SIMEON STATE HISTORIC PARK

SAN SIMEON POINT

SAN SIMEON BAY

PIER

W.R. HEARST STATE BEACH

BROKEN BRIDGE CREEK

LITTLE PICO CREEK

NORTH FORK PICO CREEK

START OF SECTION SLO-4

PICO CREEK

PICO AVE.

SOUTH FORK PICO CREEK

S A N

ARROYO DEL PADRE JUAN

S I M E O N

THE OAKS

A C R E S

PICO ROCK

VAN GORDON CREEK

(FENCE)

SAN SIMEON STATE PARK

SAN SIMEON CREEK

0 ½ 1
MILES

MOONSTONE BEACH VISTA POINT

LEFFINGWELL CREEK

CAMBRIA ROCK

LEFFINGWELL LANDING

MOONSTONE BEACH DR.

SHAMEL COUNTY PARK

LAGOON

WINDSOR BLVD.

SANTA ROSA CREEK

Cambria

660' SCOTT ROCK

San Luis Obispo County

Sections 3 & 4

Section 3 = 6⅜ miles
Section 4 = 5⅛ miles

you can walk beach or blufftop for another mile before the CCT is forced to follow the highway shoulder to section's end.

From the turnout just east of unmarked Adobe Creek, climb over the green gate and follow the trail south to the tideline. Turn left and follow the tideline east-southeast along a broad beach. You can see Hearst Castle atop the hill northeast and the high hulk above Point Buchon far down the coast. Cross the mouth of Arroyo Laguna/Oak Knoll Creek at ¼ mile, where a windswept lagoon lies on your left and tidal rocks stand offshore. Local beachcombers have built whimsical driftwood shelters beside this lagoon and at the next arroyo.

Beyond the lagoon, continue along the tideline of a narrowing beach with the eroded dun-colored face of twenty-foot-tall bluffs rising on your left. Pass more tidal rocks around ⅜ mile and continue down the beach past the mouth of a small arroyo. By ⅝ mile two peaks rise above the bluff, followed by that incongruous "castle." Continue past the mouth of a larger arroyo and some vegetated dunes.

By ¾ mile, as the dunes give way to bluffs with faces of folded rock, CCT leaves the beach to head east-southeast on a track between the dunes and the vegetated bluffs to their right. The beach-leaving point is also marked by near white rocks embedded in the bluff face.

Just 50 feet from the beach, look for a trail on your right heading south along the bluff's edge. Follow it to dip through a small gully and join another trail from the beach. Continue through ice plant on improved tread. By one mile the ice plant mostly gives way to low grasses as the path continues along the bluff edge overlooking a rocky tidal zone. Don't worry if the path is indistinct—there's always a way through.

Pass an unnamed point around 1⅛ miles and contour above a dark sand pocket beach. The only spurs down to the beach are at its midpoint and near its south end. By 1¼ miles you overlook a sparkling cove where sea otters often play and seals haul out on offshore rocks. Approach the end of the cove's beach around 1½ miles where a rough spur descends to it. Several windows punctuate the rocks below, and the cove's rocky shore sweeps south to San Simeon Point.

Soon your blufftop trail leads into a stand of cypress and forks. Bear right to follow the trail on a promenade between two parallel rows of cypress trees. Where the path forks again at 1⅝ miles, go straight along the sheltered track. Soon a spur on the right leads back to the nearby coast.

Continue along the cypress promenade, passing another spur to the coast at 1¾ miles. Just beyond that, the track forks again. CCT goes left this time, contouring southeast through a shady grove to meet a broad path at 1⅞ miles. Turn right and head south, then southeast with the surf crashing on your right.

By 2⅛ miles your trail veers left to head east, then northeast to a T junction. Though you can barely see the ocean for the trees, you've reached San Simeon Point. Take some time to turn right on the spur that explores the amazingly convoluted shore of the nearby point before following the bluff edge track as it swings north to San Simeon village.

CCT goes left at the T junction, heading northwest, then north through forest. Soon Hearst Castle reappears on the hilltop ahead, then the azure waters of San Simeon Bay appear on the right with old San Simeon village beyond. Contour past pines and eucalyptus, enjoying filtered coastal vistas. You may need to climb

Hikers approach rugged San Simeon Point.

over some fallen pines around 2⅜ miles. When your path returns to the bluff edge around 2½ miles, follow it north. Soon a barbed-wire fence is on your right. Follow it 150 feet, then duck through a break in the fence (or carefully climb over it) and continue along the bluff edge path.

By 2¾ miles you want to veer right and descend a broad track to the sandy beach, then walk the beach east. After passing a small lagoon at the mouth of Arroyo del Puerto before 3 miles, you can turn left and parallel the creek for 400 feet and duck through a gap in the chain-link fence to explore sleepy San Simeon village and the historic Sebastian Store. CCT continues east along the beach, passing through W.R. Hearst State Beach, which has picnic tables, water and restrooms.

Pass beneath the pier at 3 miles and continue along the narrowing beach. A stairway on the left 300 feet beyond the pier offers a second escape from the tideline. CCT continues east on the beach, although a narrow point beyond 3⅛ miles is impassable at high tide, requiring a detour to the blufftop via the stairway. Otherwise follow the beach east across Broken Bridge Creek beyond 3¼ miles. Leave the beach at 3⅜ miles and walk the blufftop east to 4 miles and the next arroyo, where you must head up to the highway.

CCT follows the highway shoulder toward Cambria, contouring across a low marine terrace. Cross Little Pico Creek at 4⅝ miles, dip nearly to sea level around 5⅜ miles, then climb slightly to cross the bridge over Pico Creek at 6¼ miles and enter the tourist town of San Simeon Acres. Immediately turn right on Pico Avenue and walk to its end at 6⅜ miles, start of the next CCT section.

ALTERNATE ROUTE: The only other choice would be to stay on the highway.

SUGGESTED ROUND TRIPS & LOOPS: Hike the 2⅛ miles to San Simeon Point and return the way you came more or less, 4¼ miles round trip. You can also walk out to the point from San Simeon village, only 1¾ miles round trip.

HOW TO IMPROVE CCT HERE: Acquire a non-revocable easement for the CCT across the Hearst Ranch west of Highway 1. Better yet, purchase the Hearst Ranch and turn it into San Simeon National Seashore.

Will the Hearst Corporation Get Its Way with the San Luis Obispo Coast?

The Hearst Corporation still owns 77,000 acres along the coast in northern San Luis Obispo County despite their donation of Hearst Castle to state parks in 1958. While the Hearsts have been praised for keeping this land in a natural state, this has not always been their intention. In the 1960s the Hearst Corporation announced plans to build a city of 65,000 near the tiny coastal village of San Simeon. Although that plan was scrapped, in 1980 the San Luis Obispo board of supervisors incorporated into the county's general plan the Hearst Corporation's "scaled down" wishes for San Simeon Point. It was to be a vast tourist facility with one motel and four lodges that together totaled 900 rooms, plus eight restaurants, an RV park, two eighteen-hole golf courses, two shopping centers, boat docks, and an employee housing complex.

In 1997 the board of supervisors adapted the county Local Coastal Plan (LCP) to accommodate a new Hearst development plan. That plan includes 650 lodging units at four different sites including a dude ranch, one golf course, a convention center, restaurants and shops. In January 1998 this version of Hearst's gargantuan development came before the Coastal Commission. Hundreds attended the meeting to voice their concerns. After a long, heated day of debate, the Commission unanimously rejected the county's LCP update and supported staff recommendations that the development be scaled back to 350 units clustered at one site, that the golf course be rejected, and that environmental constraints, most notably the scarcity of water, be taken into account.

As the staff report pointed out, the proposed development site sits upon "an unspoiled shoreline with hundreds of coves, dozens of uncrowded beaches, rocky headlands and clean blue water stretching to a far horizon unmarked by oil rigs or air pollution . . . one of California's premier natural wonders."

As this book went to press in April 2000, the San Luis Obispo County government was once again revising its LCP as the CCC requested. While the entire plan is complex, the most controversial element involves zoning for the Hearst Ranch. So far the County Planning Department has generated drafts of six planning options for the Hearst property, ranging from a status quo plan that would keep the ranch entirely agricultural to a full development plan reinstating the proposed 650-lodging-unit development, with a vast range of choices in between. Several of the six options include a route for the California Coastal Trail across part of or most of the Hearst Ranch west of Highway 1. At the very least, a bike lane will be built along the shoulder of Highway 1 through the Hearst property.

SECTION 4
Pico Avenue Access, San Simeon Acres, to Cambria

DISTANCE: 5⅛ miles (8.2 kilometers).

OPEN TO: Hikers, dogs. Bicyclists on road portion.

SURFACE: Beach, trail, sidewalk.

ACCESS POINT: Pico Avenue Access.

HOW TO GET THERE: Turn west off Highway 1 at north end of San Simeon Acres (motel row) 4 miles north of Cambria at Milepost 54.75 onto Pico Avenue, go straight .1 mile to end of street and park.

OTHER ACCESS: Directly south of the Cavalier Inn in San Simeon Acres a public path leads along the north bank of Arroyo del Padre Juan. Also at west end of San Simeon Creek Campground at San Simeon State Park, San Simeon Creek Access south of creek, Moonstone Beach Vista Point, Leffingwell Landing, Santa Rosa Creek Access, Shamel County Park.

DIFFICULTY: Easy.

ELEVATION GAIN/LOSS: 130 feet+/90 feet-.

CAUTIONS: Watch for rogue waves and rising tides along the beach.

FURTHER INFORMATION: San Simeon State Park (805)927-2035, San Simeon Chamber of Commerce (805)927-3500.

FACILITIES: None at access point. San Simeon State Park has a phone near the entrance kiosk and restrooms and water in the picnic area south of San Simeon Creek. Leffingwell Landing and Shamel County Park have restrooms, water and picnic tables.

CAMPGROUNDS: San Simeon State Park has 202 sites, but only the 132 sites in the San Simeon Creek unit have access to hot showers.

HOSTEL: Morro Bay Home Hostel (805)772-9005 is in Morro Bay 22 miles south.

LODGING: San Simeon Acres has several choices of motels, while Cambria has a more diverse mix of lodging.

MAP: See page 110.

The land still owned by the Hearst Corporation along the San Luis Obispo County coast finally comes to an end at San Simeon Creek, less than two miles from the north end of this section. Finally public access to the shoreline here becomes clear and specific, unlike the obscure and revocable access ways north along the coast. The number of shoreline visitors rises exponentially, especially around the Pico Avenue access and from San Simeon Creek south to Cambria. Two other significant boundaries occur along this section. The ancestral lands of the Salinan people reach their southern limit near present-day Cambria. Today's California Sea Otter Game Refuge sprawls south along the coast for 100 miles from the mouth of the Carmel River to the mouth of Santa Rosa Creek, which you pass on this section just north of Shamel County Park. The original Hearst Ranch was much larger than today's 77,000 acres. George Hearst's original 250,000-acre ranch included three vast Spanish ranchos on the northern San Luis Obispo coast—San Simeon, Piedra Blanca, and Santa Rosa— and once included 50 miles of coastline from southern Big Sur to Cambria, as well as today's Fort Hunter-Liggett, by itself a vast expanse of wild lands. George Hearst began buying the lands after the 1863-64 drought killed many of the original land grant holders' livestock, leaving the Spaniards deeply in debt. San Simeon had a whaling station when Hearst took over in 1865. He built warehouses, a pier and store on San Simeon Bay, adding to his mining fortune by exporting local products. The illiterate George Hearst brought his family to San Simeon to camp up on Camp Hill, creating a lasting impression with his only offspring, William Randolph Hearst. Only after the younger Hearst inherited the family fortune upon his mother's passing in 1919 did he retain architect Julia Morgan to design what today is known as Hearst Castle. Construction continued for more than 30 years, with Hearst using the San Simeon pier to import art treasures and fully grown trees from around the world to decorate his immense play house, visited by numerous international celebrities.

From the end of Pico Avenue, descend the stairway to a cobblestone beach. Turn left and walk the tideline south, crossing a sandstone shelf around ⅛ mile. (You can also walk the beach about ⅛ mile northwest to a point.) Beyond the shelf, continue along the beach below motel row, passing the mouth of the Arroyo del Padre Juan where another access path follows the north bank. Walk a sandy beach there, then sand alternates with cobbles and uneven rocks.

Pass the last condominium on the bluff at ⅜ mile and continue down the beach to a rocky point at ½ mile. It takes a tide of +4.0 feet or less to walk the beach around the point. Otherwise you can climb to a path along the bluff's edge. Turn around to admire the sweeping view up the coast to nearby San Simeon Point with Ragged Point beyond.

Beyond the point you walk a beach of rougher terrain than the last one, with another mix of sandstone shelves, cobbles and pockets of sand. Follow it past another small point, coming to the mouth of a small arroyo at ¾ mile. When you round the next point in 250 feet, you'll need a lower tide to walk the beach beyond. If you can't proceed along the tideline, it's easier to climb to the blufftop alternate path before you round the point. Continue along beach or blufftop, rounding another small point at ⅞ mile.

Beyond one mile you pass rocks standing both offshore and near the bluff edge. The bluff path is easiest here as many rocks make the tideline rough going. After another point around 1¼ miles, you must return to the beach before coming to the wooden fence of a private residence. The beach is passable at all but the highest tides of +5.0 feet or more. It's easier to return to the tideline well before you reach the fence, where a steep rough descent requires caution.

Continue along the beach. Around 1⅝ miles 30-foot-tall Pico Rock stands offshore and 40-foot tan cliffs rise on your left. Reach state park property beyond 1¾ miles, although it's not marked on the beach. The bluff veers inland to the nearby highway. By 1⅞ miles, the north end of the highway bridge over San

Simeon Creek lies due east of the tideline. A short walk east under the bridge would lead to the San Simeon Creek Campground of San Simeon State Park in ⅛ mile, but you'd want to stay on the north side of the lagoon.

CCT continues south along the sandy tideline, passing the seasonal outlet of San Simeon Creek, a small point around 2⅛ miles, then along sandstone bluffs that rise 40 feet on your left. Round a point at 2⅜ miles where a cluster of rocks rise offshore. Continue down the beach to 2⅝ miles where, just before another point, you want to ascend steps to the blufftop. Follow the blufftop path briefly to Moonstone Beach Vista Point at the north end of Moonstone Beach Drive.

Walk south past the parking lot to pick up the blufftop path and follow it down the coast. After a broad point at 2⅞ miles, the path veers east briefly, rounds a cove and passes another point at 3¼ miles. Contour along the blufftop to Leffingwell Landing and another parking lot at 3¾ miles. Just north of it, picnic tables in a sheltered cypress grove offer a nice spot for a break.

Continue along the blufftop path, watching the rocky tidal area below for sea otters which favor this spot. By 4 miles the path descends from the low blufftop to the parking lot for Santa Rosa Creek Access. Descend to the beach and walk the tideline south, crossing the seasonally flowing mouth of Santa Rosa Creek west of its broad, crescent-shaped lagoon. When you pass the south end of the lagoon at 4¼ miles, the CCT turns east to leave the beach and follow a path along the northern edge of Shamel County Park. While the beach extends about ⅛ mile south, it has no exit at its south end.

Around 4⅜ miles the park path comes to a parking lot at a bend on Windsor Blvd. To detour into the pleasant town of Cambria, head east on Windsor Blvd., cross Highway 1 in ¼ mile, then walk Main Street into town. For the CCT, turn right and walk the sidewalk of Windsor Blvd. through a residential neighborhood to road and section's end at 5⅛ miles. The East-West Ranch access path that traverses the bluffs ahead is described in Section 5.

ALTERNATE ROUTE: At low tide you can walk Moonstone Beach from the vista point south. Of course you could walk the highway shoulder if you're in a hurry.

SUGGESTED ROUND TRIPS & LOOPS: You can choose any one of several spots to start pleasant beach walks along this section of the CCT: Pico Avenue, Arroyo del Puerto, San Simeon Creek, Santa Rosa Creek or Shamel County Park. Another choice is to walk the blufftop path between Moonstone Vista Point and Santa Rosa Creek Access.

SECTION 5
Cambria to East Fork Villa Creek

DISTANCE: 11 miles (17.7 kilometers).

OPEN TO: Hikers. Dogs OK on trail portion. Bicyclists on road portion.

SURFACE: Trail, street, highway shoulder.

ACCESS POINT: End of Windsor Blvd.

HOW TO GET THERE: Turn west off Highway 1 in Cambria at the northernmost stoplight, Milepost 50.6, onto Windsor Blvd. and go 1.0 mile to its end.

OTHER ACCESS: Ardath Drive, Highway 1.

DIFFICULTY: Easy.

ELEVATION GAIN/LOSS: 660 feet+/680 feet-. Trail portion: 20 feet+/60 feet-.

CAUTIONS: At East-West Ranch, gates close at sunset. Stay on trail and off adjacent private property. Watch for traffic on road portions.

FURTHER INFORMATION: East-West Ranch office (805)927-0500.

FACILITIES: None.

CAMPGROUNDS: San Simeon State Park north of Cambria has 202 units. Town of Morro Bay to south has camping in 2 state parks and 2 private campgrounds.

HOSTEL: Morro Bay Home Hostel (805)772-9005 is 11 miles south of section's south end.

LODGING: Several choices in both Cambria and Cayucos.

Suddenly public access to the coast once again becomes scarce. We begin this section at the Fiscalini/East-West Ranch Blufftop Trail because public access has been agreed to there. For now the old ranch property remains undeveloped and natural, but subdivision of the property may be only a matter of time since this would join the north and south halves of Cambria west of Highway 1, with an extended Windsor Blvd. being the coastal thoroughfare.

Go enjoy this portion of the coast while it's still in a natural state. The trail has been kept open to the public because volunteer "trail guides" agree to patrol the path across private land. They may ask you to sign a liability waiver to pass through, a small enough price to pay for access to the pleasant bluffs above a rocky shore.

From there south, the Coastal Trail is currently forced to follow road shoulders for 10⅛ miles, the longest uninterrupted stretch since northern Big Sur. If you go, stay out of the roadway and walk facing traffic on this mostly straight leg of Highway 1 where traffic moves quite fast.

From the south end of the street, walk through the gap in the fence and follow the East-West Ranch blufftop path southwest. Climb gently to the path's sum-

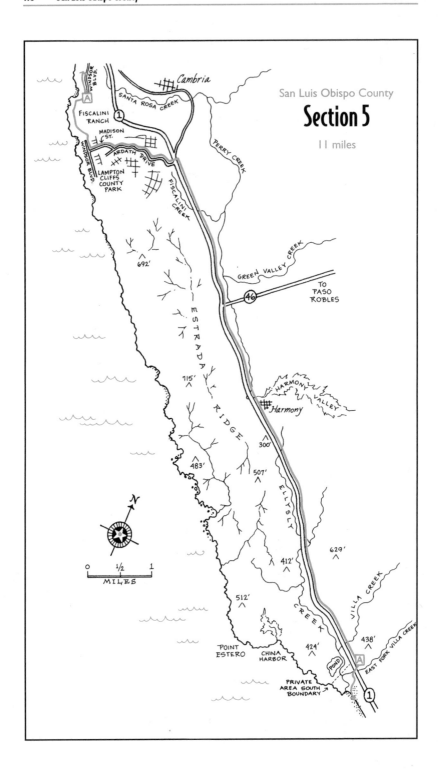

San Luis Obispo County

Section 5

11 miles

Cambria

SANTA ROSA CREEK

WINDSOR BLVD.

FISCALINI RANCH

MADISON ST.

ARDATH DRIVE

WINDSOR BLVD.

LAMPTON CLIFFS COUNTY PARK

PERRY CREEK

FISCALINI CREEK

692'

GREEN VALLEY CREEK

46

TO PASO ROBLES

ESTRADA RIDGE

715'

HARMONY VALLEY

Harmony

300'

483'

507'

ELLYSLY

N

0   ½   1
MILES

412'

629'

512'

VILLA CREEK

POINT ESTERO

CHINA HARBOR

424'

438'

POND

A

EAST FORK VILLA CREEK

CREEK

PRIVATE AREA SOUTH BOUNDARY

1

mit in 250 feet, then contour out to a point around ⅛ mile where you overlook a rocky, convoluted shoreline with a small bay to the north. Contour along the blufftop trail, passing a unique driftwood and stone bench with a great view north to Ragged Point and beyond.

The path meanders away from the shore, crossing an unusual bridge over a small arroyo at ¼ mile. By ⅜ mile the ocean is once again directly below on your right. Continue across a boardwalk through seasonal wetlands. Pass another great driftwood bench beyond ½ mile.

Contour out around one more point at ⅝ mile, then descend gently to cross another bridge. The path continues to the property's south gate around ⅞ mile. From there the only route currently available for CCT follows quiet residential streets to Highway 1, then follows the highway shoulder south to section's end. If you are looking for more coastal access, you'll find it at the ends of Wedgewood, Castle, Harvey and Lampton streets, and at Lampton Cliffs County Park near the latter.

From the East-West Ranch south gate, follow sleepy Windsor Blvd. south for three blocks, turn left and walk up Orlando Drive two blocks, then turn right and ascend Madison Street to its end at Ardath Drive at 1½ miles. Turn left and walk the shoulder of Ardath, a mildly busy thoroughfare, up to Highway 1 at 2¾ miles. Cross the highway at the traffic signal, turn right and walk the highway shoulder south. The highway descends the canyon of Fiscalini Creek to 4 miles, then climbs along Perry Creek until it reaches the tiny town of Harmony (limited services) at 6¾ miles.

Continue south along the highway shoulder, ascending to a 300-foot summit around 7¼ miles, then making a gentle descent along Ellysly Creek to return to the coastal environment. Approach a coastal valley drained by Villa Creek at 10½ miles. Cross the Villa Creek bridge at 10⅝ miles and continue along the shoulder to the next bridge at 11 miles. This section ends there at the East Fork of Villa Creek.

ALTERNATE ROUTE: From Cambria's northernmost stoplight at the north end of Windsor Blvd., you have the pleasant town option of walking Main Street through the friendly town. Main Street ends at the Ardath Drive-Highway 1 intersection.

SUGGESTED ROUND TRIPS & LOOPS: Walk the East-West Ranch blufftop path, 1¾ miles round trip.

HOW TO IMPROVE CCT HERE: Develop a route off the highway from Ardath Drive south. Much of the land on Estrada Ridge is for sale and public purchase should be pursued.

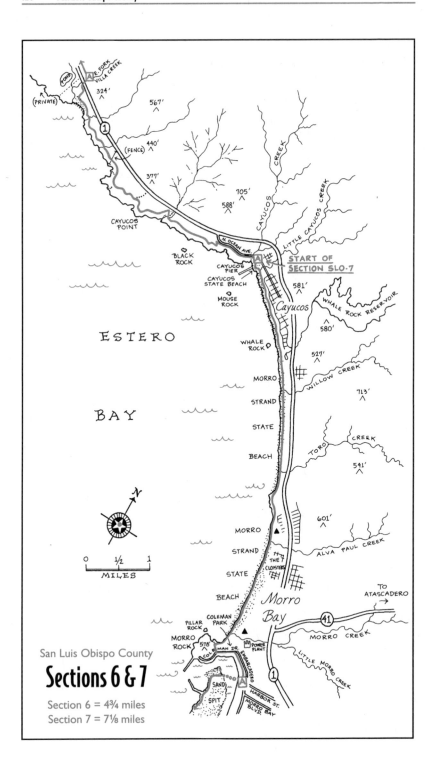

E. FORK VILLA CREEK
(ROAD)
(PRIVATE)
324'
567'
1
(FENCE)
440'
377'
CAYUCOS POINT
588'
705'
CAYUCOS CREEK
LITTLE CAYUCOS CREEK
BLACK ROCK
W. OCEAN AVE.
START OF SECTION SLO-7
CAYUCOS PIER
CAYUCOS STATE BEACH
MOUSE ROCK
Cayucos
581'
WHALE ROCK RESERVOIR
580'
ESTERO
WHALE ROCK
527'
WILLOW CREEK
MORRO
713'
STRAND
BAY
STATE
CREEK
BEACH
TORO
541'
N
601'
MORRO
ALVA PAUL CREEK
STRAND
THE CLOISTERS
STATE
0   ½   1
MILES
BEACH
Morro Bay
TO ATASCADERO
PILLAR ROCK
COLEMAN PARK
41
San Luis Obispo County
MORRO ROCK
578'
COLEMAN DR.
POWER PLANT
MORRO CREEK
LITTLE MORRO CREEK

Sections 6 & 7

Section 6 = 4¾ miles
Section 7 = 7⅛ miles

SAND SPIT
EMBARCADERO
HARBOR ST.
MORRO BAY BLVD.
1

SECTION 6
East Fork Villa Creek to Cayucos Pier

DISTANCE: 4¾ miles (7.6 kilometers).

OPEN TO: Hikers. Bicyclists on road portion.

SURFACE: Trail, beach, ranch road, road shoulder.

ACCESS POINT: East Fork Villa Creek bridge.

HOW TO GET THERE: On Highway I about II miles south of Cambria, or 3.3 miles up highway from northern Cayucos exit, park on west side of road opposite the Villa Creek Ranch sign, near Milepost 39.85.

OTHER ACCESS: Highway I east of Cayucos Point, North Ocean Avenue.

DIFFICULTY: Easy.

ELEVATION GAIN/LOSS: 135 feet+/175 feet-.

CAUTIONS: Stay on described access path. Do not disturb any natural features. No dogs please. Stay out of posted closed areas.

FURTHER INFORMATION: Trust for Public Land (415)495-5660, Cayucos State Beach (805)549-3312, Cayucos Chamber of Commerce (805)995-1200.

FACILITIES: None except pier at south end has restrooms, water, phone, picnic area at adjacent Veteran's building.

CAMPGROUNDS: San Simeon State Park north of Cambria has 202 units. Town of Morro Bay to south has camping in 2 state parks and 2 private campgrounds.

HOSTEL: Morro Bay Home Hostel (805)772-9005 is II miles south of section's south end.

LODGING: Several choices in Cayucos.

Estero Bay curves gently along the center of the San Luis Obispo County shore, spanning about 15 miles as the seagulls fly. Cabrillo spotted the bay on his 1542 voyage, naming it for the large estero, or estuary, at the center of the bay that contains the more sheltered and famous Morro Bay. In 1769 the Portola expedition camped at the mouth of Villa Creek in the northern crook of the bay. Today the route of the CCT, after the 10-mile road walk from Cambria, returns to the shoreline very near the site of Portola's camp. The broad, gently sloping marine terrace on the ocean side of the highway contrasts sharply with the high hills and steep canyons on the inland side of the road.

The Trust for Public Land acquired about 275 acres along the north shore of Estero Bay near Cayucos Point at the end of 1998, purchasing it from a group that had been trying to subdivide and develop it. The acquisition was made possible with $2.5 million from the Coastal Conservancy, $2.4 million from the Packard Foundation, and $1 million from a private donor. This land includes 3½ miles of coastline with two streams, coastal terrace grasslands, sandy coves, wetlands, and tidepools. At press time the Trust for Public Land was negotiating the details of what agency would hold title to the land and how it would be managed. Although we cannot specifically tell you to follow the route described here for the first 4 miles of this section's Coastal Trail, public access will be allowed and this is the probable route. We suggest you call the Trust for Public Land or inquire locally before you hike here.

A sign for Villa Creek Ranch stands east of the highway bridge across the creek's unmarked east fork. Find the gate on the ocean side of the highway nearest the ranch sign. This section begins there. The CCT follows the ranch road behind the gate. It quickly swings left to head east to an informal parking area on a knoll around ⅛ mile. From the knoll the CCT follows the vague ranch track as it descends south to a sandy dune area surrounding by wetlands, then continues south to the beach just east of the mouth of Villa Creek. (The newly acquired property extends west less than ¼ mile from there.) CCT turns left and follows the tideline of the beach. By ½ mile intertidal rocks lie offshore from the beach which continues for 350 feet.

From near the end of the beach, CCT climbs above the rocks along the shore to the top of a low dune which overlooks a sandy pocket beach. CCT continues southeast along the coast, either across the second beach or on the bluff edge above it. By ¾ mile it reaches a small point between the second beach and a third, smaller one. CCT contours along the bluff edge track to another small point, then follows the bluff edge as it angles east above a fourth small beach before turning southeast across the blufftop beyond ⅞ mile.

CCT reaches the most prominent point so far on this section at one mile, then continues across the blufftop before dipping through a gully on one of several steep cowpaths. It then follows the bluff's edge past an eroded point to dip through another gully at 1¼ miles. The Coastal Trail winds inland to pass above two small gullies, then crosses a rocky gully at 1⅜ miles. Contour along the grassy blufftop above rust-colored tidal rocks, coming to a fenceline west of a high hill before 1½ miles.

To continue along the CCT, one climbs carefully over a well-strung barbed wire fence, then contours along the bluff edge, crossing the heads of two gullies. The route offers good vistas southeast to Morro Rock and other volcanic peaks on its left, and south to Point Buchon beyond Montaña de Oro State Park. From 1⅝ miles CCT follows the edge of the bluff south toward a point, passing a spur at 1¾ miles that descends to a surf-scoured beach. At 1⅞ miles a second spur on the right leads 200 feet to a south-facing point. CCT continues along the bluff edge, passing another fenceline at 2⅛ miles, then following the coast east around a rocky cove with a narrow beach.

At 2¼ miles the path forks, the left fork heading for a turnout on Highway 1. CCT follows the vague right fork east across the blufftop toward an uplifted sea stack, staying inland of several eroded gullies. Beyond the last gully, CCT angles right to follow the distinct track heading southeast to a young cypress at bluff's edge beyond 2½ miles. The route veers left along the bluff edge, coming to the tip of Cayucos Point at 2⅝ miles, where a sandy beach below invites exploration.

Beyond the point CCT follows the bluff edge track northeast, then east, finally passing the uplifted sea stack to your left at 2¾ miles. From there you can see the Cayucos Pier backed by the town. Soon the track veers inland to eucalyptus trees west of a small arroyo. Where CCT reaches the trees beyond 2⅞ miles, it leaves the track heading for the highway to head southeast, descending to cross the small pocket beach near the mouth of the arroyo. It ascends to the blufftop beyond the beach at 3 miles and follows the bluff edge east. After rounding a small cove, CCT crosses another seasonal creek around 3½ miles. Contour east along a coast with many small offshore rocks, passing four small points. The latter two are more pronounced promontories, with the fourth point at 3⅞ miles having an extensive offshore reef. Beyond the fourth point, the Coastal Trail heads northeast toward the highway. It meets the west end of North Ocean Avenue near where the street meets Highway 1, beyond 4 miles.

Climb over the fence, turn right and walk the shoulder of Ocean Avenue east toward Cayucos. It crosses a creek and meets the west end of Lucerne Road at 4¼ miles. Continue along Ocean until you reach the east end of Lucerne Road around 4½ miles. Then turn right and walk Lucerne briefly, looking for a path that descends to the beach between two-story condominiums. The paved path is signed "NO MOTOR HOMES, CAMPERS, BOATS OR ORVS BEYOND THIS POINT." That means pedestrians are OK, so descend the path and stairs to the beach, reaching the tideline by 4⅝ miles. Turn left and walk the tideline past Cayucos Creek lagoon. Beyond it you enter Cayucos State Beach, continuing to Cayucos Pier at 4¾ miles, where this section ends and the next begins.

ALTERNATE ROUTE: The only other way would be to walk the shoulder of Highway 1.

SECTION 7
Cayucos Pier to Morro Rock to Harbor Street, Morro Bay

DISTANCE: 7⅛ miles (11.4 kilometers).

OPEN TO: Hikers. Bicyclists on road portion.

SURFACE: Beach, city streets.

ACCESS POINT: Pier, Cayucos State Beach.

HOW TO GET THERE: Exit Highway 1 at Cayucos onto Cayucos Drive and drive south to its end near the pier.

OTHER ACCESS: Nine public beach stairways between First Street and 22nd Street, 24th Street, north end of Studio Drive, north of Juanita Avenue, stairways at ends of Coronado, Mayer, Mannix and Cody avenues, through campground at west end of Yerba Buena Drive, Orcas Street, Hatteras Street, Easter Street, Beachcomber Drive, Atascadero Road, Coleman Drive (Morro Rock) and Embarcadero.

DIFFICULTY: Easy.

ELEVATION GAIN/LOSS: Negligible.

CAUTIONS: A few points along the beach will be impassable at high tide, although you can usually find a nearby detour.

FURTHER INFORMATION: Cayucos State Beach (805)549-3312, Morro Strand State Beach (805)772-7434, Morro Bay Harbor Office (805)772-6254.

FACILITIES: Cayucos Pier has restrooms, picnic area, water and phones at adjacent Veteran's building. Restrooms, picnic tables and water at end of 24th Street. Coleman City Park has restrooms, picnic tables.

CAMPGROUNDS: Morro Bay has two private and two state park campgrounds.

HOSTEL: Morro Bay Home Hostel (805)772-9005 is nearby. Hostel Obispo (805)544-4678 is 14 miles east in San Luis Obispo.

LODGING: Many choices in Cayucos and Morro Bay.

MAP: See page 120.

This section consists of one of the longest beach walks to this point in Volume Two, followed by a short walk through the harbor district of the town of Morro Bay. While most of the walking lies within sight of houses and commercial districts, the towns of Cayucos and Morro Bay are small with steep and mostly undeveloped coastal hills towering directly behind them, giving the walk a more natural feel.

The hike described here ends on the shore of Morro Bay. To continue south on the CCT from there, you'll want to hire a boat to take you out to the sand spit on the bay's west shore, where SLO Section 8 begins. This is the first boat shuttle in Volume Two, in fact the first since Bolinas Lagoon north of San Francisco. At press time there were no companies offering boats for hire at Morro Bay. We recommend you call the Harbor Office, (805)772-6254, and ask if they can refer you to an individual or company with boats for hire, or ask around on the docks along the Embarcadero.

From the foot of Cayucos Drive, walk down to the tideline beside the Cayucos Pier, turn left and walk the tideline of the sandy beach south, passing numerous small offshore rocks. Pass the mouth of Little Cayucos Creek by ⅛ mile. Continue past the first of many public stairways between the beach and the streets of Cayucos. Beyond this stairway from First Street, you soon leave Cayucos State Beach for Cayucos City Beach. Soon the bluffs, lined with houses, rise forty feet on your left. Cross a seasonal creek around ⅜ mile, then round a small point. Continue down the beach, which narrows at the south end of town. While it may be impassable at high tide, you can detour up one of the stairways, walk along Pacific Avenue, then return to the beach by the stairway at 24th Street.

Pass 24-foot-tall Whale Rock by 1⅛ miles, the largest of the small rocks offshore. You promptly enter Morro Strand State Beach. Soon the beach becomes broad again. Walk the broad strand down the coast, passing a lagoon on your left at the mouth of the seasonal creek that descends from Whale Rock Reservoir. The beach narrows again by 1⅝ miles, with the Highway 1 freeway not far inland, then houses lining the top of the beach.

Cross the mouth of Willow Creek beyond 1⅞ miles. Continue along the sandy tideline, leaving the north unit of Morro Strand State Beach at 2½ miles. Ironically CCT also leaves the residential neighborhood, following a broad beach with the freeway 400 feet inland. As you continue south, the mountains dip to reveal the deep canyon of Toro Creek, which you cross at 3⅛ miles. Around 3⅜ miles, walk the tideline at its nearest point to Freeway 1. Then the beach angles away from the road, running out to a point lined with low offshore rocks.

Enter the south unit of Morro Strand State Beach beyond 3⅝ miles. Continue along the tideline past the state park campground at the top of the beach to 4¼ miles. Cross the mouth of Alva Paul Creek at the south end of the campground, then continue along the beach, passing the Cloisters area of the state beach around 4½ miles.

Walk the tideline of the state beach south toward impressive Morro Rock. The beach turns very broad with sand dunes rising above its upper end and the north end of the city of Morro Bay farther east. Leave Morro Strand State Beach for Morro Rock City Beach at 5⅜ miles, with the Atascadero Road access on the east boundary. Continue along the tideline toward towering Morro Rock, passing a private campground east of the broad beach.

After you cross the mouth of Morro Creek at 5⅝ miles, the PG&E power plant towers on your left and 578-foot Morro Rock towers on your right. Continue along the tideline until you almost reach the base of Morro Rock at 6⅛ miles. Leave the tideline and walk the almost level sand spit south to meet Coleman Drive along its south shore before 6¼ miles. From here you might want to make a side trip southwest to the ocean side of Morro Rock, about ¾ mile round trip. Otherwise turn left and walk the shoulder of Coleman Drive east. Around 6⅜ miles, Coleman Park on your left offers picnic tables, restrooms and a playground, a nice spot for a break. Continue east along the waterfront street, which soon becomes Embarcadero and turns southeast. Follow Embarcadero to the foot of Harbor Street at 7⅛ miles. Turn right and walk to the harbor office. That is where this section ends and the next one begins.

ALTERNATE ROUTE: At high tide, you may need to exit the beach at the south end of Cayucos, climb one of the beach access stairways to Pacific Avenue and follow it south to the stairway at 24th Street, where you can return to the beach.

SUGGESTED ROUND TRIPS & LOOPS: Explore the tideline and beach around the base of Morro Rock. Walk the beach north or south from Morro Strand Campground or south from Cayucos Pier and return the way you came.

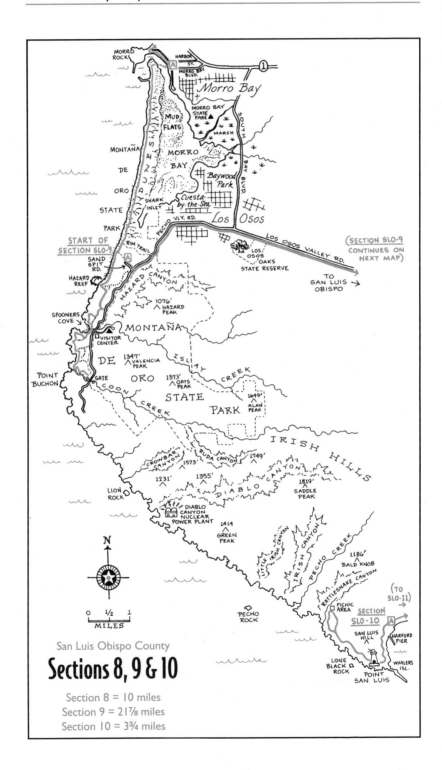

San Luis Obispo County

Sections 8, 9 & 10

Section 8 = 10 miles
Section 9 = 21⅞ miles
Section 10 = 3¾ miles

SECTION 8
Morro Bay to Sand Spit to Montaña de Oro State Park South Boundary

DISTANCE: 10 miles. 5 miles to Sand Spit Road trail, 6¼ miles to Dune Trail, 7¾ miles to Spooners Cove (16.1, 8, 10.1, 12.5 kilometers).

OPEN TO: Hikers. Equestrians on Dune Trail. Bicyclists on Bluff Trail.

SURFACE: Beach, trail.

ACCESS POINT: West end of Harbor Street, Morro Bay.

HOW TO GET THERE: Exit Highway 1 to downtown Morro Bay, take Morro Bay Blvd., which soon splits and becomes one way, putting you on Harbor Street, which you drive to the end.

ALTERNATE ACCESS POINT: To hike this section without making the boat shuttle across Morro Bay, start your hike from the end of Sand Spit Road.

HOW TO GET THERE (ALTERNATE): From the south, exit Highway 101 onto Los Osos Valley Road and head west 13 miles to state park, then turn right on Sand Spit Road and drive to its end. From the north, exit Highway 1 east of Morro Bay onto South Bay Blvd. and drive south to its end at Los Osos Valley Road, where you turn right and follow Los Osos to Sand Spit Road.

OTHER ACCESS: Montaña de Oro State Park.

DIFFICULTY: Easy.

ELEVATION GAIN/LOSS: 310 feet+/190 feet-. Negligible for first 6 miles.

CAUTIONS: To begin this section from the north, you must hire a boat to cross Morro Bay to the sand spit. Contact the Harbor Office, (805)772-6254, and ask if they can refer you to an individual or company with boats for hire, or ask around on the docks along the Embarcadero. Watch for rogue waves along beach portion. Day hikers can start at Sand Spit Road parking area at Montaña de Oro State Park and walk north to tip of sand spit or south to section's end.

FURTHER INFORMATION: Montaña de Oro State Park (805)528-0513, Morro Bay State Park (805)772-7434.

FACILITIES: Restrooms, water and phone at access point. Handicap accessible chemical toilets, picnic area and phone at Sand Spit Road parking area. Picnic area at Spooners Cove, with phone at park headquarters and water at campground nearby.

CAMPGROUNDS: Morro Bay has camping with hot showers in two state park campgrounds, Morro Strand State Beach on previous section and Morro Bay State Park about 2 miles south of town, plus two private campgrounds. Montaña de Oro State Park has primitive camping.

HOSTEL: Morro Bay Home Hostel (805)772-9005 is nearby. Hostel Obispo (805)544-4678 is 14 miles east in San Luis Obispo.

LODGING: The town of Morro Bay and vicinity offers many choices.

Montaña de Oro State Park offers 8400 acres of the wild central California coast at its best. Its seven miles of shoreline range from the low sand spit in the north through extensive vegetated sand dunes around Hazard Canyon west of the park road to spectacular, diverse rock formations along the coast in the center and south of the park. In addition to the Coastal Trail described here, the park has nearly 50 miles of trails that explore canyons, peaks and ridges east of the park road. The park's name, meaning mountain of gold, refers to the abundant blooms of mustard and California poppy found here in spring. The park visitor center occupies an old ranch house perched above Spooners Cove at the campground entrance. The visitor center is open weekends, daily during summer months. While the Chumash people lived in the area for thousands of years, this has always been a rugged and wild stretch of coast. The original Spanish land grant here came to be known as Rancho Cañada de los Osos y Pecho y Islay, literally the Valley of Bears, Bravery and Wild Cherry.

Although we describe the Coastal Trail here from the tip of the sand spit west of Morro Bay, you can also drive to the center of this section at the end of Sand Spit Road and follow the CCT either north or south from there.

If you take a boat ride to the sand spit, walk west to the tideline and follow it south. Around ¾ mile you pass the south breakwater protecting the harbor mouth, with views over Morro Bay to the east. Contour down the beach, entering Montaña de Oro State Park at 1¼ miles. CCT continues along the west shore of the sand spit, passing sand dunes of increasing height that hide the bay as you head south.

By 2⅝ miles the dunes to your east reach 90 feet in height as you follow the tideline. If you want another view of Morro Bay, detour east to climb an 80-foot dune. Otherwise follow the west shore south, passing a low gap in the high dunes around 3⅛ miles. The heart of the dunes are protected here in Morro Dunes Natural Preserve.

Pass the south end of Morro Bay to your east around 4¼ miles. Watching on your left you soon might notice a trail that forks left to head southeast into the dunes, the first of many trails in this wonderful state park. That trail connects with a path along the east shore of Shark Inlet at the south end of Morro Bay.

CCT follows the Pacific shore south. Around 4¾ miles it meets the Rim Trail climbing into the high dunes on your left. This is shortest of several choices for the CCT through route, the detour around PG&E's Diablo Canyon Nuclear Power Plant property that requires a 20-mile road walk before returning to the coast. While we highly recommend the hike described in the rest of this section, through-hikers on tight schedules may want to follow the Rim Trail east ¾ mile to Pecho Valley Road, then walk Pecho Valley Road north to Los Osos Valley Road to make the detour.

Otherwise, continue south along the tideline. At 5 miles you pass a broad, distinct side trail that ascends ¼ mile to the parking lot at the end of Sand Spit Road. By 5⅛ miles a soft sandstone layer appears beneath the high dunes on your left. The sandstone layer gets progressively taller as you walk south. Pass a deep gully in the dunes around 5⅜ miles and two smaller gullies before 5⅝ miles, where a rock shelf crosses the beach and extends into the tidal zone. Continue past a trans-Pacific cable landing to approach Hazard Reef. Reach the reef's rocky shore, then pass a high point on the bluff above around 6 miles. The shoreline cuts in to Hazard Creek flowing out of its deep canyon.

Since you can't easily get through to Spooners Cove by walking south along the shore, CCT turns left to follow the trail up the canyon to a junction. The Hazard Reef Trail on the left ascends steeply, then loops back to Sand Spit Road or the CCT road detour. The CCT, however, takes the unmarked right fork, climbing the Hazard Canyon Reef Trail on a boardwalk beside the creek, then steps up to the sandy blufftop where you come to an unmarked junction at 6¼ miles. The trail straight ahead leads ⅛ mile to a parking area on Pecho Valley Road. CCT turns right to ascend the Dune Trail, which is overgrown for the first 200 feet, then continues on better though still narrow tread through chaparral.

After the next junction before 6⅜ miles, where the left fork leads to a parking lot, the Dune Trail contours south through vegetated dunes.Pass under a power line at 6½ miles, then generally contour south along it, the coast obscured by the high dunes on your right. Descend gently at 6¾ miles with the hills of PG&E's property visible ahead.

At 7 miles you reach a trail junction where the road and the Ridge Trail parking area are nearby on the left. The equestrian Dune Trail descends south toward

The Volcanic Peaks of San Luis Obispo County

Morro Rock rises 576 feet like a sentinel above the Coastal Trail and the mouth of Morro Bay, visible for miles on a clear day. In 1542 Cabrillo named the rock "El Moro" (the Moor) for its dark countenance. But when Portola camped nearby in 1769, he noted the presence of "a rounded morro" (promontory) at the mouth of the estuary.

Morro Rock is actually a volcanic plug, the only remnant of a volcanic peak that stood over 20 million years ago. The igneous basalt of Morro Rock was the molten core of the volcano, which in this case never flowed out of the volcano's crater. Over time the softer outer rock of the volcano eroded away, leaving only the plug in place.

Only 120 years ago Morro Rock stood 1000 feet off the mainland shore, with the entrance to Morro Bay on its north side. Then, between 1880 and 1969, more than one million tons of rock were quarried from the inland face of Morro Rock, used to build the breakwaters of Morro Bay and San Luis Bay. Morro Rock was connected to the mainland and a new harbor channel dredged south of the rock and breakwater. Ironically, the quarrying sculpted a more

dramatic vertical face for the rock as viewed from shore. In 1969 the rock was preserved in Morro Rock Ecological Preserve to protect the soaring peregrine falcons that nest there.

Morro Rock is the most famous of a chain of nine volcanic peaks highlighting the landscape between Morro Bay and San Luis Obispo. All of them formed beneath the Pacific long before being uplifted onto the expanding continent. From Turri Road you can see Black Hill, Cerro Cabrillo and Hollister Peak. Cerro Romualdo and Chumash Peak are visible from Los Osos Valley Road.The tallest of the plugs, 1546-foot Bishop Peak and nearby Cerro San Luis Obispo can be seen from Foothill Boulevard and most of San Luis Obispo. Islay Hill, the southernmost of the peaks rises east of the San Luis Obispo Airport.

For a grand view from the top of one of the volcanic peaks, head for Morro Bay State Park and make the 3-mile round trip ascent of Black Hill. From the 661-foot summit you'll see several of the volcanic plugs and a breathtaking view of Morro Bay and the surrounding coast.

Spooners Cove visible ahead. The CCT turns right on a slightly longer and more scenic route, angling northwest to a T junction overlooking dunes along the shore at 7¼ miles. Turn left and contour along the bluff edge through densely vegetated dunes. Descend south from 7⅜ miles with grand views of Spooners Cove below and prominent Islay Point beyond it. Your path turns east before 7½ miles, contouring toward the park road and passing a prickly pear cactus, probably planted when this was ranch land.

Reach a junction beneath power lines at 7⅝ miles. Turn right and descend the narrow path toward the cove, soon reaching the paved road. Turn right, follow the road across the bridge over Islay Creek and turn right again to walk south across the Spooners Cove parking lot. Just beyond it at 7¾ miles, you reach the bottom of a stairway. Climb the rough steps beside a stratified rock outcrop to meet the paved road. Turn right and ascend its shoulder south, then southwest to the Bluff Trailhead at 7⅞ miles.

Take the Bluff Trail south to cross a bridge over an arroyo, then west to a junction at 8 miles. Take the right fork and head west out to the tip of Islay Point before 8¼ miles, which offers stratified rocks protruding west into the surf zone and magnificent views of Spooners Cove and the coast north. Head southwest to another facet of the point, then contour south along the bluff above a rugged rocky shore. Around 8⅜ miles a spur on the right descends to Corallina Cove's fine beach. Turn around for a view north to Morro Rock and the coast beyond it.

CCT contours along a broad blufftop track, soon swinging east around a deep canyon. When you see a bridge over the canyon, turn right and cross it, then turn right again on the Bluff Trail to head west back to the shore. By 8½ miles your trail winds south along the bluff's edge, soon coming to a junction where you stay to the right. Follow the Bluff Trail across a gully and wind to meet a spur trail on the right. CCT turns right on the spur, heading to the tip of a point.

By 8¾ miles your trail ends at the main Bluff Trail. Turn right and contour south with grand views of the rugged, convoluted shore. You pass long finger-like points with narrow ocean inlets between them. To the east the steep hills reach nearly to the shore.

By 8⅞ miles you overlook Quarry Cove, coming to a spur on the right that dips to a picnic table above the rocky cove. Follow the Bluff Trail, contouring to a junction beyond 9 miles. The broad track on your left climbs east to the road. Take the broad right fork to continue along the shore. By 9¼ miles you overlook tunnel-riddled Grotto Rock just off a rugged sculpted shore. Contour south across a level marine terrace, passing several spurs on the right that explore finger points, then a spur on the left before 9⅜ miles. From the Bluff Trail/CCT you soon overlook the pristine inaccessible beach at the mouth of Coon Creek. By 9½ miles your trail winds inland briefly, paralleling the ugly chain-link and barbed wire fence marking that PG&E property before coming to a sign, "END OF TRAIL." From here you have a view south to the level marine terrace extending south to nearby Point Buchon and beyond, with a high rounded 1424-foot peak rising on its left that perches on the state park/PG&E boundary.

You must backtrack to the trail at 9⅜ miles and follow it east through chaparral to the paved park road at 10 miles. Across the road there you'll find chemical toilets and picnic tables beside the Coon Creek Trailhead, with the PG&E gate just a few feet down the road.

Montaña de Oro's dramatic, convoluted shoreline near Islay Point.

This is all the rightful CCT route. The ideal, completed CCT would continue south across what's currently PG&E land, but until the utility giant opens that route to the public, you have only two choices:

Return north via the route you came or along the shoulder of Pecho Valley Road.

ALTERNATE ROUTE: While this entire route is highly recommended, through-hikers might choose to skip part of Montaña de Oro, heading east on either the Rim, Sand Spit, Hazard Reef, or Hazard Canyon trails to Pecho Valley Road and walking it north to begin the long road detour described in Section 9.

SUGGESTED ROUND TRIPS & LOOPS: Montaña de Oro State Park offers many great choices for day hikers. Get the park map and consider loops combining the CCT with the Coon Creek and Rattlesnake Flats trails at the south end of the park, the Reservoir Flats, Valencia Peak, Oats Peak and Badger trails near Spooners Cove, or the Bloody Nose and Manzanita trails near Sand Spit Road. These trails only scratch the surface of the many possibilities here.

HOW TO IMPROVE CCT HERE: Pacific Gas and Electric Company really has an obligation to the citizens of California to provide a route for the CCT across their Diablo Canyon property. The Pecho Coast Trail (see Section 10) is a good start but far from sufficient.

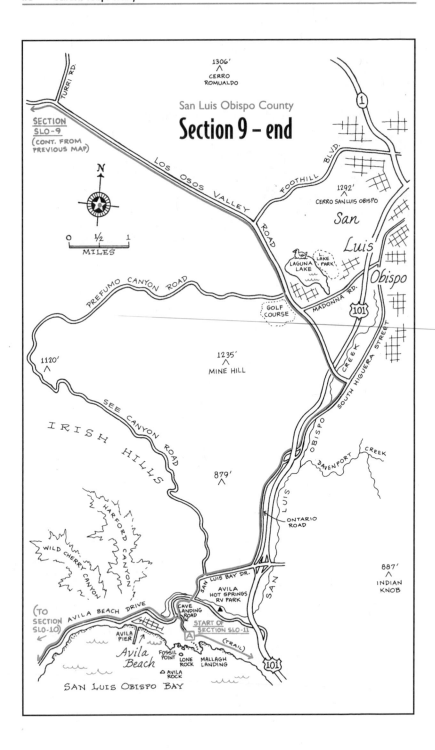

San Luis Obispo County

Section 9 – end

SECTION 9
Montaña de Oro State Park to Avila Beach

DISTANCE: 20⅛ miles or 21⅞ miles, depending on your destination (32.4 or 35.2 kilometers).

OPEN TO: Hikers, bicyclists.

SURFACE: Road shoulders, sidewalks.

ACCESS POINT: Sand Spit Road, Montaña de Oro State Park.

HOW TO GET THERE: From the south, exit Highway 101 onto Los Osos Valley Road and head west 13 miles to state park, then turn right on Sand Spit Road and drive to its end. From the north, exit Highway 1 east of Morro Bay onto South Bay Road and drive south to its end at Los Osos Valley Road, where you turn right and follow Los Osos to Sand Spit Road.

OTHER ACCESS: Anywhere along route.

SOUTH END ACCESS: Avila Beach, either at end of Cave Landing Road or at PG&E's south gate.

DIFFICULTY: Easy.

ELEVATION GAIN/LOSS: 595 feet+/715 feet- to start of Section 10, 795 feet+/725 feet- to start of Section 11.

CAUTIONS: No overnight parking in day use lot. Use extreme caution walking these busy road shoulders: walk single file, wear bright clothing, stay out of roadway.

FURTHER INFORMATION: Montaña de Oro State Park (805)528-0513, Morro Bay State Park (805)772-7434.

FACILITIES: Handicap-accessible chemical toilets, picnic area, phone at access point. Stores, phones and water in towns along the way.

CAMPGROUNDS: Montaña de Oro State Park has primitive camping. Town of Morro Bay has camping with hot showers in two state park campgrounds, Morro Strand State Beach on Section 7 and Morro Bay State Park about 3 miles north of route, plus two private campgrounds. Avila Beach area has a private campground, the Avila Hot Springs Spa & RV Resort. Pismo State Beach at end of Section 11 has 103 units.

HOSTEL: Morro Bay Home Hostel (805)772-9005 is nearby. Hostel Obispo (805)544-4678 is in San Luis Obispo.

LODGING: Many choices in Morro Bay and San Luis Obispo, a few in Avila Beach.

MAP: For access point and start of section, see map on page 130.

Until Pacific Gas and Electric allows more public access through its Diablo Canyon property, site of California's largest nuclear power plant, CCT hikers are forced to make this 20-mile road detour to get between the coast of Montaña de Oro State Park and Avila Beach to the south. It's barely ten miles as the crow flies from the southern end of the state park to Port San Luis near PG&E's south gate, or 13 miles of rugged and pristine coast, only the southernmost 3¾ miles of which are currently open to the public (see next section). The land along the Pecho Coast remains wild and undeveloped except of course for the massive nuclear plant located smack in the middle of that pristine shoreline. During Coastwalk's CCT Whole Hike in 1996, the hikers received permission to walk the entire Pecho Coast—except for five miles surrounding the plant. The exclusion of those five miles that PG&E required as a condition of gaining access split the Whole Hikers into two groups. One group accepted their terms and walked the coast through the Diablo Canyon lands, accepting a ride for the five miles. The other group followed this detour, believing that, if they did not walk five miles of the coast, they could not say they walked the entire coast.

We firmly believe that PG&E has an obligation to Californians to provide a route for the Coastal Trail across their Diablo Canyon property. While we are pleased and grateful that they've opened up access to the southern end of that coast on a guided hike basis, we don't think PG&E should be let off the hook until they establish a through route for the Coastal Trail.

If you choose to walk this detour—a provisional road route for the CCT— we hope you find comfort and camaraderie in the fact that some of the Whole Hikers walked it too. Then sit down and write PG&E a letter urging that they open more of the Pecho Coast to public access.

Be aware that you can start the detour from one of several spots. You could for example skip all of Montaña de Oro (though it would be a shame to miss such a dramatic shoreline), walking south from the town of Morro Bay on Main Street which turns into State Park Road as it winds through Morro Bay State Park. When it ends at South Bay Blvd., turn right and follow the latter to Los Osos Valley Road on the described route at 3⅞ miles. Alternately you can choose to walk a small part or all of the Montaña de Oro coast, then follow Section 9 as described.

If you're hiking south along the sand spit, you want to leave the beach at 5 miles at the broad, distinct side trail that ascends ¼ mile to the parking lot at the end of Sand Spit Road. From the lot follow the road, or the trail that parallels it to the north, uphill to Pecho Valley Road beyond ½ mile and turn left.

Walk the shoulder of Pecho Valley Road northeast, ascending to the road's summit beyond 1⅛ miles. (The Rim Trail, an alternate route from the sand spit meets the road just south of the summit.) The road contours briefly, then descends, leaving the park around 1⅜ miles. Continue your descent to 2¼ miles, entering the town of Cuesta-by-the-Sea. Soon the road turns east and becomes Los Osos Valley Road, which you'll follow all the way to Highway 101.

Follow Los Osos Valley Road on a gradual ascent, passing through the commercial center of the town of Los Osos beyond 3 miles. Reach the intersection with South Bay Blvd. at 3⅞ miles, which connects with Morro Bay to the north. Los Osos Valley Road picks up a bike lane as it continues east. Top the gentle hill you've been climbing at 4⅜ miles and begin a gentle descent.

At 4⅝ miles you pass the Los Osos Oaks State Reserve on your right, an 85-acre natural area with old growth coast live oaks and chaparral growing atop ancient dunes, a pleasant spot for a shady break. Cross Los Osos Creek at the reserve's eastern boundary and descend to 5⅛ miles, then climb over a rise with a cemetery on your left.

Continue east on a gentle descent through the rich bottom lands of the Los Osos Valley. When you pass Turri Road around 7 miles, begin a gentle ascent that continues to 8¾ miles. Descend gradually, then contour to the stoplight at Foothill Blvd. at 10½ miles. Los Osos Valley Road enters the city of San Luis Obispo at 11⅛ miles, where you pick up sidewalks to get you off the busy road shoulder. Follow the sidewalks on a mostly level walk through a busy neighborhood, passing Laguna Lake on your left, then crossing Madonna Road beyond 12¼ miles.

Continue southeast on the shoulder of Los Osos Valley Road, which has lost its sidewalks here but does have bike lanes. Descend gradually to pass beneath Freeway 101 at 13¼ miles and continue to the end of Los Osos Valley Road at 13¾ miles. Turn right on South Higuera Street and walk its shoulder south. You quickly leave town and follow a shoulder bike lane along San Luis Obispo Creek. When you cross the creek at 14¾ miles, you're back beside the roaring freeway.

Follow Higuera Street under the freeway and turn right on Ontario Road at 15½ miles, since Higuera soon merges with the freeway south. Walk the shoulder of Ontario south for 2 miles to its end at San Luis Bay Road at 17½ miles. Turn right and ascend along the shoulder of San Luis Bay Road to 17¾ miles, then descend to 18⅜ miles, where you pass See Canyon Road. Climb briefly then descend across San Luis Obispo Creek to road's end at 18⅞ miles.

Turn right and walk the shoulder of Avila Beach Drive. At 19⅝ miles it comes to Cave Landing Road on the left, where you must make a decision. Avila Beach Drive continues west, coming to First Street of Avila Beach at 20½ miles which leads to the town's commercial district opposite the beach, then continues to PG&E's south gate, start of the Pecho Coast Trail, at 21⅞ miles. If you have a reservation for a docent led hike north on the Pecho Trail, SLO Section 10, you'll want to continue west. Otherwise, the CCT through route down the coast turns left and climbs steeply up Cave Landing Road to 20 miles, then descends to the paved road's end at 20⅛ miles, start of SLO Section 11.

HOW TO IMPROVE CCT HERE: PG&E should recognize its obligation to the citizens of California to open up a route for the CCT along the entire length of their privately owned Pecho Coast, abolishing this provisional road walking detour altogether.

SECTION 10
Pecho Coast Trail: Port San Luis to Rattlesnake Canyon

DISTANCE: 3¾ miles (7½ miles round trip, add 2¾ miles if you need to walk to start of Section 11) (6.0, 12.1, 4.4 kilometers).

OPEN TO: Guided hikes by prior reservation only.

SURFACE: Trail, paved road.

ACCESS POINT: Port San Luis.

HOW TO GET THERE: From the north, exit Highway 101 south of San Luis Obispo onto San Luis Bay Road. Turn right and go 1.4 miles to road's end, then turn right on Avila Beach Drive and go 3 miles to PG&E's south gate. From the south, exit Highway 101 north of Shell Beach onto Avila Beach Drive. Turn left and drive 4.3 miles to PG&E's south gate. Park on road shoulder opposite gate.

OTHER ACCESS: None.

DIFFICULTY: Moderate.

ELEVATION GAIN/LOSS: 830 feet+/830 feet- round trip to trail's end. 650 feet+/650 feet- to lighthouse.

CAUTIONS: Pecho Coast Trail is only open for scheduled docent led hikes. You must make a reservation in advance.

FURTHER INFORMATION: PG&E Pecho Coast Trail information (805)541-8735.

FACILITIES: Chemical toilets at start, lighthouse and Rattlesnake Canyon.

CAMPGROUNDS: Avila Beach area has a private campground, the Avila Hot Springs Spa & RV Resort. Pismo State Beach at end of Section 11 has 103 units.

HOSTEL: Hostel Obispo (805)544-4678 is in San Luis Obispo.

LODGING: Many choices in San Luis Obispo, a few in Avila Beach.

MAP: See page 126.

The Pecho Coast Trail was opened for docent led tours in 1991, ending Pacific Gas & Electric Company's exclusive use of this pristine twelve miles of coast. The California Coastal Commission negotiated the public access trail with PG&E as a concession for a 1983 construction project at Diablo Canyon. PG&E spent $300,000 to open the trail, working with the Nature Conservancy and local conservation groups to organize and train docents to lead the hikes that occur here, usually held on Wednesdays and Saturdays. The California Conservation Corps constructed the well-engineered, occasionally steep trail. While the Nature Conservancy is no longer involved, you'll find the docents well-trained and knowledgeable guides, with each docent bringing their own particular knowledge and expertise to the hikes. Call in advance to reserve space on the popular hikes.

Meet your guides and fellow hikers in the wide parking area on the opposite side of the road from the PG&E gate. Your guided hike crosses the road to the security gate, then climbs stairs on the left, passing through a locked gate. From the top of the stairs, your group follows a trail through coastal sage scrub. Switchback twice around ⅛ mile and climb west to a gravel road built in the 1950s for lighthouse access.

Follow the road south, climbing gradually with views on your left over the vast expanse of San Luis Bay. A Chumash village site, where habitation has been traced back 9500 years, lies below the road. Around ⅜ mile an Indian tobacco bush grows on the right side of the road. Climb moderately past native rye grass.

Around ½ mile a road cut on your right has gray-green and black layers of serpentine rock. It's an exposed fault with sedimentary rocks underlying it. Continue a moderate ascent overlooking San Luis Bay. When it's clear you can see Point Sal at the southern end of the bay.

Beyond ⅝ mile a sign welcomes you to the Pecho Coast Trail. From here your hike descends steeply on rough steps, dropping toward the Harford Pier south of your starting point. The path switchbacks to the right around ¾ mile and descends gradually, soon dipping under shady coast live oaks where a plaque commemorates Pat Stebbins, the Coastal Commission staffer who strongly advocated for broad public access to the California coast. Here you meet part of the historic trail between the 1888 Point San Luis lighthouse and the harbor. The children of the lighthouse keepers once had to walk this trail to get to and from school.

CCT follows the original trail south, climbing across a small seasonal stream where Mexican or hummingbird sage grows. Descend briefly from one mile then contour, all with grand views of the San Luis Bay coast. A short steep ascent around 1¼ miles leads to more vista-rich contouring. Around 1⅜ miles you descend steep steps across a recent slide, then contour along the bottom of a steep rocky slope above Smith Island, approaching Point San Luis. As you descend to the point at 1½ miles, you can see Whalers Island right below, now part of a breakwater extending from the tip of the point.

After reaching the southern face of Point San Luis, CCT joins a semi-paved road, descending it toward the lighthouse. When the lighthouse was built in 1888, Port Harford was a thriving whaling community, producing abundant whale oil to fuel the light. Several of the whaling town's buildings stood along this road. The whaling station closed just after 1900.

The lighthouse finally comes into view around 1¾ miles. Walk the pavement past the caretakers' house, the signal building and the current automated light to stand before the historic lighthouse at 1⅞ miles. Picnic tables and a toilet nearby provide a respite. When it's reasonably clear here, you can see beyond Point Sal to Point Arguello 40 miles south on the Vandenberg coast. The shorter guided hikes return from the lighthouse.

If you're participating in a Rattlesnake Canyon hike, beyond the lighthouse your group climbs briefly, passes through a gate, then follows an old ranch road as it contours northwest up the Pecho coast. After crossing a gulch around 2½ miles, your rough road descends then contours across a sloping grassy marine terrace above the rocky shore. Chaparral draped ridges tower on your right.

Beyond 2¾ miles the eroded ranch road descends toward the shore. Before 3 miles you round a point at the base of a ridge, gaining a broad vista of the Pecho coast to the north. Pass through a ranch gate with Chumash shell middens nearby before 3¼ miles, then contour across a broadening gentle marine terrace through lush grasslands. Around 3⅜ miles the track becomes vague but you head for another ranch gate near the bluff's edge.

After passing through the gate, your trailless trek follows the left side of a barbed wire fence up a gentle incline. Soon you follow the rim of Rattlesnake Canyon. As you ascend, the canyon on your left becomes deeper. It's filled with colorful, wildly shaped coast live oaks. Dip through a side canyon at 3⅝ miles and come to a grassy picnic area with long-focus vistas up the Pecho coast including 1414-foot Green Peak to the northwest. The nuclear plant lies 1½ miles west of the peak's summit. You'll find an open-air toilet with a view about 300 feet east

The Battle for Diablo Canyon

Forty thousand people gathered in June 1979 to protest the construction of PG&E's Diablo Canyon Nuclear power plant. Governor Jerry Brown addressed the huge crowd in a rousing speech at this largest event to question whether a nuclear plant should be allowed to operate on an earthquake fault. PG&E eventually won the war when the Diablo Canyon plant became fully operational in 1986 after years of protests and civil disobedience where 2700 people were arrested, but the victory came at great cost to the utility giant.

It seems that PG&E had a bizarre knack for placing nuke plants on earthquake faults. The first nuclear power plant that PG&E built, the Vallecitos plant near Livermore (now shut down), was just 200 yards from the Verona fault. The plant near Eureka on Humboldt Bay, located beside a series of faults, closed down in 1976, fortunately before a magnitude 7.0 quake struck in 1980. Another early PG&E nuke, proposed to be built at Bodega Head in Sonoma County in the early 1960s, turned out to be smack on top of the San Andreas fault. That plan was scuttled by a coalition that formed where no effective environmental movement had existed before. Only five years later PG&E proposed another nuclear power plant at Point Arena in Mendocino County. It was obvious they hadn't learned their lesson: this time the site was a mile or two west of the big fault.

Perhaps when PG&E announced plans for the Diablo Canyon facility in autumn 1966, they felt they had learned their lesson about earthquake safety and nuclear power plants, boasting that the nearest fault was 45 miles away. Then in 1969 two oil company geologists discovered the Hosgri fault just 2.5 miles offshore from the Diablo plant already under construction. Later research shows that segments of the fault may run directly under the nuke plant. PG&E went into denial, disputing the existence of the Hosgri fault until 1973.

Early resistance to construction at Diablo Canyon was slight. The Sierra Club endorsed construction, saying it was far preferable to the earlier plan of building a nuke plant in the Nipomo Dunes not far south. Organized opposition to the plant slowly developed. By 1978 thousands of people were demonstrating against the Diablo reactors. Several hundred were arrested. Then in spring 1979, a near meltdown occurred at Three Mile Island Nuclear Power Plant in Pennsylvania. As public awareness of the magnitude of the mishap spread, many people joined the movement to stop the Diablo Canyon plant. Despite the 40,000 protestors blocking the Diablo Canyon gates in June, completion and opening of the Diablo Canyon plant was finally allowed. Now the big question has become "When will the Diablo Canyon Nuclear Power Plant be shut down?"

of the picnic spot.

The guided hike returns by heading east, then southeast along the top of fence, rejoining your outward route above the last gate. Enjoy the views down the coast as you return to the trailhead. When the guided hike ends, returning to PG&E's south gate, through hikers will need to walk east on the shoulder of Avila Beach Drive for 2¼ miles to Cave Landing Road, then turn right and climb ½ mile to the start of SLO Section 11.

> HOW TO IMPROVE CCT HERE: Extend the Pecho Coast Trail north along the entire PG&E-owned coast to Coon Creek at the southern end of Montaña de Oro State Park.

SECTION 11
Cave Landing, Avila Beach, to Pismo Beach Pier

DISTANCE: 6 miles (9.7 kilometers).

OPEN TO: Hikers. Bicyclists on Shell Beach Road and other streets. Dogs OK on leash.

SURFACE: Trail, road shoulder, sidewalk, beach.

ACCESS POINT: Cave Landing Trailhead.

HOW TO GET THERE: From the north, exit Highway 101 south of San Luis Obispo onto San Luis Bay Road. Turn right and go 1.4 miles to road's end, then turn right on Avila Beach Drive and go .75 mile to Cave Landing Road, turn left and go .5 mile to road's end. From the south, exit Highway 101 north of Shell Beach and go 2.05 miles to Cave Landing Road, turn left and go .5 mile to road's end.

OTHER ACCESS: From Bluffs Drive or anywhere south.

DIFFICULTY: Easy.

ELEVATION GAIN/LOSS: 140 feet+/390 feet-.

CAUTIONS: Stay out of roadway when walking road shoulders.

FURTHER INFORMATION: Pismo State Beach (805)489-1869.

FACILITIES: Near Pismo Pier at south end, you'll find restrooms, phone, water and commercial services. The only other facilities are a chemical toilet around ¼ mile and picnic tables around 1¼ and 3¼ miles.

CAMPGROUNDS: Avila Beach has a private campground, the Avila Hot Springs Spa & RV Resort. Pismo State Beach's North Beach Campground just south of section's end has 103 units.

HOSTEL: Hostel Obispo (805)544-4678 is in San Luis Obispo.

LODGING: San Luis Obispo has many choices, Avila Beach a few, Pismo Beach several.

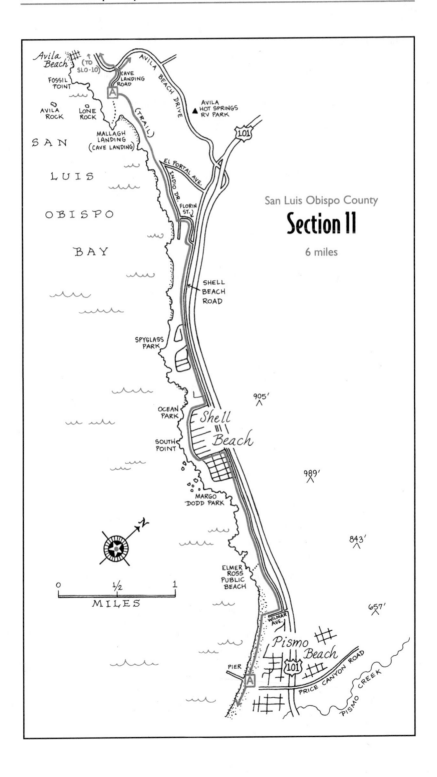

Avila Beach

(TO SLO-10)

CAVE LANDING ROAD

AVILA BEACH DRIVE

FOSSIL POINT

AVILA HOT SPRINGS RV PARK

A

AVILA ROCK

LONE ROCK

(TRAIL)

101

MALLAGH LANDING (CAVE LANDING)

S A N

EL PORTAL AVE.

INDIO DR.

L U I S

FLORIN ST.)

O B I S P O

San Luis Obispo County

Section 11

B A Y

6 miles

SHELL BEACH ROAD

SPYGLASS PARK

905'
∧

OCEAN PARK

Shell Beach

SOUTH POINT

989'
∧

MARGO DODD PARK

843'
∧

N

0   ½   1

M I L E S

ELMER ROSS PUBLIC BEACH

657'
∧

WILMAR AVE.

Pismo Beach

PIER

101

A

PRICE CANYON ROAD

PISMO CREEK

From Cave Landing Road's dirt parking lot, you can see that the shoreline south is not walkable for the next couple of miles. The Coastal Trail follows the old roadway, now closed to vehicles, down the coast. (While we begin this section's description at the parking area at the end of the drivable portion of Cave Landing Road, you might want to start at PG&E's south gate, an option described under Alternate Route.)

From the Cave Landing parking lot, a side trail descends southeast to Cave Landing itself. Also known as Mallagh Landing, this steep rocky promontory forms a natural rock pier that extends into deep water. A steep trail continues east to sheltered Pirate's Cove and a popular clothing-optional beach. Local Chumash people once fished from the rock and buried their dead in its caves. In 1860 sea captain David Mallagh built a warehouse atop the rock and a wooden chute to load local produce onto ships anchored offshore.

Walk past the rust brown gate and follow the dirt road northeast, climbing slightly for the first ⅛ mile. The road bends to the right, descending gradually then moderately with views of the rocky point called Cave Landing and Pirate's Cove below, coming to a locked gate. Continue along the road beyond the second gate, entering the city of Pismo Beach and coming to a cul-de-sac with a chemical toilet.

In another 75 feet you reach a public pedestrian path which the CCT follows down the coast. It follows the ocean side of Bluffs Drive, gated to public vehicles, sometimes as a sidewalk and occasionally as a separate path. Pass a short spur on the right beyond ⅜ mile which leads to a view of the rocky, wave-swept tidal zone below. Descend the main path to the parking area at its end around ⅝ mile, where a steep rough spur descends to the tideline.

CCT continues along Bluffs Drive, following sidewalks where available and the edge of the street where they are not. When you reach the intersection with El Portal Avenue on the left, veer to the right and continue along Indio Drive. You'll glimpse the ocean around ⅞ mile, but generally contour along a residential street lined with homes.

When you reach Florin Street around 1⅛ miles, turn left and ascend Florin. You soon pass a small park on your left which has picnic tables, a good spot for a break. Continue along Florin to its end, then go left on Hermosa Drive, quickly climbing to its end at busy Shell Beach Road just beyond 1⅜ miles.

Turn right and walk the sidewalk of Shell Beach Road down the coast, descending gradually. Reach Spyglass Drive by 2⅛ miles. It leads to access to adjacent Highway 101 to the north and coastal access at Spyglass City Park about ¼ mile south, but has no through access along the coast.

Continue along Shell Beach Road to 2⅞ miles where CCT turns right to descend Vista del Mar Avenue to its end. Turn left and follow Ocean Blvd. By 3⅛ miles it comes to the first blufftop parking area above the shore. At medium to low tide you can walk the tideline south from here. Continue along Ocean Blvd. or the tideline, passing two coastal access stairways before coming to Ocean City Park before 3¼ miles. One needs to leave the tideline here and return to the shoulder of Ocean Blvd. to follow the CCT south. Walk through a residential area, reaching the end of Ocean Blvd. at Placentia Avenue before 3½ miles. Turn left and follow Placentia up to Shell Beach Road around 3⅞ miles.

The sweeping curve of popular Pismo Beach from the town of Shell Beach.

Turn right and follow Shell Beach Road down the coast. After passing an entrance to the freeway south around 4⅛ miles, Shell Beach Road becomes Price Street and draws near the coast, but the shore lies hidden at the base of tall bluffs. Continue past two motels, then an access for the freeway north beyond 4¾ miles to Wilmar Avenue on your right at 5¼ miles. Turn right and walk Wilmar to its end, then descend the stairway to the broad strand of Pismo State Beach beyond 5⅜ miles. The beach extends almost ⅛ mile north from the stairway, but the Coastal Trail turns left and follows the beach south to the Pismo Beach Pier at 6 miles.

ALTERNATE ROUTE: If you need to hike from the south gate of PG&E's Diablo Canyon property, it's 2¾ miles to SLO 11's access point. To do so, walk east on Avila Beach Drive. At 1⅜ miles First Street on your right leads to the town of Avila Beach and Avila State Beach along its shore. Follow Avila Beach Drive to Cave Landing Road on the right at 2¼ miles. Turn right and ascend steeply on Cave Landing Road, then descend to the dirt parking area at 2¾ miles.

SUGGESTED ROUND TRIPS & LOOPS: Walk the closed portion of Cave Landing Road and the quiet path along Bluffs Drive and return, 1¼ miles round trip. Walk Pismo Beach from either the pier or the Wilmar Drive stairway, up to 1½ miles round trip.

SECTION 12
Pismo Beach Pier to Oso Flaco Trail

DISTANCE: 7¼ miles (11.7 kilometers).

OPEN TO: Hikers. Dogs OK on leash on State Beach, not allowed on Nature Conservancy lands.

SURFACE: Beach, dunes, trail.

ACCESS POINT: Pismo Beach Pier.

HOW TO GET THERE: From Highway 101 in Pismo Beach, exit Hinds Avenue southbound or Price Street northbound. Go west on Hinds Avenue to parking near pier at end.

OTHER ACCESS: Ends of Grand Avenue and Pier Avenue.

DIFFICULTY: Easy.

ELEVATION GAIN/LOSS: Negligible.

CAUTIONS: Watch for rogue waves on beach. From Grand Avenue around 1¼ miles south, most of this section is open to motor vehicles. Try not to hike through the State Vehicular Recreation Area there on a weekend, and wear bright clothing when you go.

FURTHER INFORMATION: Pismo State Beach (805)489-1869, Oceano Dunes State Vehicular Recreation Area (805)473-7220.

FACILITIES: Restrooms, water and phones at access point, with town services—groceries, food, body adornment—available to east. Restrooms and water at North Beach Campground, Oceano Campground and near the end of Pier Avenue.

CAMPGROUNDS: Pismo State Beach has 103 sites in North Beach Campground and 82 sites in Oceano Campground.

HOSTEL: Hostel Obispo (805)544-4678 is in San Luis Obispo. Bill's Home Hostel (805)929-3647 is in the town of Nipomo 9 miles east of south end.

LODGING: Many choices in the Five Cities area—Shell Beach, Pismo Beach, Grover Beach, Oceano and Arroyo Grande.

Around Pismo Beach the CCT through hiker heading from north to south once again encounters a vast accumulation of sand, in fact more sand than has been seen since the shores of Monterey Bay. This sandy world extends all the way to Point Sal in northern Santa Barbara County without interruption and sets the tone for most of the shoreline to the south. The Pismo Dunes are followed by the vast Nipomo Dunes, the second largest collection (after the Oregon Dunes) of sand on the west coast of North America.

The bad news for hikers here is that vehicles are allowed on the beach from Grover Beach south for five miles, almost to the end of the section. While CCT hikers in Humboldt and Del Norte Counties may have encountered a few vehicles driving the beach, here the off-roaders congregate in alarming numbers, ironically compressing and denuding a fragile environment. Let it suffice to say that this is

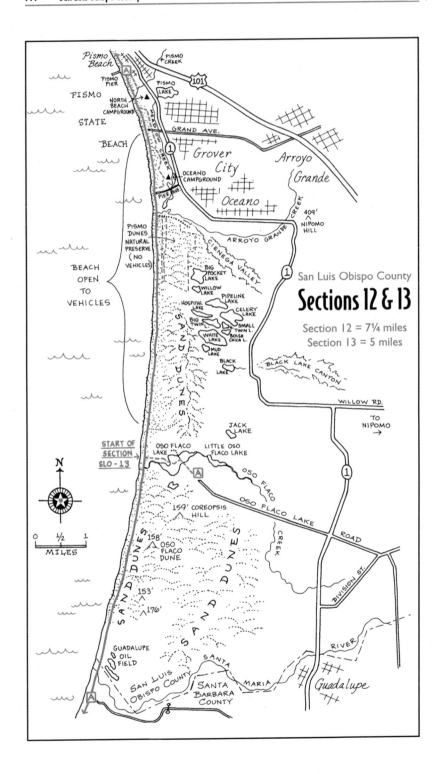

San Luis Obispo County

Sections 12 & 13

Section 12 = 7¼ miles
Section 13 = 5 miles

not our favorite part of the Coastal Trail, although it would offer delightful hiking if the State of California would take the brave stand of closing this ORV amusement park. We do recommend the Suggested Loop at the end of this section. There you'll experience enough vehicles on the beach to get the picture, then be able to leave them behind as you loop back through dunes and along wetlands fortunately protected from the onslaught of internal combustion engines.

The name Pismo comes from the Chumash word *pismu*, meaning the asphaltum tar that leaks from natural fissures in the ground or sea floor along the central California coast. The Chumash used the tar to make their baskets and pine plank canoes waterproof. Here in the Pismo Beach area CCT through hikers will likely see the first gooey balls of tar on the beach. The town of Pismo Beach first became a popular summer vacation destination shortly after it was founded in 1891. Then the Pismo clam for which the area is also famous was so abundant that farmers fed them to their animals after harvesting them by plowing the beach. Now the clam is scarce enough that it's usually found by experienced clam diggers only at low tide.

Unless you are continuing along the CCT from the previous section, make your way from the parking lot to the beach at the foot of the pier. The CCT heads south along the tideline of the broad beach, a busy and popular place on a sunny day. When the weather is clear you look south across San Luis Obispo Bay to Mussel Rock Dune and Point Sal.

Alternately you can walk south from the pier's access way across the concrete plaza, then follow the raised wooden boardwalk along the beach front. It turns to concrete as it passes the Sandcastle Inn. Then you can take the stairs or ramp that descend to the beach and follow the tideline south, or cross the cul-de-sac and walk sidewalk and parking lot south to the development's abrupt end at ¼ mile.

Either way you go, follow the tideline beyond ¼ mile, with the wetlands near the mouth of Pismo Creek to your east. When you cross the seasonally flowing mouth of the creek at ⅜ mile, the state beach's North Beach Campground lies to the east. Soon the broad beach narrows where the trees of the campground extend west. Immediately south of the campground at ⅝ mile, the second of two beach access trails heads east. The easiest CCT route continues along the tideline, but you can also walk the trail east 1000 feet, then turn south and follow the Meadow Creek Trail to its south end, cross Grand Avenue and continue south on the Grand Dunes Trail, which ends at Oceano Campground around 2 miles where you need to head west to return to the tideline.

The tideline route passes the end of Grand Avenue before 1¼ miles. Street legal vehicles are allowed on the beach south from here for the next 2 miles, with off-highway vehicles permitted from there south almost to the end of this section. As you follow the shore south, dunes of increasing height lie to the east between the tideline and Meadow Creek which parallels the shore. Pass the highest of these dunes, about 55 feet, around 1¾ miles. Continue down coast on the tideline, with Oceano Campground on the west shore of Oceano Lagoon lying to the east beyond 2 miles.

At 2⅜ miles you reach the end of Pier Avenue, the main access for Oceano Dunes State Vehicular Recreation Area (SVRA). You'll find restrooms not far to the east here. We highly recommend you wear bright clothing if you walk south

Oil Sure Can Make a Mess of the Coast

In 1969 the Santa Barbara oil spill occurred when an offshore oil well blew out, dumping 4.2 million gallons of crude oil into the Pacific. Beaches turned black and were littered with dead birds. No waves rose from the black shiny water. It was eight months before anyone could use the beach again. This isolated incident created plenty of momentum for voters passing the Coastal Protection Initiative three years later, and California has not yet had such a massive spill again.

Petroleum is toxic, however, and California pumps and refines plenty of it.

In 1990 the central coast learned that Unocal's Guadalupe Oil Field, within a mile of the beach and the CCT in southern San Luis Obispo County, had been leaking petroleum thinner, or diluent, into the Nipomo Dunes beneath it. Over the next four years it came to light that Unocal officials knew of the leaks but failed to report them. Then three experts hired by Unocal estimated the spill at between 4.6 million and 8.5 million gallons, larger than the 1969 spill and possibly twice the size. Once Unocal officials admitted to the scale of the spill, it became clear that the leaks had been occurring over 15 years. They were fined $1.5 million. Efforts to clean up the underground leaks have recovered about a million gallons of diluent, with most of the rest dispersed along the nearby coast and ocean. The Guadalupe Oil Field is surrounded by the Nature Conservancy's Nipomo Dunes Preserve.

In 1989 an Avila Beach merchant began excavating to expand his small business, but he found oil flowing under the town's main street. The discovery did not make him wealthy. A Unocal oil tank facility crowns the hill above town. When Unocal officials were confronted with the mess, they acknowledged responsibility and admitted knowing of the spill since 1977. In 1994, after further investigation, Unocal estimated the spill to be 22,000 gallons and 100 feet deep. In autumn 1998, Unocal began cleaning up the spill in the only way possible. They tore down the four blocks of the small town's business district and began digging down 40 to 60 feet to remove 100,000 cubic yards of oil-soaked sand. Estimates now place the spill at 400,000 gallons of diesel, crude oil and gasoline, with estimated final costs exceeding $200 million. The town of Avila Beach hopes to reopen in summer 2000 after ten years of anguish and a year of complete shutdown. As one merchant said, "It's basically killed the town is what it's done." But the story goes on. Unocal has been buying up the beachfront property as it cleans up. Long-time residents and visitors suspect that the oil giant will sell the prime land to developers, who will then build high rises there, turning funky Avila Beach into another Newport Beach.

Responsibility for monitoring California's more than 8000 miles of buried petroleum pipelines is divided among several state agencies and some leaks are not fixed for years. "You've got a very antiquated infrastructure of pipelines in California and they're not holding," said Steve Sawyer of the state Office of Oil Spill Prevention and Response. "We're dealing with pipes that have been buried for 40 or 50 years. After a while corrosion sets in and you get breaks."

These are only three of the many sobering stories about the messy side of oil and its toll on human and natural resources. Is petroleum's next assault on California's coast waiting to happen or already lying buried beneath the surface?

from here. As you walk the tideline south, cross the mouth of Arroyo Grande Creek around 2⅝ miles. While the tideline still offers the firmest footing, on busy days in the SVRA the tideline south from here seems more like a highway than a beach. Consider following the south shore of the creek east for about 400 feet into the Pismo Dunes Natural Preserve where vehicles are not allowed. There you can walk south through the dunes (soft sand, slow going) to the preserve boundary around 4 miles. You pass through the site of the Dunite's village there(read the feature *The Amazing Nipomo Dunes*), then return to the tideline.

From 4 miles the vehicle traffic starts to thin out since off-road vehicles are also allowed in the dunes east of the beach and street legal vehicles are not allowed at all. Between 4 and 5½ miles, several lakes nestle in the dunes about a mile east of the tideline, but you can't see them because of the 100-foot-high dune ridge about ⅝ mile east. The dunes in this area have a flat, compressed appearance because of the extensive vehicle traffic, which also destroys virtually all of their stabilizing vegetation. A few fenced enclaves with isolated green foliage only reinforce this contrast.

CCT continues south along the tideline. Around 6¼ miles a large sign proclaims a 15 mph speed limit. At 6½ miles you reach the metal fence that marks the southern end of the SVRA. Pass the fence and walk the tideline for another ½ mile to a spot where the high dune ridge to the east has a ¾-mile gap. Watch on your left for the Oso Flaco Trail, a boardwalk that climbs east into the dunes. The boardwalk marks this section's end and the beginning of the next. The side trail leads one mile to the end of Oso Flaco Lake Road. If you miss the boardwalk, you might see the small lagoon near the mouth of Oso Flaco Creek, though it may dry up in the dry season.

ALTERNATE ROUTE: Several choices included in trail report give you options for avoiding the vehicle traffic that mars the experience of walking this stretch of beach.

SUGGESTED ROUND TRIPS & LOOPS: Walk the beach to Pier Avenue, head east to Oceano Campground, then return by walking north through the campground or along the Oceano Lagoon Trail, continuing on the Grand Dunes Trail to Grand Avenue, then the Meadow Creek Trail to its north end. From there you head west to return to the beach for the final leg north, although in winter you might consider a side trip ¼ mile east into the grove of eucalyptus trees that are the winter home of thousands of monarch butterflies.

HOW TO IMPROVE CCT HERE: Close the beach to vehicles.

SECTION 13
Oso Flaco Trail to Guadalupe Dunes Parking Lot

DISTANCE: 5 miles (CCT) plus one mile from access point (8.0 plus 1.6 kilometers).

OPEN TO: Hikers. Wheelchair riders can navigate the first ¾ mile of access trail.

SURFACE: Beach for CCT. Dirt road, boardwalk, trail from parking area to beach.

ACCESS POINT: Oso Flaco Lake Natural Area.

HOW TO GET THERE: Turn west off Highway 1 north of Guadalupe onto Oso Flaco Lake Road and go 3 miles to entrance kiosk. When kiosk is not staffed, you'll need to park on road shoulder 150 feet east. Do not block gate there.

OTHER ACCESS: None.

DIFFICULTY: Easy.

ELEVATION GAIN/LOSS: None for CCT. Trail from parking area to beach: 50 feet+/75 feet-.

CAUTIONS: Open 6 am to 6 pm. No bikes, dogs, horses or fires. Watch for rogue waves when walking beach. Please stay out of plover nesting area from March 1 through September 15. During that time stay on trail or on wet sand of beach and stay off upper beach and foredunes.

FURTHER INFORMATION: Oso Flaco Dunes Natural Area (805)473-7220, Guadalupe-Nipomo Dunes Preserve (805)343-2455.

FACILITIES: Wheelchair accessible chemical toilets at parking areas at both north and south ends of section.

CAMPGROUNDS: Pismo State Beach on Section 11 has 185 sites in two campgrounds.

HOSTEL: Bill's Home Hostel (805)929-3647 in nearby Nipomo is run by Bill Denneen, an expert on the ecology and history of the Nipomo Dunes. Another choice is Hostel Obispo (805)544-4678 in San Luis Obispo.

LODGING: Arroyo Grande, Nipomo and Santa Maria have several choices.

MAP: See page 144.

Oso Flaco Lake nestles in the heart of the Nipomo Dunes, a vast complex of sand hills stretching from Oceano south for 14 miles to Point Sal in northern Santa Barbara County. The dunes cover more than 18 square miles, the largest undeveloped coastal dune ecosystem in California. You've probably seen the Nipomo Dunes even if you've never visited them. A famous Ansel Adams photograph of the dunes was taken near Oceano and part of the 1920s version of the movie *The Ten Commandments* was filmed in the dunes. The immense Hollywood-style sets that were built for that epic lie buried somewhere in the vast dunes. To learn more about the Nipomo Dunes, read the adjacent feature and visit the Dunes Discovery Center on Highway 1 in Guadalupe.

Oso Flaco Lake, crossed by the access trail, is one of two lakes along lower

Oso Flaco Creek, with a dozen more lakes scattered in the dunes in the three miles to the north. All the lakes provide important habitat for resident and migratory birds, and many unusual endemic plants grow around them. Oso Flaco Lake was named by the Portola expedition for the skinny bear they shot when camped here in 1769. The lean grizzly measured ten feet long but weighed only 375 pounds (typical grizzlies weigh 400 to 850 pounds). Still the bear fed 62 hungry men. Of course grizzlies no longer survive in California, but on my visit here I saw fresh mountain lion tracks and two young coyotes who eyed me warily as they ran across the trail.

The Coastal Trail follows the tideline at the western edge of this vast eolian landscape. To reach the CCT from Oso Flaco Lake Road requires a hike of just over one mile (2⅛ miles round trip). When you reach the tideline there, you have the choice of walking north on Section 12 or south as described in this section.

From the access point either east of the entrance kiosk or just west of it, follow the narrow road northwest, soon passing the second gate and the only chemical toilets. Contour along the paved path through a marsh filled with willows. At ¼ mile the path crosses the northern neck of Oso Flaco Lake. Turn left in the middle of the crossing and follow the bridge/boardwalk across the lake. It soon turns right to head west. Leave the bridge and lake before ½ mile to contour west on a wooden boardwalk through vegetated dunes. By ¾ mile the boardwalk ahead is closed. Veer right on a sandy path over a dune, affording your first good views of the surrounding dunes. The well-marked route soon returns to the boardwalk, which you follow west to its end around one mile. Continue west about 300 feet to the tideline, where you meet the CCT. Our mileage starts from zero here.

Follow the tideline south from the point west of the end of the boardwalk. Around ⅛ mile you may parallel a seasonal lagoon near the mouth of Oso Flaco Creek where it runs north to south. Cross the mouth of the creek, which was flowing into the Pacific on my February 1999 visit, at ¼ mile. Continue down the coast along the tideline with high vegetated dunes to your east.

Pass Coreopsis Hill around 1¼ miles, a prominent dune ridge lying about ¾ mile east where the giant Coreopsis of the sunflower family grows to eight feet, three feet taller than most individuals of the species. Beyond 1½ miles Oso Flaco Dune stands about ½ mile east, the highest dune this near the coast in the Guadalupe Dunes. Continue along the tideline, rounding a sandy point around 2⅜ miles.

By 3 miles two more high dunes rise to the east, the second dune, 176 feet, being about ¾ mile inland. Between 3 and 4 miles, the Guadalupe Oil Field lies in the dunes to the east. You may see several sandy vehicle tracks in this area, especially the southernmost two tracks between 4 and 4¼ miles where three small ponds nestle in the foredunes. No sign marks your passing into Santa Barbara County around 4¼ miles, but the high dunes give way to a low sandy swale with pockets of vegetation. This depression in the dunes marks the mouth of the Santa Maria River which flows seasonally out to sea around 4½ miles. Only after winter storms does the river offer any difficulty fording. The river's 365-acre wetland just inland from the mouth provides important bird and mammal habitat.

From around the river mouth, you may actually see cars driving over the dunes to the southeast. They follow the paved road that provides access to the

Guadalupe entrance of Nipomo Dunes Preserve. This section ends at 5 miles as the tideline draws even with the Guadalupe parking lot at the end of that road. The paved parking area lies atop a rise about 200 feet east of the tideline.

SUGGESTED ROUND TRIPS & LOOPS: Walk the beach for as many miles as you choose in either direction, leaving enough time for your return hike unless you've planned a car shuttle. For a loop hike when the plovers aren't nesting, walk the beach south for up to 3 miles, follow the dune crest east for about a mile, then head north for Oso Flaco Lake. Be sure to take a map and compass.

Santa Barbara County

A DISTINCT CAPITAL LETTER **L** describes the Santa Barbara County coast on the Golden State's shore. Santa Barbara County's wild north coast forms the L's vertical. The L hinges on rugged, inaccessible Point Conception, and the sheltered and sun-warmed south coast makes its horizontal arm. Mountains rim this entire coastline, with a narrow coastal marine terrace wedged between the precipitous mountains and the shore. Only in the southeastern county does the terrace fan out to a width of two or three miles. The steeply sloped mountains provide a spectacular backdrop to the shoreline's diversity, the Coast Range rising 2000 feet along the north coast and the Santa Ynez Range towering up to 4000 feet above the south coast.

In Santa Barbara County the Coastal Trail explores a land of contrasts. Here the CCT traverses the most populous county since San Francisco, yet hikers will marvel at how few people they'll see along 90 percent of its shore. The wind- and wave-swept north coast is remote and rugged, much of it inaccessible, while the south coast sprawls along the sunny base of the mountains, with Highway 101 running most of its length. Vast stretches of the Santa Barbara coast are preserved in parks welcoming visitors, but hikers may be arrested for visiting other coastal places. Much of Vandenberg Air Force Base's long coast is off limits to visitors, and three immense private ranches, remnants of old Spanish ranchos, and a coast guard reservation warn trespassers of arrest.

Along Santa Barbara's wild north coast, the CCT first explores the Guadalupe Dunes, climbing the flank of the west coast's highest dune to reach remote Paradise Beach. As the Coastal Trail makes a dramatic ascent of Point Sal Ridge, it overlooks the immense Vandenberg base which occupies the next 35 miles of Santa Barbara's shoreline. The CCT currently follows roads to get around this bastion of national security, but we describe Alternate Routes exploring ten miles of Vandenberg's shore. Another Alternate Route heads south from Jalama Beach County Park, getting as close to Point Conception as one can without a boat or train ride.

After more than 50 miles of road detours through coastal valleys and hills, the CCT reaches the south coast at Gaviota Pier. For nearly all of its final 50 miles through Santa Barbara County, the Coastal Trail follows beaches and bluffs along the sunny south-facing shore, where water temperatures are ten degrees warmer than north of Point Conception, with gentler surf, cruising porpoises and Channel Islands views as a bonus. From Gaviota the CCT's next 22 miles mostly follow lightly used beaches passable only at medium to low tides and notably free from development.

Once the CCT reaches the university town of Isla Vista on the western outskirts of Santa Barbara, the shoreline's popularity rises dramatically. Still, as the CCT continues along the Santa Barbara waterfront on gorgeous beaches at the base of steep towering bluffs, what most impresses one about the fine beaches is their seclusion. When the quiet beaches finally give way to an urban waterfront, the CCT passes through the city on sparkling beaches along one of the most pleasant and well loved urban shorelines in California.

East of the city, the CCT continues along beaches and bluffs through exclusive urban neighborhoods, friendly small towns, and beside rich agricultural lands. After passing through Carpinteria, famed for the safest beach in California, Santa Barbara's Coastal Trail ends after 112⅝ miles.

SECTION 1
Guadalupe Dunes, Nipomo Dunes Preserve, to Point Sal to Highway 1 at Brown Road

DISTANCE: 13¼ miles; 3 miles to Paradise Beach, 4⅞ miles to Point Sal, 7⅛ miles to Brown Road, then 6⅛ more miles to Highway 1 (21.3, 4.8, 7.8, 11.5, 9.9 kilometers).

OPEN TO: Hikers. Bicyclists on road portion. Dogs OK south of Mussel Rock Dune.

SURFACE: Beach, dunes, trail, road shoulder.

ACCESS POINT: Guadalupe Dunes, Nipomo Dunes Preserve.

HOW TO GET THERE: Turn west off Highway 1 onto West Main Street at south end of town of Guadalupe. Follow Main 3 miles to entrance kiosk for Guadalupe-Nipomo Dunes Preserve, then continue 2 miles to parking at end of road.

OTHER ACCESS: Point Sal via Brown Road.

DIFFICULTY: Moderate to strenuous.

ELEVATION GAIN/LOSS: 1660 feet+/1540 feet-. 280 feet+/280 feet- to Paradise Beach.

CAUTIONS: Parking lot at access point open 6 a.m. to 8 p.m. No overnight parking. No dogs or vehicles allowed beyond the parking lot. No fires. Road to access point is occasionally closed by drifting sand, in which case you need to add the distance walked to parking lot at end of road. Dunes up from the beach are closed March to September to protect endangered birds during nesting season. Watch for rattlesnakes, ticks and scorpions, especially on Point Sal Ridge.

FURTHER INFORMATION: Guadalupe-Nipomo Dunes Preserve (805)343-2455.

FACILITIES: Chemical toilets at access point.

CAMPGROUNDS: Private Santa Maria Pines Campground in Santa Maria is the nearest. Oceano Campground in Pismo State Beach 19 miles north has 82 sites.

HOSTEL: Bill's Home Hostel, (805)929-3647, in nearby Nipomo is run by Bill Denneen, an expert on the area's ecology and history. Bill may be willing to give a guided hike of the region. Another choice is Hostel Obispo in San Luis Obispo (805)544-4678.

LODGING: Motels in Santa Maria 13 miles east.

Looking south from the parking lot, an expansive beach ends abruptly at an immense high sand dune. Perhaps you'll rub your eyes in disbelief. While dunes are a familiar sight on the coast, the vast Guadalupe-Nipomo Dunes complex covers 18 square miles of southwestern San Luis Obispo County and northwestern Santa Barbara County. If you've been walking the Coastal Trail south from Pismo Beach, you've seen plenty of dunes, but the giant dune blocking the south end of the beach reaches an entirely different level.

In fact Mussel Rock Dune towers 480 feet above sea level, the west coast's highest dune. The CCT not only provides a closer look, it also climbs over the dune to interact with this unique feature, also the only way to get down coast to

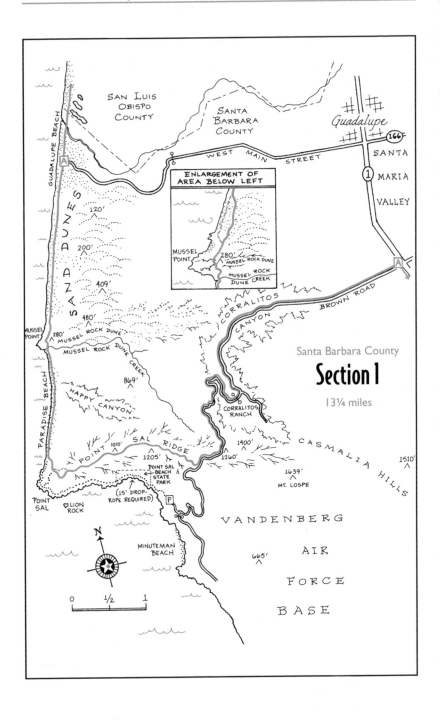

SAN LUIS OBISPO COUNTY

SANTA BARBARA COUNTY

Guadalupe

SANTA MARIA VALLEY

WEST MAIN STREET

GUADALUPE BEACH

ENLARGEMENT OF AREA BELOW LEFT

MUSSEL POINT

280'
MUSSEL ROCK DUNE
MUSSEL ROCK DUNE CREEK

S A N D U N E S

120'
200'
409'
480'
869'
1010'
1205'

MUSSEL POINT

280'
MUSSEL ROCK DUNE

MUSSEL ROCK DUNE CREEK

PARADISE BEACH

HAPPY CANYON

POINT SAL RIDGE

POINT SAL BEACH STATE PARK

(15' DROP-ROPE REQUIRED)

POINT SAL

LION ROCK

MINUTEMAN BEACH

N

0   1/2   1

CORRALITOS CANYON

BROWN ROAD

CORRALITOS RANCH

1400'
1260'
1639'
MT. LOSPE

CASMALIA HILLS

1510'

Santa Barbara County

Section 1

13¼ miles

VANDENBERG AIR FORCE BASE

665'

1½-mile long Paradise Beach just beyond. If you keep pushing through the vast sandy landscape beyond Mussel Rock, you encounter Point Sal where the CCT route turns strenuous. There one must climb steeply to get onto Point Sal Ridge, another marvelous feature that ascends east to narrow Brown Road, the only way to continue down the coast. That's because vast Vandenberg Air Force Base occupies the next 35 restricted miles of shoreline. While the CCT follows a few miles of Vandenberg's coast, those miles do not include the 16 miles from Point Sal to Ocean Beach County Park west of Lompoc.

Whether you walk all of this section, best done with a car shuttle so it's a one way hike, plan to visit Mussel Rock Dune, Paradise Beach and Point Sal, among the most amazing places on the California coast. One can carry a backpack and camp on Paradise Beach, where water can usually be found in springs or creeks. Of course carrying a backpack here tips the scale, making it a strenuous trip.

From the parking lot at the end of the road, walk west about 200 feet to the tideline. Turn left and follow the tideline south toward Mussel Point at the seaward foot of the giant dune down the coast. You first follow a beach backed by low dunes to the east. Around one mile, where the shoreline cuts inland somewhat, the low dunes on your left give way to taller dunes, first to vegetated sand hills to 40 feet in height, then to taller, larger dunes. The high sandy rise of Mussel Rock Dune looms ever larger.

By 1½ miles the immense dune thoroughly dominates the view south. The steep slope above the tideline may have you wondering at the way through, while the mountain of sand rising to the east is also daunting. Watch carefully along the top of the beach at the dune's base for a bleached wooden T-shaped marker, the base and left arm of the T imbedded in the dune. If it hasn't been obscured by drifting sand, it marks the easiest, most gradual route up onto the dune.

Alternately one can continue along the tideline, either as a side trip to see the fascinating rock formations at the dune's seaward base or for a more difficult CCT route. If you continue along the shore, beyond 1¾ miles the sandy beach is cut by

This T-shaped post marks the easiest way onto Mussel Rock Dune.

The CCT descends this steep gully to Paradise Beach.

fingers of rock protruding into the tidal zone. Walk up the beach slope to the dune's base and follow the top of the beach south, then a ledge atop the rocks. Be careful if you cross the rocks, very slippery in places. This route explores a fascinating area with seeps and black-sand pockets between the soft sandstone fingers, which have harder rocks and marine shells embedded in them. The easy walk ends before 2 miles, where it takes creative scrambling to continue. I learned the hard way when I stepped on a sloping dune only to find it underlaid with slick rock that sent me sliding ten feet down to the beach. If you get beyond that, a short stroll atop more rock fingers ends at a larger inlet at 2 miles. Cautiously pick your way around this inlet. After crossing slick rock on its far side, hop a waist-high ledge and find a vague path angling steeply east-southeast up the dune, the alternate CCT route south. (One might continue along the shore about ¼ mile, but it dead-ends.)

Back at the T guidepost, scramble about twenty feet up a slope of loose sand, then angle right to climb a more gradual slope of sand that's more firmly packed to reach an area stabilized by vegetation. Try not to step on plants as you find your way south, angling gradually up the dune. You won't find a trail unless someone came this way recently. Shifting sands on the dune's windward slope quickly cover any tracks, often within hours, certainly within days of anyone's passing. Stay off the steepest face of the dune down near the tideline, which may be undercut by sand cliffs not visible from here. At some point you'll need to traverse sidehill across steep slopes. Just be sure to keep climbing and not stray too close to the steep base of the dune near shore.

Beyond 2 miles you want to climb generally south-southwest, picking your way carefully across the sloping face of the giant dune. In places the dune is soft as silk, elsewhere it's hard as stone so take your time and watch where you're going. The lush pockets of vegetation perched on this giant sandhill may surprise you: fragrant lupine, beach strawberry, sand verbena, dune primrose plus several rare species.

By 2⅝ miles you want to be around 200 or 250 feet above sea level. Contour south ⅛ mile, then ascend steeply again to the main ridge of Mussel Rock Dune around 2¾ miles, elevation about 280 feet. The crest provides views down the steep northwest slope to an arched rock on a convoluted shore and south down coast to Paradise Beach and Point Sal. You might also pass Chumash shell middens atop the plateau on the dune's west slope.

To continue south on CCT to Paradise Beach, be sure you find a safe route down the dune. The preferred route descends a steep gully between two dune hills, winding down a vegetated slope to reach sandy Mussel Rock Dune Creek near its mouth. Once you get down to the creek, which flows out of a deep canyon, cross to the stream's south side and find the vague track that descends to Paradise Beach at its narrow north end around 3 miles.

CCT follows the tideline of Paradise Beach south. After quickly passing a rock outcrop, the beach broadens as it arcs toward vegetation-darkened Point Sal. It's a rare day you don't have this grand sweep of beach to yourself. Pass the broadest expanse of beach by 3½ miles, but the beach remains broad and backed by steep brushy slopes nearly to its south end. By 4¼ miles you pass a narrow spot on the beach before it fans out broadly again. By 4½ miles you'll see offshore rocks, then reach a double pronged covelet along the shore.

When you reach a long finger cove at 4⅝ miles, Point Sal is less than ¼ mile south, but the shoreline around the point does not offer safe passage. (To continue around the point to Point Sal Beach requires a low tide, walking narrow rock shelves, and climbing fifteen feet up an anchored rope to pass the final rock ledge.) CCT climbs southeast from the finger cove up a steep gully. Ascend the gully until you gain 200 feet elevation, where the slope eases. Contour south about ⅛ mile to where the odd plant giant coreopsis grows. As you go, watch on your left for a safe passage up onto Point Sal Ridge. You can climb southeast to gain a knob on the ridgetop around 5 miles, or you can follow the gully to the northeast which has an obvious double track, an old jeep trail through loose sand. If you follow the double track, leave it for a sandy track that climbs steeply, heading due east up the ridge. Before 5¼ miles leave the sandy track for a grassy track climbing steeply due east.

When you gain the ridgetop, you want to climb east-northeast along its crest. As you ascend, enjoy the expanding vistas of this wilderness stretch of coast. On the way up you might also want to watch for the abundant pillow basalts, spheroid-shaped lavas created long ago beneath the Pacific, then brought up with this entire ridge by tectonic plate movement.

TO REMOVE GOOEY TAR: If you get tarred when walking a central coast beach, here's how to best remove the black goo. Scrape as much tar as possible from your feet (or shoes). Rub with mineral oil or cooking oil on a rag or paper towel to remove tar residue without using harsh solvents. Be sure to clean the oil off your feet before touching the carpet of your vehicle, home or lodging.

The Amazing Nipomo Dunes

The vast Nipomo Dunes sprawl over 18 square miles between Pismo Beach and Point Sal. They form the largest undeveloped coastal dune ecosystem in California, and the second largest, after the Oregon Dunes, on the west coast. Most of the dunes have been preserved by the efforts of the Nature Conservancy, with help from the state parks department and local groups. The dunes began forming 18,000 years ago during the last ice age, with the oldest dunes lying atop Nipomo and Orcutt mesas to the east now stabilized and covered with vegetation. Much of the sand was deposited here by the Santa Maria River, a stream that carried much more water and sandy sediment during the Ice Age than it does today. More recently, sand has accumulated here from the north due to the dunes' position at the southern end of San Luis Obispo Bay, with sand drift to the south blocked by the ancient high rise of Point Sal.

The Nipomo Dune Complex actually consists of three dune fields. Oso Flaco Creek forms the boundary between the Callender Dunes to the north and east and the Guadalupe Dunes to the south. The Mussel Rock Dunes lie south of the Santa Maria River in Santa Barbara County. Mussel Rock Dune, rising precipitously about 500 feet above sea level at the promontory called Mussel Rock, is the tallest single dune in North America.

The vast dunes, the most unique and fragile ecosystem in California, harbor a wealth of surprising and unusual features, both natural and manmade. A dozen lakes clustered east of the westernmost ridge of the Callender Dunes formed in troughs between the dunes roughly 16,000 years ago, fed by groundwater from the mesa to the east. They support yellow pond lily at the southern limit of its range and provide water for abundant wildflowers, including several endangered species, that surround them. Oso Flaco Lake, along the lower end of the creek of the same name, is the largest lake in the Nipomo Dunes. From a boardwalk that crosses the lake, one can see ducks and herons year round and huge white pelicans in winter. On Coreopsis Hill just south of that lake, the giant coreopsis of the sunflower family grows larger than anywhere else.

Manmade features in the shifting dunes are more elusive, but tantalize with their presence. A group of bohemians settled in the Callender Dunes beginning in the 1910s. They lived in driftwood shacks, often built under a full moon and ornamented with mystical symbols. Most Dunites practiced astrology and social nudism, while many believed in the lost continent of Lemuria, nature spirits, and Hindu sacred writings. Dunite culture reached its height in the establishment of Moy Mell (Pasture of Honey), a commune begun in 1931 by Gavin Arthur (grandson of U.S. President Chester A. Arthur) which lasted for eight years, located near today's south boundary of the Pismo Dunes Natural Preserve. The community published six issues of an intellectual magazine called Dune Forum. The last Dunite in Nipomo Dunes died at his driftwood-and-grass shack in 1974.

Less idealistic but equally romantic are the other ruins hidden in the Nipomo Dunes. In 1923 Cecil B. DeMille filmed his silent movie classic The Ten Commandments in the dunes southwest of Guadalupe. The film's set, 750 feet long with walls 109 feet high, was left in the dunes when filming was complete. The clay-and-plaster ruins had long been buried and were thought destroyed until 1984 when two men found a six-foot-wide horse head sculpted in ancient Egyptian style nestling in the Mussel Rock Dunes. Subsequent efforts to uncover the ruins have not been successful. Take a wander in the Nipomo Dunes—you just can't tell what you might find.

Climb steadily up the ridgetop, but not as steeply as the surrounding slopes, especially those to the south which drop precipitously to Point Sal Beach, an undeveloped state park. By 5¼ miles you gain 400 feet elevation. After a knob the track dips briefly then makes another steady ascent, gaining 800 feet elevation by 5⅝ miles where you again ascend steeply.

By 5¾ miles you approach a ridgetop knob 1010 feet in elevation. Veer right to follow a path that contours along the ridge's south face, enjoying amazing vistas down the wild Vandenberg coast to Honda Point and Point Arguello. Contour past a 1040-foot knob around 5⅞ miles, passing native beavertail cactus and hummingbird sage. Return to the ridgetop at a grassy saddle at 6⅛ miles and ascend the ridgetop east. Top a 1100-foot hill with a metal post at 6⅜ miles, then continue up the ridgetop to the 1205-foot summit at 6¾ miles. Follow the undulating ridgetop east-southeast, dipping to a saddle around 6⅞ miles before ascending a final 1200-foot crest beyond 7 miles. From there the track descends southeast, losing about 50 feet in elevation before meeting Brown Road at a big north-facing bend beyond 7⅛ miles.

The CCT turns left to follow Brown Road as it winds generally east. (A right turn would descend to Point Sal Beach in about 2½ miles.) Brown Road ascends past an abandoned air force missile tracking station to this section's summit beyond 7¾ miles, 1260 feet. There the road turns north to leave Point Sal Ridge and descend into Corralitos Canyon. Drop by two switchbacks to cross the canyon's creek and come to a gate (locked on my May 1999 visit) at 9⅜ miles, just below the heart of historic Corralitos Ranch. The paved track continues, meeting the ranch road at 9½ miles, where you turn left on improved surface to descend steadily down the canyon. Descend to 400 feet by 10½ miles where the road and canyon turn east. Continue down Brown Road until the canyon broadens around 11¾ miles, then contour or descend gradually to Highway 1 and section's end at 13¼ miles.

ALTERNATE ROUTE: The only choice would be to stay on Highway 1 and miss this wondrous stretch of coast.

SUGGESTED ROUND TRIPS & LOOPS: Walk south from the Guadalupe Dunes lot, following the tideline to the rock fingers, or if you're careful and realize the dangers, all the way to the dead end at 2¼ miles and return. You can climb to the crest of Mussel Rock Dune for grand views, 5½ miles round trip, or continue to Paradise Beach, 6 miles or more round trip. Another choice is to park at the 4-mile gate or the 6.1-mile point on Brown Road and walk down Point Sal Ridge to Paradise Beach. Or drive to the end of the rough road, if it's open, and descend the steep trail to Point Sal Beach.

HOW TO IMPROVE CCT HERE: When and if Vandenberg Air Force Base is ever decommissioned, establish a through-route along its entire marvelous wild coast for the Coastal Trail. In the interim, the state might pursue an easement along the base's shoreline for the CCT, usable by permit.

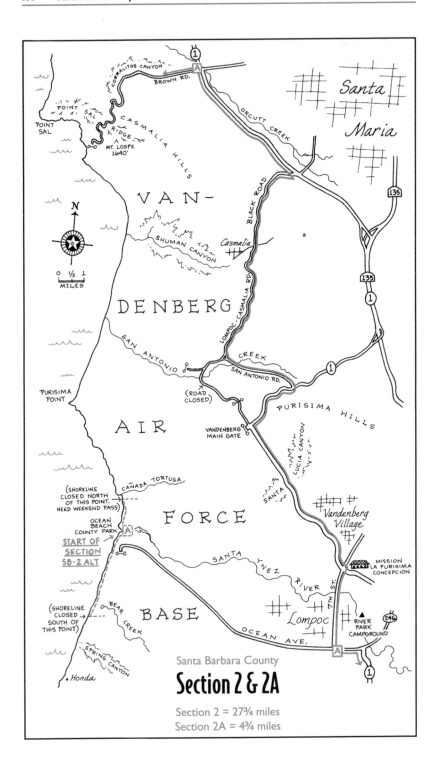

Santa Barbara County
Section 2 & 2A
Section 2 = 27¾ miles
Section 2A = 4¾ miles

SECTION 2
Highway 1 at Brown Road to Lompoc

DISTANCE: 27¾ miles (44.7 kilometers).

OPEN TO: Hikers, bicyclists.

SURFACE: Highway shoulder, road shoulder, city sidewalks.

ACCESS POINT: Highway 1 at Brown Road.

HOW TO GET THERE: On Highway 1 about 2 miles south of Guadalupe, turn west on Brown Road and park on shoulder. Or from Highway 101 in Santa Maria, exit onto Main Street and drive west 9 miles to Highway 1, then drive Highway 1 south 1.8 miles to Brown Road.

OTHER ACCESS: Anywhere along route.

DIFFICULTY: Moderate.

ELEVATION GAIN/LOSS: 1575 feet+/1615 feet-.

CAUTIONS: Stay out of roadway and on shoulder. Use extreme caution when crossing road.

FURTHER INFORMATION: Santa Barbara County Road Department (805)568-3094.

FACILITIES: None until Lompoc, except small store in Casmalia ⅜ mile off route.

CAMPGROUNDS: The nearest campground to north end is private Santa Maria Pines Campground in Santa Maria. Other than that, Oceano Campground in Pismo State Beach 19 miles north has 82 sites. Or try River Park, a private campground near Lompoc.

HOSTEL: Bill's Home Hostel, (805)929-3647, 10 miles northeast of access point in Nipomo is run by Bill Denneen, an expert on area ecology and history.

LODGING: Both Santa Maria and Lompoc have several motels, but you'll find nothing between the towns at either end of this long road walk.

Since Vandenberg Air Force Base occupies 35 miles along the coast south of Point Sal, the California Coastal Trail is forced to follow Highway 1 and rural roads to get south to the town of Lompoc (pronounced Lom-Poke). This long road section has no camping or lodging for nearly the entire route, making it problematic if you plan to hike through and don't want to do a 28-mile day. You'll actually reach the first lodging at Vandenberg Village 4⅝ miles north of downtown Lompoc, but the Spaceport Inn, which caters to NASA and other Vandenberg AFB visitors, is far more expensive than the budget motels in town. On the positive side, most of the section follows lightly travelled two-lane roads through ranch lands with pretty rolling hills dotted with oaks. Only the final 11 miles, which follows Highway 1, offers much traffic.

Walk the narrow shoulder of Highway 1 south from its intersection with

Brown Road. The highway generally contours with agricultural fields on the left and the Casmalia Hills rising on the right. Climb an overpass to cross the main railroad line at one mile, then descend back to farm level with the tracks now on your right. As you contour down the highway, watch the tracks rising on your right. They soon turn south heading for Casmalia. The CCT soon does the same. Climb a gentle hill around 4 miles with views of the farms around Orcutt Creek, then contour or ascend slightly to meet Black Road at 5½ miles.

CCT turns right and follows quiet, two-lane paved Black Road, climbing south. After crossing the railroad tracks at 7 miles, Black Road generally follows them south. After a short descent to 7¼ miles, resume climbing to 8⅛ miles, passing oil fields. Follow Black Road as it descends gently south down Shuman Canyon.

You reach Casmalia Junction at 9¼ miles. CCT continues straight, but a right turn on Point Sal Road leads to tiny Casmalia in ⅜ mile, which has a post office, store and steak house but little else. An amusing sign at the junction refers to Casmalia as the gateway to Point Sal—the road that goes through Casmalia on its way down Shuman Canyon, which like the railroad turns west here, has not gone through to Point Sal since the 1950s. Just beyond town, the road has a locked gate with grass growing in the roadway beyond it. The sign indicates how off the beaten track you are.

CCT climbs south from the junction on Lompoc-Casmalia Road, crossing the westbound tracks at 9⅝ miles, then dipping through a valley before ascending moderately through a corner of Vandenberg AFB. Climb through ranch lands, then across brushy slopes with scattered oaks to reach the section's summit at Bishop Road at 11 miles. Descend moderately along a pleasant oak-filled canyon beneath steep brushy slopes, passing Vandenberg's Titon Gate at 13 miles.

Beyond 13⅝ miles the road forks. If the right fork, Lompoc-Casmalia Road, has reopened, it offers the shortest route south, reaching the Vandenberg Main Gate at Highway 1 at 17⅞ miles. (At press time it was closed by a washout at San Antonio Creek.) Otherwise turn left at the fork and head east on San Antonio Road, gently ascending San Antonio Valley to reach Highway 1 at 16¾ miles. From there CCT heads south on the highway, climbing to a summit at Firefighter Road at 17½ miles, then descending to Vandenberg's Main Gate at 18⅞ miles.

CCT follows Highway 1 as it turns left and climbs slightly before descending a long hill to Santa Lucia Canyon at 22 miles. Continue on Highway 1, climbing to 22⅞ miles, descending to 23⅜ miles, then climbing briefly to the Vandenberg Village exit, which offers the first lodging on this section, beyond 23⅝ miles.

CCT continues down Highway 1, descending to 24¾ miles, then climbing briefly before descending again. Before 25⅝ miles the highway comes to a stoplight where you turn right to follow Highway 1 downhill into the town of Lompoc. After you cross the Santa Ynez River at 26⅜ miles, you pass the airport and pick up city sidewalks to take you downtown to section's end at Ocean Avenue at 27¾ miles. Highway 1 turns left on Ocean Avenue, the start of Santa Barbara Section 3, another long road walking section, the CCT's provisional route until Vandenberg Air Force Base gives up a route along the coast.

If you would like to visit and walk the Vandenberg coast in the interim, check out alternate Santa Barbara Sections 2A and 3A. While they don't offer a through route, they explore miles of wonderful shoreline.

ALTERNATE ROUTE: Perhaps your group can get permission from the Air Force for an escorted trip along the entire 35 miles of the Vandenberg coast like Coastwalk's Whole Hike did in 1996.

> HOW TO IMPROVE CCT HERE: Establish an off-road route for the CCT, ideally one along the spectacular coast where Vandenberg Air Force Base is today.

SECTION 2A
Heart of Vandenberg Coast from Ocean Beach County Park

DISTANCE: 4¾ miles total one way (9½ miles round trip), up to 1¼ miles north and up to 3½ miles south. With a weekend day-use pass you can walk up to 5⅝ miles north (7.6, 15.3, 2.0, 5.6, 9.1 kilometers).

OPEN TO: Hikers, dogs. Bicyclists on road from Lompoc to park.

SURFACE: Paved trail, beach.

ACCESS POINT: Ocean Beach County Park.

HOW TO GET THERE: From Highway 1 in downtown Lompoc, head west on Ocean Avenue for 8.4 nearly level miles, then turn right on road marked "Ocean Beach" and go one mile to parking at end of road.

OTHER ACCESS: None.

DIFFICULTY: Easy.

ELEVATION GAIN/LOSS: Negligible.

CAUTIONS: Park open 8 a.m. to sunset. Portions of the park's sand dunes above the beach may be closed from March through September to protect nesting least terns, an endangered shore bird. You are not allowed on the bluffs of Vandenberg Air Force Base, outside of the County Park, without written permission from VAFB. No swimming or wading on beach due to bacterial contamination.

FURTHER INFORMATION: Ocean Beach County Park (805)934-6148.

FACILITIES: Restrooms, water, picnic area at Ocean Beach County Park.

CAMPGROUNDS: River Park, a private campground on the Santa Ynez River east of Lompoc has 34 RV units plus a large open area for tenters.

LODGING: Many economical motels in Lompoc.

MAP: See page 160.

Here you can explore the heart of the Vandenberg coast, which consists of 35 miles of some of the wildest, most untouched beaches and rocky shorelines in the state. From the access point here at Ocean Beach County Park, you will see missile silos and other military installations up on the bluffs, but you won't see significant human-made intrusions on the beach and tidal zone except for the concrete seawalls built to protect the railroad right of way that follows the bluff edge along the southern half of the base. The wild coast provides important habitat for marine mammals and shore birds, which have lost so much of the rest of their California coastal habitat to development. Of course that means you're likely to see more marine wildlife when you hike here.

While most of Vandenberg Air Force Base is closed to public access for security reasons, the base does issue 50 day-use passes on weekends and holidays to explore other parts of the coast. These day use permits usually go to fishermen, but if you tell the game warden who issues the passes that you're here to look at or photograph marine wildlife, he'll probably give you a pass. The game warden's office is in building 13401 near the main base entrance on Highway 1 north of Lompoc, or call him at (805)606-1110, ext. 51275. If you get a pass, consider visiting Purisima Point to the north, where several miles of trails explore the bluffs south of the point with paths descending the bluffs to pocket beaches.

Even without obtaining the pass you can walk the intertidal zone from Ocean Beach County Park, heading north for up to 1¼ miles and south for up to 3½ miles. You can also explore Vandenberg's southern coast for up to 3¾ miles, described north from Jalama Beach County Park in Santa Barbara Section 3A. For any of these explorations, you want to avoid high tides and plan your trip to coincide with the tide ebbing to the lowest possible tide. The lower the tide, the more you're likely to see. You definitely do not want to explore here during particularly high tides and stormy weather. Under those conditions, you would see less and also might be forced to trespass up onto the bluffs, where you are subject to arrest by the military police.

Here at Ocean Beach, we'll describe the route south from the park, then the route north.

From the parking area at the end of the park road, follow the cement path under the train trestle and out to the beach where the pavement ends before ⅛ mile. Continue west on the loose sand to the tideline around ¼ mile, where the mouth of the Santa Ynez River is directly on your right. Turn left and follow the firm wet sand south along the tideline.

Walk a broad beach defined by the raised bed of the railroad. By ¾ mile you pass the Air Force community called Surf, perched on a 50-foot bluff along the tracks. As you continue down the beach, the sloping bluffs soon rise to 80 feet in spots. By 1⅛ miles the tracks swing away from the beach. Continue south on the tideline passing three small canyons along the bluffs between 1⅝ and 1¾ miles.

By 2¾ miles the train tracks once again follow the top of the bluff. You may not notice them, however, since the bluffs now rise to 120 feet high. At 3⅛ miles where you pass the mouth of Bear Valley, which has extensive wetlands up from the tracks along Bear Creek, the bluffs rise to a towering 160 feet. You can continue along the beach below the high bluffs to a small point at 3½ miles, where the Air Force asks that you turn back. Above the high bluffs here, there is no level or gently sloping marine terrace. The land rises to an 887-foot peak about 1½ miles from the beach.

Walk back the way you came to Ocean Beach County Park.

Vandenberg Air Force Base as Nature Preserve

Vandenberg Air Force Base, established in 1958 when it absorbed the older Camp Cook (founded 1941), occupies 98,500 acres (154 square miles) along the central California coast in northern Santa Barbara County. With 35 miles of wild shoreline, Vandenberg qualifies as one of the most important large parcels of property on the California coast.

Vandenberg AFB currently has about 4,000 military and 4,000 civilian personnel. The Base hosts several important activities including a Strategic Air Command base, the center for missile-combat training, a center for Intercontinental Ballistic Missile (ICBM) testing, a satellite launching area for NASA, and the west coast base for the Space Shuttle. With so many activities and programs, Vandenberg Air Force Base will likely be operational for a while. Should the Base ever be decommissioned, we strongly hope and urge that its extensive lands be turned over to the state of California for a public park.

Fortunately the Air Force takes its stewardship of this invaluable land very seriously. Of the 98,500 acres, only about 20,000 acres have facilities, with the other 78,500 acres remaining mostly wild, undeveloped and virtually inaccessible to the public. The wild portions of Vandenberg harbor abundant mountain lions, coyotes, wild pigs and lesser land mammals, plus some of the healthiest deer herds in California. The coast itself features some of California's richest tidepools as well as healthy populations of both resident and migratory marine mammals.

Participants in Coastwalk's 1996 Whole Hike took an escorted walk along Vandenberg's entire coast, but public access is generally quite limited. This book describes walks along 8½ miles of the Vandenberg coast in Santa Barbara Sections 2A and 3A, plus another 4⅜ miles from Purisima Point south that you can walk with a weekend pass from the Air Force. All those miles are among the least travelled miles on the entire CCT. The pristine and wild nature of the Vandenberg coast and the solitude you're likely to experience there make it well worth a visit.

To walk north from the Ocean Beach parking lot, you need to cross the mouth of the Santa Ynez River. This can be either extremely easy or a mild challenge. It's easiest in late summer and early autumn when the river stops flowing at the barrier beach. Then you can follow the trail from the park to the tideline and walk north with dry feet. In early summer, you may still be able to ford the shallow outlet of the river at its mouth, but at press time the river water and nearby ocean were signed "NO SWIMMING OR WADING—BACTERIAL CONTAMINATION." When the water is shallow and you have waterproof boots, you'll easily get across. When the contamination is cleared up, you'd be able to ford the river at its mouth in all but the wettest months. If you cannot cross the river at its mouth, the only way north (other than a boat) is to walk across the railroad trestle, then walk west along the river's bank to the tideline.

Whichever way you go, you'll be on the tideline north of the river mouth by ⅜ mile, where the beach swells to its widest point. Walk the broad, curving beach north. The beach narrows as you go. By one mile, the dunes to your east end, replaced by a 20-foot-tall bluff. As you continue north, the bluffs rise gradually higher. By 1⅛ miles the beach becomes quite narrow, perhaps impassable at high tide. Layered rock underlies the soil of the bluffs now with a few small caves add-

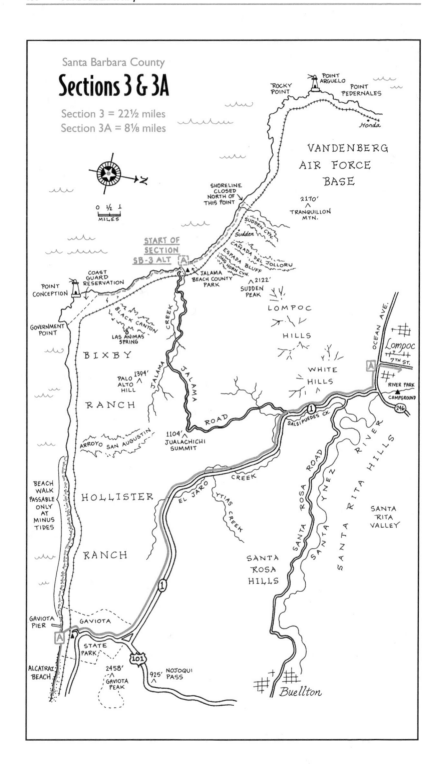

Santa Barbara County

Sections 3 & 3A

Section 3 = 22½ miles
Section 3A = 8⅛ miles

N

0 ½ 1
MILES

POINT
ARGUELLO
ROCKY
POINT
POINT
PEDERNALES
Honda

VANDENBERG
AIR FORCE
BASE

2170'
TRANQUILLON
MTN.

SHORELINE
CLOSED
NORTH OF
THIS POINT

SUDDEN CYN.
Sudden
CAÑADA DEL JOLLORU
ESPADA BLUFF
LONG HORN CYN.

START OF
SECTION
SB-3 ALT

A

JALAMA
BEACH COUNTY
PARK

2122'
SUDDEN
PEAK

LOMPOC

HILLS

WHITE
HILLS

OCEAN AVE.

Lompoc
7TH ST.

A

RIVER PARK
CAMPGROUND

246

COAST
GUARD
RESERVATION

POINT
CONCEPTION

GOVERNMENT
POINT

BLACK CANYON

LAS ANIMAS
SPRING

CREEK

BIXBY

PALO
ALTO
HILL

1394'

JALAMA

JALAMA

ROAD

1

SALSIPUEDES CK.

RANCH

ARROYO SAN AUGUSTIN

1104'
JUALACHICHI
SUMMIT

CREEK

EL JARO

YTIAS CREEK

SANTA ROSA ROAD

SANTA YNEZ

SANTA RITA HILLS

RIVER

SANTA
RITA
VALLEY

BEACH
WALK
PASSABLE
ONLY
AT
MINUS
TIDES

HOLLISTER

RANCH

SANTA
ROSA
HILLS

1

GAVIOTA
PIER
A

GAVIOTA

STATE
PARK

ALCATRAZ
BEACH

2458'
GAVIOTA
PEAK

101

925'
NOJOQUI
PASS

Buellton

ing interest.

By 1¼ mile you reach a big arched rock blocking the beach. An inconspicuous sign atop it warns that this is the end of public access. The arch provides an intriguing view of the rocky shore to the north. Even if you have a day-use pass from the base's game warden, you couldn't walk far beyond the arched rock, and even then only at low tide. If you have a pass, walk back south about ⅛ mile and find a path up onto the bluffs. With your pass you can walk north along the bluff's edge or on the road just inland. By 3⅝ miles the road peters out as it enters extensive sand dunes, but one can continue along the west face of the dunes above the convoluted rocky shore until you reach Purisima Point around 5⅝ miles. However far you walk, you must return to Ocean Beach County Park since the CCT has no through route along the coast.

SUGGESTED ROUND TRIPS & LOOPS: Walk the beach north or south as described and return the way you came.

> HOW TO IMPROVE CCT HERE: When Vandenberg Air Force Base is decommissioned, establish a through route for the Coastal Trail along this entire 35-mile shoreline.

SECTION 3
Lompoc to Gaviota State Park Pier via Highway 1

DISTANCE: 22½ miles (36.2 kilometers).

OPEN TO: Hikers. Bicyclists on road portion.

SURFACE: Highway shoulder, sidewalk.

ACCESS POINT: Downtown Lompoc, Ocean Avenue and H Street, where Highway 1 makes a 90-degree turn.

HOW TO GET THERE: Drive Highway 1 to Lompoc's downtown area, where the highway turns from north-south on H Street to east-west on Ocean Avenue.

OTHER ACCESS: Anywhere along route.

DIFFICULTY: Moderate.

ELEVATION GAIN/LOSS: 1370 feet+/1450 feet-.

CAUTIONS: Wear bright clothes, walk single file and be careful on this highway route.

FACILITIES: City services near access point. The rest area one mile before section's end and Gaviota State Park have restrooms, water, phone and picnic tables.

CAMPGROUNDS: River Park, a private campground only a mile off the route on the Santa Ynez River east of Lompoc has 34 RV units plus a large open area for tenters. Gaviota State Park has 55 units available on a first come, first serve basis.

LODGING: Lompoc has many choices.

The shoreline here continues to have very limited access due to the combination of Vandenberg Air Force Base and large private ranches north and east of Point Conception. You have the opportunity to walk some of this remote, spectacular coast from Ocean Beach County Park as described in Section 2A and Jalama Beach County Park as described in Section 3A, but if you're through-hiking the CCT, you'll need to follow this section's route to get through, whether or not you detour to explore the dead-end routes along the coast.

Head east along the sidewalk of Ocean Avenue (also Highways 1 and 246) from its corner with H Street, walking through a mostly abandoned commercial district, then through a newer neighborhood of malls and eating establishments. By the time you reach Seventh Street at one mile, you'll see enough room to fly kites beside this main drag. Follow Highway 1 as it veers left towards the eastern city limit.

Beyond 1¼ miles the road forks. Highway 246 continues straight, soon crossing the Santa Ynez River and coming to River Park Campground on the left in ¾ mile. At the highway intersection, CCT turns right to follow Highway 1 south. Follow the two-lane road, with city sidewalks soon replaced by broad shoulders as you ascend into coastal hills, a lovely lush green in spring replaced by golden brown in summer. By 2¾ miles you reach the first summit, where Santa Rosa Road forks left.

CCT continues along Highway 1, descending slightly to 3⅜ miles, then contouring beside passing lanes before climbing gently to a second summit at 3⅞ miles. After a slight descent to 4¾ miles, ascend gradually along the highway shoulder as it follows the canyon of Salsipuedes Creek. Cross the creek at 5 miles and climb slightly to the turnoff on the right for Jalama Road at 5⅝ miles. Jalama Road leads 14 miles to Jalama Beach County Park on the other side of the Santa Ynez Range. See Section 3A for coastal access there.

CCT's provisional highway route continues along Highway 1, descending east to 6¾ miles, then climbing fitfully along El Jaro Creek. After crossing the creek beyond 7¼ miles, descend briefly, then climb to 7¾ miles before dropping to cross El Jaro Creek again at 9⅜ miles. Ascend gently along the highway as it follows El Jaro Creek Canyon, crossing Ytias Creek at 10½ miles, then El Jaro Creek again. The highway contours or climbs gradually to its final crossing of El Jaro Creek at 15 miles. Contour east to 15½ miles, then climb to the section's summit at 16⅝ miles.

From the summit you descend a long steady hill to 19½ miles where Highway 1 joins Highway 101 as it descends from nearby Nojoqui Pass. Turn right and cautiously walk single file down the shoulder of the busy combined highways. Around 21⅜ miles you'll want to veer off the busy road and walk through the rest area for a short break from speeding traffic.

When you return to the highway shoulder, you only have a short walk downhill to the turnoff for Gaviota State Park at 22 miles. Turn right and walk down the park entrance road, crossing Gaviota Creek and coming to the park's entrance kiosk at 22⅜ miles. If you're camping here, take the first left beyond the kiosk.

Otherwise continue straight through the day-use parking lot to the end of the pavement and section's end at 22½ miles. The next section starts here near the Gaviota Pier and follows the tideline down the coast, which actually runs east from here to the Santa Barbara/Ventura County line.

ALTERNATE ROUTE: None unless you can get permission to walk the coast through the privately owned Bixby and Hollister Ranches from Point Conception to Gaviota.

HOW TO IMPROVE CCT HERE: Establish a route that gets the trail off the highway.

SECTION 3A
Southern Vandenberg Coast and Point Conception from Jalama

DISTANCE: 8⅛ miles total one way (16¼ miles round trip), up to 3¾ miles north and up to 4⅜ miles south (13.1, 26.2, 6.0, 7.0 kilometers).

OPEN TO: Hikers, leashed dogs OK on beach. Bicyclists on road to Jalama.

SURFACE: Beach, rocky shore.

ACCESS POINT: Jalama Beach County Park.

HOW TO GET THERE: Turn west off Highway 1 about 5.5 miles south of downtown Lompoc onto Jalama Road. Drive 14.3 miles to county park at end.

OTHER ACCESS: None.

DIFFICULTY: Easy to moderate.

ELEVATION GAIN/LOSS: Negligible.

CAUTIONS: Stay along the tideline and off adjacent private and Air Force Base property. Hike north requires a tide lower than +3.5 feet. Hike south requires progressively lower tides for each mile you walk. Watch for dangerous surf and rogue waves.

FURTHER INFORMATION: Jalama Beach County Park (805)736-3504.

FACILITIES: Restrooms, water, picnic area, phone, small store at access point.

CAMPGROUNDS: Jalama Beach County Park has 110 sites available on a first come, first serve basis. A few group sites can be reserved in advance.

LODGING: Lompoc has the nearest lodging.

MAP: See page 166.

The popular campground at Jalama Beach draws enthusiastic visitors nearly year round despite chilly winters, often foggy summers and cool coastal breezes most of the year. The park's gorgeous setting gets overwhelmed by the crowds at times, but it's a pleasant place even if rowdy on weekends. The real treasure here is the

What Will Be the Fate of Santa Barbara County's Large Coastal Ranches?

Three giant ranches cover most of the land between Vandenberg Air Force Base and Gaviota State Park, roughly 20 miles of the California coast. Rancho San Julian, inland from the coast along Highway 1, is owned by heirs of Jose Noriega, the original Spanish land grantee in the early 1800s. It's still used for cattle and sheep grazing. On the coast, the El Cojo-Jalama Ranch (also called the Bixby Ranch), covering 24,400 acres north and just east of Point Conception, is owned by the Bixby Corporation, the legal descendent of the Bixby family that bought it for a song around 1850.

East of the Bixby land lies the Hollister Ranch. The Hollister family owned the ranch for nearly 100 years until 1965 when they sold it to pay property taxes. The corporation that bought it subdivided the 15,000-acre ranch into 100-acre parcels and sold them for residential development. The sales included deed restrictions that limited access to residents and governed the way owners could site their homes. Today about a hundred homes dot the Hollister Ranch, accessible only via a gravel road that leaves Highway 101 near the Gaviota State Park entrance kiosk. Gaviota State Park was created from the Hollister Ranch when it was subdivided.

The 1976 California Coastal Act specifically named the Hollister Ranch as a place where the public should be allowed access, and directed the Coastal Conservancy to develop that access. The Hollister Ranch Association and residents have successfully resisted public access for 24 years since that legislation and for 35 years since the subdivision was created. The official position of the Hollister Ranch is that the State has the right to develop public access, but that it would need to offer owners just compensation. Still, many residents oppose any access.

Today the Santa Barbara coast west and north of Goleta remains largely undeveloped, but intense pressures may soon change that. Areas currently proposed or being considered for development include: Ellwood Shores subdivision on the western edge of Goleta, the Dos Pueblos Golf Course immediately west of Ellwood, Naples subdivision just west of the golf links, and El Capitan Ranch adjacent to El Capitan State Park. Owners of the Bixby Ranch are currently attempting to redraw the boundaries of the ranch's 52 legal lots, a move county planners consider a prelude to efforts to develop some of the ranch.

Since 1995 a group called the Gaviota Coastal Conservancy has been working to establish a national seashore along the undeveloped shores west and north of Santa Barbara. The proposed boundary would span from Coal Oil Point in Isla Vista north to the crest of the Santa Ynez Range, then west and north along the crest to the northern county line where it would include Point Sal and Mussel Rock Dune. No feasibility study has yet been funded, always a first step in such a move. Local conservationists generally support the effort and the local Sierra Club chapter has made it their top priority. Local ranchers, however, remain highly skeptical of the idea, and it's primarily their lands that would be affected. Many ranchers are still fuming over the 1980 establishment of Channel Islands National Park, where a century old ranch sold out to the feds on the stipulation that they could remain for 25 years, only to have a local environmental lawsuit force the feds to close down the ranch 13 years before the agreement ended. On the pristine and undeveloped northern Santa Barbara County coast, the stakes are high and each development or preservation issue is hotly contested. The largely pristine nature of this dramatic coast hangs in the balance.

near wilderness quality of the shoreline extending north and south. Very few people walk north more than ½ mile even though a medium-low tide allows passage up the rugged shore of the Vandenberg coast for up to 3¾ miles. Given the appropriately low tides, a few adventuresome souls walk the shoreline south just for the chance to get near Point Conception, the otherwise inaccessible point where the California coast makes an amazing dogleg turn east. The land at Point Conception is a Coast Guard Reservation, but unlike some lighthouses and their reservations, visitors are not allowed there. This entails more than just a government regulation. The Chumash people consider Point Conception the "Western Gate." The Chumash believe that all land visible from the point is sacred, and that disaster will befall anyone who disturbs the land. Thus they asked the Coast Guard to restrict access.

We highly recommend both the beach walks north and south from Jalama Creek, but you need to be aware that, while tideline walking is allowed, you can be arrested for trespassing on the bluffs of Vandenberg Air Force Base. The wild hills and bluffs south and east of Jalama Park are all part of the huge Bixby Ranch, a privately owned ranch dating back to the 19th century. Ranch hands for the Bixby don't appreciate trespassers either. Some of these ornery cowpokes have been known to rough up those who ignore the fences and private property. So be sure to schedule your hike(s) with the appropriate low tides. First we'll describe the hike north, then the walk south.

From the north end of the Jalama Park day-use parking lot, walk west to the tideline and head north along the damp sand. You soon pass the mouth of Jalama Creek, which may require a ford during the wet season. Before ¼ mile the bluffs rise 30 feet on your right. The point here may not be passable at the highest tides. Be sure you have a receding tide low enough to continue.

By ½ mile you pass rocks and tar deposits littering the tidal zone as the sheer bluffs rise 50 feet. Pass a cave in the cliff around ⅝ mile. At ⅞ mile a steep narrow gully cuts through the 80-foot-high unstable cliff. The beach is broad here but narrows to a rocky shelf beyond one mile. Pick your way carefully along the rocky shelf to 1⅛ miles.

Follow another sandy beach, then a rocky beach, with gullies bisecting the bluffs above and towering Espada Bluff looming ahead. Around 1¼ miles your route requires scrambling around a rocky point, with the roughest passage lying at the very point before 1⅜ miles. Walk north on the narrow rocky beach littered with abalone and spiny lobster shells, enjoying the views toward shovel-head-shaped Espada Bluff ahead. When you reach Espada, you won't be able to see it towering overhead.

Beyond 1½ miles you need to scramble around a double point beneath an 80-foot-high bluff. While the first point is easy, the second, marked by a small rock arch at tideline, offers the roughest passage yet on this section. Still, you'll find a vague footpath here. Amidst this scramble you meet the steep narrow gully of Long Horn Canyon where escaped celery, watercress and fennel crowd the stream along with native mallow and sunflower. The canyon features a double waterfall when its stream is flowing.

By 1⅝ miles you can see the railroad line above. Drop to a narrow beach and follow it north, soon leading to more rock scrambling. By 1¾ miles you reach a

On the way to Point Conception on Jalama Beach.

seawall that shields the rail line from powerful wave action. Walk the top of the seawall along the base of Espada Bluff which towers 378 feet only ⅛ mile from the beach. From there the steep slopes rise to 2014-foot Oak Mountain 2 miles from the beach.

The seawall, dated 1923, ends at 2 miles, passing a raised culvert. To continue you must scramble around another point. Your passage is easy until the narrow spot at the point itself around 2⅛ miles, where you'll need a tide of +3.5 feet to get through. Walking turns easy again on low-tide sand or rock shelves above.

Espada Bluff ends before 2¼ miles where a gully cuts through a 40-foot cliff above the beach. If you can continue, you reach another sandy beach by 2⅜ miles, backed by low bluffs. Walk it to a sandy point at 2⅝ miles where Canada del Jolloru has cut a broad path to the sea, then continue along the sand until it ends around 3 miles. The railroad siding called Sudden, named for the family that ranched here for generations, perches 90 feet overhead on the marine terrace above the bluffs.

If the tide is low or receding, you can continue along the tideline by rock scrambling. If you go, you'll pass the mouth of Sudden Canyon at 3⅛ miles. By 3½ miles, where you pass another deep unnamed canyon, you're once again able to walk a sandy beach. Follow it to the low sandy point at 3¾ miles, where you are asked to turn back and return the way you came. If the weather is clear enough on your way back to Jalama Beach, enjoy the long vistas down the coast to the high bluff of Point Conception.

From the Jalama Park day-use parking lot, walk west to the tideline and head south. By ¼ mile the bluffs rise 40 feet on your left. Follow the sandy beach toward the nearby point, passing a few rocks at tideline around ⅜ mile, then a small seasonal creek that cascades down the rock shelf of the bluff in winter and spring. Pass another seasonal stream beyond ⅝ mile, then a cross atop the bluff. An arroyo at ⅞ mile has a small waterfall during the wet season.

At one mile you round the point that has limited your view down the coast and encounter a broad rock shelf extending into the low tide zone. You also gain a view of Point Conception and its lighthouse to the south. The bluffs rise 100 feet on your left. Continue south, rounding a secondary point at 1⅛ miles.

Beyond the second point, walk the sandy beach around a shallow curving bay. At an arroyo beyond 1½ miles, you can see the railroad tracks 160 feet above. Round a small rocky point at 1⅝ miles that marks the end of the bay. Most of your walking here follows rock shelves where you probably could not get by at high tide. Curving rock strata shape the cliffs on your left.

By 1¾ miles your walking again turns easy along a sandy beach. Around 1⅞ miles you pass the first seawall south of Jalama, with unstable sloping bluffs above it. You cannot see the Point Conception Lighthouse beyond this point. Soon the tidal zone features mostly level stratified rock shelves. By 2⅛ miles you reach the second seawall and a small cascade that drops down the high bluff. Reach the third seawall at 2¼ miles. At higher tides you may need to walk above it to get down the beach. That seawall ends beyond 2⅜ miles.

Around 2½ miles you pass the final seawall before Point Conception. An old wooden flume here carries a seasonal creek jammed with mimulus to the beach. From here the railway line angles inland and the sandy beach offers easy walking. Pass Black Canyon around 3 miles, notable as the only named canyon on this stretch of coast and the last place you see the train tracks from the beach. After a nameless canyon at 3⅜ miles, you head straight down the beach toward the point. Pass a steep canyon at 3⅝ miles that descends from Las Animas Spring.

At 3⅞ miles you reach a deep dry canyon that sits just north of a rocky ledge. A ranch road runs from near the mouth of the canyon up onto the headlands, but you're not supposed to use it since it sits on private property. If the tide allows you to continue along the shore, scramble over the tarry rock ledge called Perch Rock and continue south on the beach.

From 4 miles you must have a tide of 0 feet or lower to continue. Even then you'll need to walk on slippery seaweed-covered rocks (or make a difficult rock scramble over a protruding bluff) to continue south. It's only about 200 feet to the next beach, essentially the final accessible beach before the impassable cliffs of Point Conception. That beach continues almost ⅜ mile before ending with vistas of the nearby 200-foot cliffs of Point Conception and its inaccessible Coast Guard Reservation. This final beach has an emergency escape route if rising tides cut you off. You'll find the vague emergency track climbing the steep bluffs at 4⅛ miles, but since it puts you on private property try not to use it and instead re-trace your steps to Jalama Beach.

SUGGESTED ROUND TRIPS & LOOPS: Walk the beach north or south for as long as time and tides allow.

HOW TO IMPROVE CCT HERE: Establish a through route along the coast.

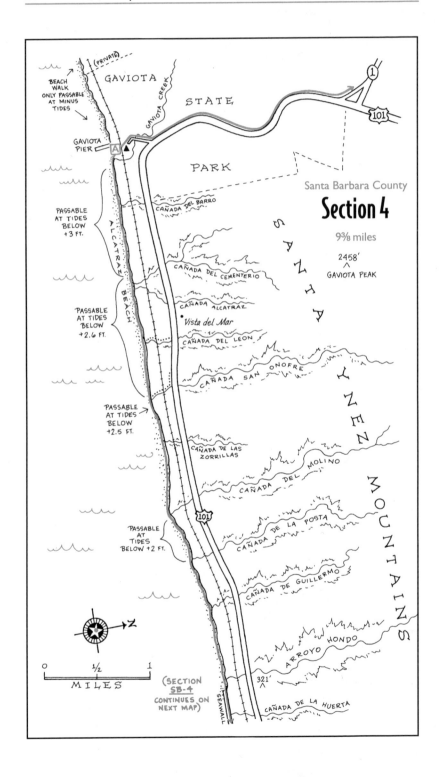

(PRIVATE)

GAVIOTA

BEACH WALK ONLY PASSABLE AT MINUS TIDES

GAVIOTA CREEK

STATE

1

101

GAVIOTA PIER

A

PARK

Santa Barbara County

Section 4

9⅜ miles

2458'
∧
GAVIOTA PEAK

CAÑADA DEL BARRO

PASSABLE AT TIDES BELOW +3 FT.

SANTA

CAÑADA DEL CEMENTERIO

ALCATRAZ BEACH

CAÑADA ALCATRAZ

PASSABLE AT TIDES BELOW +2.6 FT.

• Vista del Mar

CAÑADA DEL LEON

CAÑADA SAN ONOFRE

Y

PASSABLE AT TIDES BELOW +2.5 FT.

CAÑADA DE LAS ZORRILLAS

N

CAÑADA DEL MOLINO

E

101

Z

PASSABLE AT TIDES BELOW +2 FT.

CAÑADA DE LA POSTA

M

CAÑADA DE GUILLERMO

O

U

N

ARROYO HONDO

T

N

½   1

A

MILES

321'

I

(SECTION SB-4 CONTINUES ON NEXT MAP)

SEAWALL

CAÑADA DE LA HUERTA

S

SECTION 4
Gaviota State Park Pier to Refugio Creek, Refugio State Park

DISTANCE: 9⅜ miles (15.1 kilometers).

OPEN TO: Hikers.

SURFACE: Beach, trail at end.

ACCESS POINT: Gaviota State Park day-use parking lot and Pier.

HOW TO GET THERE: Turn west off Highway 101 at the Gaviota State Beach exit, 33 miles west of Santa Barbara. Drive past kiosk and campground to day-use parking area below railroad trestle.

OTHER ACCESS: From Highway 101 at Vista del Mar/Cañada del Leon at MP.44.3, Cañada San Onofre at MP.43.85, Cañada de Guillermo at MP.41.7, Arroyo Hondo/Vista Point at MP.41.0, Tajiguas Creek at MP.38.4.

DIFFICULTY: Easy to moderate.

ELEVATION GAIN/LOSS: 70 feet+/70 feet-.

CAUTIONS: Requires tide below +2.0 feet to pass. In winter, displaced sand may require an even lower tide, may be impassable in spots. Section also requires a short, rough steep climb about 1⅜ miles before south end. Day use open 8 a.m. to sunset. No overnight parking in day-use lot.

FURTHER INFORMATION: For Gaviota State Park and Refugio State Park, call Channel Coast District of California State Parks (805)968-1033.

FACILITIES: Restrooms, water, phones, picnic areas and seasonal stores at both Gaviota and Refugio State Parks. No facilities in between except the picnic table at 9 miles.

CAMPGROUNDS: Gaviota State Park has 55 units available on a first come, first serve basis. Refugio State Park has 85 units, all on the state park reservation system.

HOSTEL: Banana Bungalow is in Santa Barbara, (800)346-7835.

LODGING: Several choices at Buellton 11.5 miles north on Highway 101, many more in Santa Barbara to east.

MAP: Section 4 map continues on page 180.

The CCT finally returns to the coast at Gaviota to follow a mostly narrow strip of sandy and rocky beach along the east-west running shore. You'll need a medium to low tide to get around the first rocky point just beyond Gaviota Creek, and encounter more tidal bottlenecks along the way. None of them are as tight as the final 1⅜ miles of beach before Refugio Creek, passable in summer only at tides below +1.4 feet. That low-tide stretch has an alternate path through a defunct nursery up on the blufftop, but it requires a steep rocky scramble to get up to the nursery from the trail's 8-mile point. Before starting this section, you might walk out the Gaviota Pier to peruse the narrow coastal strip you'll be walking.

State parks plan to build a bicycle/pedestrian path all the way along the blufftop between Gaviota and Refugio. This project was to begin in 1999, but El Niño winter storms caused washouts and landslides along much of the route, requiring further planning with no firm completion date set yet. The paved path eventually will link with the Aniso Trail between Refugio and El Capitan State Beaches (see next section).

West of Gaviota Pier lies a rocky shoreline passable only at minus tides in summer. Only a mile west of the pier, the area above the tideline belongs to the vast Hollister Ranch which allows no public access to the blufftops. If you time a shoreline walk west from Gaviota at the lowest tides in summer (definitely requires a minus tide), you can walk west along the tideline of the Hollister Ranch coast. It's 7½ miles one way to Arroyo San Augustin, 14 miles to Government Point, beyond which there's no beach to walk and thus no legal way to hike the final 1½ miles to Point Conception. Without gear for an overnight bivouac along the high tideline, there's no way, even at the lowest tides, to cover more than the 15 miles round trip to San Augustin in a day hike. Even that distance offers a difficult trek that must be timed with the tides. Hikers who walk the Hollister Ranch bluffs without written permission have been arrested for trespassing.

Walk south from the south end of the Gaviota State Park day-use parking area, passing beneath the tall railroad trestle and meeting the foot of the pier in 200 feet. Turn left and walk the tideline east. Before ⅛ mile you must ford Gaviota Creek and round a rocky point with the narrowest passage in the first ½ mile, passable in May 1999 at tides below +3.0 feet.

Follow the narrow beach down coast, walking beneath cliffs of near-white Monterey shale that soon rise 100 feet on your left. At ½ mile pass the tiny creek of Cañada del Barro flowing from a tunnel, then scramble past a rock shelf requiring a tide similar to the first point. Beyond the shelf, the beach is broader except for a scramble past a recent slide at ¾ mile. Around one mile a small creek provides a seasonal waterfall.

CCT continues along the tideline. Walk the section's narrowest beach to this point from 1⅛ to 1¼ miles, then meet a broad canyon. The fenced canyon, jammed with lush foliage, is the mouth of both Cañada del Cementerio and Cañada Alcatraz. Continue around a high rocky point if you can, remembering that you may need to return this way at an equally low tide. After scrambling past another tight spot at a high cliff at 1⅜ miles, walk a slightly broader beach with eucalyptus trees on the bluff above you until 1⅝ miles, then a sandy beach scattered with low rocks.

Pass a concrete abutment at 1¾ miles marking the mouth of Cañada del Leon, where people walk down to the beach from the nearby highway. Continue along a broad pleasant beach toward a point with a beached sea stack. Scramble past a rocky point at 2⅛ miles and walk another broad beach to the 30-foot sea stack at 2¼ miles marking the mouth of Cañada San Onofre. The wooded canyon, jammed with lush foliage, has a well-beaten path up the west side of its stream that climbs steeply to the highway. CCT rock hops down the beach past the canyon's broad mouth, which extends to 2⅜ miles.

Beyond Cañada San Onofre, you reach a narrow passage requiring a tide of +2.5 feet or lower. Then walk east along a sandy beach sprinkled with large rocks. Pass slabs of layered light shale around 2½ miles. By 2⅝ miles you walk a broadening sandy beach below jumbled cliffs, passing a tunnel marking the mouth of Cañada de las Zorrillas.

Before 3 miles you pass a monolithic panel of Monterey shale. Continue past a minor narrow spot to round a point with slabs of shale, passing the deep mouth of Cañada del Molino at 3⅜ miles. Pick your way over uneven loose rocks of assorted sizes, then walk a narrow sandy beach northeast, with fingers of rocks crossing the narrow strand. The above-head-high rock finger at 3½ miles offers a close scramble at tides above +2.0 feet, the tightest passage yet.

Follow a narrow beach with greatly layered and twisted cliffs. A rock ledge at 3¾ miles offers the trickiest passage yet only because it requires brief rock scrambling at tides above +2.0 feet. Be sure to use good all-hands-and-feet scrambling technique. Pass Cañada de la Posta around 3⅞ miles and walk a narrow beach beneath scrambled and patterned blond cliffs, passing a few narrow rocky points that may require scrambling.

Beyond 4¼ miles the bluffs dip to only 30 feet tall with a rock outcrop forming an alcove, a sheltered spot to pause beside a waterfall and greenery. CCT continues east on a narrow beach with more rock fingers. Pass the usually tiny stream of Cañada de Guillermo at 4½ miles. It doesn't have much of a canyon at its mouth, but has a striking setting and an escape trail. Round a jumbled point around 4¾ miles, then walk a broadening beach to Arroyo Hondo at 5 miles.

As you approach the broad, deep mouth of Arroyo Hondo, the sandy beach gives way to a striated, mostly level rocky tidal zone at the base of sculpted cliffs. People often surf fish here. Pass the mouth of the creek at 5 miles, where the railroad trestle towers overhead with a five-arch highway bridge just upstream.

Continue to the canyon's east wall, where you'll find a seawall that runs along the top of the beach for the next ⅝ mile. Because the wall is nearly eight feet tall and protrudes into the low tide zone, you need to climb onto it and walk it east at all but the lowest minus tides. The first part of the seawall is very old, deteriorating and broken—be careful. By 5⅛ miles, where you pass a jumble of varied rocks on the land side of the wall, the wall walking improves but you still must watch your step. Round the first bend in the wall by 5¼ miles with the railroad tracks often visible above you. Cross a spillway at the mouth of Cañada de la Huerta.

By 5⅜ miles you reach a newer section of seawall dated 1919. The seawall walking becomes easy from here except for ducking under or around big culverts around 5½ and 5⅝ miles. Reach the end of the seawall at 5⅝ miles. It's a bit tricky to get down to the beach here, about a ten-foot drop to the rocky and sandy beach below. Scramble down carefully only after considering that it's even harder to get back onto this end of the seawall if you need to return this way.

Beyond the seawall, it's easy walking east along the beach at anything but high tide. A few eucalyptus trees grow atop the bluff above the seawall's end. As you walk east, the railroad tracks angle away from the edge of the bluff. By 6 miles the beach broadens with more eucalyptus on the bluffs above. Pass some houses perched on the bluff edge between the beach and the trees, then pass the mouth of Arroyo Quemado at 6¼ miles. Continue along a narrowing beach to another seawall at 6¾ miles. Walk along its base or top, depending upon the tide, until the seawall ends around 7⅛ miles. Then walk the beach to a point at 7¼ miles. From the point, a broad beach cuts back in to the mouth of Tajiguas Creek.

CCT then follows a narrow beach east with the railroad tracks perched on the bluff 60 feet above. The beach narrows with the sandy beach soon ending. Round a point of jumbled rocks, pass two tall palms on the bluff above, then a seawall around 7⅞ miles. It isn't long but is ten feet tall, so it's fortunate you can usually walk along its seaward side.

By 8 miles, you've entered the unmarked west end of Refugio State Park, rounding another rocky point beneath sloughing, jumbled bluffs. Beyond the point, look east along the bluffs to see an old chain link fence descending part way to the beach from the blufftop. A rough, steep track climbs up the bluff and along the east side of the fence. It requires a scramble but can be done with caution. If you're afraid of heights or crumbly cliffs, don't do it alone. At the top of the bluff, you'll gain a narrow level terrace just south of the fenced railroad tracks with the highway beyond.

Turn right and head east along the blufftop. After crossing a gully, the path passes to the left of pines, then a palm at 8⅛ miles. Continue east along the narrow strip of blufftop between the tracks and beach. Where the path forks before 8¼ miles, stay to the right. You quickly hit pavement. On your left a gap in the fence leads across the tracks to the highway. Continue east across the head of another gully. Contouring east, you might notice flowering plants on your left, then a seawall on the beach below on your right. Continue winding east along the path through the old nursery grounds, passing more pines, palms and eucalypti.

By 8½ miles you cross a larger gully on a makeshift bridge. Pass a short overgrown stretch and return to pavement. Contour through the heart of the nursery past an array of naturalized plants. Before 8¾ miles the blufftop terrace narrows and you leave the nursery. Continue along a path beside the railroad tracks—if a train comes, give it plenty of room.

Before the tracks bend left, your trail veers to the right to follow the bluff's edge. Reach a junction before 9 miles. The right fork leads 250 feet to a wonderfully sited picnic table atop the point overlooking palm-lined Refugio Beach and cove. CCT takes the left fork and descends to the day-use parking lot for Refugio State Beach at 9⅛ miles. Continue east along road or beach until you see the mouth of Refugio Creek, then walk north to find the bridge where the road crosses the creek at 9⅜ miles. This section ends here, with Section 5 beginning at the start of Aniso Bike Trail on the east side of the creek.

ALTERNATE ROUTE: The only other choice follows busy Highway 101, mostly freeway.

SUGGESTED ROUND TRIPS & LOOPS: From Gaviota, walk east to Arroyo Hondo and back, 10 miles round trip. Another pleasant choice heads west from Refugio's day-use lot up to the nursery and return, up to 2½ miles round trip. For the latter hike, consider a picnic at the bird's-eye picnic spot overlooking Refugio Beach.

HOW TO IMPROVE CCT HERE: Develop a safe path or stairway between the beach at the west end of Refugio State Park to the old nursery. Build the Gaviota-Refugio bike trail.

SECTION 5
Refugio Creek, Refugio State Park to El Capitan State Park

DISTANCE: 2½ miles (4.0 kilometers).

OPEN TO: Hikers, bicyclists.

SURFACE: Paved trail.

ACCESS POINT: Refugio State Park day-use parking lot.

HOW TO GET THERE: Turn west off Highway 101 at the Refugio State Beach exit, 23 miles west of Santa Barbara, 10 miles east of Gaviota. Drive past the kiosk and under the railroad bridge to where the road forks. CCT follows the paved bike trail on your left, but turn right and drive to day-use parking area southwest of campground.

OTHER ACCESS: Highway 101 at MP.35.2 for Corral Beach, MP. 34.4 for easy CCT access.

DIFFICULTY: Easy.

ELEVATION GAIN/LOSS: 170 feet+/130 feet-. If you leave trail for beach at 1¼ miles: 60 feet+/90 feet-.

CAUTIONS: Day use open 8 a.m. to sunset. No overnight parking in day-use lots.

FURTHER INFORMATION: For Refugio State Park and El Capitan State Park, call Channel Coast District of California State Parks (805)968-1033.

FACILITIES: Restrooms, water, phones, picnic areas and seasonal stores at both Refugio and El Capitan State Parks.

CAMPGROUNDS: Refugio State Park has 85 units, all on the state park reservation system. El Capitan State Park has 142 units on the state park reservation system plus several hike/bike sites right beside the trail at west end of the campground.

HOSTEL: Banana Bungalow is in Santa Barbara, (800)346-7835.

LODGING: Many choices in Santa Barbara and Goleta to the east.

Since it takes a very low tide and summer beaches full of sand to walk the shoreline east from Refugio State Park, the CCT follows the paved Aniso Hike and Bike Trail to get to El Capitan State Park. It not only affords a break from sand and tideline walking, but also offers views of the surrounding countryside. Aniso is the Chumash word for seagull.

The paved trail starts just east of Refugio Creek near the spot where the campground road forks. Follow the level track east along the edge of the campground. By ⅛ mile you pass the last restrooms and leave the campground. Follow the paved trail as it climbs onto the marine terrace, offering a good view west across the flat around the mouth of Refugio Creek. The Santa Ynez Range rises to the north, the westernmost portion of the Transverse Ranges that run east-west through southern California. On the clearest days you can see the Channel Islands 25 miles offshore, yet another spur of the Transverse Ranges.

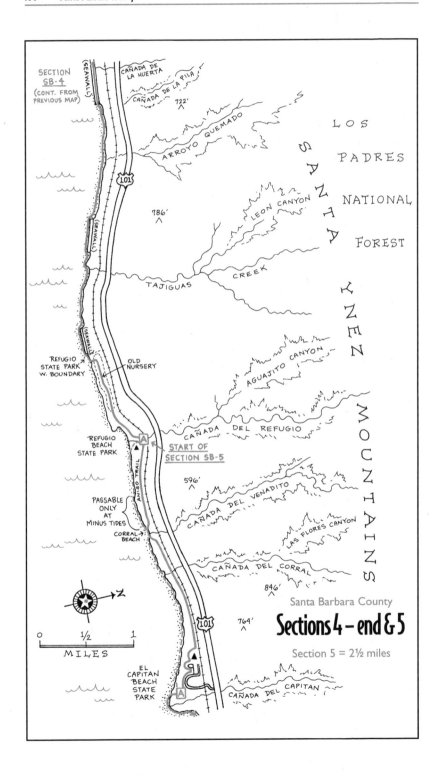

SECTION
SB-4
(CONT. FROM
PREVIOUS MAP)

(SEAWALL)

CAÑADA DE
LA HUERTA

CAÑADA DE LA PILA

CAÑADA DE LA PILA

722'
∧

ARROYO QUEMADO

101

786'
∧

LEON CANYON

TAJIGUAS

CREEK

(SEAWALL)

(SEAWALL)

REFUGIO
STATE PARK
W. BOUNDARY

OLD
NURSERY

AGUAJITO CANYON

REFUGIO
BEACH
STATE PARK

A

CAÑADA DEL REFUGIO

START OF
SECTION SB-5

596'
∧

ANISO TRAIL

PASSABLE
ONLY
AT
MINUS TIDES

CAÑADA DEL VENADITO

LAS FLORES CANYON

CORRAL
BEACH

CAÑADA DEL CORRAL

846'
∧

101

764'
∧

LOS

PADRES

NATIONAL

FOREST

S A N T A   Y N E Z   M O U N T A I N S

N

0   1/2   1
MILES

EL
CAPITAN
BEACH
STATE PARK

A

CAÑADA DEL CAPITAN

Santa Barbara County
Sections 4 – end & 5

Section 5 = 2½ miles

The paved path contours through coastal scrub paralleling the railroad tracks on your left. Pass a palm tree on your right at ½ mile and get a glimpse of the sandy beach below. Ascend a gentle hill around ⅝ mile. At the top of the hill you gain a good view of the coast to the east, all the way to Coal Oil Point on Santa Barbara Section 6, perhaps even beyond.

Descend to a small pocket beach around ⅞ mile—it's Corral Beach of El Capitan State Park. (Crucial low tide passages lie along the shoreline both west and east of Corral Beach.) The paved trail climbs back onto the marine terrace by one mile, with a view of Canada del Venadito to the north.

Soon the Aniso Trail/CCT descends, passing just above a beach. You can take side trails on the right at either 1¼ or 1⅜ miles to descend to the beach and walk the tideline east at all but high tide. Our described route, however, stays on the paved Aniso Trail. Beyond 1⅜ miles it ascends to the blufftop. By 1⅝ miles you're within sight of the highway sign, "EL CAPITAN STATE BEACH – 1 MILE." The path continues beside the railroad tracks to 1⅞ miles, then bends right.

Immediately after the bend, you enter the large, pleasant campground of El Capitan State Park. Aniso Trail passes the four choice hike/bike sites—yours for certain if you reserved in advance. If they're vacant, you can still inquire at the park's entrance kiosk. Then the paved track winds along the bluff's edge beside the campground. After a restroom beyond 2 miles, your trail dips through a gully. Pass the park's lifeguard headquarters around 2¼ miles which has a great view up the coast. Continue along the blufftop through alternating wooded and coastal scrub vegetation, passing several spur trails to the beach.

Both this section and the paved trail end at the day-use parking lot at 2½ miles. If you are continuing on Santa Barbara Section 6, turn right and walk 150 feet past the El Capitan store, then take the path that descends to the beach.

ALTERNATE ROUTE: At very low tides in summer, you may be able to walk the shoreline between Refugio and El Capitan.

SUGGESTED ROUND TRIPS & LOOPS: Walk or bike the paved path from either end and return, an easy 5 miles round trip.

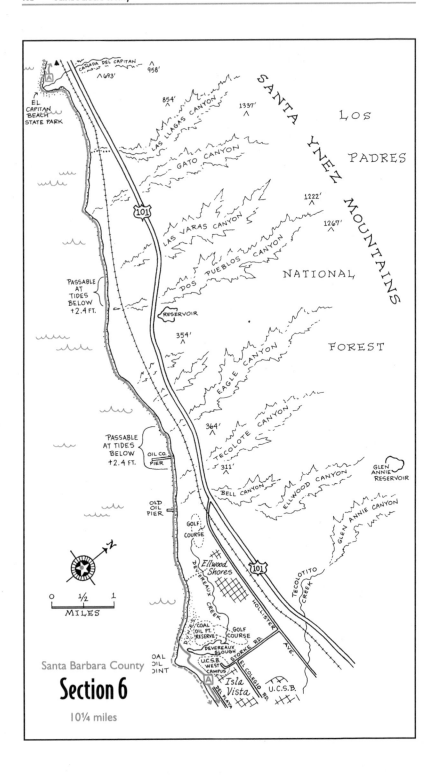

SANTA YNEZ MOUNTAINS

LOS

PADRES

NATIONAL

FOREST

CAÑADA DEL CAPITAN
∧958'
∧693'

EL
CAPITAN
BEACH
STATE PARK

854'
∧

1337'
∧

LAS LLAGAS CANYON

GATO CANYON

1222'
∧

1267'
∧

101

LAS VARAS CANYON

DOS PUEBLOS CANYON

PASSABLE
AT
TIDES
BELOW
+2.4 FT.

RESERVOIR

354'
∧

EAGLE CANYON

364'
∧

PASSABLE
AT TIDES
BELOW
+2.4 FT.

OIL CO.
PIER

311'
∧

TECOLOTE CANYON

BELL CANYON

ELLWOOD CANYON

GLEN
ANNIE
RESERVOIR

OLD
OIL
PIER

GOLF
COURSE

GLEN ANNIE CANYON

Ellwood
Shores

101

DEVEREAUX CREEK

TECOLOTITO
CREEK

N

0   ½   1
MILES

D.S.
COAL
OIL PT.
RESERVE

GOLF
COURSE

HOLLISTER RD.

DEVEREAUX
SLOUGH

STORKE RD.

AVE.

Santa Barbara County

Section 6

10¼ miles

COAL
OIL
POINT

U.C.S.B.
WEST
CAMPUS

EL COLEGIO RD.

Isla
Vista

U.C.S.B.

EL PLAYA

SECTION 6
El Capitan State Park to Isla Vista

DISTANCE: 10¼ miles(16.5 kilometers).

OPEN TO: Hikers. Bicyclists ride the dirt trails on the marine terrace at Coal Oil Point Reserve.

SURFACE: Beach, trail.

ACCESS POINT: El Capitan State Park day-use area.

HOW TO GET THERE: Exit Highway 101 at El Capitan State Beach exit. Go south to park entrance kiosk, then go straight to day-use parking.

OTHER ACCESS: From Highway 101 at MP.32.5 down Las Llagas Canyon. From the west end of Hollister Avenue, take Santa Barbara Shores Drive to its end to reach the beach at Ellwood Shores.

DIFFICULTY:: Easy.

ELEVATION GAIN/LOSS: 40 feet+/40 feet-.

CAUTIONS: Day use open 8 a.m. to sunset. No overnight parking in day-use lot. Requires a tide lower than +2.4 feet to get through.

FURTHER INFORMATION: El Capitan State Park (805)968-1411.

FACILITIES: Restrooms, water, phone, picnic area and seasonal store at El Capitan State Park.

CAMPGROUNDS: El Capitan State Park has 142 units on the state park reservation system plus several hike/bike sites right beside the trail at west end of campground. El Capitan Canyon, a private campground just north of Highway 101, has 235 sites.

HOSTEL: Banana Bungalow, Santa Barbara (800)346-7835.

LODGING: Many choices in Santa Barbara and Goleta to the east.

The long, tide-dependent trek along the rural western Santa Barbara coast concludes with this section which ends at the west campus of the University of California at Santa Barbara in the student town of Isla Vista. Despite some onshore oil facilities, this long trek remains essentially rural until you pass the new Bacara Resort at 7 miles. Once again you'll want to plan your hike to coincide with an appropriate low tide.

From the El Capitan Beach store by the day-use lot, take the trail down to the beach, passing a restroom in 200 feet. Turn left and walk down coast (east), either on the paved path at the base of the bluff or the tideline of the sandy beach. By ⅛ mile the paved path ends at a grassy picnic area, which extends east to the point at ¼ mile. From the start of the picnic area, an adjacent gravel path offers easier walking than the rocky tideline.

At El Capitan Point, the gravel path veers inland but you continue on a dirt path paralleling the shore. It soon crosses the usually tiny creek and passes a final chemical toilet on your left. Around ⅜ mile the path ends at a cobblestone beach. Turn left and walk down the coast which heads north briefly from the point surrounding the creek.

By ½ mile the rocky beach ends. CCT continues along the sandy beach, which quickly turns east, heading toward Santa Barbara at the base of 100-foot cliffs. From ⅝ to ⅞ mile you parallel a seawall built to protect the railroad on the blufftop above. Before one mile you round a small point where the beach may be inundated at tides higher than +3.0 feet.

Continue east on the beach, passing Las Llagas Canyon and a path to the highway at 1½ miles, then walking a narrow beach beneath 60-foot-high bluffs. Where you pass a gully jammed with bamboo-like carrizo at 2⅛ miles, the near-white cliffs you've been following give way to fractured orange-brown bluffs.

Round a prominent point at 2⅜ miles. If the day is clear, look west for a view along 28 miles of mostly wild coast to Government Point near Point Conception. Usually when the air is that clear, you can also see the Channel Islands offshore about the same distance to the south, with Santa Cruz Island, largest of the Channel group, due south from here. Beyond the point at 2⅜ miles, you must rock hop to get down the coast. Try to stay above the slippery rocks at tideline. After you cross the mouth of Gato Canyon, a path follows the high tideline above the rocks, reaching a sandy beach before 2⅝ miles.

Beyond 2¾ miles, where eucalyptus trees grow atop the bluffs, several small canyons allow escape to the railroad tracks in a high-tide emergency. Walk a broad beach beneath eroded bluffs. Around 3⅜ miles, only the raised landfill bed of the train tracks stands on your left. Pass the creek of Las Varas Canyon flowing from a tunnel beneath the tracks.

At 3½ miles you encounter the first of several rock ledges protruding into the tidal zone. You need a tide lower than +2.4 feet to walk the next ½ mile of shore and stay dry. The very first rock ledge offers the tightest passage, although it doesn't look like the worst from there. That ledge consists of a diagonal shelf of hardened orange sandstone extending about 40 feet from the cliff. If you can't get around its tip, you can probably scramble over its chest-high mid-section. If you cannot, you can retrace your steps about 50 feet to an emergency escape trail climbing to the train tracks. Though it would be trespassing, one could walk the tracks east, then descend across oil company property to the mouth of Dos Pueblos Canyon at 4 miles.

Assuming you get around the ledge, walk east along a secluded narrow beach strewn with medium to large rocks and crowded by golden bluffs. Cliff swallows nest on the cliffs around 3¾ miles in summer. From there you can see the broad mouth of Dos Pueblos Canyon. Walk the narrow beach east to cross the canyon's mouth at 4 miles. It's a pretty spot with oil company property upstream.

Continue east along a sandy, rock-strewn beach backed by bluffs of massive slabs of white rock. Round a tall point topped by a white pole at 4⅛ miles, gaining a coastal view east that ends at Coal Oil Point near section's end. After rounding the point at 4⅛ miles, another nearby point comes into view. This happens twice more before 5 miles. After passing these small points, you can see the prominent V of Eagle Canyon ahead with an oil company pier beyond it and Coal Oil Point extending seaward beyond.

The Native Californians: Here Before History Began

Before contact with white civilization, the abundant natural resources of California supported one of the highest population densities in North America. Most estimates place the California native population around 250,000, some argue two or three times that, about 10% of the native U.S. population. Like today's pattern, the highest concentration of people lived on or near the coast. The ancestors of many of California's tribal groups settled here at least 5000 years ago, in some cases more than 12,000 years ago.

California in 1800 supported about 110 major tribes or language groups, with twenty-eight of those spread along the coast. Many other tribes made regular sojourns to the coast to harvest the ocean's bounty and trade and visit with the locals. Of the twenty-eight coastal nations, Volume One traverses the territories of sixteen groups, while Volume Two visits a dozen.

We don't have space to discuss all these diverse cultures, so we recommend that you seek out the rich and varied literature on California's Native Americans. For now, let's take a quick overview.

Forget your stereotypes of Native Americans. No California natives lived in tipis. Rather they inhabited a diverse array of dwellings. None rode horses before white contact. California natives were among the most peace loving people on earth, though ritual war did occur. Elders of most tribes spoke several neighboring languages in response to the diverse tribal landscape. Tribes near and far conducted trade along well established trails usually open to all. Intertribal gatherings were important social events in which the whole village interacted with visitors, feasting, dancing, storytelling and game-playing, often over several days.

The Chumash were the largest of all California tribal groups, inhabiting the coast from Estero Bay to Malibu as well as the Channel Islands offshore. Some of the permanent Chumash villages in the Santa Barbara area housed more than 1000 residents. The Chumash were also among the most prosperous of California's native groups, thriving on the abundant fish and shellfish available in the Santa Barbara Channel plus the diversity of plants thriving in the mild coastal climate. The stable and populous Chumash culture regularly produced a surplus of food to trade with their surrounding tribes. They made clamshell disk currency that was highly valued and widely distributed among their neighbors.

The Chumash culture was both innovative and complex. Circular houses, framed with willow poles and covered with tules, were often 50 feet in diameter, housing several families whose spaces might be divided into rooms by hanging mats. Unlike other California tribes, they built beds covered with rush mats and rush pillows for sleeping. The Chumash were the only California tribe to make and use fishhooks, which they carved from abalone shell. While the Yurok people in the far north also had seaworthy canoes, only the Chumash built tomols, boats built of pine planks sewn together with plant fibers, then caulked with the abundant tar found in local seeps. A tomol, one of the glories of Chumash civilization, was about 30 feet long, could carry two tons, and could be rowed as fast as a person could run. You can see a fine example of a tomol in Fleischmann Auditorium at the Santa Barbara Museum of Natural History.

Walk the narrow rock-strewn beach east beneath 60-foot bluffs. As you pass two small canyons at 5⅜ and 5¾ miles, you may get a glimpse of the extensive oil drilling activities hidden atop the marine terrace beyond the bluffs. This area was developed long ago for its abundant oil reserves. Fortunately most of this industrial buildup is hidden from the marvelous beach.

The bluffs reach 90 feet high and the beach once again becomes a narrow strip only passable at tides below +2.4 feet before you reach Eagle Canyon at 6¼ miles. After crossing the mouth of the canyon, you must once again navigate a narrow strip of beach at tides below +2.4 feet. If you cannot get through, you could get around it by climbing to the tracks, walking them east to the oil pier, then trespassing across oil company property to return to the tideline. Of course it's far better to time your walk with the tides, avoiding trespassing and possibility of arrest.

Continue along alternately sandy and rocky narrow beach, reaching the oil company pier at 6⅝ miles. Another 250 feet of rock hopping follows, passing the section's narrowest tidal passage at a protruding rock ledge with a natural window. Just 100 feet more of rock hopping leads finally to long sandy Haskells Beach, much broader than the strand you've followed since the 3½-mile-point.

Reach the west rim of Tecolote Canyon at 6⅞ miles. Not long ago it was a wild canyon, but at press time the massive new Bacara Resort was being built, due to open in 2000. Amidst the wetlands east of the hotel, a towering landfill rises above the natural landscape. Phase two of this controversial development would include tennis courts built on this huge fill pile. The sight of this immense commercial development after one has walked all these miles of pristine shoreline leads one to ponder. Will the current fate of Tecolote Canyon be the eventual fate of too many other Santa Barbara coastal canyons?

Reach the canyon's east rim in 300 feet, where a dirt road currently provides public access to the beach. Walk the beach beneath 100-foot bluffs topped with giant eucalyptus trees to Bell Canyon at 7⅛ miles. Walk the strand below the mouth of this broad canyon, first passing undisturbed wetlands, then paralleling the lush green of a golf course until 7⅜ miles where the canyon ends and the golf links climb onto the terrace above the bluff.

Walk the beach beneath 40-foot bluffs where prickly pear cacti have naturalized, paralleling an old oil company service road along the base of the bluffs. It soon leads to another short oil company pier, perhaps linked more than aesthetically with the abandoned drilling platform visible ¼ mile offshore, not to mention the slightly less obtrusive active rig farther offshore.

Walk this otherwise pleasant beach east toward Coal Oil Point, once again in view across the waves. Along the base of the bluff you'll notice the ruins of a wooden retaining wall which once supported an extension of the oil company road. Pass wild bluffs towering 100 feet overhead with no sign of the golf course hiding on top.

As you walk east, the long curve of beach and cliffs slowly reveals the extensive sand dunes and open space surrounding Coal Oil Point. Beyond 8⅛ miles where you round the penultimate point, the full sweep of dramatic beach is revealed. The tall bluffs, mostly draped in vegetation here, continue all the way to the shallow canyon around 8⅝ miles. Then, as the wooden retaining wall finally ends, follow a broad beach backed by 60-foot dun cliffs with patchy vegetation.

Around 8⅞ miles you pass a popular access trail marked by three palms. It descends to the beach through Ellwood Shores, a proposed subdivision mired in a dispute with the California Coastal Commission. As you walk east along the broad beach, the bluffs on your left gradually become lower, giving way to dunes around 9⅛ miles. You soon pass twenty-foot sandhills cloaked in vegetation.

When you see the lagoon on your left at 9⅜ miles, the CCT veers left along its shoreline, entering the Coal Oil Point Reserve. (In summer you can continue along the beach, rounding Coal Oil Point and following the strand to the stairway that leads to section's end.) Watch for and follow a sandy track into the dunes between the wetlands and the fenced dune preserve. The track veers left of the fence and up the first sandhill at 9⅝ miles, then climbs onto a level marine terrace, passing through the west campus of UCSB. Turn right to head southeast past a dirt parking lot at 9¾ miles. Turn right and follow a dusty track south for 200 feet, then turn left at the first opportunity to follow a dirt bike path that contours east, soon returning to ocean vistas.

When this path forks around 10¼ miles, the right fork leads to both the blufftop path that begins the next section and a stairway that descends to the beach. The left fork heads 200 feet to the on-street parking area for Section 7 and the south end access for Section 6 at the corner of Camino Majorca and Del Playa Drive in the student community of Isla Vista.

SUGGESTED ROUND TRIPS & LOOPS: In summer you can make a short, pleasant loop hike from the Isla Vista parking at section's end through the west campus and Coal Oil Point Reserve, then turn left to walk the beach around the point and on up the stairway to return to your starting point, 1¾ miles. Or take a longer round trip hike along the beach from either end of the section, with Dos Pueblos Canyon a good destination from the west end and Eagle Canyon a good goal from the east.

Grand sweep of shore north of Coal Oil Point.

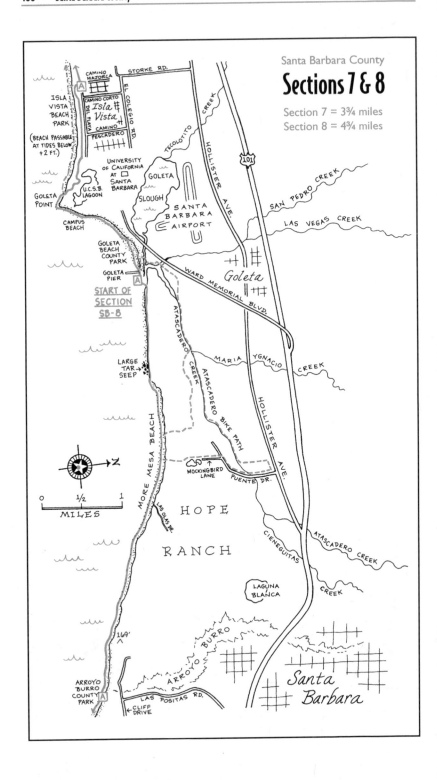

Santa Barbara County

Sections 7 & 8

Section 7 = 3¾ miles
Section 8 = 4¾ miles

SECTION 7
Isla Vista to Goleta Beach County Park

DISTANCE: 3¾ miles(6.0 kilometers).

OPEN TO: Hikers, dogs. Bicyclists on street and blufftop portions.

SURFACE: Trail, streets, beach.

ACCESS POINT: In Isla Vista at the corner of Camino Majorca and Del Playa Drive.

HOW TO GET THERE: Exit Highway 101 at Storke Road west of Santa Barbara and go south for 1.3 miles, then go left on El Colegio Road for one long block, then go right on Camino Corto to its end. Turn right and drive Del Playa Drive for 2 blocks to its end at Camino Majorca.

OTHER ACCESS: Anywhere along Del Playa Drive.

DIFFICULTY:: Easy.

ELEVATION GAIN/LOSS: 20 feet+/40 feet-.

CAUTIONS: Use caution on slippery tidal rocks.

FURTHER INFORMATION: Goleta Beach County Park (805)967-1300.

FACILITIES: Restrooms and water at 2⅝ miles. Restrooms, water, phones, picnic areas and seasonal store at south end.

CAMPGROUNDS: El Capitan State Park 10 miles west has 142 units on the state park reservation system plus several hike/bike sites.

HOSTEL: Banana Bungalow, Santa Barbara (805)963-0154.

LODGING: Many choices in Santa Barbara and Goleta.

This short section follows the residential blufftop through the student community of Isla Vista, then passes through a corner of the University of California, Santa Barbara campus before dropping to follow a tideline popular with the students. It ends by passing the length of Goleta Beach County Park. If you plan your visit to coincide with a tide below +2.0 feet, you can avoid the student ghetto and walk the shoreline for virtually the entire section's length.

From the on-street parking area, follow the dirt path south toward the shore. In 250 feet you approach the top of a stairway to the beach. At tides below +2.0 feet you may be able to walk the beach east below residential Isla Vista to get to Goleta Point at 2⅛ miles, but since the beach is impassable at most tides except perhaps in summer, our described CCT route turns left before the top of the stairs and follows the blufftop path east, coming to the lawn of Gaffney Park at ⅛ mile. Walk the path through the park, coming to Del Playa Drive by ¼ mile.

Follow the street or its intermittent sidewalks east. By ⅜ mile you pass a coastal access stairway at the end of Camino del Sur. (These stairs were closed at press time.) Continue along Del Playa to ⅝ mile where the Pescadero Bluff mini-

Park offers another stairway where you can descend to the beach. In May 1999 you could walk the beach east from here at tides below +3.0 feet.

If you cannot head east on the beach from there, continue east on Del Playa, soon passing a vehicle barrier that prevents through auto traffic. At ⅞ mile the street ends. Follow the path that veers to the right where a bike path veers left, and cross a cul-de-sac. Then follow the dirt path east along the blufftop. The area of vacant lots looks like an urban wasteland but you're following a designated "coastal access path" on the UC Santa Barbara campus. The trail descends to the beach at 2 miles, joining the beach route there. Turn left and walk the tideline east to Goleta Point at 2⅛ miles.

After rounding the point, walk a rocky beach, soon coming to sandy Campus Beach. Cross the usually dry outlet to a wetland on your left between 2¼ and 2⅜ miles. After passing a restroom, you must scramble over rocks briefly, then walk a narrow beach below 50-foot bluffs with university buildings on top. After you pass a stairway at 2⅝ miles (closed at press time), the narrow beach broadens then narrows again at a rocky point on the cliff before 2¾ miles. It broadens until another narrow point beyond 2⅞ miles where you need to pick your way over seaweed draped rocks or perhaps wade briefly if the tide is above +3.0 feet.

Walk a sandy beach to its end at 3⅛ miles. Then you need to walk a slick rock shelf briefly, then scramble up rocks to the low blufftop to get around a low rocky point with a natural bridge. Turn right and walk the dusty blufftop east for 200 feet to the westernmost paved parking lot of Goleta Beach County Park.

Walk east along the tideline of the beach or through the parking lot. You reach the Goleta Pier at 3 11/16 miles. Continue east through the parking lot to its east end at 3¾ miles, start of Santa Barbara Section 8.

ALTERNATE ROUTE: Walk the beach all the way if the tide is below +2.0 feet.

SUGGESTED ROUND TRIPS & LOOPS: Walk the beach from either end, preferably at low tide.

HOW TO IMPROVE CCT HERE: Reopen the closed coastal access stairways.

SECTION 8
Goleta Beach County Park to Arroyo Burro Beach County Park

DISTANCE: 4¾ miles (7.6 kilometers).

OPEN TO: Hikers, dogs.

SURFACE: Beach.

ACCESS POINT: Goleta Beach County Park.

HOW TO GET THERE: Exit Highway 101 west of Santa Barbara onto Highway 217, Ward Memorial Blvd. Go 2 miles, take the Airport/Sandspit Rd. exit. Go left for Sandspit Rd., follow it to the park, go right to enter, then left to parking lot at end of road.

OTHER ACCESS: More Mesa Beach, a clothing optional portion of the larger beach. Exit Highway 101 at Turnpike Road, go south to Hollister Avenue and turn left. Take the second right onto Puente Drive which leads to Vieja Drive from which you turn left on Mockingbird Lane and park at its end. Walk the ½-mile trail to the beach.

DIFFICULTY:: Easy.

ELEVATION GAIN/LOSS: 30 feet+/30 feet-.

CAUTIONS: Day use open 8 a.m. to sunset. No overnight parking in day-use lot.

FURTHER INFORMATION: Goleta Beach County Park (805)967-1300, Arroyo Burro Beach County Park (805)687-3714.

FACILITIES: Restrooms, water, phone, picnic areas, snack stand and cafe at both ends.

CAMPGROUNDS: El Capitan State Park 12 miles west has 142 units on the state park reservation system plus several hike/bike sites. Another choice is El Capitan Canyon, a private campground north of the highway at the same exit.

HOSTEL: Banana Bungalow, Santa Barbara (805)963-0154.

LODGING: Many choices in Santa Barbara and Goleta.

MAP: See page 188.

You wouldn't expect to find a wild, lightly used beach amidst such a large urban area as Santa Barbara, but most of this section is lightly visited except on the warmest days. The west end gets very light use beyond the ford of Goleta Slough. Although numerous houses lie up from the beach around the big tar seep, the beach offers more seclusion than crowding. In this section's middle you'll find More Mesa Beach, a popular clothing-optional strand, the use of which is lessened by the ½ mile walk required to reach it. East of there, the residents of the exclusive Hope Ranch subdivision on the bluffs above use the beach lightly for walking, sunning and horseback riding. Only on the section's east end will you find more beach users. They make the easy walk west from Arroyo Burro Park to enjoy the shore. Much of the charm and remote feeling you'll find here result from the high cliffs shielding the shoreline from the busy residential areas above it.

From the east end of the parking lot, walk the sand spit along its slough side until you near its end, about ⅛ mile. Find a safe place to ford the slough near the mouth of Atascadero Creek, planning your ford to reach the opposite shore to the right of the cliff and be able to walk east. The ford is about fifty feet across, knee to waist deep depending on the tide.

Once across, walk east on a gorgeous, usually empty beach. Pass eucalyptus trees atop the low bluff on your left by ⅜ mile. The light-colored cliffs get higher as you walk east, with their highest point near the radio towers around ½ mile.

Before ⅞ mile you see houses atop the bluff as the beach narrows, ending at a house-sized tar seep. At very low tide you can walk the water line around the tar seep. At tides of +3.0 feet or less you can climb over the mostly hardened tar along the top of the seep, but watch for wet, oozing spots. If the tide is higher, you might want to take the inconspicuous stairway just before the elephantine seep that links to a rough path across the sloughing bluff above the seep.

Whichever way you pass it, you're beyond the tar seep by one mile. Walk the broad beach east, passing smaller tar seeps along the top of the blond beach. Pass a few more houses visible atop the 60-foot bluffs, but by the high gray-cliffed point beyond 1⅛ miles no more homes are visible. You can see the high cliffs down coast that give this city walk its remote feeling. Except at the highest tides it's usually easy to walk around the two more large tar seeps at the base of the cliffs around 1¼ miles.

Walk a broad beach east. It narrows at a high rocky point at 1½ miles that's passable at all tides, then broadens as you continue east. No boundary marks the start of More Mesa Beach, a favorite clothing-optional sunning and bathing spot for the locals, but by 1¾ miles you're definitely on More Mesa Beach. Its access path descends from the high bluff around 2 miles. It offers an escape route that leads to Mockingbird Lane in west Santa Barbara if you walk the ½ mile path north.

CCT follows the beach east as the high bluffs on your left reach a marvelous 120 feet high. Continue along the shore beneath the Hope Ranch, a gated community with no other public access. Watch for equestrians on the beach. At 2½ miles you pass a canyon where Hope Ranch's Las Olas Drive descends to the beach. Beyond the canyon as the high bluffs rise again, you walk the shoreline of Hope Ranch Park, with lands above the high tideline open only to Hope Ranch residents and guests. Beyond the park, you'll probably once again have the beach almost all to yourself.

The beach narrows on the way to a small point. After you round the point at 3 miles, the beach broadens again. Soon the bluffs on your left have a slightly less vertical slope and support more vegetation, but they soon become even higher, towering 140 feet. CCT continues east on the beach, passing another small point at 3¾ miles. Pass an indentation or cove on the bluff around 4 miles and quickly enter Santa Barbara city limits where a few houses perch part way up the bluff. After the cove along the bluff ends, pass the highest bluff of all, towering 169 feet overhead. Walk a narrow beach beyond it where you might not get through and stay dry at high tide.

Assuming you can pass the narrow spot, walk the beach as it angles due east below descending bluffs. By 4¾ miles the bluffs end at the mouth of Arroyo Burro. Walk 200 feet to section's end where the parking lot for Arroyo Burro County Park lies just north of the beach. The next section continues along the bluff-sheltered beach beyond the mouth of Arroyo Burro's creek.

ALTERNATE ROUTE: At high tide the first two miles of beach may be impassable or difficult to pass at several points. If so you can follow the Atascadero Creek Bike Path
east from the park entrance, then descend to the beach via More Mesa Trail.

SUGGESTED ROUND TRIPS & LOOPS: Walk the beach from either end for as long as you like.
Make a loop at the west end by looping back on More Mesa Trail and Atascadero
Bike Path.

SECTION 9
Arroyo Burro Beach County Park to Stearns Wharf, Santa Barbara

DISTANCE: 3⅞ miles (6.0 kilometers).

OPEN TO: Hikers. Dogs OK on leash.

SURFACE: Beach, paved trail.

ACCESS POINT: Arroyo Burro Beach County Park.

HOW TO GET THERE: Exit Highway 101 in west Santa Barbara onto Las Positas Road. Go
south on Las Positas 1.8 miles to its end, go right on Cliff Drive .2 mile, then left
into Arroyo Burro Park lot.

OTHER ACCESS: Mesa Lane stairs, Shoreline Park, Leadbetter Beach.

DIFFICULTY:: Easy.

ELEVATION GAIN/LOSS: Negligible.

CAUTIONS: Day use open sunrise to sunset. No overnight parking in day-use lot.

FURTHER INFORMATION: Arroyo Burro Beach County Park (805)687-3714.

FACILITIES: Restrooms, water, phone, picnic area and snack stand at access point,
where the Brown Pelican Restaurant serves excellent breakfasts.

CAMPGROUNDS: El Capitan State Park 16 miles west has 142 units on the state park
reservation system plus several hike/bike sites.

HOSTEL: Banana Bungalow (805)963-0154 is only seven blocks from the beach near
Stearns Wharf.

LODGING: Many choices in Santa Barbara.

This section completes the transition to a fully urban waterfront. At the west end,
the high bluffs east of Arroyo Burro Park offer seclusion and drama to the beach.
The shore becomes increasingly urban as you pass below or through splendid
Shoreline Park, then lose the bluffs altogether at Leadbetter Beach. On this

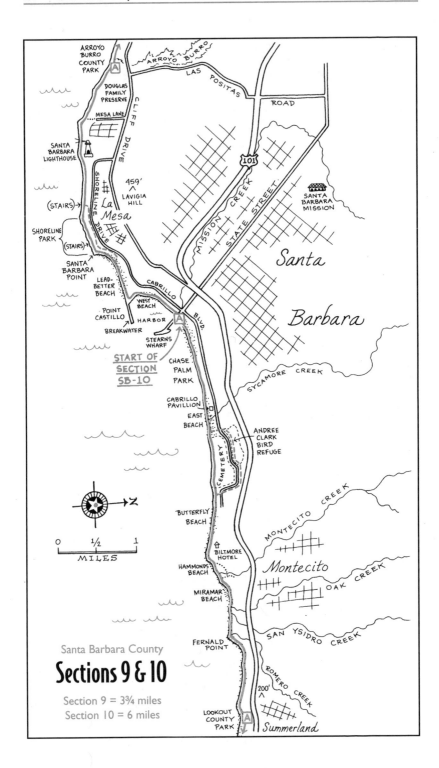

ARROYO BURRO COUNTY PARK

ARROYO BURRO

LAS POSITAS

ROAD

DOUGLAS FAMILY PRESERVE

MESA LANE

CLIFF DRIVE

SANTA BARBARA LIGHTHOUSE

101

MISSION CREEK

STATE STREET

SANTA BARBARA MISSION

459' ∧ LAVIGIA HILL

(STAIRS)→

SHORELINE DRIVE

La Mesa

Santa

SHORELINE PARK

(STAIRS)

SANTA BARBARA POINT

LEAD-BETTER BEACH

CABRILLO

Barbara

POINT CASTILLO

WEST BEACH

HARBOR

BREAKWATER

BLVD.

STEARNS WHARF

START OF SECTION SB-10

CHASE PALM PARK

CABRILLO PAVILLION

EAST BEACH

SYCAMORE CREEK

ANDREE CLARK BIRD REFUGE

CEMETERY

MONTECITO CREEK

BUTTERFLY BEACH

BILTMORE HOTEL

Montecito

OAK CREEK

HAMMONDS BEACH

MIRAMAR BEACH

SAN YSIDRO CREEK

N

0   ½   1
MILES

FERNALD POINT

ROMERO CREEK

Santa Barbara County

200' ∧

Sections 9 & 10

Section 9 = 3¾ miles
Section 10 = 6 miles

LOOKOUT COUNTY PARK

Summerland

section's final mile, you'll find motels, restaurants, a college, city parks, ball fields, tennis courts, boat rentals, fishing charters, municipal pool, harbor, 2000-foot-long Stearns Wharf, even concerts and crafts fairs all within ¼ mile of the CCT.

Walk down the path at the south end of the parking lot and cross the beach to the tideline, about 150 feet. Turn left and walk the tideline east. After you cross the mouth of the little creek that flows seasonally out of the slough, high bluffs rise 150 feet on your left, now protected as the Douglas Family Preserve.

CCT continues east along the narrowing, wild beach to round a point at ½ mile. Beyond the minor point, the beach turns broad again as you walk east. Reach the Mesa Lane stairs at ⅞ mile, a coastal access path that ascends 150 feet to the suburban bluff. Follow the beach east, rounding another point around one mile. The beach narrows on the way to a canyon before 1½ miles. You can usually get through at all but high tide, except during storm surf in winter. Above the canyon the Santa Barbara Lighthouse perches on the bluff 100 feet above.

Walk the beach east with the bluffs becoming shorter as you go. When you reach the stairway ascending to the end of Santa Cruz Boulevard at 1⅞ miles, the bluff is about 60 feet high. At high tide you'll probably need to climb these stairs, known as One Thousand Steps, and walk Shoreline Drive east, then continue east on the paths of Shoreline Park.

If you can, continue east along the narrow beach below the bluffs. By 2 miles, Shoreline Park perches atop the bluff. Continue to the Shoreline Park stairway at 2⅜ miles, which offers another escape if you cannot get around Santa Barbara Point at 2⅝ miles, which requires a tide below +3.0 feet.

If you round the point, follow the tideline of the beach north. As you go, the beach broadens and the cliffs angle away from the shore and become lower. By 2¾ miles follow the tideline of broad Leadbetter Beach northeast. Soon a grassy park at the top of the beach offers restrooms, picnic tables and a snack stand.

Reach the east end of Leadbetter Beach by 3⅛ miles. Continue along the waterfront to Point Castillo at 3¼ miles. Straight ahead lies the breakwater protecting Santa Barbara Harbor. Turn left and walk the waterfront past the Yacht Club and Naval Reserve Center, then follow the shoreline as it turns right to head north overlooking more docks. Pass the municipal pool on your left, then the pier at 3⅝ miles that defines the east end of the marina.

Beyond the pier, you come to West Beach. You can walk the tideline of the often crowded beach or follow the pedestrian boardwalk that's also popular with bicyclists and skaters. By 3⅞ miles West Beach and this section end at Stearns Wharf, a mecca for seafood lovers, fishermen, tourists and strollers. See the next section for more about the wharf.

ALTERNATE ROUTE: At high tide, you may need to bypass the shoreline between One Thousand Steps and the west end of Leadbetter Beach. In that case, follow Shoreline Drive and the paths of Shoreline Park between those points.

SUGGESTED ROUND TRIPS & LOOPS: From the access point, walk the secluded beach east as far as time or tides will allow. Another choice would be to stroll through pleasant Shoreline Park and down to Leadbetter Beach. If the tide is low enough, you can loop back on the beach around Santa Barbara Point, returning to the blufftop via the Shoreline Park stairs or One Thousand Steps.

SECTION 10
Stearns Wharf, Santa Barbara, to Lookout County Park

DISTANCE: 6 miles (9.7kilometers).

OPEN TO: Hikers, dogs on leash.

SURFACE: Beach.

ACCESS POINT: Stearns Wharf.

HOW TO GET THERE: Exit Highway 101 in Santa Barbara onto Castillo Street and go south .4 mile to its end, then turn left on Cabrillo Blvd. and go east .4 mile to Stearns Wharf at the foot of State Street. (Downtown Santa Barbara is north on State Street.) You'll find limited parking on the wharf and hourly parking three blocks east at city lots on Cabrillo Blvd.

OTHER ACCESS: East Beach on Cabrillo Blvd., Butterfly Beach off Butterfly Lane, stairway at Biltmore Hotel, Hammonds Beach off Eucalyptus Lane, Miramar Beach in front of Miramar Resort Hotel on Jamison Lane.

DIFFICULTY: Easy.

ELEVATION GAIN/LOSS: Negligible.

CAUTIONS: The tideline from the east end of East Beach to Butterfly Beach is only passable at tides of +2.5 feet or less.

FURTHER INFORMATION: Santa Barbara City Department of Parks and Recreation (805)564-5418, Lookout County Park (805)969-1720.

FACILITIES: West Beach, Palm Park, East Beach and Lookout County Park have restrooms, water, phones and picnic tables.

CAMPGROUNDS: Carpinteria State Beach, 12 miles east, has 262 campsites.

HOSTEL: Banana Bungalow, (805)963-0154, is only seven blocks from the beach near Stearns Wharf.

LODGING: Santa Barbara has many choices from budget to deluxe. In the latter category are two grand hotels adjacent to the CCT, the Four Seasons Biltmore and the Miramar Hotel.

MAP: See page 194.

This section follows the beach for its entire route. In the event of rising tides, you'll find several escape routes. The hike passes two classic hotels, the Biltmore and the Miramar, and a row of attractive beach homes. The section begins at Stearns Wharf, which was damaged by fire in 1998. You can still stroll out on the wharf for a great view of the shoreline and city backed by the Santa Ynez Range. While there, visit the free Sea Center, which has exhibits on the marine aspects of the Channel Islands offshore, and the Nature Conservancy, with exhibits about several of its California preserves including Santa Cruz Island in the Channel group. You might also have a seafood meal or buy some fresh seafood at the open air market. The wharf is open 24 hours.

Stearns Wharf was originally constructed in 1872 when local commerce with the rest of the world was conducted largely by ship. When local lumber merchant J. P. Stearns completed the wharf, it was the longest pier between San Francisco and Los Angeles. For twenty years streetcars ran between the wharf and downtown. When the first restaurant was built on the wharf in 1941, it marked the end of the wharf's use for shipping and passenger traffic.

From the foot of the Wharf at the end of State Street, walk east along the beach or on the pedestrian walkway. Pass through mile-long Chase Palm Park, with a strip of lawn lined with tall palms. Beyond the park you reach East Beach, another Santa Barbara-style park with picnic tables, grills and a children's playground near the street and a gorgeous broad beach along the shore. After you pass the 1925-vintage Cabrillo Pavilion, the top of the beach is filled with volleyball courts, a popular local pastime.

At 1⅞ miles Cabrillo Boulevard turns inland, East Beach officially ends and the bluffs begin, soon rising 50 feet above the broad beach they shelter. Across the street here you'll find the Andree Clark Bird Refuge, with a paved bike path along its south and east shores. If the tide is above +2.5 feet, you need to cross the street and follow the bike path east, then follow Channel Drive to return to the CCT at Butterfly Beach.

If the tide is below +2.5 feet, walk the beach east along the base of the bluffs. Around 2⅛ miles you pass a wonderfully comfortable rest spot at the base of the bluff with a rock perfectly contoured for two backs. Continue east along the narrowing beach beneath golden cliffs topped by cypresses and palms. As you approach the narrow point around 2⅜ miles, large stones litter the sandy beach. If tide and surf allow you around the point, the stones soon give way to a broadening beach at the base of descending bluffs.

After you pass a remnant seawall beyond 2½ miles, follow the broad beach below the bluffs to Butterfly Beach at 2¾ miles, passing the stairway to Channel Drive and Butterfly Lane. Walk the broad beach, also a popular spot, along bluffs that dip even lower, passing the stairs from the Biltmore Hotel around 3⅛ miles.

Beyond the resort, the beach swings out to a rounded point around 3⅜ miles. At the point's southernmost arc, the Surfrider Trail heads inland across the northwest corner of Hammonds Meadow, a 22-acre rolling grassland and natural area on the low bluff above the beach. Continue east along Hammonds Beach, crossing the mouth of Montecito Creek at 3⅝ miles. On the east side of the creek, the Bakewell Trail provides beach access from the end of Eucalyptus Lane. After Hammonds Beach, the low bluff up from the beach is lined with homes.

Where the coast veers north briefly around 4 miles, walk narrow Miramar Beach, shared with the Miramar Hotel across the railroad tracks. Continue past stately beachfront homes, crossing the mouth of Oak Creek at 4¼ miles, then San Ysidro Creek shortly beyond. The beach broadens heading for Fernald Point.

Cross the indistinct mouth of Romero Creek at Fernald Point at 4¾ miles. As you make the turn around the point, vistas expand to the high tan bluffs around Loon Point with the high peaks of Ventura County rising beyond. After crossing a low seawall at 4⅞ miles, walk the beach, passing the last beachfront house around 5⅛ miles. The beach narrows and turns east with the bluffs rising high

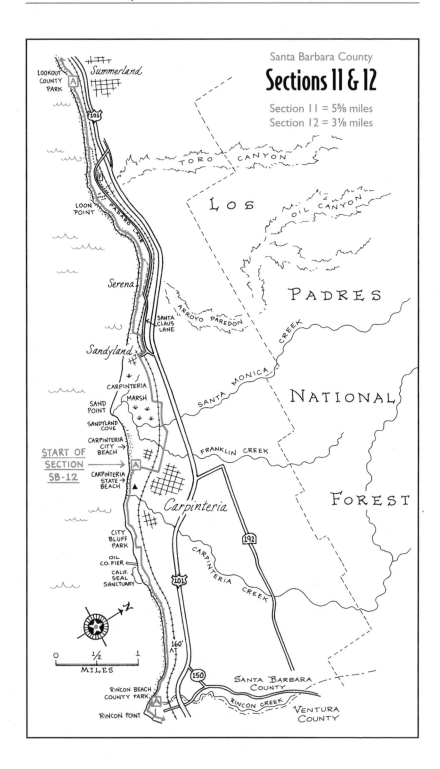

Santa Barbara County

Sections 11 & 12

Section 11 = 5⅝ miles
Section 12 = 3⅛ miles

LOOKOUT
COUNTY
PARK

Summerland

101

TORO CANYON

LOON
POINT

PASEO LANE

LOS

OIL CANYON

PADRES

Serena

ARROYO PAREDON

SANTA
CLAUS
LANE

Sandyland

SANTA MONICA CREEK

CARPINTERIA
MARSH

SAND
POINT

NATIONAL

SANDYLAND
COVE

CARPINTERIA
CITY
BEACH

FRANKLIN CREEK

START OF
SECTION
SB-12

A

CARPINTERIA
STATE
BEACH

Carpinteria

FOREST

CITY
BLUFF
PARK

192

OIL
CO. PIER

CARPINTERIA CREEK

CALIF.
SEAL
SANCTUARY

101

0   ½   1
MILES

160'

150

SANTA BARBARA
COUNTY

RINCON BEACH
COUNTY PARK

RINCON CREEK

VENTURA
COUNTY

RINCON POINT

above topped by Freeway 101. Follow seawalls protecting the tracks halfway up the sloping bluffs. When the second seawall ends at 5½ miles, you may need to scramble briefly over riprap or get wet along the tideline to reach Lookout Beach.

Follow a third seawall from 5⅝ to beyond 5¾ miles. By the time it ends near one more beachfront home, you're on the broad beach of Lookout County Park. Before 6 miles, watch for the paved trail climbing ⅛ mile from the beach to Lookout County Park's parking and picnic areas. The sloping path, lined by a chain link fence, marks this section's end and the start of Santa Barbara Section 11.

ALTERNATE ROUTE: At tides above +2.5 feet, you must leave CCT's main route at the east end of East Beach, cross Cabrillo Blvd. and head east on the bike path along the south boundary of Andree Clark Bird Refuge, then follow Channel Drive east and south to Butterfly Lane to descend the stairs and return to the CCT.

SUGGESTED ROUND TRIPS & LOOPS: Walk the beach from either end for as long as you like or tides will allow.

SECTION 11
Lookout County Park to Carpinteria State Beach

DISTANCE: 5⅝ miles (9.1 kilometers).

OPEN TO: Hikers, dogs. Bicyclists on streets and path along tracks.

SURFACE: Beach, sidewalks, trail.

ACCESS POINT: Lookout County Park.

HOW TO GET THERE: Exit Highway 101 at Summerland/Evans Avenue east of Santa Barbara. Go left, then left again on Evans, following it downhill to its end at Wallace Avenue opposite the Lookout County Park entrance.

OTHER ACCESS: Around Loon Point from Padaro Lane, either west along railroad tracks or south down Toro Canyon along its creek to Loon Point. From Santa Claus Lane, walk across railroad tracks and riprap to beach.

DIFFICULTY:: Easy.

ELEVATION GAIN/LOSS: Negligible.

CAUTIONS: Lookout Park is open 8 a.m. to dusk. The beach between Serena and Sandyland is passable at tides below +4.0 feet.

FURTHER INFORMATION: Lookout County Park (805)969-1720, or call Santa Barbara County Parks and Recreation (805)568-2460, Carpinteria State Beach (805)684-2811, Carpinteria City Beach (805)684-5405 ext. 449.

FACILITIES: Lookout County Park and Carpinteria State Beach have water, picnic tables, restrooms and phones.

CAMPGROUNDS: Carpinteria State Beach has 262 campsites.

LODGING: Carpinteria has a variety of accommodations.

This route follows an isolated beach at the base of high bluffs before entering the flat landscape of Carpinteria Valley where it follows the beach if tides allow, then the road shoulder briefly through the little settlement of Santa Claus Lane with its permanent Christmas facade. It continues on a path along the railroad tracks to get around Carpinteria Marsh, the oceanside mouth of which is generally impassable at its tide-scoured channel. The route then follows city streets back to the beach. If you start from the Lookout Park parking lot, you need to descend the paved trail ⅛ mile to the beach to join the CCT.

Summerland had the dubious distinction of having the first offshore oil drilling rig in the nation. Offshore drilling began here in 1896, and by 1906 more than 400 wells covered Summerland beaches. Then in 1958, the first modern oil rig on offshore state lands was built two miles out from Lookout Beach. In 1969, a rig five miles offshore had a blowout, causing a huge spill that blackened beaches all along the Santa Barbara coast, effectively closing them to public use for eight or nine months.

From the paved ramp at Lookout County Park, walk the beach east toward the high bluffs of Loon Point. Beyond ⅜ mile a seasonal creek has carved a canyon in the 50-foot bluffs, spanned by a railroad trestle. The bluffs resume as you walk down the beach. Around ⅞ mile the railroad veers away from the shore, with a volunteer coastal access path following the tracks to the Loon Point parking lot. CCT follows the narrow sandy beach east. As you approach Loon Point, the sand gives way to a rocky intertidal zone beyond 1¼ miles. The bluffs get

The Chumash long used this tar seep, now in Carpinteria State Beach.

lower as you near Loon Point, then they are bisected by Toro Canyon where another volunteer path ascends along the creek to the Loon Point lot on Padaro Lane ¼ mile north. Native sycamore and coast live oak line the stream up canyon, mingling with introduced cypress and eucalyptus trees that shelter monarch butterflies. Beds of giant kelp grow more than ½ mile offshore here.

After you round Loon Point at 1½ miles, continue along a meandering tideline of a mostly narrow beach below 40-foot bluffs. You begin to see houses atop the wooded bluffs beyond 2 miles. Soon the bluffs disappear, yielding to low marine terraces that support specialty crops like avocados and citrus. Beyond 2¼ miles the beach angles southeast past scattered beach houses in the community of Serena. If the tide is high, around 2⅜ miles you may need to detour inland to follow Padaro Lane. Otherwise continue along the beach crowded by houses, coming to riprap around 3 miles that may require scrambling at tides above +3.5 feet.

Beyond the rocks you can walk the beach to around 3⅜ miles before it ends at a wall of riprap shielding a private Arabesque house perched on a small point. Just before the beach ends, turn inland and walk northeast across the riprap and train tracks. Look for a path between the Padaro Beach Grill on the left and Santa Claus/Toyland on the right. It leads to Santa Claus Lane, where you turn right and walk past Toyland. At the end of this clapboard tourist Mecca, turn right and head south through bamboo to the railroad tracks. Turn left and follow the volunteer path beside the railroad right-of-way, a route frequently used by locals.

You reach a cross street, Estero Way, that crosses the tracks to enter the Carpinteria Marsh at 4¼ miles. Turn left and walk Estero Way briefly to Carpinteria Avenue, then turn right and follow this into town. Turn right on 7th Street at 4¾ miles and follow it southeast to Linden Avenue before 5¼ miles. Turn right on Linden and follow it to its end at the beach at 5⅝ miles where this section ends and the next one begins. Carpinteria City Beach extends west on your right and Carpinteria State Beach extends east.

ALTERNATE ROUTE: If the tide is higher than +3.0 feet, around 2⅜ miles you may need to detour inland to follow Padaro Lane to Santa Claus Lane.

SUGGESTED ROUND TRIPS & LOOPS: Walk east from Lookout Park for as long as you like. Or hike to the beach at Loon Point and hike west or east on the CCT.

HOW TO IMPROVE CCT HERE: Put a pedestrian bridge across the mouth of Carpinteria Marsh so that the CCT can stay on the shoreline for the last part of the section.

SECTION 12
Carpinteria State Beach to Rincon Beach County Park

DISTANCE: 3⅛ miles (5.0 kilometers).

OPEN TO: Hikers.

SURFACE: Beach, trail.

ACCESS POINT: Carpinteria State Beach at Linden Avenue.

HOW TO GET THERE: Exit Highway 101 in Carpinteria east of Santa Barbara at Linden Avenue. Turn right and drive Linden to its end at the beach in .7 mile. (The main entrance to Carpinteria State Beach, where you enter the campground, is at the end of Palm Avenue four blocks south.)

OTHER ACCESS: City Bluffs Beach Park, the newly purchased public coastal land at Ballard Road, has an informal path to the CCT.

DIFFICULTY: Easy.

ELEVATION GAIN/LOSS: 50 feet+/60 feet-.

CAUTIONS: Watch for tar balls on the beach. Stay out of the seal pupping area from December through March. Dogs OK on leash on the county beach. Dogs not allowed on state beach.

FURTHER INFORMATION: Carpinteria State Beach (805)684-2811, Rincon Beach County Park, (805)568-2460.

FACILITIES: Water, picnic tables, restrooms and phones at Carpinteria State Beach and Rincon Beach County Park, picnic tables at City Bluffs Beach Park.

CAMPGROUNDS: Carpinteria State Beach has 262 campsites.

LODGING: Carpinteria has ample accommodations from budget to deluxe.

MAP: See page 198.

This final Santa Barbara section offers a pleasant, diverse walk despite passing extensive oil drilling and storage facilities. The beach at Carpinteria is known as "the safest beach in California" because a shallow offshore shelf prevents rip currents and minimizes rogue waves. Beyond the state park, the CCT passes through City Bluffs Beach Park, recently purchased after a dogged fundraising effort by local coastal advocates saved the land from development. Beyond the oil drilling facilities, you'll pass through the California Seal Sanctuary, one of only four onshore harbor seal pupping areas in the state. Beyond that CCT follows a wild span of beach to Rincon Point, a Mecca for surfers, just short of the Ventura County line.

A village of the native Chumash people long occupied the banks of Carpinteria Creek near its mouth. When Spaniard Gaspar de Portola visited the site in 1769, he was so impressed by the Chumash boat building activities that he called the village La Carpinteria, Spanish for carpenter shop. The Chumash gathered planks from inland pine trees and hauled them to coastal villages where craftsmen would split them with whale-rib wedges that had abalone shell blades. They used plant fibers to sew the planks together, then caulked them against leakage with tar from local seeps. The Chumash used their boats to travel across the Santa Barbara Channel, a powerful testimony to their seaworthiness. On the Channel Islands they would hunt and fish, also trading with other Chumash villages there.

From the end of Linden Avenue, walk down to the tideline and turn left. Follow the tideline of Carpinteria State Beach down the broad beach in front of the campground. Watch for tar balls on the beach that come from active tar seeps ahead. Pass the Palm Drive access to the State Beach around ¼ mile and continue east to cross the mouth of Carpinteria Creek at ⅜ mile.

Soon the beach narrows, with a low bluff above the strand being part of the state park campground. Pass active tar seeps in the low bluff along the narrowing beach from ½ to ¾ mile. Beyond ⅝ mile you may need to walk through the campground when the tide is high since the beach may be inundated. Continuing along the beach, the bluffs get higher.

When you reach a stairway near the eastern boundary of the state beach at ¾ mile, walk up the steps and turn right to follow the blufftop trail east, passing through mostly undeveloped City Bluffs Beach Park. At ⅞ mile the path dips through a gully with beach access, then returns to the blufftop to follow the bluff edge east. Around one mile you pass some picnic tables on a small point near a few scattered cypress trees on the blufftop.

CCT continues east on the blufftop path for about 400 feet beyond the point, then veers northeast to 1⅛ miles where it joins and follows an oil company service road east. Take the paved track and parking lot nearest the railroad tracks, the only way through. Pass the oil company pier by 1¼ miles and continue to the end of the parking lot.

Continue southeast on the dirt blufftop track. It soon returns to the bluff's edge, passing a sign about the harbor seal pupping area, the California Seal Sanctuary, on the beach below. That area of the beach is closed every year from December 1 until May 31 to allow the seals to breed and pup without interruption. You can watch the action from the blufftop.

CCT continues east on the blufftop trail for another J mile. Before 1½ miles, you come to the first of two paths that descend to the beach. If your hike here isn't during the seal pupping season closure and it isn't high tide, you can descend this path to a rocky beach at 1½ miles. Walk the rocky beach around the point at 1⅝ miles, then follow the beach east, soon meeting the second path between blufftop and beach around 1¾ miles. Continue on down the mostly rocky beach, passing more tar seeps around 2 miles. The bluffs rise 120 feet on your left around 2¼ miles as you walk a beach of cobbles and sand. By 2½ miles the bluffs tower 160 feet overhead. After you pass some fine tidepools around 2¾ miles, the bluffs get lower and the beach becomes very wide as you head towards wooded Rincon Point.

By 3⅛ miles, where the bluffs rise only about 30 feet above the beach, you'll come to both a gentle ramp and stairs rising to the parking lot for Rincon Beach County Park. If you're continuing down the coast, the next section starts here. If you left a vehicle at the Rincon Park lot, ascend to reach it before 3¼ miles. Day hikers might want to walk the ¼ mile to Rincon Point itself before turning back.

SUGGESTED ROUND TRIPS & LOOPS: Walk the beach from either end, up to 6½ miles round trip. Walk or bicycle the bluffs of City Bluffs Beach Park where small loops can be made between the shore and the train tracks.

Ventura County

T HE VARIED 43-MILE* VENTURA COUNTY COASTLINE offers everything
from quiet sandy beaches and exceptional Point Mugu State Park
to some of the worst excesses of beach armoring on the entire
coast of California. Mountains crowd the coastline both north and south
where Highway 101 runs between the base of the mountains and the
ocean replete with miles of seawalls constructed to protect the roadbed
from erosion.

Between the bookend mountains, the Oxnard Plain and the Santa
Clara Valley support a thriving agricultural industry and bustling, growing towns. The City of Ventura boasts one of the best historic downtown
districts anywhere on the California coast with a Spanish mission, muse-
ums, a significant archeological site marking the earliest mission, and an
old Main Street retaining the flavor of a what a town was like before

shopping malls.

The county hosts the Channel Islands National Park Visitor Center, a fine place to find out more about the five islands lying between 10 and 45 miles offshore, and the Visitor Center and Headquarters for Santa Monica Mountains National Recreation Area, located inland at Thousand Oaks.

Oil production is prevalent in the county with older onshore facilities on the north coast and newer offshore platforms on the ocean horizon. The Naval Air Weapons Station protects a significant marine estuary and wetland, Mugu Lagoon. Amidst the shoreline development, truly fine beaches offer places to stroll, swim, surf, fish or rest in the mild semi-desert climate. Inland, the rugged mountains of Los Padres National Forest offer camping, hiking and backpacking and contain the Sespe Condor Sanctuary and the Sespe, Matilija and Chumash Wilderness Areas.

Ventura County's CCT starts at the famous surfing spot Rincon Point and then negotiates Highway 101 for several miles before reaching relatively uncrowded Old Pacific Coast Highway. At Emma Wood State Beach, the CCT abandons the road and hits the beach along an untamed stretch of shoreline before reaching the Ventura city waterfront. Beyond the Ventura City Pier, our route takes to the long sandy beach fronting the plains. This middle part of Ventura County's Coastal Trail on pleasant beaches suffers interruption by man-made barriers. Three detours result from two small boat harbors carved out of coastal dunes and marshes, deep water Port Hueneme and two Navy bases.

At the south end of the county, our CCT route negotiates a combination of the road shoulder and beaches at the base of the scenic and dramatic Santa Monica Mountains through Point Mugu State Park. Starting at Mugu Rock, the historic Chumash Trail climbs into the mountain back country. Down coast a little farther the Santa Monica Mountains Backbone Trail begins at the Ray Miller Trailhead in La Jolla Canyon. Ventura County's Coastal Trail ends at Leo Carrillo State Beach just across the Los Angeles County line.

---

* Ventura County's Coastal Trail is 52 miles because of detours.

SECTION 1
Rincon Beach County Park to Faria Beach County Park

DISTANCE: 7 to 7¾ miles (11.3 or 12.9 kilometers) depending on route.

OPEN TO: Hikers. Bicyclists on most.

SURFACE: Beach, riprap, road, bike lane on highway shoulder.

ACCESS POINT: Rincon Beach County Park.

HOW TO GET THERE: Take the Bates Road exit from Highway 1 at the Santa Barbara/ Ventura County Line. Drive Bates Road to its end where free parking lies both on right and left at the entrance to a gated community.

OTHER ACCESS: Rincon Point, Hobson County Park, Faria Beach County Park.

DIFFICULTY: Easy.

ELEVATION GAIN/LOSS: 60 feet-. Modest gains and losses climbing riprap.

CAUTIONS: Use extreme caution while walking the highway, climbing on riprap, or following the railroad right of way.

FURTHER INFORMATION: Rincon Beach County Park (805)568-2460, Faria Beach County Park and Hobson County Park (805)654-3951.

FACILITIES: Parking, restrooms, water, picnic tables, phone at Rincon Beach County Park. Restrooms, water, picnic tables at Faria Beach County Park.

CAMPGROUNDS: Hobson County Park has 31 sites and hot showers. Faria Beach County Park has 42 sites and hot showers. Carpinteria State Beach to the north has 262 campsites and hot showers.

LODGING: Carpinteria Valley has many rooms of all kinds. Mussel Shoals near La Conchita has the moderately priced Cliff House.

The first Ventura County CCT section begins at picturesque Rincon Point, passes the little settlement of La Conchita and historic oil wells, then takes to Old Pacific Coast Highway. Unfortunately, this section has perhaps the worst example of a damaged coastline because of the thoughtless and intense use of riprap to protect shoreline property from erosion. CalTrans, Ventura County and homeowners have dumped tons of huge boulders right into the surf and on the beach to build Highway 101 at the base of steep eroding coastal hills. For more about the negative effects of riprap, read *The Case Against Shoreline Armoring*.

The highway built right on the shoreline makes the first part of this section difficult. After leaving Rincon Point, you have three ways to make it to the Old Pacific Coast Highway at Sea Cliff. The route then becomes more pleasant and straightforward on its way to Ventura.

Before 1900 the Ventura-Santa Barbara stage followed the tideline along the coast here. Often the stage would have to wait for the tide to recede to get around Rincon Point.

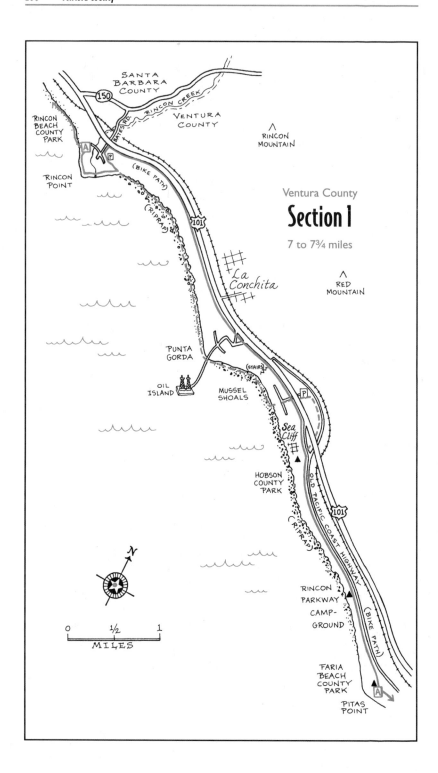

SANTA BARBARA COUNTY

150

RINCON CREEK

VENTURA COUNTY

RINCON MOUNTAIN

RINCON BEACH COUNTY PARK

A

P

BATES RD.

RINCON POINT

(BIKE PATH)

(RIPRAP)

101

Ventura County

Section 1

7 to 7¾ miles

La Conchita

RED MOUNTAIN

PUNTA GORDA

(STAIRS)

OIL ISLAND

MUSSEL SHOALS

P

Sea Cliff

HOBSON COUNTY PARK

(RIPRAP)

OLD PACIFIC COAST HIGHWAY

101

RINCON PARKWAY CAMP- GROUND

(BIKE PATH)

N

0   ½   1
MILES

FARIA BEACH COUNTY PARK

A

PITAS POINT

Wooded Rincon Point marks the county line.

To start this walk from Rincon Beach County Park, take the stairs or the ramp down to the beach. At most tides the route around Rincon Point is passable. If the beach is flooded, you will have to walk on the low riprap that lines the point to protect the houses. Off the point, surfers ride what they describe as one of the best winter breaks in the world, providing beautifully shaped waves and long rides. Just before the rocky point at ⅜ mile, cross Rincon Creek into Ventura County. Continue down the rocky shoreline. At the end of the row of houses before ¾ mile, a path descends from a parking lot. At extremely low tides you can continue on the sand at the base of the riprap. You can also rock hop on the large boulders when the ocean is calm, but to do so requires steady feet and good balance. The riprap route offers quieter but slower going than the highway.

If the beach or riprap look impassable or too difficult, take the path up to the parking lot. From there you can follow the bike lane down the highway. A third route, not recommended, follows the railroad tracks at the base of the hills to La Conchita, then follows a utility right-of-way from La Conchita to the end of Old Pacific Coast Highway near the Bush Oil Company. Whichever route you take, the goal remains to make it to Sea Cliff 5⅜ miles down the coast from Rincon Point. From there the route follows lightly traveled Old Pacific Coast Highway.

To walk the riprap or low tide beach, continue on the beach past the last house on Rincon Point to the riprap at ⅞ mile. If the route proves unsafe or uncomfortable after you get started, you can carefully climb up the rocks to the bike lane, but you would also need to climb over a fence. It would be better to decide early if the route is feasible so that you can return to Rincon Point and walk the bike path if necessary.

To get to the bike lane from Rincon Point, take the path next to the last house. Follow it to the parking lot, exit the lot on the entrance drive and walk up the access ramp to the highway and the bike lane. This section of highway, although not a freeway, is very busy with noisy and fast traffic.

To get to the tracks, take Bates Road under the freeway and scale the embankment up to the tracks. Take the dirt track paralleling the tracks, then follow the street through La Conchita, then the utility road before reaching the end of Old Pacific Coast Highway where it deadends about ¾ mile north of Sea Cliff. Follow Old Pacific Coast Highway under the freeway, then along the coast.

On both the recommended routes, you walk past houses on Punta Gorda at 3¼ miles. An oil pier marks the point. If you are scrambling on the rocks, you reach a narrow road around 4½ miles which tunnels under Highway 101 to Old Pacific Coast Highway, where you turn right. You can also continue on the rocks and pick up the Old Pacific Coast Highway at Sea Cliff. Whether you follow the rocks or the bike path, you reach Sea Cliff at 5⅜ miles.

From Sea Cliff walk the wide road shoulder past a row of houses, or you can instead walk in front of the houses at low tide until you get to Hobson County Park. Beginning at Hobson County Park at 5⅞ miles, the road parallels the surf atop the wicked looking riprap, so the bike path is the best choice. Around 6¼ miles you reach Rincon Parkway with RV campsites on the road shoulder. In summer and winter the road is lined bumper to bumper for more than a mile with large RVs. Rincon Parkway ends at Faria Beach County Park at 7¾ miles and so does this section.

The Case Against Shoreline Armoring

Shoreline erosion occurs as a natural process. The planet's surface shifts in a dynamic, ever changing interplay of wind, water and earth. This constant movement plays out most dramatically and rapidly on the shoreline, creating circumstances for disaster. Crashing waves, exposed geology, fresh air, sandy beaches, and vivid scenery attract millions of people to the California coastline. The problem: some like it so much that they build their homes or businesses directly on this rare, shifting, restless and hazardous shore. If it's not private property owners challenging nature for the views, then the state builds roads in unstable places and spends millions to protect them.

Once we have made the mistake of building in hazardous locations, engineering steps up to solve the problem, but not always with satisfactory results. When the Mississippi River flood of 1993 overwhelmed millions of acres of farmland and many towns, causing $15 billion in damage, the Army Corp of Engineers admitted

that $50 billion spent on dikes over more than 100 years did not solve flooding problems. The solution proposed for this failed policy: it's cheaper to buy out flood-prone property and let the river return to its natural cycle of flooding.

On the California coast thousands of structures sit directly in the path of unstoppable natural forces. About 950 miles of the 1100-mile-long shore are actively eroding. Along 125 miles of that shoreline, erosion threatens structures. The solutions used to protect the inappropriate development generate more mistakes. Owners and/or the state install piles of unsightly boulders (riprap), or cold concrete seawalls to stop erosion. Groins and jetties stick out into the surf and inland dams clog rivers.

Such interference with natural process is disastrous and costly. The dams stop the flow of sand particles from inland, starving the beaches. The jetties and groins stop sand flow along the beach, called littoral drift. The seawalls create a barrier to wave energy disbursement, causing a backwash

SUGGESTED ROUND TRIPS AND LOOPS: You can explore the sandy Rincon Beach, then walk around Rincon Point to explore tidepools and watch the hot surfing action, 1½ miles round trip, or cut across the point by taking the path up to the two parking areas.

HOW TO IMPROVE THE CCT HERE: The idea of improvement for the first few miles of Ventura County's CCT seems daunting because of the highway right on the edge of the armored shoreline. Short of tearing out Highway 101 and restoring the coast (yay), it is at least feasible to move the bike lane to run between the railroad tracks and the highway from Bates Road to Sea Cliff. Another solution would be to construct a walkway atop the riprap from Rincon Point to Sea Cliff, but this seems unlikely because of high costs and the problem of washouts during major storms.

Shoreline Armoring – continued

that scours the shore of sand. Shoreside buildings are threatened, leading to costly repairs or construction of more seawalls and expensive sand replenishment projects. This all comes at huge expense to the public. The beaches simply disappear under a barrage of rock or concrete. The public loses the legally mandated right to walk the shoreline while their taxes often pay the bill.

There are only three ways to cope with erosion damage to structures: continue hardening the shoreline, replenish beach sand on a regular basis, or retreat. Hardening and replenishing are short term solutions that need continual maintenance and/or repair. The ocean's constant dynamic forces continue to batter such defenses. Retreat remains the only real long term solution; surrender to the forces of nature. It's time to halt all shoreline development and move or tear down threatened structures. Presently California state law allows seawall construction, if a structure is threatened, as well as repair and maintenance of seawalls. On the Pacifica

shoreline south of San Francisco, soft sandstone bluffs rapidly erode, threatening a row of homes. Construction of a 1000-foot-long seawall at the base of the bluff directly on the beach gained government approval. The public gets stuck with the bill, losing a beach in the bargain.

Government should buy threatened structures and tear them down, allowing the open-space bluffs to retreat as nature dictates. This solution seems difficult and harsh but in the long term saves money and our beaches.

The opposition to seawalls grows daily as the public sees more beaches lost. Until elected officials make the hard decision to end seawall construction, rezone threatened shoreline areas to open space, and move or remove threatened buildings, we will continue to see damage to the coastal environment for the benefit of the few coastal landowners at the expense of the citizens of California.

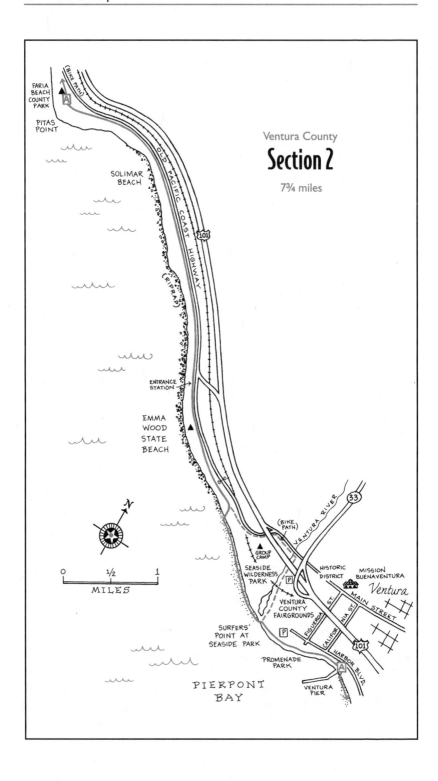

Ventura County
Section 2
7¾ miles

SECTION 2
Faria Beach County Park to Ventura City Pier

DISTANCE: 7¾ miles (12.5 kilometers).

OPEN TO: Hikers, bicyclists.

SURFACE: Road shoulder, beach.

ACCESS POINT: Faria Beach County Park.

HOW TO GET THERE: Take the Sea Cliff exit off Highway 101 and go south 2.5 miles on Old Pacific Coast Highway to Faria Beach County Park.

OTHER ACCESS: Anywhere along Old Pacific Coast Highway, Emma Wood State Beach, Ventura County Fairgrounds, Promenade Park.

DIFFICULTY: Easy.

ELEVATION GAIN/LOSS: Negligible.

CAUTIONS: The Ventura River mouth may be impassable during storms and/or high tides.

FURTHER INFORMATION: Faria Beach County Park (805)654-3951, Emma Wood State Beach (805)648-4807, Promenade and Seaside Wilderness parks (805)652-4550.

FACILITIES: Faria Beach and Emma Wood State Beach have restrooms, picnic tables and water. Promenade Park has restrooms and picnic tables. It and Ventura City Pier have all the city amenities nearby.

CAMPGROUNDS: Faria Beach County Park has 42 campsites and hot showers. Emma Wood State Beach has hike and bike sites plus four group sites at the south end plus 61 sites run by the county at the north end.

LODGING: Ventura has abundant lodging including the moderate Vagabond Inn and the deluxe Holiday Inn right near the pier at section's end.

This section offers a pleasant, easy walk along Old Pacific Coast Highway, followed by a refreshing walk on the relatively natural beach and parkland at the mouth of the Ventura River before reaching the developed beachfront of the city of Ventura.

From Faria Beach County Park, walk south on Old Pacific Coast Highway, rounding Pitas Point and passing the community of Solimar. If the tide is low, you can walk the exposed beach in front of the houses. At 1⅝ miles the houses end while our route continues along the shoulder overlooking the riprap and what little sand remains on Solimar Beach.

Continue along Old Pacific Coast Highway past more houses, with the Santa Ynez Range towering inland from nearby Highway 101. At 4 miles take the entrance road into Emma Wood State Beach. The park features campsites along the park road overlooking a cobble beach which you can walk at all but high tides. The park road ends at 5¼ miles, but continue on the path a short distance before turning down to the widening beach.

Walk the cobble beach south. You soon enter Seaside Wilderness Park which seems quite wild with the cobbled beach, sand dunes, large cypresses and Monterey pines, and the highway finally ⅜ mile distant. As you approach the river mouth and the Ventura City limits, you see thick riparian foliage, then the estuary at the mouth of the river.

You reach the Ventura River mouth at 6⅛ miles, usually sand barred or some-times flowing but shallow. In the event it's flooded, return to the bike path at the south end of Emma Wood State Beach and follow it inland across the Main Street bridge and back to the coast. The main CCT route continues past the estuary, climbing the river bank to meet the bike path where it comes down the east bank of the river. Follow the bike path down coast (east at this point) toward Surfers Point with the Ventura County Fairgrounds on the left. The path was damaged by 1997 winter storms, so several short detours take you briefly into the fairgrounds parking lot. At low tide you can also walk the beach around Surfers Point, well known among surfers for the fine break. When the fairgrounds end, you reach formal Promenade Park at 6⅜ miles. After passing in front of the high-rise Holi-day Inn, you reach the Ventura City Pier and section's end at 7¾ miles.

SUGGESTED ROUND TRIPS AND LOOPS: From Emma Wood or the Fairgrounds walk out and back on the Seaside Wilderness Park beach for a taste of what this coastline was like before development.

To get a sense of the history of Ventura, walk a few blocks inland to the truly historic, interesting and somewhat unappreciated old downtown district. The city gets credit for a fine job of preserving the area even as they allowed a multitude of shopping malls to sprawl into the suburbs and farmland. To get there take either Figueroa Street from Promenade Park or California Street from just north of the pier. Features clustered next to the business district in a park setting include the San Buenaventura Mission, the Ortega Adobe, Ventura County Museum of His-tory and Art, Figueroa Plaza and the Albinger Archaeological Museum, with the archeological dig of the original mission featured. Main Street maintains a '30s and '40s downtown character. Although many of the old businesses have been lost to shopping malls, the antique stores, thrift stores, restaurants, coffee houses and bookstores do a lively business. A block off Main at the end of California Street, the remarkable neo-Classic Ventura County Courthouse sits as a monu-ment to the power of authority.

SECTION 3
Ventura City Pier to McGrath State Beach

DISTANCE: 7¾ miles (add ½ mile to McGrath Campground) (12.5 + .8 kilometers).

OPEN TO: Hikers. Bicyclists on bike path.

SURFACE: Beach, bike path, sidewalk.

ACCESS POINT: Ventura City Pier.

HOW TO GET THERE: Take the Downtown Ventura exit off of Highway 101. The pier is adjacent to downtown Ventura near the end of California Street at Harbor Blvd.

OTHER ACCESS: San Buenaventura State Beach, and anywhere on the harbor part of the route.

DIFFICULTY: Easy.

ELEVATION GAIN/LOSS: None.

FURTHER INFORMATION: San Buenaventura State Beach (805)654-4610, Ventura City Department of Parks and Recreation (805)652-4594, McGrath State Beach (805)654-4744, Channel Islands National Park (805)658-5700.

FACILITIES: City amenities at Ventura City Pier and around the Ventura Harbor. Marina Park and the Channel Islands Visitor Center have restrooms, picnic tables and water. McGrath State Beach has water, picnic tables and restrooms.

CAMPGROUNDS: McGrath State Beach has 174 sites and hot showers.

LODGING: The Ventura area has abundant accommodations including the moderate Vagabond Inn and the deluxe Holiday Inn right near the pier.

This section offers a fine beach walk interrupted by the man-made Ventura Harbor carved out of dunes. Consider visiting the Channel Islands National Park Visitor Center perched on the south shore at the harbor mouth or checking out the good birding at the mouth of the Santa Clara River at McGrath State Beach.

After strolling on the 1700-foot long Ventura Pier for a boat captain's view of the Ventura beachfront, walk down the wide sandy beach past the huge picnic area and parking lot of San Buenaventura State Beach before one mile. Continuing down the beach, in the second mile you pass houses covering what was once a dune environment.

You reach Marina Park nestled in sand dunes on the north peninsula of Ventura Harbor at 2 miles. The only way to avoid walking residential streets around the large harbor is to arrange a boat ride from Marina Park over to the Channel Islands National Park Visitor Center. Unless you take a boat, turn into Marina Park at a large masted playground boat and walk east. Walk along the shore of the harbor briefly before turning north through the parking lot to follow Pierpont Blvd. for about ⅜ mile. From Peninsula Street you make your way on residential streets to get around the harbor.

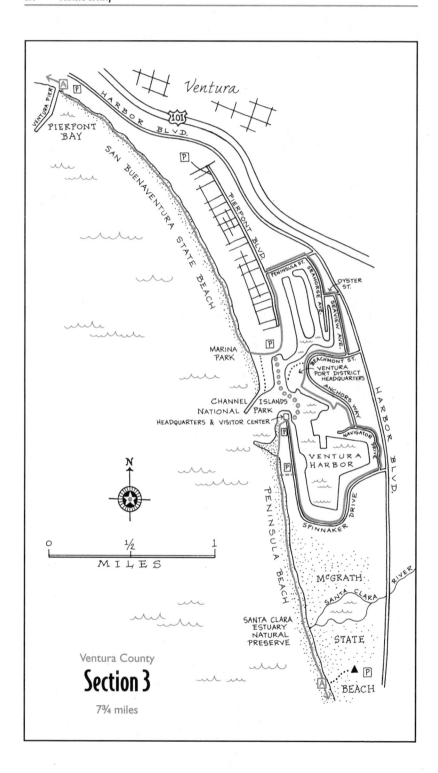

Ventura

PIERPONT BAY

VENTURA PIER

HARBOR BLVD.

101

SAN BUENAVENTURA STATE BEACH

PIERPONT BLVD.

PENINSULA ST.

SEAHORSE AVE.

OYSTER ST.

SEAVIEW AVE.

MARINA PARK

BEACHMONT ST.
VENTURA PORT DISTRICT HEADQUARTERS

ANCHORS WAY

CHANNEL ISLANDS NATIONAL PARK
HEADQUARTERS & VISITOR CENTER

NAVIGATOR DR.

HARBOR BLVD.

VENTURA HARBOR

N

SPINNAKER DRIVE

PENINSULA BEACH

McGRATH

SANTA CLARA RIVER

0   ½   1
M I L E S

SANTA CLARA ESTUARY NATURAL PRESERVE

STATE

Ventura County
Section 3
7¾ miles

BEACH

Channel Islands National Park

On clear days a tantalizing vision appears as you hike the Santa Barbara or Ventura coastline. Five islands comprising Channel Islands National Park rise from the blue Pacific Ocean, sparking curiosity about what's out there. While the five islands lie between 10 and 40 miles across the sea, extensive information about the park dwells a few yards from the CCT at Channel Islands National Park Visitor Center beside Ventura Harbor. As interpretive displays there show, the islands are largely uninhabited by humans, a landscape like California before the westward movement, full of natural wonders on land and sea.

The Channel Islands chain actually has eight islands. In 1980 Congress designated the five northern islands—Anacapa, Santa Cruz, Santa Rosa, San Miguel and Santa Barbara—plus 125,000 acres of ocean floor as a national park to protect the unique natural and cultural resources of the area. Later that year the islands gained more protection with creation of a National Marine Sanctuary extending six miles around each island. The other three islands—San Nicolas, San Clemente and Santa Catalina—lie farther south between 20 and 63 miles off the Los Angeles shore.

Chumash and Kumivit Indians made the islands home, traveling to and from the mainland in pine plank boats called tomols. Hundreds of largely undisturbed and protected archeological sites remain from the 6000-year habitation of these tribal peoples. When Juan Cabrillo landed on the islands in 1542 and claimed them for Spain, the natives must have wondered what the future held. However, it wasn't until the early 1700s that fur traders from Russia, Britain and America came and stripped the shoreline of sea otter, and hunters nearly wiped out the seal population. When Gaspar de Portola came to California to establish Spanish settlements in the late 1700s, it marked the beginning

of the end for the native residents. By the early 1800s, the Spaniards removed the island natives to mainland missions, opening the way for ranchers. Soon the ranchers were shipping sheep, cattle, honey, olives and wine to the mainland. Later the U.S. military established bases on most of the islands, providing coastal defense.

Channel Island natural resources still suffer greatly from historic cultivation and grazing, and non-native species such as ice plant, sheep, cats and rabbits. Nonetheless the unique scenic beauty, flora and fauna remain. Endemic species and large populations of pinnipeds exist here due to special conditions. First, many animals depend on both land and sea. For example, pelicans nest on Anacapa and fish for anchovies in the sea. No less than seven species of seals and sea lions, including elephant seals and California sea lions, numbering over 120,000 on San Miguel alone, use the beaches for pupping.

Second, isolation from the mainland created species related to but distinct from mainland cousins. The island fox, related to the mainland gray fox, is the size of a house cat. A dwarf mammoth roamed the islands during the Pleistocene era when the sea level was lower and the islands were connected. On San Miguel Island, mammoth fossils and peculiar sand castings (caliche) of the extensive trees that once covered the islands remain. On Santa Rosa Island, the rare Torrey pine, also from the Pleistocene, stands in two small groves.

Third, the mingling of warm and cold ocean currents creates conditions for rich kelp forests offshore and abundant tidal life. Abalone, anemones, sea urchins, purple hydrocorals, fishes and seals represent a fraction of over 1000 species living in the top 60 feet of water beneath the kelp canopy.

Severe restrictions apply in most of the park to protect natural and cultural continued on next page

From Pierpont Blvd. turn right on Peninsula Street, then right on Seahorse Avenue at 2⅞ miles. Go left on Oyster Street at 3⅛ miles, then right on Seaview Avenue to its end, where you turn right on Beachmont Street. Where Beachmont Street swings south it becomes Anchors Way Drive. At this point you can walk west out to the Ventura Port headquarters and along the waterfront in front of a hotel for about ¼ mile. Walk either on the sidewalk or along the sportsfishing docks, but then you must return to Anchors Way Drive and continue to its end. Go left on Navigator Drive to the southeast corner of the harbor, then turn right on Spinnaker Drive where boat slips and dockside businesses abound. Make your way along the waterfront on a walkway, with some detours around buildings.

After Spinnaker Drive turns north around 6 miles, you have a choice of routes. You can cut over to the beach past the sign for Ventura Harbor Village, or walk north to the end of Spinnaker and the Channel Islands National Park Visitor Center to find out about the islands and how to get a boat ride out to them. The nearest, Anacapa Island, lies 10 miles offshore while Santa Barbara Island lies 45 miles offshore.

From the Visitor Center, walk across the street to the beach and follow the tideline south. Around 7½ miles (6¾ miles if you took the shortcut), you cross the mouth of the Santa Clara River, usually crossable except during heavy rainfall or higher tides. The 160-acre Santa Clara River Estuary Natural Preserve protects the thickly vegetated estuary. At 7¾ miles the CCT continues down the beach on Ventura Section 4 and this section ends. To get to McGrath State Beach Campground, turn inland across a wide beach, then follow one of the numerous unmarked volunteers paths through the dunes to the large campground at 8¼ miles.

SUGGESTED ROUND TRIPS AND LOOPS: Walking south from the Ventura City Pier or north from McGrath Beach to the harbor mouth offers two fine round trip strolls of about 4 miles each.

McGrath Beach State Park has a short nature trail exploring the Santa Clara Estuary Natural Preserve, starting near the entrance station.

Check with the National Park Service-licensed Island Packers next to the Visitor Center about booking a trip out to the Channel Islands. Great hiking, camping and diving opportunities abound on the islands. Call (805)642-7688 for information.

Channel Islands – continued

features. The Nature Conservancy owns 90% of the largest, wildest island, Santa Cruz, with access limited to permit holders.

The islands are hard to reach, affording extra protection. The nearest, Anacapa, is 10 miles out, Santa Barbara more than 60. Wind and rough seas often create difficult landings that keep visitation low. If you can tolerate these conditions, be sure to visit the most remote California coastlines on the Channel Islands. The best time to visit is March to July, but you can go year round. Activities include boating, diving, swimming, fishing, camping, hiking and wildlife watching. Primitive camping remains the only way to stay overnight. If you want to camp, apply early (preferably at least six months in advance) to the National Park Service for a free permit.

For information on camping, hiking, permits, commercial boat and air service, and restrictions, contact:

Channel Islands National Park
1901 Spinnaker Drive
Ventura CA 93001, (805)658-5730

SECTION 4
McGrath State Beach to Port Hueneme Beach Park

DISTANCE: 8½ miles (13.7 kilometers).

OPEN TO: Hikers. Bicyclists on road.

SURFACE: Beach, sidewalk.

ACCESS POINT: McGrath State Beach.

HOW TO GET THERE: Exit Highway 101 in Ventura onto Victoria Avenue and go south to Olivas Park Drive. Turn right and drive west to Harbor Blvd., then turn left and go about one mile to the McGrath State Beach Campground entrance.

OTHER ACCESS: Mandalay County Park via 5th Street, various points along Mandalay Beach Road including Oxnard State Beach, anywhere along route on Channel Islands Blvd. and Ventura Road, Port Hueneme Beach Park.

DIFFICULTY: Easy.

ELEVATION GAIN/LOSS: Negligible.

FURTHER INFORMATION: McGrath State Beach (805)654-4744, Oxnard Department of Parks and Facilities (805)385-7950, Port Hueneme Recreation and Community Services (805)986-6555.

FACILITIES: Restrooms, water, picnic tables at McGrath State Beach, Mandalay County Park, Oxnard State Beach and Port Hueneme Beach Park.

CAMPGROUNDS: McGrath State Beach has the largest campground on the Ventura coast with 174 sites and hot showers.

LODGING: Oxnard and Port Hueneme have abundant accommodations.

This CCT section in the middle of the Ventura Coast starts out on the wide, long pleasant strand of McGrath State Beach, one of those lesser known spots in southern California where you can get away from it all in a natural setting. Then it passes several expansive, grassy parks, detours inland around not one, but two man-made harbors and a Navy base, and returns to the beach at Port Hueneme.

Day hikers need to cross the dunes from McGrath State Beach Campground to reach the Coastal Trail where it runs along the beach, about ½ mile. Follow the tideline of the sandy beach south with low vegetation-stabilized dunes above the beach. From ¾ mile, freshwater McGrath Lake lies hidden in the dunes. By one mile you might walk up to the top of the beach and follow the lake's shore to 1¼ miles. Return to the tideline and continue south. By 1⅝ miles the Mandalay Power Plant rises in the dunes on your left. You pass its water outlet jetty on the beach.

At 2 miles you reach Mandalay County Park, with 104 acres of beach and vegetated dunes, a pleasant natural habitat. The dunes reach their broadest point here, extending inland about ⅝ mile. Beyond the park around 2⅜ miles, the Ox-

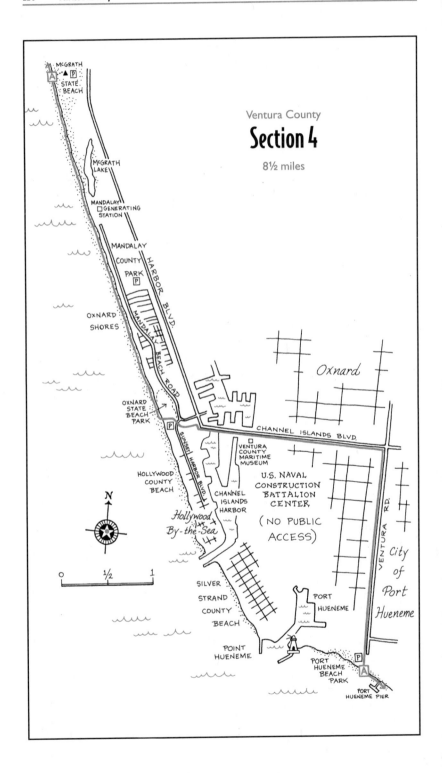

Ventura County
Section 4
8½ miles

nard Shores subdivision begins. It lies up from the beach until around 3¼ miles. The CCT continues along the beach.

At 3½ miles you come to Oxnard State Beach where low dunes once again lie up from the awesomely broad beach. Behind the dunes lies a large expanse of grass with picnic areas, athletic fields and restrooms. Continue along the beach past the main park area and a hotel until you see tall palm trees at 3¾ miles. Turn inland through a small park there to begin the walk around the harbors and the Navy base.

Walk diagonally through the park a few hundred feet to pick up a bike path at the corner of Mandalay Beach Road and Sunset Lane. The path comes out at the corner of Harbor Blvd. and Channel Islands Blvd. at 4 miles. Cross Harbor Blvd. and follow the south side of Channel Islands Blvd., crossing two bridges over the upper end of Channel Islands Harbor. On the other side, find a faux fishing village full of the usual collection of tourist shops plus a hidden jewel, the Ventura County Maritime Museum with its excellent collection of model boats.

The rest of the route follows bike lanes or sidewalks. Walk Channel Islands Blvd. on either the sidewalk on the left side or the bike lane on the right. Turn right at Ventura Road at 6 miles and follow the paved path beneath eucalyptus trees on the right side of Ventura Road that runs along the edge of the Navy base. Your route changes to sidewalk at Pleasant Valley Road at 7¾ miles and the beginning of the Port Hueneme business district. Continue along Ventura Road to its end at the Port Hueneme Beach Park at 8½ miles where you will find restrooms, picnic tables, and a fishing pier. This section and the town walk also end here.

SUGGESTED ROUND TRIPS AND LOOPS: Starting from either McGrath State Beach or Oxnard State Beach, walk out and back for an exceptional 7-mile beach stroll. You might also consider a visit to Hollywood Beach or Silver Strand Beach, two long sandy strands bypassed by the CCT.

Hollywood Beach lies just south of Oxnard State Beach. To reach Silver Strand, go south on Victoria Avenue (just east of the Maritime Museum) to its end at Ocean Avenue where the beach spans the entire oceanfront between the two harbors.

HOW TO IMPROVE THE CCT HERE: Presently the Naval Construction Battalion Center does not allow civilian foot traffic except by special permission. A multi-use public path from Janelle Park at the north jetty to Port Hueneme Beach Park through the base and around the port would eliminate the long detour inland. Locals and CCT hikers would no doubt find it a better way to get from one side of town to the other.

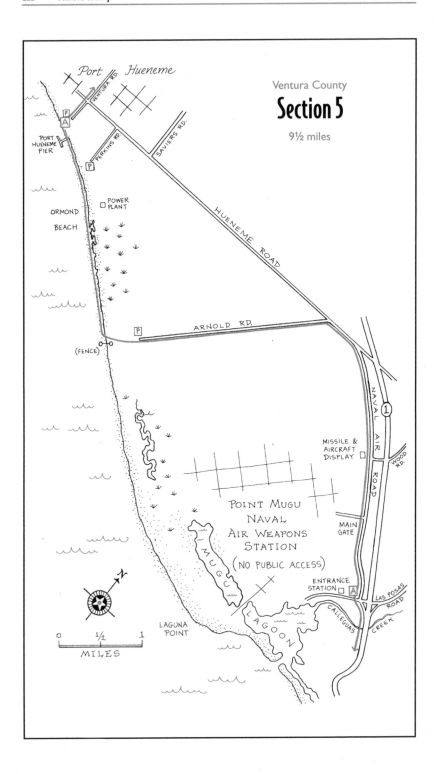

Port Hueneme

Ventura County
Section 5
9½ miles

VENTURA RD.

P
A

PORT
HUENEME
PIER

P PERKINS RD.

SAVIERS RD.

POWER
PLANT

ORMOND
BEACH

HUENEME ROAD

P ARNOLD RD.

(FENCE)

MISSILE &
AIRCRAFT
DISPLAY

NAVAL AIR ROAD

1

WOOD RD.

MAIN
GATE

POINT MUGU
NAVAL
AIR WEAPONS
STATION
(NO PUBLIC ACCESS)

MUGU LAGOON

LAGUNA
POINT

ENTRANCE
STATION A

CALLEGUAS CREEK

LAS POSAS ROAD

0   ½   1
MILES

SECTION 5
Port Hueneme Beach Park to Point Mugu Naval Air Station Entrance at Las Posas Road

DISTANCE: 9½ miles (15.3 kilometers).

OPEN TO: Hikers. Bicyclists on road.

SURFACE: Beach, road shoulder.

ACCESS POINT: Port Hueneme Beach Park.

HOW TO GET THERE: From Highway 101 take the Oxnard Blvd. exit. Head south about 6 miles to Hueneme Road and turn west (Oxnard Blvd. becomes Saviers Road). In one mile turn south on Ventura Road and drive to its end (.5 mile). From Highway 1 take Hueneme Road west to Ventura Road. Turn left and go south to its end at Port Hueneme Beach Park.

OTHER ACCESS: You can reach Ormond Beach from Perkins Road or Arnold Drive.

DIFFICULTY: Easy.

ELEVATION GAIN/LOSS: 20 feet+/10 feet-.

FURTHER INFORMATION: Oxnard Dept. of Parks and Facilities (805)385-7950, Port Hueneme Recreation and Community Services (805)986-6555, Naval Air Station Public Affairs Office (805)989-8094.

FACILITIES: Port Hueneme Beach Park has restrooms, water and picnic tables, with the usual city amenities nearby. There are no other facilities on the route.

CAMPGROUNDS: Point Mugu State Park on the next section has 54 improved sites in Sycamore Canyon Campground and 88 primitive sites at Thornhill Broome State Beach.

LODGING: Port Hueneme and Oxnard have abundant accommodations.

This walk starts out on a great sandy swath of beach that soon leaves the hustle and bustle behind, only to be forced inland after 3 miles by a barrier, in this case the Point Mugu Naval Air Station, requiring a long walk on the road shoulder.

From Port Hueneme Beach Park, head south on the beach past the pier and the developed beachfront, leaving it behind at 1¼ miles where you reach Ormond Beach. The undeveloped beach has extensive wetlands behind the low dunes, home to endangered species, numerous wetland-unfriendly businesses, a power plant and agriculture. Not surprisingly, it's a battleground between environmentalists and developers. The value of southern California land, even if it's wet, creates tremendous pressures to develop. An important remnant of a vast wetlands hangs on here, and the Ormond Beach Observers continue to make great strides towards protecting it.

At the end of the lightly used beach you come to the Navy Base fence at 3 miles. Follow the fence inland across the wide beach to the end of Arnold Road at 3⅜ miles. Walk the shoulder of Arnold Road through agricultural fields. At 5⅞ miles the CCT turns right to follow Hueneme Road through more farms. Turn right again at 6¼ miles onto Naval Air Road paralleling Highway 1. At 7⅞ miles you pass a roadside display of historic missile weaponry and airplanes tested and evaluated at the base.

At 8⅜ you pass the main gate and the base security office. Past the main gate the road narrows, so use caution walking its narrow shoulder. The hike ends at 9½ miles at Las Posas Road just down the road from another entrance station.

SUGGESTED ROUND TRIPS AND LOOPS: Ormond Beach from the Port Hueneme Pier south to Arnold Road and back makes a fine 6-mile stroll on a little-visited beach with great opportunities for wildlife viewing.

HOW TO IMPROVE THE CCT HERE: The Naval Air Station, with 6½ miles of relatively un-damaged beach and dunes and 2000 acres of wildlife rich wetlands around Mugu Lagoon, operates an environmental and archeological program. They take care to protect the several endangered species, keep the wetland healthy and offer environmental tours to civic groups and schools. The base is otherwise closed to the public. The possibility exists that a public trail may be allowed through the base on a restricted basis sometime in the future. Also, the Santa Monica Mountains National Recreation Area has an agreement in hand that if the base closes, they will take over the beach and wetlands area, managing it to protect these remarkable natural features. The Naval Air Station also occupies San Nicholas Island, a highly protected environmental and archeological area, and the farthest offshore of the eight Channel Islands.

SECTION 6
Point Mugu Naval Air Station Entrance at Las Posas Road to Sycamore Cove Beach, Point Mugu State Park

DISTANCE: 6¼ miles (10.1 kilometers).

OPEN TO: Hikers. Bicyclists on road.

SURFACE: Beach, road shoulder.

ACCESS POINT: Las Posas Road at Highway 1 (Pacific Coast Highway).

HOW TO GET THERE: Take Las Posas Road exit off Highway 1 and go south just a few hundred feet to the intersection of Las Posas Road and Naval Air Road.

OTHER ACCESS: Mugu Beach, Thornhill Broome Beach and along Highway 1.

DIFFICULTY: Easy.

ELEVATION GAIN/LOSS: 70 feet+/80 feet-.

CAUTIONS: Watch for steep drop-offs at Mugu Rock. Use caution when walking highway shoulder.

FURTHER INFORMATION: Angeles District, California State Parks (818)880-0350.

FACILITIES: Thornhill Broome Beach and Sycamore Cove Beach have water, picnic tables and restrooms. While no facilities currently exist at Las Posas Road, a Santa Monica Mountains National Recreation Area Visitor Center is planned near this location in the future.

CAMPGROUNDS: Thornhill Broome State Beach with 88 primitive sites, Sycamore Canyon Campground with 54 sites and flush toilets, and La Jolla Group Camp are all at Point Mugu State Park.

LODGING: Port Hueneme and Oxnard have the nearest lodgings.

Less than a mile from Las Posas Road, the northern end of the scenic, rugged Santa Monica Mountains rises dramatically from the Oxnard Plain. Congress designated the state, federal, and county parks and beaches within the region as the Santa Monica Mountains National Recreation Area (SMMNRA), which reaches 70 miles down coast into Los Angeles County. The SMMNRA abounds in opportunities for hiking, biking, swimming, surfing, camping, sightseeing and even backpacking. The NRA brims with archeological sites, historic locations, and an ecosystem rich in plant and animal life. Read more about this great area in the adjacent feature article.

From Las Posas Road, walk down onto the wide bare strip of land between the highway onramp and the Navy base fence. Follow it ¼ mile to the Calleguas Creek bridge. Since the freeway ends at the north end of the bridge, cautiously cross the bridge and follow the wide shoulder of the Pacific Coast Highway. Beyond the fence inside the base and off limits to the public, extensive pickle weed

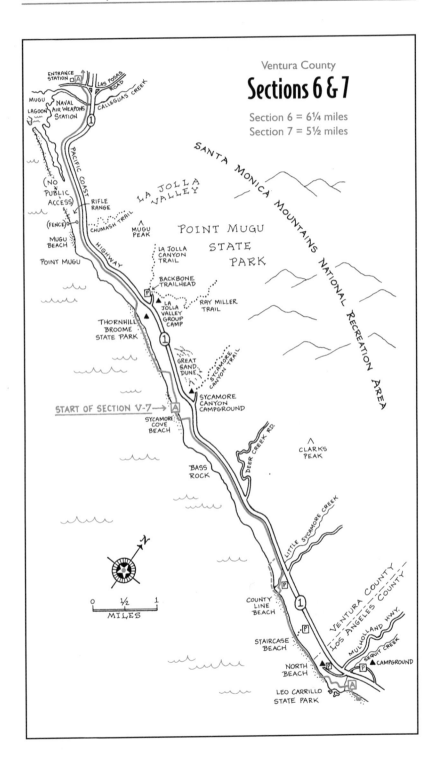

Ventura County
Sections 6 & 7

Section 6 = 6¼ miles
Section 7 = 5½ miles

ENTRANCE STATION
LAS POSAS ROAD
CALLEGUAS CREEK
MUGU LAGOON
NAVAL AIR WEAPONS STATION
PACIFIC COAST

SANTA MONICA MOUNTAINS NATIONAL RECREATION AREA

(NO PUBLIC ACCESS)
RIFLE RANGE
CHUMASH TRAIL
(FENCE)
MUGU BEACH
POINT MUGU
HIGHWAY

LA JOLLA VALLEY
MUGU PEAK

POINT MUGU STATE PARK

LA JOLLA CANYON TRAIL
BACKBONE TRAILHEAD
LA JOLLA VALLEY GROUP CAMP
RAY MILLER TRAIL

THORNHILL BROOME STATE PARK

GREAT SAND DUNE
SYCAMORE CANYON TRAIL

START OF SECTION V-7 →
SYCAMORE COVE BEACH
SYCAMORE CANYON CAMPGROUND

BASS ROCK

DEER CREEK RD.

CLARKS PEAK

LITTLE SYCAMORE CREEK

N

0   ½   1
MILES

COUNTY LINE BEACH

VENTURA COUNTY
LOS ANGELES COUNTY

MULHOLLAND HWY.
SEQUIT CREEK
CAMPGROUND

STAIRCASE BEACH

NORTH BEACH

LEO CARRILLO STATE PARK

marshes of Mugu Lagoon reach to the dunes. At 1½ miles you reach a wildlife viewing deck overlooking the marsh. A boardwalk is planned from the proposed Visitor Center at Las Posas Road to this deck. Continue along the wide shoulder. After passing a fence marking the southern limit of the closed area of the base, you overlook Mugu Beach at 2¾ miles with monolithic Mugu Rock looming at the other end. On the inland side of the highway, the Chumash Trail climbs over a pass to secluded La Jolla Valley. For the main CCT route, either continue on the road shoulder or drop down to the beach for the short stroll to Mugu Rock at 3 miles. The newer Pacific Coast Highway runs straight to pass through a huge man-made slash in Mugu Rock, cutting it off from its mother mountains.

For a short side trip, take the old roadbed angling around the seaward side of the rock to see why the highway was moved. In a few hundred yards the pavement of the old roadbed abruptly ends at a jagged edge, cut by an eroding ravine. On the big tidal rocks below, just before the broken off highway, you will find an impressive bed of fossil shells imbedded in the rock. Do not attempt to make your way around the upper end of the ravine on a narrow and dangerous volunteer trail. Return to the highway shoulder to continue south.

After passing through the man-made slash in the rock, the highway hugs the riprapped coast, so the only practical route stays on the highway shoulder to the beginning of Thornhill Broome Beach at 4⅞ miles. Across the highway you can see the mouth of La Jolla Canyon where the Backbone Trailhead marks the western end of the 64-mile Santa Monica Mountains Backbone Trail, a CCT High Route Alternate. For a description of that route, see Ventura Section 6A.

For the main CCT route, make your way down to the cobble and sand of Thornhill Broome Beach. Walk along the tideline past the campground. At the other end of the beach, climb up to the highway atop a low rise at 5⅞ miles. Walk the highway shoulder for only a short way, with the Great Sand Dune rising on the other side of the road, then descend from the highway to Sycamore Cove Beach with a State Park Ranger Station and picnic area. The section ends at the picnic area at 6¼ miles. Sycamore Canyon Campground, also the start of the Sycamore Canyon Trail, sits across the highway.

ALTERNATE ROUTE: The 64-mile-long Backbone Trail begins at La Jolla Canyon. When completed in a few years, it will provide a fine inland backpack trip along the rugged scenic ridges of the Santa Monica Mountains. See Ventura Section 6A for more on the Backbone Trail.

An alternate walk from Mugu Rock to Sycamore Canyon takes the Chumash Trail, which starts across the highway from the gunnery range, the La Jolla Loop Trial, and the Backbone Trail down to Sycamore Canyon Trail and back to the coast for a beautiful hike of about 8 miles.

SUGGESTED ROUND TRIPS AND LOOPS: The best thing any hiker dedicated to hiking and exploring can do is get a trail map of Santa Monica Mountains National Recreation Area which includes 15,000-acre Point Mugu State Park and many other public lands. We offer three trails here to explore the wild and scenic backcountry of Point Mugu State Park. All three trails intersect inland offering various loop possibilities. The Chumash Trail, across the highway from Mugu Beach, climbs steeply up a hillside on a trail used by the Chumash to get from their La Jolla Val-

Santa Monica Mountains National Recreation Area

The 150,000-acre Santa Monica Mountains National Recreation Area (SMMNRA), established in 1978, preserves the region's unique ecosystems and rich cultural and natural history. This beautiful, diverse area, bounded by Mugu Lagoon and the Oxnard Plain on the west, Conejo Valley and San Fernando Valley on the north, and the coast on the south, reaches all the way to the edge of downtown Los Angeles 46 miles east of Point Mugu.

A patchwork of 60,000 acres of parks and the famed Malibu coast comprise the Recreation Area. With a resident population of about 80,000 people, it nestles in the midst of the vast urban development of Los Angeles and Ventura counties. It offers diverse recreational opportunities including hiking on 570 miles of trails, camping, backpacking, cycling, horseback riding, plant and wildlife observation, and visiting cultural sites such as Chumash villages, historic ranches and movie sets. The coast offers many water-oriented pursuits on miles of beaches. A variety of cultural events such as art shows and concerts occur at various locations.

The unique Mediterranean climate, hot summers and cool, wet winters, creates a varied ecosystem with chaparral, oak woodlands, coastal sage scrub, and riparian woodlands. Fifty-three species of mammals live here including mountain lions, deer, gray fox, badger, striped skunk and coyote. Birds of 263 species reside or visit here, including more types of raptors than are seen anywhere in the United States except one area in Idaho.

The National Park Service oversees the SMMNRA, coordinating planning activities among more than 60 government agencies and countless private landowners, acquiring new parkland, and informing the public. Park literature lists 47 individual features, with California State Parks running the largest units including 15,000-acre Point Mugu State Park (with the only officially designated wilderness area), 7000-acre Malibu Creek State Park and 10,000-acre Topanga Canyon State Park.

Other highlights of the SMMNRA include:

• Will Rogers State Historic Park – Highlighted by the ranch house the famed humorist built in 1928, which contains abundant artifacts from his life, the park also includes an active polo field, stables and several miles of trails including the eastern trailhead of the Backbone Trail.

• Circle X Ranch – This old Boy Scout camp now administered by the National Park Service features a campground and the highest point in the Santa Monica range, 3111-foot Sandstone Peak. The popular Mishe Mokwa Trail circles the peak through spectacular mountain scenery.

• Leo Carrillo State Beach – This coastal park features several miles of beach and a campground under giant sycamore trees along the creek. Nicholas Flat Trail leads to an upland oak valley with a small lake.

• Paramount Ranch – Western Town, an active movie set open to the public even during filming, is the main attraction here. Since the 1920s, hundreds of movies and TV series used the location. Several trails explore the area, with links to Malibu Creek State Park and the Backbone Trail.

• Santa Monica Pier and Beach – The wide sandy beach, the most popular on the west coast, hosts millions of visitors each year, with everything from rollerblading to surfing to body building. The pier amusement park features an antique carousel with 44 hand-carved horses. Downtown Santa Monica sits adjacent to the beach and pier.

• Rancho Sierra Vista/Satwiwa – Here you'll find historic evidence of the equestrian heritage of Spanish and American settlers and of the Chumash Indian culture at the Native American Indian Culture Center.

• Malibu Creek State Park – This park

ley village down to the coast. The Ray Miller Trailhead at the La Jolla Canyon parking lot starts the Backbone Trail. See more about the Backbone Trail in Ventura Section 6A. The Big Sycamore Canyon Trail from the end of the Sycamore Canyon Campground explores a lovely canyon full of huge sycamore trees and lush vegetation.

SECTION 6A
Backbone Trail, Santa Monica Mountains National Recreation Area
Ray Miller Trailhead to Will Rogers State Park

DISTANCE: 64⅛ miles plus 2 miles to Will Rogers State Beach (103.2 + 3.2=106.4 kilometers).

OPEN TO: Hikers and equestrians. Bicyclists on part.

SURFACE: Trail, road shoulder.

ACCESS POINT: Ray Miller Trailhead.

HOW TO GET THERE: Ray Miller Trailhead is on the inland side of Highway 1 across from Thornhill Broome State Beach, about 7 miles west of the Ventura/Los Angeles County line.

OTHER ACCESS: Circle X Ranch, Mishe Mokwa Trailhead, Kanan Dume Road/Newton Canyon Trailhead, Latigo Canyon Road Trailhead, Corral Canyon Road Trailhead, Malibu Creek State Park, Tapia Park, Piuma Trailhead, Dark Canyon Trailhead, Saddle Creek Road, Stunt Road/Saddle Peak Road/Schueren Road junction, Topanga State Park: Dead Horse Trailhead, Trippet Ranch.

SMMNRA – continued
features astounding natural features and a campground. Malibu Creek, with the second southernmost steelhead run on the west coast, winds through the wild Goat Buttes area, oak woodlands and rich riparian zones before descending a deep canyon to the sea. Twenty trails take hikers into wild and remote country in this 7000-acre park.

Information for this article was adapted from Mountains to Ocean, A Guide to the Santa Monica Mountains National Recreation Area, published by the Southwest Parks and Monuments Association.

For more information on the SMMNRA, contact these agencies:

National Park Service
SMMNRA Visitor Center
30401 Agoura Road
Agoura Hills, CA 91301
(818)597-9192

California State Parks
1925 Las Virgines Road
Calabasas, CA 91302
(818)880-0350

Santa Monica Mountains Conservancy
3700 Solstice Canyon
Malibu, CA 90265
(310)456-5046

DIFFICULTY: Strenuous.

ELEVATION GAIN/LOSS: 8800 feet+/8300 feet- for Backbone Trail. 8800 feet+/8800 feet-including final two miles to beach.

CAUTIONS: Carry ample water. Beware of rattlesnakes, ticks, poison oak, deer flies, harvester ants and possibly Africanized bees. In summer, the days are hot, black flies can be a nuisance, and most of the route is very dry. Extreme fire hazard in summer and fall. No smoking or fires along the Backbone Trail.

FURTHER INFORMATION: Santa Monica Mountains National Recreation Area Visitor Center, National Park Service, 401 West Hillcrest Drive, Thousand Oaks CA 91360 or call (805)370-2301. California State Parks, 1925 Las Virgines Road, Calabasas CA 91302 or call (818)880-0350.

FACILITIES: Water, tables, restrooms or chemical toilets at Ray Miller Trailhead, Danielson Camp, Malibu Creek State Park, Tapia Park, Trippet Ranch, Musch Camp, Will Rogers State Historic Park.

CAMPGROUNDS ON OR NEAR THE BACKBONE TRAIL: Point Mugu State Park: Thornhill Broome State Beach Campground, La Jolla Group Camp, La Jolla Canyon Wilderness Camp, Danielson Multiuse Camp. National Recreation Area: Circle X Ranch Group Camp. Malibu Creek State Park Campground. Topanga State Park: Musch Camp.

CAMPGROUNDS IN AREA: Point Mugu State Park: Sycamore Canyon Campground. Leo Carrillo State Beach Campground.

HOSTEL: Santa Monica Hostel, downtown Santa Monica (310)393-9913.

LODGING: You have a wide choice of hotels and inns located in various communities surrounding Santa Monica Mountains National Recreation Area.

The 30-year-old dream of a Santa Monica Mountains Backbone Trail from the Griffith Observatory in Hollywood to the coast at Point Mugu failed to materialize in the early years. It seemed doomed to failure because of daunting private property holdings and development. Now after years of work by hundreds of dedicated people and several organizations, the Backbone Trail From Point Mugu to Will Rogers State Park nears completion. Much work remains including land acquisition for the last segment, installing signs, and providing water supplies for backcountry camps.

The completion of the Backbone Trail calls attention to a remarkable feat. It traverses some of the most rugged topography on the California coast as well as some of the most threatened by development. The area found new life by the creation of the Santa Monica Mountains National Recreation Area in 1978 and by the large State Parks pre-dating the Recreation Area. For more on the history and features of this remarkable area, read the feature article *Santa Monica Mountains National Recreation Area.*

At 66⅛ miles this alternate CCT High Route takes 29 miles longer than the coastal route and a whopping 8600 feet more elevation gain and loss, but it definitely has plenty to recommend it if you are game and fit.

A brief description of the Backbone Trail follows which we hope will whet

Hikers pass dramatic cliffs and peaks on the Backbone Trail.

your appetite to explore this wonderful region, walk the Backbone Trail, and become an advocate for the protection of the area and the completion and upkeep of the trail. The trail, rough and vague in parts, remains unsigned in some areas. In some cases the final route remains undetermined out of several possible existing or potential trails. Furthermore, long distances between trail camps with water discourage backpacking. Plans call for more camps. If you are through-hiking the CCT and choose this route over the much more populated coastal route, then a car pick up at day's end and a return ride back to the trailhead the next day permits comfortable day hiking. The sixteen road crossings along the route support this method.

To find out more about the status of the trail, check in at the Santa Monica Mountains National Recreation Area Visitor Center for maps and updates. Maps showing the Backbone Trail and other trails in the region can be ordered from Tom Harrison Cartography, (415)456-7940, or Trails Illustrated, (800)962-1643. The Backbone Trail gets covered briefly in a book by Milt McAuley, the dean of Santa Monica Mountains trails and one of the major forces in creating the Backbone Trail. Order *Hiking Trails of the Santa Monica Mountains*, 6th edition, from Canyon Publishing Company, 8561 Eatough Avenue, Canoga Park CA 91305.

PART I: Ray Miller Trailhead to Mishe Mokwa Trailhead.

DISTANCE: 16⅞ miles (27.2 kilometers).

The Backbone Trail starts in La Jolla Canyon at the Ray Miller Trailhead across Highway 1 from Thornhill Broome State Beach. This section through the wild and scenic Point Mugu State Park requires a two-day backpack trip or a one-day marathon hike because you meet no intersecting roads until 16⅞ miles at the

East Gate Trailhead on Yerba Buena Road. Danielson Camp at 7½ miles has water and a restroom.

The equestrian route takes the Ray Miller Trail and intersects with the Sycamore Canyon Trail at 5⅞ 1miles. The longer hiking route follows La Jolla Canyon into the lovely grassy flats of the upper canyon, the site of a significant Chumash village and the La Jolla Valley Walk-in Camp at 4 miles. The trail descends to the Sycamore Canyon Trail at 5⅞ miles (That popular tree-lined multi-use trail transects the mountains between Rancho Sierra Vista in Potrero Valley and Sycamore Canyon Campground at the ocean). You take Sycamore Canyon Trail to reach Danielson Camp with water, toilets and tables at 7½ miles. The trail then ascends the flank of scenic Boney Mountain. This waterless route climbs steadily for 7 miles from 400 feet to almost 3000 feet just below the highest point in the Santa Monica Mountains, Sandstone Peak (so called despite its volcanic origin) at 3111 feet. A short, steep spur trail climbs to the summit. The Backbone Trail route flanks the peak and descends to the Mishe Mokwa Trailhead at 16⅞ miles.

PART 2: East Gate Trailhead to Kanan Dume Road.
DISTANCE: 12⅛ miles (19.6 kilometers).

The first 5¼ miles of this route stays on the road. At press time, the National Park Service nears acquisition of the land needed to complete this last link in the Backbone Trail. Cautiously walk the shoulder of Little Sycamore Canyon Road, crossing the Ventura/Los Angeles County line at 2½ miles, then take Mulholland Highway to the Clarke Ranch Motorway Trailhead at 4¾ miles. Walk ½ mile on this trail to reach Encinal Canyon Road at 5¼ miles. Follow Encinal Canyon Road for 1¾ miles to Zuma Ridge Motorway at 7 miles. A new section of the Backbone Trail completed in early 1999 intersects the Zuma Ridge Motorway at 7¾ miles and reaches Kanan Dume Road at 12⅛ miles (29 miles from start).

PART 3: Kanan Dume Road to Tapia Park.
DISTANCE: 10¾ miles (17.3 kilometers).

You have a choice of two routes for the last half of this section. The official route continues more or less directly to Tapia Park while the more interesting and longer alternate route goes through Malibu Creek State Park, taking you through a bit of old Hollywood movie making history.

Take the Backbone Trail from the Kanan Dume parking lot. At ⅜ mile you cross the ridge over the road tunnel. At 2⅛ miles you reach Latigo Canyon Road and the Bulldog Motorway junction at 4⅜ miles. The Bulldog Motorway takes you on the Malibu Creek State Park alternate route. You'll pass the site of the movie and TV series *M.A.S.H.* and Century Ranch, the location for many westerns. You'll also see some great scenery as you pass lovely little Century Lake, walk among oak woodlands, then along Malibu Creek at the base of the striking Goat Buttes. You'll find a campground in Malibu Creek State Park. A connector trail from the campground joins the official route at Tapia Park.

The main route follows the Castro Crest, reaching a parking lot at Corral Canyon Road at 5¼ miles. You reach Peak 2049 at 7¾ miles, then descend 1500 feet into Malibu Canyon and Tapia Park at 10¾ miles (39¾ miles from start).

PART 4: **Tapia Park to Dead Horse Trail parking lot on Topanga Canyon Blvd.**

DISTANCE: 13⅜ miles (21.6 kilometers).

Dominated by Saddle Peak, this section climbs 2700 feet in 6⅝ miles before making the long descent down Hondo Canyon.

From the Tapia Park parking lot, the trail crosses Malibu Canyon Road at Piuma Road, parallels Cold Creek for ¼ mile, and then starts the long, steady climb up the flanks of Saddle Peak. It crosses Piuma Road at 1½ miles and continues winding up the mountain. You reach Saddle Peak at 6⅝ miles before starting down the other side. You come to the Stunt/Saddle Peak/Schueren Road junction at 7⅝ miles. Parallel the road for a short distance, then start down into Hondo Canyon. Cross Old Topanga Canyon Blvd. at 12¼ miles before crossing Topanga Canyon Road to the Dead Horse Trail parking lot off of Entrada Road at 13⅜ miles (53⅛ miles from start).

PART 5: **Dead Horse Trail parking lot to Will Rogers State Historic Park.**

DISTANCE: 11 miles (13 miles to Will Rogers State Beach) (17.7, 20.9 kilometers).

Take the Dead Horse Trail from the parking lot off Entrada Road above Topanga Canyon Blvd. and reach Trippit Ranch at 1⅛ miles. You'll find a Topanga State Park ranger station here with water, restrooms, picnic tables and a phone. Take the Musch Ranch Trail to reach Musch Camp at 2⅛ miles. This first-come first-served walk-in camp can be used by groups or as eight individual camps. You reach Eagle Junction at 3⅛ miles. Take either the North Loop via Eagle Rock or the South Loop via Eagle Springs. They come together at the Hub junction at 4½ miles. From the Hub, take the Rogers Trail to reach Will Rogers State Historic Park at 11 miles (64⅛ miles from start).

To complete the coast-to-coast connection, continue down the park entry road, turn right and follow Sunset Blvd., go left on Chatauqua Blvd. to its end, and carefully cross Highway 1 to Will Rogers State Beach. On the beach you meet the CCT's main route on L.A. Section 5, a sharp contrast to the chaparral-covered slopes of the last 66⅛ miles, to continue your journey to the Mexican border.

VENTURA SECTION 7
Sycamore Cove Beach, Point Mugu State Park, to Leo Carrillo State Beach

DISTANCE: 5½ miles (8.9 kilometers).

OPEN TO: Hikers. Bicyclists on road.

SURFACE: Beach, road shoulder.

ACCESS POINT: Sycamore Cove Beach.

HOW TO GET THERE: On Highway 1 about 4.5 miles north of the Los Angeles/Ventura County line, turn west into the Sycamore Cove Beach parking lot entrance opposite the campground on the inland side of the highway.

OTHER ACCESS: Anywhere along Highway 1.

DIFFICULTY: Easy.

ELEVATION GAIN/LOSS: 80 feet+/80 feet-.

FURTHER INFORMATION: Angeles District, California State Parks (818) 880-0350.

FACILITIES: Sycamore Cove Beach and Leo Carrillo State Beach have water, picnic tables and restrooms.

CAMPGROUNDS: Sycamore Canyon Campground east of the highway at Point Mugu State Park has 54 sites. Leo Carrillo State Beach has 127 sites and hot showers.

LODGING: Oxnard, Port Hueneme and the Malibu coast to the south all have accommodations.

MAP: See page 226.

This last Ventura County section offers, like most of the Ventura walks, sharp contrasts in the condition of the coastline and the trail. The first part follows the road because of extensive riprap, while the second half follows relatively undisturbed scenic beaches.

From the Sycamore Cove Beach picnic area, walk up to the bike lane on Pacific Coast Highway and head south. The highway and the riprap protecting it obliterate most of the beach and tidal rocks. At medium to low tides you can scramble down the rocks to several pocket beaches marked by coastal access signs along the road, but for the most part, the bike lane or road shoulder offers the easiest alternative. Along the shoulder you round a point at ½ mile where the mountains tower on your left, then dip to the mouth of a small canyon. The highway dips close to sea level to cross another canyon at ⅞ mile, then passes Bass Rock at 1¼ miles. Contour east to the highway's intersection with Deer Creek Road around 1⅞ miles, where a stairway descends to a beach.

Contour east along the shoulder before dipping almost to sea level around 2¼ miles. Climbing back to a narrow shelf at the base of the steep mountains, the highway crosses the mouth of another small canyon at 2½ miles, then contours above the surf. By 3⅛ miles you reach a row of houses on the low bluff. At low tide you can climb down the rocks to the exposed beach and walk in front of the houses and around a little point at the mouth of Little Sycamore Creek. Otherwise, stay on the road to cross Little Sycamore Creek bridge at 3⅝ miles.

Once across the bridge, turn right and follow the path out to the point and an informal parking area overlooking County Line Beach, also called Yerba Buena Beach. Descend to the beach, where surfers are usually catching rides on the point break, and walk the tideline east. As the beach narrows around 3¾ miles, you have to negotiate around riprap if the tide is low enough, otherwise return to the road until Staircase Beach.

If you can make it around the riprap, continue along the beach to a massive seawall protecting a condo project. If the beach in front of the seawall is flooded, take the stairs marked "NO TRESPASSING" up the seawall. The sign refers to the sandy flat in front of the building, not the stairs. You can walk on the seawall for 600 feet to the other end and another set of stairs leading down to the beach where you will find scenic natural bluffs. Note the remarkable contrast of these bluffs to the seawall you have just negotiated.

Around a rocky tidal point you reach public steps coming down to Staircase Beach beyond 4 miles. A small parking lot and a chemical toilet sit on the marine terrace above. Continue down the beach and watch for concrete steps coming down the bluff around 4¼ miles. These decorative steps, built by the owners of a house now gone, are worth a short detour to explore.

Beyond the steps you cross the Ventura/Los Angeles County line. At 4¾ miles you reach North Leo Carrillo State Beach and the beachside campground and parking lot. Walk to the far end of the beach beyond 5 miles.

At low tide you can stay on the beach and walk through an ocean cave under Sequit Point to reach the other side. Otherwise, walk up to the campground ac-

The beach at the Ventura-Los Angeles county line.

cess road and follow it up to the flat top of Sequit Point. A wooden stairway from Sequit Point drops to a pocket beach and access to the cave. To continue over the point, take the path leading out to the point overlooking dramatic tidal rocks, then follow the trail around the point where fencing along the trail protects habitat restoration work. Near the second lifeguard station, take the paved path leading down to Sequit Creek and the beach at 5½ miles. Both the access road and a walkway under the highway next to the creek lead to the day-use parking and canyon campground at Leo Carrillo State Park. The usually dry creek is rarely impassable during storms, but if it is, carefully walk across the highway to the parking lot.

SUGGESTED ROUND TRIPS AND LOOPS: Walk the beach from either County Line Beach or Sequit Point out and back for a 4-mile round trip. The eroding cliffs above the attractive beach bloom profusely with giant coreopsis and other coastal plants in spring.

The Nicholas Flat Trail starts near the Leo Carrillo Campground entrance station. The 8-mile round trip climbs through fragrant chaparral slopes to oak-studded Nicholas Flats and a remarkably scenic pond.

Los Angeles County

MILLIONS OF PEOPLE HAVE SETTLED in the southern California region for its great weather, endless outdoor recreation opportunities and wonderful scenery. Los Angeles County and vicinity boast spectacular snow capped, forested mountain ranges, vast scenic deserts, and a sparkling coastline rimmed by mountains in the north and backed by a level plain in the south. The L.A. coast has great scenery, fascinating history, warm water to swim in, remoteness if you walk for it, and mile upon mile of public beaches for sunbathing, swimming, fishing, beach-combing, and hiking. The more than 65 million visits locals and tourists make annually attest to the popularity of the beaches. To some people Los Angeles County conjures images of endless subdivisions, clogged freeways and smog-filled air. While L.A. does have its problems, most of them are left behind when people head for the coast, where most of the beaches are fun, remarkably safe and easily accessible.

In the county's northwest, the Santa Monica Mountains National Recreation Area not only provides a dramatic backdrop to the westernmost coast, but also offers the 64-mile Backbone Trail, a wilderness ridgetop alternative to the coast route (see Ventura County Section 6A). In the south, the Palos Verdes Peninsula is like an island separated from the city by steep terrain and strict development restrictions. It offers the 26-mile Palos Verdes Loop Trail through hidden canyons with vistas of ocean, coast, harbor and city.

Los Angeles County also boasts Catalina Island, with a partially intact southern California ecosystem, 26 miles off the coast. The Santa Catalina Island Conservancy protects 86% of the 76 square miles in a semi-wilderness condition, permitting public access to beaches, trails and campgrounds. Boats depart daily from Long Beach and San Pedro in Los Angeles County and from Newport Beach and Dana Point in Orange County for the two-hour crossing.

The California Coastal Trail in Los Angeles County starts at the Ventura County border a little west of Leo Carrillo State Beach, then skirts the base of the Santa Monica Mountains along the famous Malibu coast, the wildest part of the county's coast, winding on and off beaches and streets and even under houses built on the sand, before hitting the paved South Bay Trail and the beaches of Santa Monica Bay. The CCT passes unique beach towns such as Venice and Manhattan Beach, several marinas and four piers before reaching the Palos Verdes Peninsula.

On the mountainous Palos Verdes Peninsula, the trail follows the mostly rocky tideline at the base of steep, dramatic cliffs, then follows streets and winds through parks. At the southern end of the peninsula, San Pedro overlooks the vast Long Beach and Los Angeles ports that fill the sheltered harbor. After a walk through Point Fermin Park with its historic lighthouse and a look at the Cabrillo Marine Museum, the route circles the vast Los Angeles/Long Beach Harbor complex before reaching downtown Long Beach. If you arrange a boat ride from Ports O'Call Village in San Pedro to the city of Long Beach, you can avoid that long industrial leg. The last part of the walk traverses the long beach after which the city is so aptly named, then circles around Naples Marina before arriving at the San Gabriel River and Orange County.

SECTION 1
Leo Carrillo State Beach to Zuma Beach County Park

DISTANCE: 8 miles (12.9 kilometers).

OPEN TO: Hikers.

SURFACE: Beach, streets, highway shoulder.

ACCESS POINT: Leo Carrillo State Beach.

HOW TO GET THERE: Turn off Highway 1 14.3 miles north of the Malibu town center (about 25 miles north of Santa Monica) or 20 miles south of Oxnard. Turn into the clearly marked Leo Carrillo State Beach entrance road on the inland side of the highway just down the coast from the Mulholland Highway intersection and drive past the entrance kiosk to the day-use parking lot.

OTHER ACCESS: Nicholas Canyon County Beach, stairs to the beach at the 31100 & 31300 blocks of Broad Beach Road, parking for El Pescador, El Matador and La Piedra State Beaches, all signed on the highway.

DIFFICULTY: Easy.

ELEVATION GAIN/LOSS: Negligible.

CAUTIONS: Rocky points and coves are flooded at high tide.

FURTHER INFORMATION: Leo Carrillo State Park (818)880-0350, Malibu Division, California State Parks (310)457-8140, Los Angeles County Lifeguard Service, Northern Section(310)457-9891.

FACILITIES: Toilets, water, picnic tables and parking at Leo Carrillo, El Pescador, La Piedra, El Matador State Beaches and Zuma Beach County Park.

CAMPGROUNDS: Leo Carrillo State Beach has 127 sites and hot showers.

LODGING: The Malibu coast has ample accommodations.

Leo Carrillo was a popular movie, TV and Broadway actor, most notably as the sidekick of the Cisco Kid in that 1950s TV series. ("Oh Pancho!, Oh Cisco!" exclaimed the characters to each other to close every story.) Governor Earl Warren appointed Carrillo to the State Beaches and Parks Commission, and he played an instrumental role in public acquisition of much of the land between Malibu Lagoon and Point Mugu. Leo Carrillo State Beach includes almost two miles of coast plus rugged canyons and ridges inland.

The route, passing along some of the most beautiful beaches in southern California, can be negotiated in its entirety only at lower tides. If the tide is in, you must walk along the highway with a chance to visit beaches using several of the accesses mentioned in Other Access above. Beach hikers should keep in mind those same accesses to escape rising tides.

To begin this walk, park in the Leo Carrillo day-use parking lot across the highway from the beach. From the parking lot, find the concrete walkway that

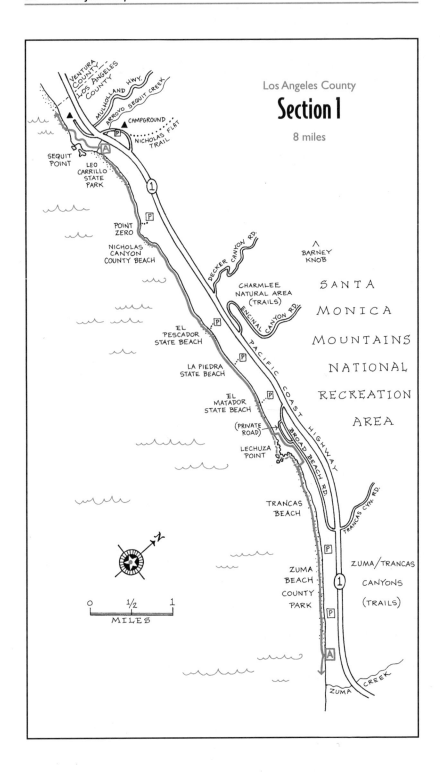

crosses under the highway alongside Arroyo Sequit Creek. During a rare winter storm, the walkway may be flooded which would mean carefully crossing the highway. The beach lies in the lee of scenic Sequit Point, a popular surfing and tidepooling spot. After turning south on the beach, you soon walk on cobblestones and sand. As the highway rises onto the bluff, the beach becomes secluded and highway sounds dwindle. At 1¼ miles a lifeguard station sits atop the bluff at what surfers call Point Zero, part of Nicholas Canyon County Beach. Continue around the point on the beach.

Two houses down the beach block access in the next mile at anything but low tide. You can exit the beach at Nicholas Canyon County Beach if necessary. If the tide is low enough to get by on the beach, you reach the El Pescador State Beach stairs at 2¾ miles, stairs at La Piedra State Beach at 3¼ miles, and El Matador State Beach stairs around 3⅜ miles. The three beaches together comprise R.H. Meyer Memorial State Beach. The rocky shoreline is passable at moderate to low tide.

Continue on the beach to rocky Lechuza Point at 5⅛ miles. The rough tidal rocks require some scrambling and climbing to pass, safe only at lower tides. Beyond the point lies house-lined Trancas Beach. The high tide route exits the beach at the first rocky ledges before Lechuza Point. Take the short stairs up to the private road (open to public foot traffic) and turn right. Follow it up to Broad Beach Road and turn right before 5¼ miles. The closed but unlocked gate on the right side of the drive is for public access, although it is not clearly marked from inside. Descend to the beach beyond the point via a nearby informal path, or take the beach access stairs at 31300 Broad Beach Road.

Now on Trancas Beach, you head down coast (east) along the tideline at the base of low bluffs. After you pass the mouth of Trancas Canyon around 6⅜ miles, continue down the coast (southeast now) on Zuma Beach, one of the county's classic beaches. Watch for rip currents here. Walk the long sloping beach to its end at the far end of the Zuma County Beach parking lot adjacent to the entrance station and section's end at 8 miles.

ALTERNATE ROUTE: If the tide is blocking your way, the only alternatives are waiting it out or walking the shoulder of Pacific Coast Highway and Broad Beach Road. The series of public access ways means that you can explore each beach somewhat regardless of the tides. If you are inclined to drive between points, keep in mind that paying the parking fee at one state park allows you to park at any others on the same day.

SUGGESTED ROUND TRIPS AND LOOPS: From any of the access points you can explore varying lengths of coastline out and back. The Nicholas Flat Trail starts near the Leo Carrillo State Park entrance station. This superb trail climbs 4 miles into the beautiful and fragrant chaparral-covered hills, providing stunning views of the coast, ending in oak studded flats around a lovely pond.

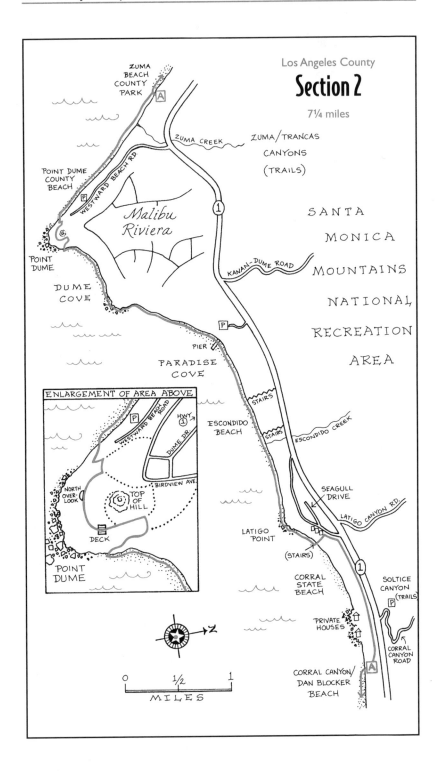

SECTION 2
Zuma Beach County Park to Dan Blocker State Beach

DISTANCE: 7½ miles (12.1 kilometers).

OPEN TO: Hikers.

SURFACE: Beach, trail, road shoulder.

ACCESS POINT: Zuma Beach County Park.

HOW TO GET THERE: Zuma Beach is on Highway 1 about one mile west of Kanan-Dume Road and 8.7 miles west of Malibu town center.

OTHER ACCESS: Point Dume County Beach at the end of Westward Beach Road, Paradise Cove private parking lot ($15 fee), path to Escondido Beach in the 27200 block of Highway 1, steps to beach at Seacliff condos on Seagull Street.

DIFFICULTY: Moderate.

ELEVATION GAIN/LOSS: 200 feet+/200 feet-.

CAUTIONS: Beaches close at sunset. Points and coves here are often flooded at high tide so it's best to time your hike with an outgoing tide.

FURTHER INFORMATION: Los Angeles County Lifeguard Service, Northern Section (310)457-9891, Paradise Cove (310)457-2511.

FACILITIES: Restrooms, water and picnic tables at Zuma Beach and Point Dume County Beach. Food, water and restrooms at Paradise Cove. Chemical toilets at Dan Blocker State Beach.

CAMPGROUNDS: Leo Carrillo State Beach has 127 sites and hot showers. Malibu Creek State Park campground, 5.5 miles inland on Malibu Creek Road, has 63 sites and hot showers. Malibu Beach RV Park south of Corral Canyon Road has 50 tent sites.

LODGING: You'll find motels and fancier digs along the Pacific Coast Highway.

This hike features a spacious beach, expansive views from the top of Point Dume, sensitive natural habitat, and a walk along scenic sandy coves and tidal rocks at the base of cliffs removed from the development on the bluffs above. This hike is best done on an outgoing tide since the rocky areas, particularly between the south end of Dume Cove and Paradise Cove, flood at high tide.

From the south end of Zuma Beach County Park near the entrance station, head down the beach towards Point Dume rising in the distance. Before ⅜ mile you pass the mouth of Zuma Creek, then continue on Point Dume County Beach. It's also called Westward Beach and has Westward Beach Road running along the base of 100-foot bluffs. Westward Beach ends at the base of Point Dume, the point towering 203 feet above the shore.

At the base of the cliff north of the point at 1⅝ miles, a well-used trail goes through an opening in the fence and zigzags up the side of Point Dume. Where you intersect two trails on the ascent, take a right turn on each of them to reach

Zuma Beach from Point Dume.

an overlook at 2 miles. From this north overlook, you peer almost straight down into the ocean 200 feet below. It's a great vantage point for watching whales and some rock outcrops frequented by climbers as well. From the overlook the trail becomes sandy and informal, skirting the edge of the drop-off as it curves left around the point. Take one of several paths contouring to the point's south side.

Around 2¼ miles you reach an overlook deck at the end of a boardwalk. This place is favored for seeing porpoises, gray whales and other marine mammals. From here you look out on scenic Dume Cove and the Malibu coast to the south. Continue to the end of the boardwalk, passing cacti and various chaparral plants. Where a side trail forks left, you can take a short walk to the top of the hill for a striking 360° view. To reach Dume Cove, stay to the right at the end of the board-walk. At 2½ miles take the trail and stairs, lined by a low chain link fence, that descends sharply to the beach.

Walk the quiet beach of Dume Cove at the base of steep cliffs to a secondary rocky point at 3 miles. The cove offers a pleasant place to wait if the point is flooded. When the point is passable, make your way along tidal rocks and pictur-esque sandy coves where you will find finely layered sedimentary rocks and good tidepooling.

At 4⅛ miles you reach Paradise Cove, a privately run beach with a small pier, restaurant, snack bar, picnic tables and restrooms. Beyond the pier, continue on narrow Escondido Beach, a favorite for divers that's lined with houses at the base of low bluffs and passable at all but the highest tides. Public access is via stair-ways, the first around 4⅞ miles (27200 Pacific Coast Highway). These stairways and others in following sections can best be identified by the fact that they are *not* marked with "NO TRESPASS" or "PRIVATE" signs. The first staircase is clearly visible as an imposing upright grey steel structure clinging to the cliffs. You'll find the second access around 5⅛ miles, just before where Escondido Creek empties into the ocean.

The CCT continues around rocky Latigo Point at 6¼ miles. About a mile beyond the point, two houses built on large boulders at the tideline block the beach. CCT exits the beach well before you reach the houses, at the public stairway at the south end of a row of white condominiums at 6⅝ miles. At the top of the stairs, turn right on Seagull Drive and walk to its end, then turn right again to follow the shoulder of Highway 1 along a chain link fence to pass the beach-hogging houses. Continue to the north end of Dan Blocker State Beach and the end of the section at 7½ miles. You'll find chemical toilets there. Across the highway a service station and an upscale restaurant sit adjacent to Corral Canyon Road.

SUGGESTED ROUND TRIPS AND LOOPS: From Zuma Beach explore Point Dume, Dume Cove

California's Coastal Conservancy

California's Coastal Conservancy is a state agency that protects and improves coastal and San Francisco Bay natural resources and helps the public get to and enjoy the coast. It works in partnership with local governments, other public agencies, non-profit organizations and private landowners.

The Coastal Conservancy has undertaken more than 700 projects along California's 1,100-mile coastline and around San Francisco Bay. Through such projects the Conservancy:

• Protects and improves coastal wetlands, streams, watersheds, and wildlife habitat.

• Helps people get to the coast and bayshores by building trails and stairways and by acquiring land and easements. It also assists in the creation of low-cost accommodations along the coast, including campgrounds and hostels.

• Works with local communities to revitalize urban waterfronts.

• Protects agricultural lands and supports coastal agriculture.

• Helps to solve complex land-use problems.

The state of California created the Coastal Conservancy to serve as intermediary among government, citizens, and the private sector, recognizing that creative approaches would be needed to preserve California's coast and San Francisco Bay lands for future generations.

Since its establishment in 1976, the Coastal Conservancy has:

• Completed more than 450 projects, with over 150 projects currently active. These projects include construction of trails and other public access facilities, restoration and improvement of wetlands and other wildlife habitat, restoration of public piers and urban waterfronts, and preservation of farmland and open space.

• Built more than 230 accessways and trails, including major portions of the California Coastal Trail and San Francisco Bay Trail, thus opening more than 70 miles of coastal and bay lands for public use.

• Assisted in the completion of 100 urban waterfront projects, including work on nearly every public pier on the coast.

• Helped preserve more than 50,000 acres of wetlands, dunes, wildlife habitat, parks, farmland and scenic open space.

• Retired more than 600 inappropriately planned subdivision lots.

• Joined in partnerships with more than 100 local land trusts and other nonprofit groups in all parts of the coast and San Francisco Bay.

The Coastal Conservancy serves all Californians and visitors to the state who are interested in enjoying, improving, and protecting the spectacular natural resources of the California coast and San Francisco Bay.

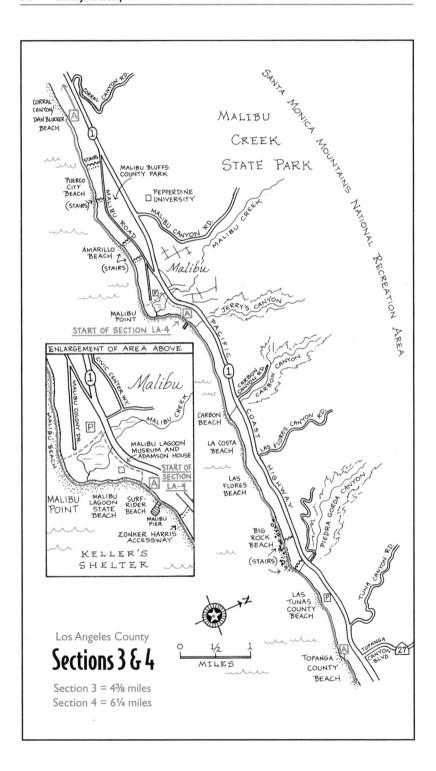

MALIBU CREEK STATE PARK

SANTA MONICA MOUNTAINS NATIONAL RECREATION AREA

CORRAL CANYON RD.

CORRAL CANYON/ DAN BLOCKER BEACH

STAIRS

PUERCO CITY BEACH (STAIRS)

MALIBU BLUFFS COUNTY PARK

PEPPERDINE UNIVERSITY

MALIBU ROAD

MALIBU CANYON RD.

MALIBU CREEK

AMARILLO BEACH (STAIRS)

Malibu

MALIBU POINT

JERRY'S CANYON

START OF SECTION LA-4

PACIFIC COAST HIGHWAY

CARBON CANYON RD.

CARBON CANYON

ENLARGEMENT OF AREA ABOVE

CIVIC CENTER WY.

Malibu

MALIBU COLONY DR.

MALIBU CREEK

MALIBU BEACH

MALIBU LAGOON MUSEUM AND ADAMSON HOUSE

START OF SECTION LA-4

MALIBU POINT

MALIBU LAGOON STATE BEACH

SURF-RIDER BEACH

MALIBU PIER

ZONKER HARRIS ACCESSWAY

KELLER'S SHELTER

CARBON BEACH

LA COSTA BEACH

LAS FLORES BEACH

LAS FLORES CANYON RD.

PIEDRA GORDA CANYON

BIG ROCK BEACH (STAIRS)

TUNA CANYON RD.

LAS TUNAS COUNTY BEACH

TOPANGA COUNTY BEACH

TOPANGA CANYON BLVD.

27

N

Los Angeles County

Sections 3 & 4

Section 3 = 4⅜ miles
Section 4 = 6¼ miles

0   ½   1
MILES

and Paradise Cove and return for a fine 8¼ miles round trip. Or walk up to the highway from Paradise Cove where local bus #434, connecting Santa Monica and Trancas hourly, can carry you back to Zuma Beach.

On the inland side of Highway 1 near this section's end, Solstice Canyon offers a pleasant three-mile circuit along a stream and through the hills. The park is the home of the Santa Monica Mountains Land Conservancy. The entrance to the park is .4 mile up Corral Canyon Road.

SECTION 3
Dan Blocker State Beach to Malibu Pier

DISTANCE: 4⅜ miles (7 kilometers).

OPEN TO: Hikers.

SURFACE: Beach.

ACCESS POINT: Dan Blocker State Beach.

HOW TO GET THERE: Road shoulder parking for the beach is in the 26000 block on Highway 1, about 3.5 miles north of the Malibu city center and just down coast from the corner of Corral Canyon Road.

OTHER ACCESS: Malibu Lagoon State Beach and stairways at 24700, 24500, 24400, 24300 blocks of Malibu Road.

DIFFICULTY: Easy.

ELEVATION GAIN/LOSS: Negligible.

CAUTIONS: Best to start your hike with the outgoing tide since parts of the beach may be impassable at high tide. In winter Malibu Creek is sometimes too deep to ford.

FURTHER INFORMATION: Malibu Division, California State Parks (310)457-8140, Los Angeles County Lifeguard Service, Northern Section (310)457-9891.

FACILITIES: Roadside parking and chemical toilets at Dan Blocker State Beach. Parking, water, tables at Malibu Beach. Urban amenities abound along Pacific Coast Highway.

CAMPGROUNDS: Malibu Creek State Park campground, 5.5 miles inland on Malibu Canyon Road, has 63 sites. Malibu Beach RV Park (310)456-6052, adjacent to Dan Blocker State Beach, has 50 tent sites and 140 RV sites.

LODGING: There are many accommodations in the area.

This easy walk features some "beach politics." The famed Malibu Colony of expensive homes lining the broad sandy beach competes with the public's desire for beach access to the tidal zone and surf there. This section begins at Dan Blocker State Beach, also called Corral Beach, a long narrow strip of sandy and rocky beach with riprap protecting the highway from pounding high-tide waves.

After rounding Malibu Point, the section concludes by passing Malibu Lagoon State Beach and the historic Adamson House operated by State Parks.

From the highway take the dirt ramp at the beach's north end down to the beach. If the tide is too high, we suggest waiting atop the bluff for it to start going out. Otherwise one would need to walk the busy highway and Malibu Road. Walk down the narrow beach. At the south end of Dan Blocker State Beach at ¾ mile, the highway climbs and veers inland, while Malibu Road and its pricey houses parallel the beach. Continue down the beach in front of the houses to Puerco City Beach. From roughly one mile to around 3 miles, four public stairs pass between the houses. The first two run between Malibu Road and Puerco Beach. Then after a small point around 2 miles, you pass two more stairs climbing from Amarillo Beach. The public stairways are identifiable because they don't have "private–no trespassing" signs on them. These serve as high tide exits as well as beach accessways.

Note also frequent signs stating that the beach behind the sign is private. It does not, however, ban the public from walking on the beach because the California state Constitution guarantees public access to the state tidelands. So not only can hikers walk the beach below the "mean high tide line," they also can walk above the line if it is unsafe to walk below it. The line fluctuates with the seasons, depending on the amount of sand on the beach, and depending on who says what about the line! Walking along the wet sand at the tideline instead of directly in front of the houses avoids confrontation.

From 3⅜ miles you walk the tideline in front of the super exclusive gated Malibu Colony, home to many Hollywood celebrities and other wealthy Angelenos. The folks you usually see in the backyards are the domestic help who sweep the patios and tend the gardens. The Colony ends at 4 miles, marked by a high fence running from the last house out into the sand. As you pass the fence, turn around to read the big "NO TRESPASSING" sign hanging from the fence. Everyone ignores the sign since the public has access rights.

Just past the fence, you reach the estuarine Malibu Lagoon, part of Malibu Lagoon State Beach. If the lagoon's opening to the ocean is sand barred, continue down the beach as it veers left around Malibu Point. Soon you pass state park's Adamson House on the left, walking Surfrider Beach to the Malibu Pier and section's end at 4⅜ miles.

If you can't get past the mouth of the lagoon, retrace your steps a few yards and take the trail that heads inland along the west side of the lagoon. Follow it across two bridges, reaching a parking lot and picnic area ¼ mile inland. The Malibu city center lies across the highway. Leave the parking lot and walk the bridge south over Malibu Creek and the lagoon. Across the creek, the Adamson House and grounds and Malibu Lagoon Museum overlook the beach. The Adamsons were descendants of the holders of the Spanish Malibu Land Grant. State Park docents conduct tours of the Spanish Colonial Revival house noted for its beautiful tile work. You are welcome to walk the grounds and gardens which stay open during the day free to the public. After passing the house, go through a parking lot, descend to Surfrider Beach, turn left and walk to section's end at the Malibu Pier.

SECTION 4
Malibu Pier to Topanga County Beach

DISTANCE: 6¼ miles (10.1 kilometers).

OPEN TO: Hikers.

SURFACE: Beach, tidal rocks. Road shoulder if the tide is high.

ACCESS POINT: Malibu Pier.

HOW TO GET THERE: Malibu Pier is south of Highway 1 in the 23000 block, 12 miles west of Santa Monica and a few blocks east of the Malibu City Center.

OTHER ACCESS: Zonker Harris Accessway, 22670 block of Pacific Coast Highway. Stairways at 20300 and 19900 Pacific Coast Highway. Las Tunas County Beach, 19400 block of Pacific Coast Highway.

DIFFICULTY: Easy.

ELEVATION GAIN/LOSS: Negligible.

CAUTIONS: Beaches close at sunset. Beaches and rocky areas impassable at higher tides so time your walk with a low or outgoing tide.

FURTHER INFORMATION: Adamson House, State Parks (310)456-8432, Los Angeles County Lifeguard Service, Central Section (310)394-3264.

FACILITIES: Parking, restrooms, picnic tables and urban facilities at Malibu Beach and Topanga County Beach.

HOSTEL: Santa Monica Hostel (310)393-9913 is near Section 5.

CAMPGROUNDS: Malibu Creek State Park campground, 5.5 miles inland on Malibu Canyon Road, has 63 sites. Malibu Beach RV Park (310)456-6052, adjacent to Dan Blocker State Beach, has 50 tent sites and 140 RV sites.

LODGING: Many motels and hotels can be found along Pacific Coast Highway.

MAP: See page 246.

This unique walk along the Malibu coast takes the hiker on beaches lined almost solidly with houses. The route takes you under the houses built out on the beach on pilings, but at higher tides the only alternative is to follow the shoulder of busy Pacific Coast Highway for the entire distance. Be cautious on either route. Along most of the beach, private access is gated and retreat is limited. Inland from the shore and highway, the Santa Monica Mountains rise to towering heights.

At Surfrider Beach on a dramatic cove next to the Malibu Pier, a good surf break and the warm climate encourages surfers to indulge their passion here and all along the Malibu coast year round.

From Surfrider Beach walk under the pier and down the beach past the mouth of Jerry's Canyon to pass the beach accessway at ¼ mile named for the famous Doonesberry comics tanning champion, Zonker Harris. Beyond it, houses crowd narrow Carbon Beach, so you may be dodging in and out among the house pilings, especially at higher tides. You may wonder how long these houses can stand up to winter-storm surf.

Walk around a small rocky point at 2 miles where the seasonal creek from Carbon Canyon empties into the Pacific. After rounding the point, continue on La Costa Beach, also lined with homes. At the next point at 2¾ miles, the CCT crosses the mouth of Las Flores Canyon's creek to encounter a large restaurant perched on riprap. Carefully negotiate the rocks to reach Las Flores Beach. If you reach the point when it's impassable, you have two choices. If you are there at high tide, the best choice is to wait for the tide to go out so you can continue down the beach. The only other choice is to turn back because there are no public access points in this area.

Assuming you find a way through, continue along Las Flores Beach, lined with more houses. Around 3½ miles the beach and tidal zone becomes rocky at aptly named Big Rock Beach. Continue along that narrow strand with more

Hostels Along California's Coast

Coastal hostels offer a welcome alternative to campgrounds and hotels as you explore California's Coastal Trail. Imagine brisk walks on the CCT while staying at a cozy, perhaps historic, hostel with an ocean view. Cook hot meals in a well-lit kitchen, sleep in a comfortable bed and meet friendly people from around the world.

Each hostel's warm, friendly atmosphere, shared kitchen, and cozy sleeping rooms are affordable, usually around $16 per person. Young world travelers still make up most hostel's clientele, but each year more older travelers and families bunk at hostels, attracted by low prices and no smoking/no alcohol policies.

Some great locations also make hostels attractive. From north coast redwood forests to central coast small towns to happening coastal cities, locations vary as much as the unique buildings: farmhouses, lighthouses, a former library and an army barracks, for example. Most California hostels are run by Hostelling International–American Youth Hostels (AYH), while a few are independent.

The varied locations of AYH hostels reflect the diverse nature of the California Coastal Trail. DeMartin Hostel in Redwood National Park sits overlooking the ocean in an historic farmhouse beside the CCT. Area trails offer coastal hiking at its finest. Marin Headlands Hostel, housed in a handsome old army building near the CCT in Golden Gate National Recreation Area, is just a short walk from Rodeo Beach. A more ambitious hike climbs over a ridge to the Golden Gate Bridge in only four miles. Point Reyes Hostel, located right beside the CCT, offers a 20-minute hike to dramatic Limantour Beach. San Francisco has a hostel at Fort Mason on the bayfront about two miles from the CCT and another downtown at Union Square. San Mateo County offers two hostels in historic lighthouses at small-town Montara and rural Pigeon Point. The Santa Cruz Hostel is centrally located near downtown, two blocks from the beach, boardwalk and CCT.

In the southern half of the state, Hostel Obispo provides lodging in the charming college town of San Luis Obispo. In the Los Angeles area, the Santa Monica Hostel provides a lively downtown setting only blocks from the pier, beach and CCT. San Pedro Hostel, on a hill near the huge Korean Friendship Bell, sits a few blocks from the CCT as it passes Point Fermin, Cabrillo

houses lining the top of the beach, particularly on its east end. At 4⅛ miles a long metal stairway that descends from 20000 Pacific Coast Highway reaches the beach. Our path rounds a point before 4½ miles, passing another stairway then the mouth of Piedra Gorda Canyon. The beach here is lined with yet more houses, but passable.

Continue along the tideline to Las Tunas County Beach starting around 5⅛ miles, where you find a break in the houses lining the beach for the next ¼ mile. The narrow rocky beach here floods at high tide. You can scramble up to the road shoulder if the tide blocks your passage. If the beach is passable, walk on down the beach along eroding low bluffs. After the mouth of Pena Canyon at 5⅜ miles, walk past more houses lining the top of the beach.

Pass the mouth of Tuna Canyon around 5¾ miles, then continue to the next point where a lifeguard station and parking lot mark the section's end at Topanga County Beach at 6¼ miles. The rocky point here also marks the end of the famed 27-mile Malibu Coast.

Hostels - continued

Marine Aquarium and Los Angeles Harbor. San Clemente Hostel in Orange County occupies an old library just a few blocks from the beach and the CCT. San Diego's two hostels sit near the coast and the CCT. Point Loma Hostel is a few blocks from Ocean Beach. The Downtown San Diego Hostel near the bayfront offers great bike riding, beaches, 1400-acre Balboa Park and its famous zoo, and a trolley that runs to the border at Tijuana in 20 minutes.

This book mentions several independent coastal hostels where you might stay. Santa Barbara's Banana Bungalow sits right in town six blocks from the beach and Stearns Wharf. In the small San Luis Obispo County town of Nipomo, Bill Denneen not only runs his unique Bill's Home Hostel, but also leads excursions to natural sites like Nipomo Dunes and Point Sal. Farther north in that county is Morro Bay Home Hostel. You'll find two more independent hostels near the coast in Los Angeles: Hostel California is about 15 minutes walk from Venice Beach while the small Marina Hostel is in nearby Marina del Rey. In Orange County's Huntington Beach, the Colonial Inn Hostel is just four blocks from CCT and beach. In recent years development of hostels slowed as government support and funding dwindled. However, with a booming economy and a new move towards coastal protection and awareness, hostels could open in places such as the Monterey Peninsula and the Mendocino coast.

Finishing the CCT, opening more hostels, and creating more coastal parks and campsites helps save the coast from unwanted development while boosting the coastal region's economy. When the CCT finally gets completed—gaps closed, trail signs in place, abundant places to stay at convenient locations—the long distance CCT hiker can anticipate an enjoyable, safe and reasonably comfortable trip, finding a choice of hostels, campgrounds, bed and breakfast inns, motels and hotels for overnight stays. American Youth Hostels envisions a string of hostels, perhaps as many as 36, placed along the coastline about 40 miles apart to serve an international cast of visitors.

For more information about Hostelling International—American Youth Hostels, contact the Golden Gate Council (415)701-1320, the Los Angeles Council (310)393-3413, the San Diego Council at (619)338-9981. Or check out the website: www.hostelweb.com

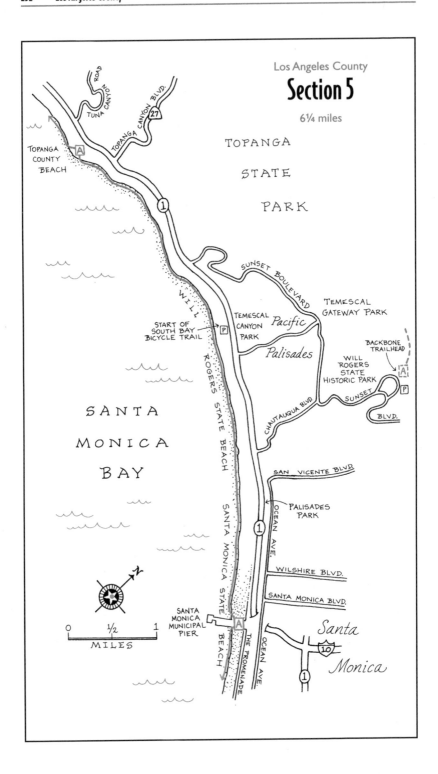

Los Angeles County
Section 5
6¼ miles

SECTION 5
Topanga County Beach to Santa Monica Pier

DISTANCE: 6¼ miles (10.1 kilometers).

OPEN TO: Hikers. Bicyclists on most.

SURFACE: Beach or paved multi-use trail.

ACCESS POINT: Topanga County Beach.

HOW TO GET THERE: Topanga County Beach is at 18500 Pacific Coast Highway (Highway 1) at the east end of the city of Malibu and just west of Topanga Canyon Boulevard.

OTHER ACCESS: Almost the entire route is accessible from Pacific Coast Highway.

DIFFICULTY: Easy.

ELEVATION GAIN/LOSS: Negligible.

FURTHER INFORMATION: For Topanga County Beach, call the Los Angeles County Lifeguard Service, Northern Section (310)457-9891. For Will Rogers State Beach, call the Los Angeles County Department of Beaches and Harbors (310)305-9503. For Santa Monica State Beach, call the Los Angeles County Lifeguard Service, Central Section (310)394-3264.

FACILITIES: Urban amenities exist at both ends of this hike and along the route.

HOSTEL: Santa Monica Hostel is in downtown a few blocks from the beach (310)393-9913.

LODGING: Motels and hotels abound in Pacific Palisades and Santa Monica.

From Topanga County Beach to Torrance Beach more than 20 miles distant, the character of the Los Angeles coastline changes dramatically from the mountainous Malibu coast. While in Malibu development spreads out somewhat, intensely developed Santa Monica Bay from Topanga County Beach to Torrance Beach features a row of distinctive beach cities. Even more contrasting, access to the Malibu coast remains difficult in many places because of beachfront development and bluffs, while Santa Monica Bay flaunts nearly all sandy public beach for the entire 20 miles. It's paradise for beach hungry residents. Notably, a multi-use bike path covers the entire distance.

Will Rogers State Historic Park nestles in the hills about 2 miles inland from Will Rogers State Beach, part of this section. The garrulous Rogers moved there in 1928 with his wife and three kids, staying until his death in 1935. The 186 acres, the house and horse facilities became a park in 1944. Activities include picnicking, touring the house full of Rogers artifacts, horseback riding and hiking. The southern terminus of the Santa Monica Mountains Backbone Trail is in the park.

You have a choice here of either cycling the entire length in an easy day or walking the beach or the bike path in several days. The walk rewards you with wild and crazy Venice Beach, and several other beach towns, five piers, a marina and a harbor. You get a sense of the enormity of Los Angeles after seeing the massive Hyperion Water Treatment Plant and hearing and seeing passenger airliners taking off over Dockweiler Beach from Los Angeles International Airport every minute all day long.

From the front of the Topanga County Beach lifeguard station, walk down the sandy beach to its end at riprap protecting a building at ⅜ mile. Walk up and around the building, then return to the beach at ½ mile. Will Rogers State Beach begins here, extending down the coast for 3 miles. The sandy beach starts out quite narrow on the north end with the highway not far from the tideline and quite distracting. The beach broadens from 1⅝ miles to 2 miles where you come to the hotspot Gladstone's Restaurant at 2 miles. Take the concrete ramp up the riprap in front of the building to the parking lot, walk through the lot and take stairs back to the beach before 2¼ miles. Continue along a broad beach past the end of Sunset Blvd. Then the beach narrows again until around 2⅜ miles. From

Saving the South Coast: Heal the Bay

The huge human population of southern California lives there in large part because of the mild desert climate and warm, inviting coast and ocean. The 4000 square miles of Los Angeles County alone hold a population of over 10.5 million. Several feature articles in this book discuss the results of historic, persistent abuse by government and development forces on the natural resources of the region. These abuses continue (seawalls, attempts to develop wetlands, fierce pollution problems) but dedicated, enlightened individuals and groups have learned to fight back with education, activism, and when all else fails, lawsuits. One of those dedicated groups is Heal the Bay.

One of the most important natural resources in Los Angeles County is 266-square-mile Santa Monica Bay. The Bay and its environs provide habitat to about 5000 species. The 50-mile bay shoreline, while featured as an amenity for the people of L.A., was at the same time being used as a dumping ground. That coastline, consisting of 22 beaches and 9 communities, attracts a whopping 45 million visitors every year. As of 1985, the enormous Hyperion Sewage Treatment Plant dumped millions of gallons of barely treated wastewater and sludge right into the Bay.

No wonder that in 1985 a small group of people discovered bay dolphins full of tumors, a large patch of virtually dead bay, and increasing complaints by swimmers and surfers of stomach flu, sinusitis and other illnesses. This small group led by Dorothy Green founded Heal the Bay, organized to bring the City of Los Angeles to task. They signed up members, held rallies and testified before regulatory agencies. The group also joined the Environmental Protection Agency lawsuit against the city. The weight of local public opinion and the lawsuit compelled the city to comply with the Clean Water Act and rebuild the sewer plant to treat water to a much higher standard. Today, the dead zone in the bay shows signs of life and swimming is safer, demonstrating that the problems of human impact on resources can be reversed.

The battle remains far from over, and Heal the Bay continues to fight for a clean environment. Their next big battle is to clean up non-point pollution. This refers to runoff from the built upon surface of the city. The 5000 miles of channels, gutters and drains, devised to keep urban Los Angeles from flooding, dumps 30 billion gallons of runoff annually into the bay from 70 outfalls. The untreated runoff carries a brew of at least 160 toxic chemicals including motor oil and automotive fluids,

there you walk a broad beach along the shore of Santa Monica Bay.

Farther down Will Rogers State Beach, you reach the beginning of the South Bay Bicycle Trail in the parking area at 3⅛ miles. From here to Torrance Beach, you can walk the paved path, dodging bikes and inline skaters, or wade through the sand down by the surf. In addition, in Santa Monica and several other beach communities, there is also a promenade adjacent to the sand.

If you continue along the beach, it becomes very broad by 3¼ miles, where Temescal Canyon Park lies across the Pacific Coast Highway. Follow the tideline of the broad beach. At 4⅜ miles the Backbone Trail (see Ventura Section 6A), an alternate CCT High Route, returns to the beach via Chatauqua Blvd., which ends opposite the beach beside the mouth of Santa Monica Canyon.

Now you have less than 2 miles remaining to the Santa Monica Pier. By 4⅝ miles Will Rogers State Beach ends and Santa Monica State Beach begins. Soon

South Coast – continued

fertilizers, herbicides, pesticides, animal wastes and human viruses. Presently the only response to this untreated mess is to advise no swimming near flowing outfalls and avoiding the water for 72 hours after a major storm.

Heal the Bay started the movement to clean up the Bay. The Santa Monica Bay Restoration Project continues to develop a comprehensive plan to ensure the long term health of Santa Monica Bay. In addition to developing the Bay Restoration Plan, this coalition of environmentalists, governments, scientists, businesses and the public conducts studies on the overall health of the bay and the impact of pollution on humans and resident species, and establishes educational programs for schools, groups, and municipalities about pollution prevention methods.

The work of healing the bay, now in its second decade, still must deal with huge public and bureaucratic obstacles. As just one example, in a recent report, Heal the Bay states that the local Water Quality Control Board in charge of enforcing clean water laws continually fails in its enforcement. The report says in part:

• Only 14 penalty actions have occurred over the last six years, totaling a mere $578,000 in fines.

• Over 99.5% of discharger violations do not result in the imposition of penalties.

The report concluded, "This is not aggressive enforcement and does not serve to deter future violations of the law. Penalties issued by the Board do not capture the economic benefit from noncompliance, as is required under federal and state enforcement policies. In essence, it pays to pollute if you are doing business in Los Angeles and Ventura Counties. The Regional Board writes off or substantially reduces penalties if a business simply agrees to comply with the law. Enforcement response is slow and, when violations continue, the Regional Board rarely escalates its response." The report goes on to outline serious non-enforcement of oil and chemical spills, illegal runoff violations, sewage spills and septic tank problems.

Despite the still dire conditions, those working hard to clean up and protect Santa Monica Bay have made great strides. They reversed the ugly human trend towards fowling the nest, created water safer for swimming, healthier wildlife, and held government agencies accountable. The goal in the next decade calls for a completely clean and safe environment for humans and wildlife alike.

Information in this article came from Heal the Bay and the Santa Monica Bay Restoration Project.

Santa Monica's beach hosts millions annually.

buildings line the top of the broad beach, with Palisades Park hiding atop the 100-foot-high bluffs beyond the highway. The closer you get to the looming pier, the busier the beach gets, especially in the summer. Millions of people of every cultural and ethnic stripe visit this beach and pier every year. By 5½ miles the Promenade runs along the top of the beach between the tideline and the Pacific Coast Highway. By 6⅛ miles the broad beach is 1/5 mile across. Whether you are traveling via beach or bike path, the section ends at 6¼ miles at the stairs to the pier. Consider climbing the stairs for a tour of the Santa Monica Pier with its old fashioned carousel, amusement park with giant ferris wheel, and enough fast food stands and souvenir shops to feed and entertain the legions of beach goers and empty their wallets.

SUGGESTED LOOPS AND ROUND TRIPS: Temescal Canyon Park offers one of the few trail connections to the Santa Monica Mountains backcountry. It's about 1½ miles up through the grassy picnic grounds to Temescal Gateway Park. From here the Temescal Canyon and Ridge Trails take you to the Backbone Trail inland about 8 miles from the coast.

Will Rogers State Historic Park warrants a visit and can be found by driving or walking up Chatauqua Blvd. in Santa Monica Canyon to Sunset Blvd. and the entrance about 2 miles inland. Several short trails in the park lead to the south end of the Backbone Trail. For the Backbone Trail, see Ventura Section 6A.

SECTION 6
Santa Monica Pier to Manhattan Beach Pier

DISTANCE: 13 miles (20.9 kilometers).

OPEN TO: Hikers. Bicyclists on bike path.

SURFACE: Beach, promenade, paved bike path.

ACCESS POINT: Santa Monica Pier.

HOW TO GET THERE: The Santa Monica Freeway (I-10) ends in Santa Monica near the pier. The Santa Monica Pier is seaward of the corner of Ocean Avenue and Colorado Avenue adjacent to downtown Santa Monica.

OTHER ACCESS: Anywhere on the route.

DIFFICULTY: Easy.

ELEVATION GAIN/LOSS: Negligible.

FURTHER INFORMATION: For Santa Monica State Beach and Venice Beach, call the Los Angeles County Lifeguard Service, Central Section (310)394-3264. For Dockweiler State Beach and Manhattan County Beach, call the Los Angeles County Lifeguard Service, Southern Section (310)832-1179.

FACILITIES: Urban amenities abound along much of the route.

HOSTELS: Santa Monica Hostel (310)393-9913 is a few blocks from the Santa Monica Pier. Venice has the Hostel California (310)305-0250 about 15 minutes walk from the beach. The small Marina Hostel (310)301-3983 is in Marina del Rey.

CAMPGROUNDS: Dockweiler State Beach RV Park near the L.A. Airport flight path has RV spaces only. Tent spaces are a rarity in Los Angeles. To find tent camping, one needs a car to get the nearest choices, two RV Parks near Disneyland that allow tents (about 50 miles, reservations advisable)—Travelers World RV Park (714)991-0100 and C.C. Camperland (714)750-6747.

LODGING: Abundant choices range from luxurious to basic. In the basic category, try the Venice Beach Hotel, just a bit fancier than a hostel, with private rooms. In the moderate range three blocks from Venice Pier, try the Inn at Venice Beach.

This lengthy section lends itself to bike riding, or to a good one-way hiking workout with a return bus ride back to your car. Much of the route can be done either on the beach along the firmer wet sand at the shoreline, or you can walk the bike path with the awareness that bikes and inline skates rule, or you might want to do some of both to get the real variety and interest of this walk.

The hike starts at the Santa Monica Pier, in a way an extension of downtown Santa Monica. You might take a look at Santa Monica Pier with its old time carousel and amusement park, funky arcade games, and fast food joints serving the likes of corndogs and cotton candy. Grassy Palisades Park north of the pier and Crescent Bay Park south occupy the bluff overlooking the beach. Across Ocean Avenue from the parks sits classic downtown Santa Monica, an older southern

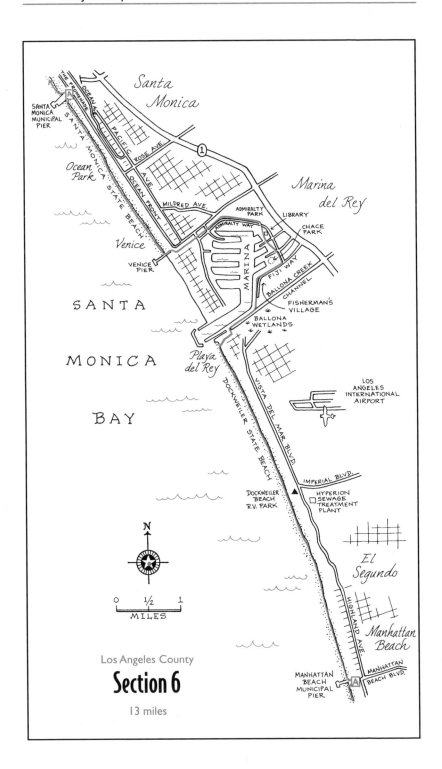

Los Angeles County

Section 6

13 miles

California city enjoying unprecedented renewal. Although the January 1994 Northridge earthquake epicenter was miles away, many older downtown buildings were damaged and now have been repaired to their striking original opulence.

After a walk on the pier, head on down the beach toward Manhattan Beach. The most interesting route for the first few miles follows the promenade along the beachfront businesses. You can also walk the wide sandy beach.

You reach Venice Beach at 1⅜ miles. Venice may be one of the most unusual towns anywhere, even along the California coast. Ocean Front Walk is home to a myriad of tourist businesses and a range of street people and vendors from new age spiritualists to cutting edge artists (or so it may seem to the gullible tourists) to beyond-hope bums, winos and panhandlers. Interspersed into this mix are body builders at a famous location known as Muscle Beach (located just south of the Santa Monica Pier, while a newer one is in Venice), girls on skates and barely in bikinis, and joggers taking a break from the office. A good dose of uncomprehending rubbernecking tourists and a contingent of totally incomprehensible yet interesting locals populate the sidelines. If you are a tourist and want to blend in, just act crazy!

A long history of incomprehensibility characterizes Venice. Conceived by entrepreneur Abbot Kinney, he thought he would build a town just like the famous Venice, Italy. In 1900 he dug canals and brought gondolas and gondoliers from Italy to help sell the canal-side lots. When that had less than the desired effect, Kinney built an amusement park, wildly popular in the 1910s. It all failed after Kinney's death in 1920, primarily due to an inadequate sewage system. After filling in most of the canals, oil was discovered in Venice. Over the years Venice changed but stayed the unique place it started out to be. Now the remaining canals are lined with Kinney's original dream houses. Inland a few blocks you can take the Canal Walk between Rose Avenue and Washington Blvd. passing well-tended and eclectic residences.

Ocean Front Walk ends at 2⅛ miles. The bike path winding through the sand continues. You reach Venice Pier at 2¾ miles. From here you begin the walk around Marina Del Rey, a wealthy counterpart to Venice with its 6000 boat slips and multitude of moderate to upscale restaurants. From the pier, walk up the sidewalk of Washington Blvd. At 3⅞ miles watch for Mildred Avenue intersecting Washington from the left. Follow the bike path as it turns right into Admiralty Park. Walk through the park and follow the bike path across Admiralty Way. The path is painted on the library and marina parking lots. Turn right after crossing through a grassy area adjacent to Chace Park and either walk the sidewalk or stroll by the marina businesses.

At the end of the street at 5¾ miles, the bike path continues on the Ballona Creek jetty. Cross Ballona Creek on a bridge at 6⅜ and enter Playa del Rey, where you might consider an interesting side trip. If you go left at the end of the bridge and walk inland along nearby streets, you can view a remnant of what used to be thousands of acres of marine estuary backed up against the beach. The Ballona wetlands and the adjacent Hughes Aircraft property are a battleground facing off environmentalists who want to save the tiny fraction of wetlands left in Los Angeles and those who want to develop it.

The CCT's route from the bridge heads toward the beach. Again the choice is between the bike path and the sand. At 7¾ miles you enter Dockweiler State Beach. This wide beach is lightly used compared to the rest of L.A.'s beaches because it lies directly under the departure flight path for Los Angeles International Airport. Hundreds of flights a day roar a few hundred feet overhead, drowning out every other sound and dousing everything with jet fuel fumes. The high dunes across the street from the beach used to be a housing tract that became unlivable as the jets got ever bigger and more numerous. Now a few endangered species make this dune environment home. A small band of conservationists wear ear protection when they work here trying to restore the dunes.

Farther down the beach past the jet noise, you come to Dockweiler Beach RV Park, a state park unit, before 9¼ miles. Continue down the beach past the looming, gigantic Hyperion Sewage Treatment Plant, which dominates the eastern skyline. The beach and bike path continue along very wide El Segundo Beach, then El Porto Beach, skirting an industrial area.

Cross into Manhattan Beach at 11⅜ miles, where low hills blanketed with

Los Angeles River Basin – Past, Present & Future

Imagine the Los Angeles basin as a rolling grassland with the Los Angeles, San Gabriel and Santa Ana Rivers flowing through riparian lowlands of cottonwood, alder and sycamore. Further imagine marshes, lagoons and large lakes interlaced with thickets of willow, grape and brambles, chaparral and oak forests draping the hills, numerous springs bubbling to the surface, even hot springs and tar seeps. Snowclad mountains provide the water, and marine estuaries and the ocean receive the clear, clean streams. Marshes, lagoons and dunes lie along the coast. Peaceful villages of the native Kumi vit dot the landscape from the mountains to the coast.

That's what Spanish explorer Gaspar de Portola saw when he rode into the Los Angeles basin in 1769. Portola soon established the first mission at San Gabriel. In 1781 twelve families numbering 46 people founded the pueblo that would become Los Angeles, located at a village site of the Kumi vit (renamed Gabrielinos by the Spaniards) overlooking the river. Before long the Spaniards drained the marshes and farmed the rich soil. The natives were forced to provide the labor as the era of a natural landscape populated

by a peaceful people ended.

Today, the Los Angeles River pours into Long Beach Harbor near downtown Long Beach. The CCT crosses the river on Anaheim Street before entering downtown, coming out on the river channel at Shoreline Village. The river is unrecognizable, encased in a concrete lined ditch designed to hasten flood waters through the intensely developed Los Angeles basin. Almost all of the 51 miles of the main stem and the 400 miles of tributaries suffer the same indignity, funnelled into a huge storm drain to protect the area from the short but occasionally intense rainy season and naturally occurring flooding of lowlands. As the population grew and the economy flourished, the open flood plains and marshes lured development irresistibly. After a severe flood in 1914, the Los Angeles County Flood Control District formed to interdict the natural patterns of the river. Dams and basins attempted to tame the river to no avail. The river flooded severely in 1934 and again in 1938, killing 113 people and causing $800 million in damage (1990 dollars). In 1936 Congress approved the Flood Control Act. Soon 15,000 depression era people went to

residences rise to the east. Follow the broad, pleasant and long beach until you reach the Manhattan Beach Pier and section's end at 13 miles.

SUGGESTED ROUND TRIPS AND LOOPS: Take your choice of long or short beach walks, a walk into downtown Santa Monica and the pier, or check out the wild and wacky Ocean Front Walk in Venice.

For a 3-mile loop, take Ocean Front Walk and the beachfront between Rose Avenue and Washington Blvd. from either end, then cut inland a few blocks and take the Canal Walk and Main Street back in the direction you came.

River Basin – continued

work on the project. By 1954 almost the whole river system suffered imprisonment while development continued unabated.

The population keeps growing, creating more hard surface. With rain unable to penetrate the paved ground, even more water hits the drainage ditches. The Corp of Engineers warns that low lying areas (former marshes) along the river risk flooding in an exceptionally heavy rainy season. The solution proposed by the county's Public Works Department, a $280 million project to increase the river's carrying capacity, places concrete parapets up to eight feet high along the banks for 21 miles.

Not everyone accepts that solution or has given up on the river. The failure of Mississippi River dikes in 1993 floods showed that channelizing rivers to get the water downstream as quickly as possible is a doomed approach. Friends of the River, a group started in 1989, proposes to work with natural forces, making the river an environmental asset for the people and wildlife of the region. Several stretches of the river remain in a semi-natural state, with soft bottom and natural vegetation lining the banks. The Friends want to see any further flood control measures more in line with nature. Proposals include wider soft-bottomed channels, flood basins with riparian habitat, permeable surfaces in the watershed to reduce runoff and direct the runoff into the aquifer. They envision a greenway from mountains to sea with trails along naturalized banks connecting parks and natural areas with neighborhoods.

With environmentalists and developers at odds, the contentious discussion continues over the best approach. The city and county prefer engineering methods. Supported by developers, they want the land along the river for projects instead of open space and flood basins. The city and county began a watershed master plan project with many jurisdictions and interest groups participating. While acknowledging the concept of a river greenway, authorities seem to favor the parapet plan.

Friends of the River and the environmental coalition Unpave L.A. continue to press for parks, greenways and trails, using a campaign of education and information. Will the river remain simply a concrete drainage ditch, or can it again resemble at least in part the river of old, meandering through wildlife-rich riparian forests and marshes? Can the people of L.A. again come to appreciate the river flowing in their midst?

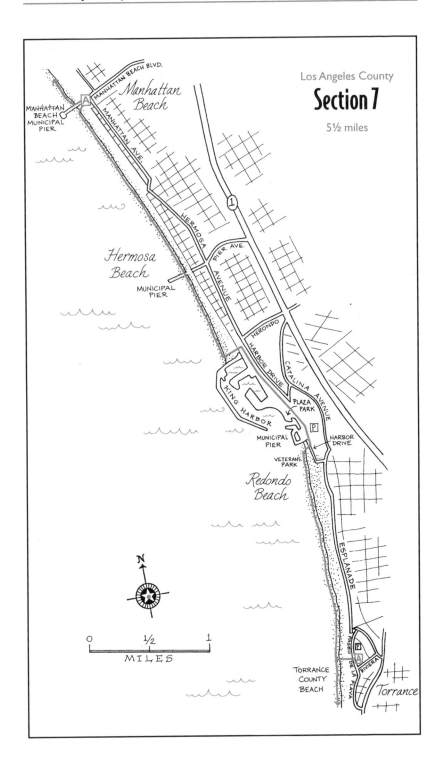

Los Angeles County
Section 7
5½ miles

SECTION 7
Manhattan Beach Pier to Torrance County Beach

DISTANCE: 5½ miles (8.9 kilometers).

OPEN TO: Hikers. Bicyclists on paved bike path.

SURFACE: Beach, paved bike path.

ACCESS POINT: Manhattan Beach Pier.

HOW TO GET THERE: From the San Diego Freeway (I-405) or Highway 1, turn west on Manhattan Beach Blvd. and drive to its end at the foot of Manhattan Beach Pier, two blocks from Manhattan Avenue.

OTHER ACCESS: Many accessways along the route including Manhattan Avenue, Hermosa Avenue, Harbor Drive, Esplanade, and various streets in Torrance.

DIFFICULTY: Easy.

ELEVATION GAIN/LOSS: Negligible.

FURTHER INFORMATION: All of the beaches on this route are served by the Los Angeles County Lifeguard Service, Southern Section (310)832-1179.

FACILITIES: You can find everything all along the bike path, including bike and skate rental shops.

HOSTELS: Santa Monica Hostel (310)393-9913 is a few blocks from the Santa Monica Pier. Venice has the Hostel California (310)305-0250 about 15 minutes walk from the beach. The small Marina Hostel (310)301-3983 is in Marina del Rey.

CAMPING: See Section 6.

LODGING: Lodgings of all kinds are abundant in the area.

The CCT traverses the shorelines of the three similar yet distinctive beach towns of Manhattan Beach, Hermosa Beach, and Redondo Beach. This section takes you on a straightforward route either along the busy bike path, full of bikes and inline skaters, or the more peaceful stroll among the tanned sun worshipers down by the water. Consider visiting the pier in each town for an entertaining side trip. The Manhattan Beach Pier has a small aquarium. The route also takes you along the street for a short distance around King Harbor in Redondo Beach.

If you want to check out the mostly residential Manhattan Beach's bustling small town atmosphere, walk two or three blocks east to Manhattan Avenue and Highland Avenue.

From the pier walk down the pleasant beach along the tideline, unless you prefer following the South Bay Bicycle Trail. Beach volleyball courts lie along the top of the beach for much of the way to Hermosa Beach.

At 1⅝ miles you arrive at the Hermosa Beach Pier. The town center is similar to its neighbor, a busy small-town core with a laid back and comfortable ambi-

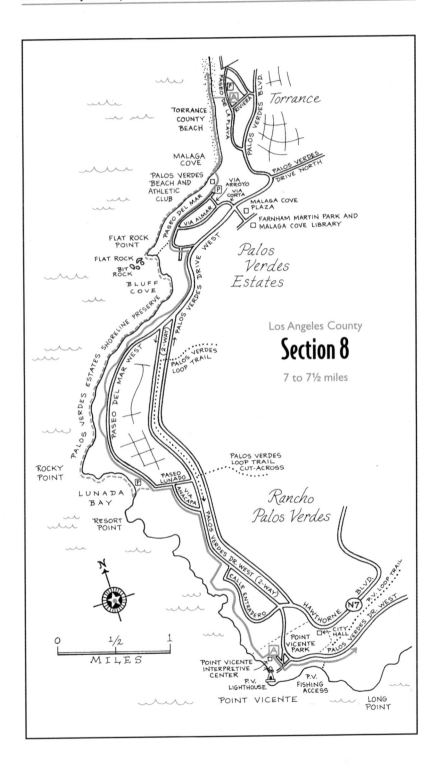

Torrance

TORRANCE
COUNTY
BEACH

MALAGA
COVE

PALOS VERDES
BEACH AND
ATHLETIC
CLUB

VIA
ARROYO
VIA
CORTA

MALAGA COVE
PLAZA

FARNHAM MARTIN PARK AND
MALAGA COVE LIBRARY

PALOS VERDES
DRIVE NORTH

FLAT ROCK
POINT

FLAT ROCK
BIT
ROCK

BLUFF
COVE

*Palos
Verdes
Estates*

Los Angeles County

Section 8

7 to 7½ miles

PALOS VERDES
LOOP TRAIL

(2-WAY)

ROCKY
POINT

LUNADA
BAY

RESORT
POINT

PASEO
LUNADO

VIA
ANACAPA

PALOS VERDES
LOOP TRAIL
CUT-ACROSS

*Rancho
Palos Verdes*

PALOS VERDES DR. WEST (2-WAY)

CALLE ENTRADERO

HAWTHORNE

BLVD.

N7

P.V. LOOP TRAIL

PALOS VERDES DR. WEST

POINT
VICENTE
PARK

CITY
HALL

N
0   ½   1
MILES

POINT VICENTE
INTERPRETIVE
CENTER

P.V.
LIGHTHOUSE

P.V.
FISHING
ACCESS

POINT VICENTE

LONG
POINT

PASEO DE LA PLAYA

RIVIERA

PALOS VERDES BLVD.

PASEO DEL MAR

VIA ALMAR

PALOS VERDES DRIVE WEST

PASEO DEL MAR WEST

PALOS VERDES ESTATES SHORELINE PRESERVE

ance just off the beach up Pier Avenue. Continue down the spacious strand. It gets even broader as you head south from Hermosa Beach Pier.

The beach ends abruptly at the north end of the ersatz King Harbor at 2¼ miles. Take a short jog inland on the bike path to Herondo Street, watching for bikes on the blind corner. Then turn right and follow the sidewalk along Harbor Drive. At 3 miles Harbor Drive ends at Plaza Park. The bike path goes through the park and parking garage, but pedestrians can find their way through the horseshoe shaped Redondo Municipal Pier area with its shops, restaurants, and fishing pier. You emerge from this complex into Veteran's Park at 3⅜ miles. Walk from there onto the beach or bike path.

Along the sandy tideline you follow beach all the way to Torrance. You first pass high-rise apartment buildings lining the beach, then continue on the sandy expanse of steeply sloping Redondo State Beach. After passing public restrooms at 4¾ miles, you come to Torrance County Beach although you can't tell because it's unmarked. The city of Torrance's short ¾ mile stretch of beach doesn't qualify it as a beach town like the others in these parts because the hub of the city actually lies several miles inland. Follow the beach at the base of undeveloped bluffs to section's end at 5½ miles. It's also the south end of the South Bay Bicycle Trail, where it angles up the steep sloping bluff to a parking lot near the corner of Paseo de la Playa and Riviera Street.

SUGGESTED ROUND TRIPS AND LOOPS: Stroll along the beach between any of the three piers on this route. Exploring the piers and the three beach towns offers several opportunities of varying length.

SECTION 8
Torrance County Beach to Point Vicente

DISTANCE: 7 miles high route, 7½ miles tidal (low) route (11.3 or 12.1 kilometers).

OPEN TO: Hikers. Bicyclists on streets.

SURFACE: Beach, trail, streets.

ACCESS POINT: Torrance County Beach.

HOW TO GET THERE: From the Redondo Pier take Catalina Avenue to Esplanade (which becomes Paseo de la Playa) for two miles to a large parking lot overlooking Torrance Beach. The South Bay Bicycle Trail ends adjacent to Riviera Street.

OTHER ACCESS: The entire high route is accessible. The tidal route has access trails at Malaga Cove, Bluff Cove and Lunada Bay.

DIFFICULTY: High route easy, tidal route difficult.

ELEVATION GAIN/LOSS: 240 feet+/100 feet-.

CAUTIONS: Take extra care climbing the steep, treacherous trail up the cliff at Lunada Bay. Informal trails south of Bluff Cove all the way to the Point Vicente Fishing access are dangerous.

FURTHER INFORMATION: For Torrance Beach, Malaga Cove, and Abalone Cove, call Los Angeles County Lifeguard Service, Southern Section (310)832-1179, Point Vicente Interpretive Center (310)377-5370.

FACILITIES: Torrance Beach has all the amenities. Point Vicente Interpretive Center has water, restrooms, picnic tables and parking.

HOSTELS: See Section 6 or 7.

CAMPING: See Section 6.

LODGING: Motels and hotels abound in Redondo Beach and Torrance.

Palos Verdes Peninsula rises steeply from the sea with cliffs as high as 300 feet. Steep terrain and winding roads isolate the peninsula from the rest of greater Los Angeles, placing it far from the convenience of the freeway system so heavily used by the populace. The steep hills, now relatively well developed with expensive homes and gated neighborhoods, consist of a series of thirteen marine terraces indicating that both the sea and the land have risen many times over millions of years. The terraces indicate the old shoreline sea beds. The youngest terrace can be seen as tidal flats being formed by waves.

In geologic time the peninsula was only recently an offshore island like Catalina is today. Sediments from the surrounding mountains filled the channel, what is now the Los Angeles Basin, with alluvium up to 20,000 feet deep. Re-markably, parts of the peninsula continue to slide toward the sea, taking houses and roads and leaving tangled landscapes like "sunken city" and Portuguese Bend.

The first of the three adventurous Palos Verdes Peninsula sections offers two routes. The bluff route is an easy footpath affording views of the tidal rocks and ocean far below. On the alternate tidal route the walker will encounter rocks rather than sand to walk on and experience the rugged nature of the shoreline at the base of steep cliffs.

From Torrance County Beach at the end of the South Bay Bicycle Trail, walk south toward the cliffs where the sand gives way to rock. You can usually make it around the small point to Malaga Cove at most tides in calm weather. At 1⅛ miles, before you come to the Palos Verdes Beach and Athletic Club, a trail climbs to a parking area. You need to make a choice of routes here. To do the low tide walk described in Alternate Route below, continue on the rocks from here.

The high route and main CCT route follows the trail up the bluff, then fol-lows the path heading west along the ocean side of Paseo del Mar. Much of the bluff edge is developed. Follow the path as it meanders along undeveloped por-tions of the bluff and then onto the street in front of upscale homes and back to the bluff. Stay on the blufftop and in front of the houses on Paseo del Mar. On clear days spectacular views include a sweep of ocean and shoreline from Santa Monica Bay to Malibu. Beyond two miles Paseo del Mar passes Flat Rock Point, then swings inland and ends at Palos Verdes Drive West. Turn right and follow Palos Verdes Drive West for about ⅞ mile to Paseo del Mar West at 2⅞ miles.

Turn right and walk along the bluff paralleling Paseo del Mar West. Where houses stand on the bluff in places you need to wind back and forth between the bluff and the street. Catalina Island rises from the sea 25 miles offshore. Watch for whales a mile offshore while near shore dolphins and seals often frolic. At 4⅛ miles you round Rocky Point, also called Palos Verdes Point, then pass above Lunada Bay.

At 4½ miles Paseo del Mar West meets Paseo Lunado. On your right open land overlooking Lunada Bay provides space for the low tide Alternate Route to ascend from the tidal rocks.

Follow Paseo Lunado as it heads inland paralleling Agua Amarga Canyon. The gorge, surrounded by a narrow strip of open space amidst residential neighborhoods, cuts deeply into the marine terrace. At 4¾ miles turn right on Via Anacapa to cross the canyon,and follow it to its end before 5¼ miles. Turn right on Palos Verdes Drive West, the main drag along the coast here, and cross its southbound lanes to the trail in the center median.

After walking the median trail for about ½ mile, cross to the west side of Palos Verdes Drive West. Turn right through a pedestrian gate in the elaborate fence. Stay on the trail that goes straight to bluff's edge. Turn left onto the improved trail beside the native habitat preserve and descend through Point Vicente Park to the Point Vicente Interpretive Center and section's end at 7 miles. The center hosts a gift shop, museum, deck for whale watching, restrooms, picnic tables and a short trail along the cliff edge.

ALTERNATE ROUTE: The tidal route from Malaga Cove offers several miles of rugged scrambling on rocks and boulders. You reach Flat Rock Point at 2 miles. You can take a wide trail up the bluff here to shorten your tidal walk, joining the high route at the top. If you continue along the tidal zone, you cross a dramatic landscape beyond Flat Rock and along Bluff Cove where the cliffs tower 300 feet. Your best reward here is the sense of remoteness and quiet as you are surrounded by rugged cliffs and breaking waves right in busy, crowded Los Angeles. After the cove watch for chunks of a freighter that ran aground in the fog in 1961. You round Rocky Point at 4¼ miles, then begin to circle horseshoe-shaped Lunada Bay. As you circle the bay, watch for a steep path coming down the bluff at 5 miles just before the deep abyss of Agua Amarga (bitter water) Canyon. Carefully make the strenuous climb to the park above. The described CCT route from here is all on the bluff. If you are feeling very adventurous, you can tackle the remaining rough, rocky and difficult shoreline that is only passable at low tide and calm weather. The end of this route takes the fishing access path up to a parking lot on Palos Verdes Drive West just around Point Vicente, extending the hike to 8 miles.

SUGGESTED LOOPS AND ROUND TRIPS: Park at the Malaga Cove school parking lot as the tide is going out (the lower the low tide the better), take the trail down to the beach east of the Palos Verdes Beach and Athletic Club and follow the tidal rocks to Lunada Bay. Return on Paseo del Mar for a loop of about 9½ miles.

For an interesting side trip walk up Via Corta to the Malaga Cove Plaza, Farnham Martin Park and the Malaga Cove Library. The park and structures are fine examples of American attempts to recreate the old world, in this case the Tuscany region of Italy. It is such a special place that an ordinance was passed to charge professional photographers for using the area.

The Palos Verdes Peninsula has about 200 miles of trails. The Palos Verdes

Palos Verdes' Portuguese Bend Cove from Half-Way Point.

Loop Trail Project is a grassroots effort to complete a 26-mile multi-use loop trail around the peninsula, connecting its four cities with paths. While the CCT and the Palos Verdes Loop Trail share less than a mile of their routes, they run more or less parallel through the peninsula. The Loop Trail Project includes the concept of a series of trails forming the connecting spokes of a wheel, the wheel's rim being the Loop Trail itself. The maps for sections 8 and 9 show where the P.V. Loop Trail and one of its spokes connect with the CCT. For more information on the Loop Trail, contact the Palos Verdes Loop Trail Project, c/o Sunshine, 6 Limetree Lane, Rancho Palos Verdes, CA 90275 or call (310)377-8761.

SECTION 9
Point Vicente to Royal Palms State Beach

DISTANCE: 7¼ miles (11.7 kilometers).

OPEN TO: Hikers. Bicyclists on streets and new development trails.

SURFACE: Beach, trail, road shoulder, bike path.

ACCESS POINT: Point Vicente Interpretive Center.

HOW TO GET THERE: From Highway 1 in Torrance, take Hawthorne Blvd. (N7) south to its end at Palos Verdes Drive West in the city of Rancho Palos Verdes. Turn left on Palos Verdes Drive West and go .25 mile to the Point Vicente Interpretive Center.

OTHER ACCESS: Point Vicente Fishing Access, Abalone Cove Shoreline Preserve, archery range access road, Ocean Trails Golf Club.

DIFFICULTY: Moderate.

ELEVATION GAIN/LOSS: Tidal Route, 300 feet+/440 feet-. High route, 400 feet+/ 540 feet-.

CAUTIONS: The tidal route is mostly cobble, rock and boulder hopping.

FURTHER INFORMATION: For Point Vicente Fishing Access, Abalone Cove Shoreline Park, and Royal Palms State Beach, call the Los Angeles County Lifeguard Service, Southern Section (310)832-1179, City of Rancho Palos Verdes (310)544-5260.

FACILITIES: Point Vicente Interpretive Center, Ocean Trails Golf Club, Abalone Cove Shoreline Preserve and Royal Palms State Beach have restrooms, water, picnic tables and parking.

HOSTELS: Los Angeles South Bay Hostel (310)831-8109 is in San Pedro.

LODGING: Redondo Beach and San Pedro have motels and hotels.

This middle section of the three Palos Verdes Peninsula sections offers even more diversity than the previous one. The route explores secluded coves, passes near the dramatic Wayfarers' Chapel, crosses a major active landslide, and ends at the site of a hotel claimed by the ocean many years ago.

Consider a visit to the Point Vicente Interpretive Center where you'll find displays on the marine life, geology, history, plants and animals of the Palos Verdes Peninsula. The center also has exhibits on the native Gabrielino people and culture which thrived here before white settlement, plus a big relief map of the area.

After taking a look at the Point Vicente Interpretive Center, spotting a whale, or buying a gift, walk up the driveway to the bike lane along Palos Verdes Drive West. To the right Point Vicente Lighthouse, completed in 1926, still sends a light seaward to warn off ships but is closed to the public. Walk south past the Point Vicente Fishing Access at ½ mile where a side trail leads steeply down to the rocky shoreline. Continue along the bike lane, at 1¼ miles passing the entrance to the defunct Marineland atop Long Point. The aquarium, built in 1954, was doomed because of its remoteness, aging facilities, and competition from more modern aquariums and amusement parks. The land lies mostly empty now, its future uncertain. Continue along the bike lane beside the road to Abalone Cove Shoreline Preserve at 2 miles.

About ⅝ mile before Abalone Cove, consider a detour down residential streets to Vanderlip Park where a ⅜ mile blufftop path in front of some houses offers a look at the tidal rocks below, but little else. To do it, go right on Seaward Drive, right on Beachview Drive, left on Nantasket Drive, then follow the utility driveway to the bluff. Make a left onto the path which ends at a fence after ⅜ mile. Take the path left through the empty lot to Coastsite Drive, jog left on Beachview Drive and right on Seahill Drive which ends at Palos Verdes Drive South. Turn right to continue the main CCT route.

At Abalone Cove Shoreline Preserve, walk through the parking lot down to the low fence along the bluff's edge. As you descend you might glimpse the

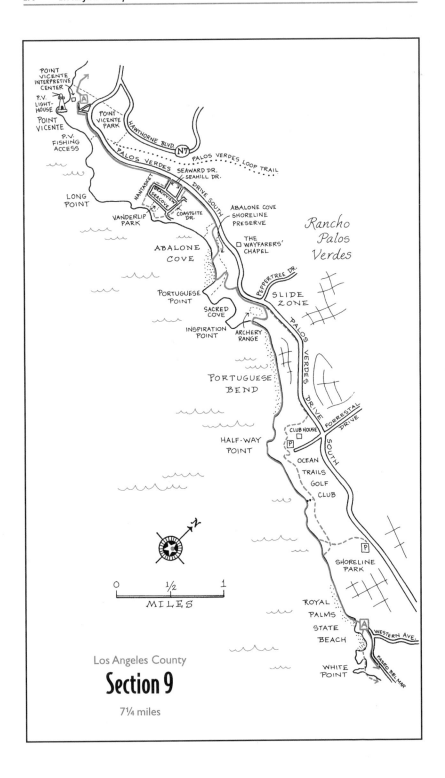

POINT
VICENTE
INTERPRETIVE
CENTER
P.V.
LIGHT-
HOUSE
POINT
VICENTE
POINT
VICENTE
PARK
HAWTHORNE BLVD.
N7
P.V.
FISHING
ACCESS
PALOS VERDES
PALOS VERDES LOOP TRAIL
SEAWARD DR.
SEAHILL DR.
DRIVE SOUTH
NANTASKET
BEACHVIEW
SEACOVE
COASTSITE
DR.
LONG
POINT
VANDERLIP
PARK
ABALONE COVE
SHORELINE
PRESERVE
Rancho
Palos
Verdes
ABALONE
COVE
THE
WAYFARERS'
CHAPEL
PORTUGUESE
POINT
PEPPERTREE DR.
SLIDE
ZONE
SACRED
COVE
INSPIRATION
POINT
ARCHERY
RANGE
PALOS VERDES DRIVE SOUTH
PORTUGUESE
BEND
FORRESTAL
DRIVE
HALF-WAY
POINT
CLUB HOUSE
P
OCEAN
TRAILS
GOLF
CLUB
P
SHORELINE
PARK
N
0   1/2   1
MILES
ROYAL
PALMS
STATE
BEACH
A
WESTERN AVE.
PASEO DEL MAR
WHITE
POINT

Los Angeles County
Section 9
7¼ miles

unique, beautiful Wayfarers' Chapel up on the hill above Palos Verdes Drive. Follow the fence to an opening at the corner where the fence turns inland. Take the path down the bluff through thick vegetation to an asphalt road and turn right. The road ends at a small building on the cove. Walk around the building and onto the beach to walk the rocky shore to the cliff of Portuguese Point at 2¾ miles. From the small deck with an old rock enclosure, take the gravel road uphill to the top of Portuguese Point. You can take a short detour out onto the Portuguese Point for a look at Sacred Cove and Inspiration Point to the south, or simply continue along the road as it contours around the hill and ends at Palos Verdes Drive South at 3⅛ miles.

Walk the bike lane along the road, heading south beside a big pipeline. Shortly you come to one of the most striking geologic features anywhere along the CCT. The road suddenly takes a severe dip just after a traffic warning sign. The dip marks the edge of the oldest active landslide on the planet, the Portuguese Bend landslide. Above the road, the gated community of Portuguese Bend, located on the edge of a bowl shaped canyon, sits perched in the slide zone. In the 1950s after numerous houses were constructed, the land suddenly started sliding toward the sea at a rate of up to six inches a day. Many houses were destroyed, but some survive by keeping them propped up on adjustable house mover cribbings as they move. The slide slowed somewhat in recent years with engineered fixes, yet some of the houses still moved as much as 600 feet over time while remaining occupied. Against the odds the owners keep the houses intact and continue to defend this horsey enclave against the inevitable sliding.

A few hundred feet past the gated Peppertree Drive, the main CCT route turns right on a dirt road. A small sign marks it as an archery range and indicates if the range is in use. If in use, you can still enter but should stay on the road. The high route along Palos Verdes Drive South is described in Alternate Route below. The road cuts down through the jumbled, moving earth. Just after starting down it, you'll see two houses by the road that used to be on the other side of Palos Verdes Drive. As the earth moved, dragging the highway and houses with it, the road was straightened, leaving the houses downhill from the road on their slow descent to the sea.

Past the archery range at the end of the road, take the rough path down to the beach at 4 miles. From here you can follow the tideline below the slide. In calm weather and during all but the highest tides, the CCT follows the tideline all the way to Royal Palms State Beach. Walk the long sweeping beach in front an exclusive beach club (you're out of the slide zone now). Then follow the tideline beneath 200-foot cliffs out around Half-Way Point, rounding the point at 5½ miles. If you need it, there's an escape trail just beyond the point that climbs to a road ascending to Palos Verdes Drive.

Continue rock hopping along the scenic shore at the base of more towering cliffs. The cliffs reach their highest extreme around 6⅜ miles. Continuing along the rocky tidal zone, you reach tall palm trees, then picnic tables, restrooms and a parking lot at the end of this section's hike at 7¼ miles. Look around the area to find the remains of the Royal Palms Hotel, built in 1883 to take advantage of a natural hot sulfur spring. Earthquakes reduced the flow of hot water, so the hotel closed and was left to be destroyed by storms in the 1920s.

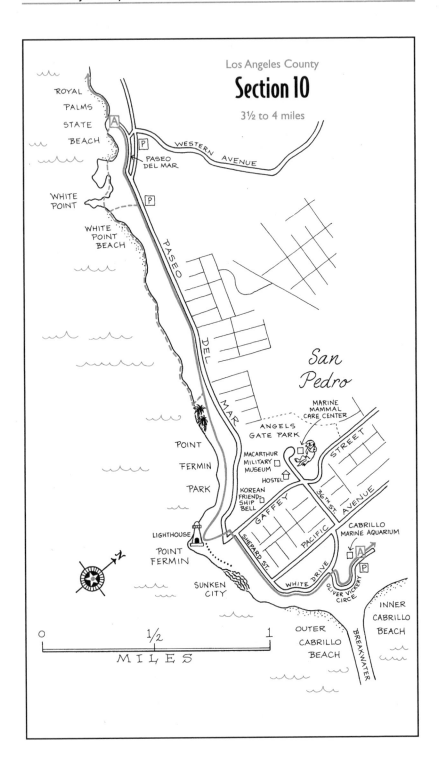

Los Angeles County
Section 10
3½ to 4 miles

ROYAL PALMS STATE BEACH

A

P

PASEO DEL MAR

WESTERN AVENUE

P

WHITE POINT

WHITE POINT BEACH

PASEO DEL MAR

San Pedro

MARINE MAMMAL CARE CENTER

ANGELS GATE PARK

MACARTHUR MILITARY MUSEUM

HOSTEL

KOREAN FRIENDSHIP BELL

POINT FERMIN PARK

36TH STREET

GAFFEY

PACIFIC

AVENUE

CABRILLO MARINE AQUARIUM

A

P

LIGHTHOUSE

POINT FERMIN

SUNKEN CITY

SHEPARD ST.

WHITE DRIVE

OLIVER VICKERY CIRCE

INNER CABRILLO BEACH

BREAKWATER

OUTER CABRILLO BEACH

0   1/2   1

MILES

ALTERNATE ROUTE: From the archery range road, continue on Palos Verdes Drive South past the Portuguese Bend Club gated community to Conqueror Drive around 5 miles. From here you look down on a huge golf course and residential development being built as this book went to press. Turn right onto the new access path and follow it down to the bluff. Take any of several trails down to the beach. If you want to minimize the rock hopping, stay on the bluff trail until it drops into a big open valley with a mobile home park on the far side. Look for a steep trail and take it down to the beach. From here it is about one mile on tidal rocks to Royal Palms State Beach at 7¼ miles.

SUGGESTED ROUND TRIPS AND LOOPS: From the Ocean Trails Golf Course look inland for a huge bare cliff, once a bentonite quarry. The bowl beneath the cliff has naturalized into a special native habitat. To see it, go up Forrestal Drive on the other side of Palos Verdes Drive from the golf course entrance. To get to the cliff's base for fossils and crystals, go straight past the barricade. The Discovery Room in the community center to the left is also worthwhile.

Consider visiting the Wayfarers Chapel above Abalone Cove. The unique structure, designed by Lloyd Wright (Frank's son), is open daily from 11am to 4 pm.

> HOW TO IMPROVE THE CCT HERE: If the short blufftop trail between Nantasket Drive and Coastsite Drive were extended northwest through the old Marineland property to Point Vicente and southeast to Abalone Cove, it would eliminate walking along Palos Verde Drive for two miles.

SECTION 10
Royal Palms State Beach to Cabrillo Marine Aquarium

DISTANCE: 4 miles for tidal route, 3½ miles for sidewalk route (6.4 or 5.6 kilometers).

OPEN TO: Hikers. Bicyclists on street.

SURFACE: Beach, sidewalk.

ACCESS POINT: Royal Palms State Beach.

HOW TO GET THERE: Take Western Avenue/Highway 213 south to its end. Go left on Paseo del Mar for .25 mile, turn right and follow Kay Fiorentino Drive to the beach. Or, from San Pedro follow Paseo del Mar for 2 miles from the Point Fermin Lighthouse, then go left on Kay Fiorentino Drive to the beach.

OTHER ACCESS: Point Fermin Park, White Point access path.

DIFFICULTY: Easy.

ELEVATION GAIN/LOSS: 120 feet+/100 feet-.

CAUTIONS: Parks close at sunset. Use caution on tidal rocks.

FURTHER INFORMATION: For parks and beaches in this section, contact the Los Angeles County Lifeguard Service, Southern Section (310)832-1179.

FACILITIES: Water, restrooms, picnic tables at Royal Palms State Beach, Point Fermin Park and Cabrillo City Beach.

HOSTEL: Los Angeles South Bay Hostel (310)831-8109 is in San Pedro's Angels Gate Park, 6 blocks up Gaffey Street from Point Fermin Park.

LODGING: San Pedro has an abundance of motels and hotels.

From the rugged shore of the Palos Verdes Peninsula to the Pacific edge of the city of Los Angeles represented by the port city of San Pedro, this section has much to offer along and near the route. Highlights include a Victorian lighthouse in a pretty park, a marine aquarium, and an apocalyptic view of the possible future of much of the California coastline. Two routes are offered: a tidal route that runs most of the way, and a sidewalk route preferable during high tides and/or bad weather.

For the sidewalk route, walk up the Royal Palms State Beach entrance road to Paseo Del Mar, turn right and walk along Paseo Del Mar's sidewalk to Point Fermin Park. You'll recognize the park by the abundance of tall palm trees at one mile. The tidal route ascends the bluff adjacent to the residential area where the park begins.

To take the more adventurous and ½-mile longer tidal route, walk through the Royal Palms State Beach parking lot at the base of the cliffs, then continue on the rocks at the tideline. Watch for the swimming pool foundations awash in the shallow water just off the beach. After rounding a small cove, walk around rugged White Point at ⅝ mile and come to a wide path going up to the bluff from White Point Beach. You can exit the beach here, but the CCT tidal route continues on the rocks at the base of 120-foot cliffs.

At 1½ miles watch for the first of the palm trees of Point Fermin Park. They mark the path you climb to its top to meet the high route beside Paseo del Mar. Point Fermin juts prominently into the sea ahead. Although it is possible to make it around the point at low tide, it's a rough proposition and not recommended. If you elect to try it, scramble on the rocks around the point, then take one of several informal paths up to the park.

After climbing the path up to the bluff, turn right and walk east through narrow Point Fermin Park, hemmed in by house-lined Paseo del Mar above and the sea cliff below. Soon Paseo del Mar and the vertical cliff converge. The CCT takes to the road's sidewalk along the edge of the eroding cliff. You reach the larger part of verdant Point Fermin Park at 2¼ miles.

Take the park path along the cliff, guarded by a railing, to the elaborate Victorian building of the retired Point Fermin Lighthouse at 2½ miles. It was built in 1874 not many years after Los Angeles Harbor began to develop, but long before the container ports and cruise ships of today's massive harbor. After the lighthouse ceased operation in 1941, it was used as a residence until the late 1960s when the Coast Guard considered tearing it down. Alarmed local residents came to the rescue, saving and refurbishing the structure. The house is a park employee

The land in turnoil at Point Fermin Park's Sunken City.

residence closed to the public, so you can only inspect it from behind the fence.

Before continuing on the main route, take a brief side trip to look at Sunken City—the past and possibly the future of the coastline—eroding, sinking, slumping and eventually disappearing. Follow the walkway past the lighthouse to the imposing gray metal fence designed more as a warning than as a barrier to keep people out. Step around the end of the fence at bluff's edge and walk out along the bluff. This was once part of Point Fermin Park and a residential area. In 1929 six acres of land started slipping, leaving the place today only a jumble of large blocks of earth and slabs of street and sidewalks tilted in all directions. It's reminiscent of the last scene in the movie *Planet of the Apes* with the Statue of Liberty buried up to its neck on a sandy beach. It demonstrates the foolhardy nature of building on the edge of a naturally eroding and unstoppable shoreline.

After the side trip, return to the lighthouse and walk north up to Gaffey Street directly inland where CCT follows sidewalks through a residential area. After a quarter block on Gaffey Street, go right on Shepard Street, left on Bluff Place, then straight on White Drive. Turn right on Oliver Vickery Circle at 3¾ miles and enter Cabrillo City Beach Park. After the entrance station, turn left and walk through the picnic area and over to the front of the Cabrillo Marine Aquarium at 4 miles where this section ends.

SUGGESTED ROUND TRIPS AND LOOPS: Walk up Gaffey Street, then go left on 36th Street to Angels Gate Park. The park features the massive Korean Friendship Bell, the Marine Mammal Care Center and the Fort MacArthur Military Museum. The Marine Mammal Care Center is open during regular business hours for self-guided tours. The museum preserves an intact coastal battery with all the equipment in place except for the huge disappearing guns which were cut up for scrap after World War II.

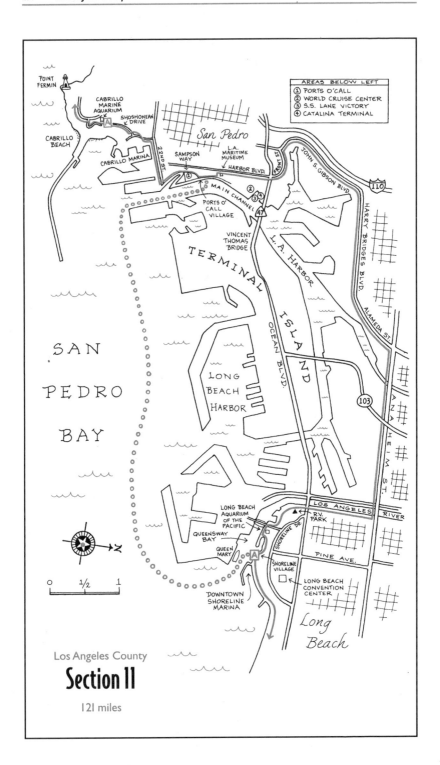

POINT FERMIN

CABRILLO MARINE AQUARIUM

SHOSHONEAN K DRIVE

CABRILLO BEACH

CABRILLO MARINA

San Pedro

SAMPSON WAY

L.A. MARITIME MUSEUM

HARBOR BLVD.

22ND ST.

MAIN CHANNEL

PORTS O' CALL VILLAGE

VINCENT THOMAS BRIDGE

47

FRONT ST.

JOHN S. GIBSON BLVD.

110

HARRY BRIDGES BLVD.

ALAMEDA ST.

TERMINAL ISLAND

L.A. HARBOR

OCEAN BLVD.

SAN

PEDRO

BAY

LONG BEACH HARBOR

103

ANAHEIM ST.

LONG BEACH AQUARIUM OF THE PACIFIC

R.V. PARK

LOS ANGELES RIVER

QUEENSWAY BAY

QUEEN MARY

SHORELINE DR.

PINE AVE.

SHORELINE VILLAGE

LONG BEACH CONVENTION CENTER

DOWNTOWN SHORELINE MARINA

Long Beach

0   1/2   1

AREAS BELOW LEFT
1. PORTS O'CALL
2. WORLD CRUISE CENTER
3. S.S. LANE VICTORY
4. CATALINA TERMINAL

Los Angeles County
Section 11
121 miles

SECTION 11
Cabrillo Marine Aquarium to Shoreline Village, Long Beach

DISTANCE: 12¾ miles, or 2½ miles plus 8-mile boat ride (20.5, or 4 + 13 kilometers).

OPEN TO: Hikers, bicyclists.

SURFACE: Sidewalk.

ACCESS POINT: Cabrillo Marine Aquarium, Cabrillo Beach.

HOW TO GET THERE: From the end of the Harbor Freeway (I-110) take Gaffey Street through San Pedro to 22nd Street, then go left to Pacific Avenue, turn right and follow Pacific to Oliver Vickery Circle, where you go left to the Cabrillo Beach parking lot (fee parking).

OTHER ACCESS: Ports O'Call Village, downtown San Pedro and anywhere along the walking route.

DIFFICULTY: Moderate (long hike), easy with boat crossing.

ELEVATION GAIN/LOSS: Negligible.

CAUTIONS: The inland route passes through miles of rundown industrial areas and some depressed city areas.

FURTHER INFORMATION: Cabrillo Marine Aquarium (310)548-7562, Long Beach Convention and Visitors Council (562)436-3645, Water Taxi Service: U.S. Port Services (310)519-8260.

FACILITIES: The first 2½ and last 2½ miles have urban amenities.

HOSTELS: L.A. South Bay Hostel (310)831-8109 is in San Pedro's Angels Gate Park.

CAMPING: Golden Shore RV Resort (562)435-4646 is in Long Beach.

LODGING: San Pedro and Long Beach have abundant motels and hotels.

The Los Angeles and Long Beach harbors present one of the most difficult man-made challenges to an uninterrupted alignment of the CCT. Whereas many other interruptions to the CCT are a matter of policy or private property that someday can be overcome, the huge harbor complex provides a daunting challenge. We offer two alternatives and at the end of the section, some possible long range solutions. A walk around the harbors on surface streets for 12¾ miles can be done in about five hours at a brisk pace. Riding a bicycle is a good option. The alternative is to walk the first 2½ miles to Ports O'Call Village and arrange a boat ride to Long Beach.

The major problem with the boat ride is the cost of the only established water taxi service between San Pedro and Long Beach. Call U.S. Port Services at (310)519-8260 and ask for their water taxi service and how many people they can carry. Try to arrange as many people for the shuttle as possible so everyone can share the cost. You must make advance arrangements to be picked up either at Cabrillo Beach or Ports O'Call village and dropped off at Shoreline Village in Long Beach.

The Profits and Pleasures of the Harbor

The Los Angeles/Long Beach Harbors exemplify the huge L.A. economy. The harbors abut each other inside San Pedro Bay and are among the world's biggest ports. The Port of Los Angeles alone throbs with commerce at 29 cargo terminals. In 1998 it handled 3.2 million containers with a cargo value of $73.8 billion. Add about a million cruise passengers to the mix each year and it's no surprise it creates 259,000 jobs.

This success came with a price. The natural San Pedro Bay disappeared completely, obscured by 35 miles of artificial shoreline, 3800 acres of water and 3700 acres of landfill. Aanticipating a booming economy, the Port of Los Angeles' plans to double capacity with new container berths and dredging projects to deepen the channels for the world's largest ships. Mitigation for disturbing the harbor's last natural resources involves funding for Orange County's Bolsa Chica wetlands (see the feature Coastal Wetlands), restoration of San Diego's Batiquitos Lagoon, and creating shallow water habitat in the harbor for fish-eating birds and as a nursery for fish.

Aside from shipping, the area hosts several historic and educational features. Two big port-oriented developments attract visitors, Shoreline Village in Long Beach and San Pedro's Ports O' Call Village. Both front the CCT as do downtown San Pedro and Long Beach. Other features include Angels Gate Park and its Korean Friendship Bell, Fort McArthur Military Museum, Point Fermin Park and lighthouse, and the mammoth Long Beach Convention Center.

If you're interested in the maritime realm, consider visiting the following places:

• The Cabrillo Marine Aquarium in San Pedro hosts exhibits about beaches, mudflats, rocky shoreline, and warm water species of the open ocean. The aquarium also does education and research, inviting public participation in the conservation of southern California marine life. It offers tours, classes and programs. Admission is free, parking $6.50 per car, a great deal for families or a car load of friends, even better for walkers, cyclists and those using public transportation. For information call (310)548-7562, or check out the website at www.cabrillo.org.

• The Queen Mary rests inside its own breakwater in Long Beach Harbor. After long service, it's now a floating hotel and conference center run by the City of Long Beach. The Queen Mary, one of the largest ships ever built, stretches 1,019.5 feet long, 118 feet wide, and weighs 81,237 tons. The 10 million rivets holding it together and 2000 portholes testify to its vastness. Its twelve decks held 2000 passengers and 1100 staff. The 1936 maiden voyage began 1001 Atlantic trips. As a troop carrier in World War II, it hauled over 750,000 troops, logging 569,429 miles. The final October 1967 cruise ended at Long Beach and the City took ownership.

• The Maritime Museum in San Pedro is the largest of its kind in California with 75,000 square feet. Originally built as the base for an auto ferry shuttling workers across the harbor to Terminal Island shipping yards, the handsome "Streamline Moderne" building fell into disrepair after the bridge was built, and was saved only by citizens dedicated to historical preservation. Today it houses 700 ship models, ship equipment, sea-related Native American artifacts, ship figureheads, maritime arts, crafts, an 18-foot model of the Titanic, exhibits on the whaling industry, the Navy and Merchant Marine. The museum offers classes like scrimshaw and small boat handling. The affiliated L.A. Maritime Institute offers sailing programs for youth aboard the historic sailboats Swift of Ipswich and Bill of Rights. Admission to the museum at the foot of 6th Street in downtown San Pedro, is just $1.

Our route starts in front of the Cabrillo Marine Aquarium, heading inland on the sidewalk to pass a gate blocking Shoshonean Drive, which you then follow north. You pass a small manmade wetlands here that tries to represent the thousands of acres of marine estuary in this area before harbor development began. At the far end of Shoshonean Drive at ⅜ mile, you can either take the walk on the left angling uphill to a small overlook park, or cross the street and continue on the sidewalk along Cabrillo Marina overlooking the small boat harbor.

At 22nd Street turn right and walk to its end, then go left on Signal Street at 2¼ miles. Along Signal you get a close look at the real working harbor, with a wharf full of gear for the fleet of commercial fishing boats lining the dock. In the distance huge container shipping cranes rise skyward.

At the end of the dock turn right at an old and colorful historic restaurant, Utro's. Have some refreshment at this interesting place, then follow the pedestrian walkway painted on the parking lot to Ports O'Call Village. If you arranged a boat ride, it features a close look at the outer harbor and the mammoth Queen Mary docked in Long Beach. You want to be dropped off at Shoreline Village in Long Beach, the beginning of Section 12.

To continue on the walking route, proceed along the row of businesses at Ports O'Call Village and then along Sampson Way to the handsome Los Angeles Maritime Museum in downtown San Pedro at 3¼ miles. Walk a short block up 6th Street, then go right on Harbor Blvd., soon passing the Los Angeles World Cruise Center where huge cruise ships dock. Continue under the even more mammoth Vincent Thomas bridge at 4 miles where Harbor Blvd. becomes Front Street.

The next 8 miles pass through a grim old decaying industrial area and into downtown Long Beach. They are not recommended. Continue on Front Street. At Pacific Avenue, you veer right on John S. Gibson Blvd. and follow it beside the Harbor Freeway. Around 6 miles that road turns east and becomes Harry Bridges Blvd. Follow it with the harbor district on your right and the area of Los Angeles called Wilmington on your left.

Around 7¼ miles that street angles left and becomes Alameda Street, which you follow paralleling the railroad tracks. Around 8⅛ miles turn right on Anaheim Street and walk its sidewalk east. You pass beneath the Terminal Island Freeway before 9¼ miles, then continue along Anaheim Street to pass under the Long Beach Freeway at 10¼ miles. Beyond the freeway you cross the channelized Los Angeles River and enter Long Beach.

Immediately turn right onto the bike path on the river levee and follow it to the waterfront. At 12 miles the path turns east past an RV park on the left and a newly created wetlands on the right. You then pass the Catalina ferry landing, then the new Long Beach Aquarium of the Pacific. At the Aquarium go left (north) and circle around Queensway Bay Harbor before reaching Shoreline Village and section's end at 12¾ miles.

ALTERNATE ROUTE: Instead of taking the bike path along the river, continue on Anaheim Blvd. and make a right on Pine Avenue through the middle of downtown Long Beach. At Ocean Blvd. make a short jog to the left toward the huge Long Beach Convention Center where you will find a wide boardwalk and plaza running along the length of the building. The boardwalk crosses Shoreline Drive on an overpass and descends a staircase to Shoreline Park. Turn left, skirting the edge

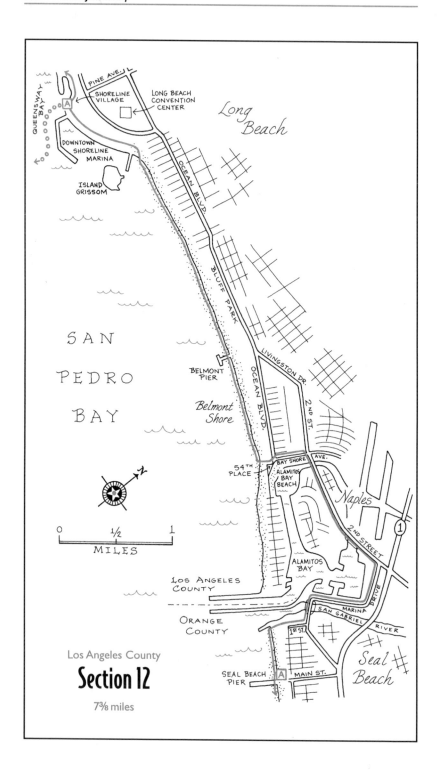

Los Angeles County

Section 12

7⅜ miles

of the lagoon and a small boat marina to arrive at Shoreline Village and the end of the walk at 12¾ miles.

SUGGESTED ROUND TRIPS AND LOOPS: A pleasant and interesting walk from the Cabrillo Marine Aquarium to the Los Angeles Maritime Museum and back makes a 6½-mile round trip. Visiting the aquarium, the museum and detouring into San Pedro's Old Town makes this walk worthwhile.

At the other end of the route, walk around downtown Long Beach, the Convention Center and Shoreline Aquatic Park to get a taste of this port town. One of the many astounding sights is the mural of full-sized whales painted on the Long Beach Arena. View the Queen Mary docked across the channel from the end of the jetty at Shoreline Village. Also be sure to visit the Long Beach Aquarium of the Pacific. A free shuttle, a red bus called the Passport, takes passengers all around the waterfront and downtown areas. There is also a water taxi from Shoreline Village to the Queen Mary.

HOW TO IMPROVE CCT HERE: It is a tough proposition, but the inland route described above goes through a huge area in need of serious redevelopment. With vision and foresight the redevelopment could include clean industry, housing, offices, restoration of former wetlands, ample greenways and a multi-use path winding through it all. Also, a bike lane is needed on the Vincent Thomas Bridge and along Ocean Avenue connecting San Pedro and Long Beach.

SECTION 12
Shoreline Village, Long Beach, to Seal Beach Pier

DISTANCE: 7⅜ miles (11.9 kilometers).

OPEN TO: Hikers. Bicyclists on streets.

SURFACE: Beach, sidewalk.

ACCESS POINT: Shoreline Village, Long Beach.

HOW TO GET THERE: Take the Long Beach Freeway (I-710) to the Shoreline Drive exit in Long Beach. Go 1.2 miles on Shoreline Drive to the foot of Pine Avenue. Shoreline Village is on the waterfront east of the Shoreline Park Lagoon and west of the marina near downtown Long Beach.

OTHER ACCESS: Anywhere on the route.

DIFFICULTY: Easy.

ELEVATION GAIN/LOSS: Negligible.

FURTHER INFORMATION: For Long Beach City Beach, Belmont Shore and Alamitos Bay Beach, call Long Beach Lifeguard Service (562)570-1341. For Seal Beach, call the Seal Beach Lifeguard Station (562)430-2613.

FACILITIES: Shoreline Aquatic Park and Bixby Park have restrooms, picnic tables and water with the usual urban amenities just inland from Shoreline. Belmont Pier has restrooms and a snack bar. Alamitos Bay Beach has restrooms.

LODGING: Long Beach has many hotel rooms. Stay on the Queen Mary for a unique experience.

This section features a walk from the big city of Long Beach, the fifth largest in California with a population of 442,000, to the relatively lazy backwater town of Seal Beach with a population of 26,000 and a short, tree-lined Main Street ending at the pier. The massive Long Beach Convention Center represents one view of what's important and the locals hanging out in Eisenhower Park at the base of Seal Beach Pier represent another.

Before heading for Seal Beach, take a short detour on the jetty sidewalk in front of Shoreline Village for a closer look at the 1,020-foot long *Queen Mary* across the channel. The world's largest ocean liner landed here for keeps in 1967 after being retired in 1964.

From Shoreline Village walk the bike path east past the small boat marina to the 4-mile long beach for which the city was named. Walk down the tideline of the wide, sandy, usually surfless beach. The islands in the bay, designed to look like modern high rise buildings, hide oil rigs pumping black gold from beneath the bay. Walk down the long beach which is tucked at the base of 40-foot bluffs that partially hide the dense city just inland.

Around 1⅜ miles Bixby Park sits on a knoll above the beach. Continue down the beach, passing Bluff Park from 1¾ miles to 2½ miles. You reach Belmont Pier, 1620 feet long, at 2⅞ miles. Continue down the beach with the bluffs soon giving way to the nearly level Belmont Shore neighborhood.

Further down the beach at 4 miles, turn inland at 54th Place, identified by a house on the beach. You start the walk around Alamitos Bay through Naples here. You can walk either pleasant Alamitos Bay Beach on the bay side or Bayshore Avenue above it. Turn right onto Second Street and walk through the lively business district to Marina Drive at 5½ miles, where you turn right. Walk either along the marina frontage or stay on the sidewalk of Marina Drive.

At 6½ miles follow Marina Drive as it makes a left turn to cross a bridge over the San Gabriel River into Orange County and Seal Beach. Turn right on First Street, walk to its end and walk onto the beach. Turn left for a short stroll to the Seal Beach Pier and the end of the section at 7⅜ miles.

SUGGESTED ROUND TRIPS AND LOOPS: To stretch out your legs and get some exercise, walk the entire 4½-mile length of Long Beach City Beach from 1st Place by Shoreline Aquatic Park to 72nd Place at the entrance to Alamitos Bay.

Orange County

THIS SMALL COUNTY WITH A SPARKLING COASTLINE portrays the ultimate images of southern California living: a herd of southern California teenagers swimming and tanning on a lazy summer day while vigorous surfers cut the waves, wealth and a bastion of conservative politics (either a blessing or a curse depending on your point of view), an onslaught of irreversible development on ridges, in valleys, coastal bluffs and citrus groves, protected wildlands in the Laguna Hills, the art town of Laguna Beach. Orange County ranks second in population of California's 58 counties and only 54th in land area.

For the adventurous walker Orange County offers more than image on its 44½-mile-long coast. Warm weather dominates the climate with a yearly daytime average of 70 degrees while the coast basks in cool ocean breezes. You can visit a truly laid back throwback of a small beach town, walk mile upon mile of warm sandy beaches past those lazy tanners, discover coastal land untouched by development, find some scenic uncrowded coves washed by clear clean water, come upon a rustic beach colony still intact from the 1920s and early 1930s, explore a significant wetland, wander around an art town and visit art galleries, visit five state parks and beaches and six piers. You can swim, snorkel and surf, or shop in the towns you pass. The Orange County Marine Institute offers information on the marine environment.

Orange County's Coastal Trail starts amid the laid back ambiance of Seal Beach. After a short detour around Anaheim Bay, a long wonderful beach walk stretches all the way to Balboa Pier. The route then turns inland, taking to the water on a brief ferry ride to Balboa Island. CCT returns to the beach at Crystal Cove State Park with the beach colony of rickety old cottages and 3½ miles of undeveloped coastline. The route then takes to the highway to pass a locked gate community blocking coastal access. The Coastal Trail then meanders on and off coves, beaches and streets all the way through Laguna Beach before again being forced to the highway by an exclusive, locked gate development in South Laguna. You once again hit the beach at Salt Creek Beach Park before walking over Dana Point, the last significant piece of unprotected open land on the Orange County coast. Beyond Dana Point Harbor the CCT hits the sand at Doheny State Beach. From here our route stays mostly on the beach through Capistrano Beach and San Clemente all the way to San Clemente State Beach just before the county line.

SECTION 1
Seal Beach Pier to Huntington Beach Pier

DISTANCE: 9¾ miles (15.7 kilometers).

OPEN TO: Hikers. Bicyclists on paved path.

SURFACE: Beach, paved bike path.

ACCESS POINT: Seal Beach Pier.

HOW TO GET THERE: From the San Diego Freeway (I-405) take the Seal Beach Blvd. exit and head south for 3.5 miles. Turn west on Pacific Coast Highway (Highway 1) for .5 mile then south on Main Street. Go three blocks to the pier at the end of the street.

OTHER ACCESS: Almost all of the route is accessible from Pacific Coast Highway.

DIFFICULTY: Easy.

ELEVATION GAIN/LOSS: Negligible.

FURTHER INFORMATION: Seal Beach Lifeguard Station (562)430-2613, Bolsa Chica State Beach (714)846-3460, Huntington State Beach (714)536-1454, Huntington City Beach (714)536-5281.

FACILITIES: Restrooms, water, picnic tables and parking at Seal Beach and Bolsa Chica State Beach. Restrooms at Huntington Beach Pier.

HOSTEL: Colonial Inn Hostel is in Huntington Beach (714)536-3315.

CAMPGROUNDS: Bolsa Chica State Beach has an enroute RV campground for self-contained vehicles only. Huntington City Beach also has an enroute RV camp but reservations are only available within 30 days of your planned stay. For reservations call (714)536-5280. Several private RV parks near Disneyland about 8 miles inland accept tenters. Try Travelers World RV Park, Canyon RV or C.C. Camperland.

LODGING: Seal Beach and Huntington Beach have abundant lodging.

Seal Beach retains some of the earthy charm of another time with a tree-lined Main Street only three blocks long ending at the foot of the pier. In contrast to its big neighbor Long Beach, Seal Beach has little going on, and it looks like they would like to keep it that way. If the huge population inland ever discovers the old beach town, the quiet ambiance will disappear. Locals hang out in Eisenhower Park and on the pier where Orange County's Coastal Trail begins. The route follows the beach except for a detour around the mouth of Anaheim Bay.

From the pier walk south on the wide sandy beach or on the sidewalk in front of the beachfront buildings to the Anaheim Bay north jetty at ½ mile. Turn left at the end of the last building, walk one block, then jog ½ block right to Seal Beach Blvd. and follow it inland to Highway 1 at ⅞ mile.

Turn right and follow the shoulder of Pacific Coast Highway. Beyond 1¼ miles the wetlands of the Seal Beach National Wildlife Refuge lie on your left. Cross the bridge over Anaheim Bay at 1¾ miles and continue past the gated

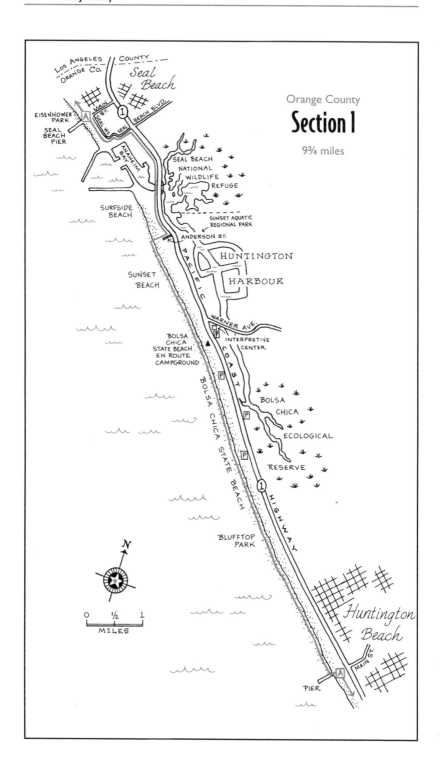

Los Angeles County
Orange Co.
Seal Beach

EISENHOWER PARK
SEAL BEACH PIER

Orange County
Section 1
9¾ miles

MAIN ST.
SEAL WY.
SEAL
BEACH BLVD.

ANAHEIM BAY

SEAL BEACH NATIONAL WILDLIFE REFUGE

SURFSIDE BEACH

SUNSET AQUATIC REGIONAL PARK

ANDERSON ST.

PACIFIC

HUNTINGTON
HARBOUR

SUNSET BEACH

WARNER AVE.

BOLSA CHICA STATE BEACH EN ROUTE CAMPGROUND

INTERPRETIVE CENTER

COAST

BOLSA CHICA STATE BEACH

BOLSA CHICA ECOLOGICAL RESERVE

HIGHWAY

BLUFFTOP PARK

N

0   ½   1
MILES

Huntington Beach

MAIN ST.

PIER

The Coastal Wetlands of Southern California

In the last 150 years, thousands of acres of California's marine estuaries disappeared under the development of harbors, marinas, industrial building and housing tracts. Wetlands became the Los Angeles, Long Beach and San Diego Harbors. Downtown San Francisco and the Marina District sit atop bay mud, much of San Francisco Bay wetlands has been converted to salt evaporation ponds, Del Mar Racetrack sits atop a wetlands in San Diego, luxury yachts float in marinas scooped out of pickleweed flats. In all, 80% of California's coastal wetlands have vanished.

The wetlands of southern California remain among the most diverse and threatened in the world. Several dozen ecosystems from Point Conception to the Mexican border continually suffer pollution and the threat of filling. The Mediterranean climate, young geologic features, and infrequent but strong winter storms create conditions for distinctive coastal wetlands species. These conditions include wide fluctuations in water levels, salinity, oxygen, and temperature, sometimes magnified by human intervention. The resulting species with unique adaptive traits make the wetlands exceptionally worthy of conservation. The clapper rail, an endangered bird, exemplifies special adaptation. It builds a platform nest tethered to cord grass, allowing it to rise and fall with varying water levels. The native Belding's savannah sparrow, which nests in the pickleweed marsh, can drink sea water.

Even where wetlands enjoy protection, uplands development generates erosion and pollution that heavily impacts the ecosystem. The degradation puts tremendous pressure on wildlife, exterminating many species and endangering others.

The importance of wetlands, the most productive ecosystems of any in the world, cannot be over emphasized. They create the base of the food chain for many species, serving as spawning and nesting site, incubator and nursery to many kinds of birds, fish and crustaceans. The south coast wetlands, an integral part of the Pacific Flyway, hosts one of the largest bird migrations on the planet. Wetlands also serve as a filter for storm water, releasing clean water to the ocean.

In spite of the dire condition of wetlands, and even though in recent years laws more strongly protect them, battles still rage in some locations over development in wetlands and pollution from upland. In Orange County, the foothills above the Upper Newport Bay estuary suffer clearing for development by the Irvine Company, among others, exposing the soil and creating silt-laden runoff that flows directly into the bay down channelized creeks. It's estimated that just one creek deposited about 400,000 cubic yards of silt into the bay in 1993. At the 1000-acre Ballona wetlands, the last significant piece left in Los Angeles, developers obtained approval for dense development on the inland part of the wetlands. Approvals allow thousands of residential units and millions of square feet of commercial space in spite of intense opposition by environmental groups and thousands of local residents. The Wetlands Action Network filed suit to stop the project based on a variety of environmental issues including the question of runoff. Development remains stalled by the suit, giving Ballona supporters a fighting chance to finally save this vital parcel.

The Bolsa Chica wetlands in Orange County contain 1300 acres of historic wetlands and 300 acres of mesa. For 30 years citizens, environmental groups, agencies and developers have battled over the fate of the site. The Amigos de Bolsa Chica wanted the entire site saved for its environmental value. Developers wanted to build, even in wetlands, although it goes continued on next page

Surfside community on your right into Sunset Beach. Turn right on Anderson Street at 2⅞ miles, marked by a large wooden tower, and walk down the street along the edge of the gated community to the beach.

Turn left at the tideline and walk down the beach to the end of the houses at 4¼ miles. This marks the beginning of Bolsa Chica State Beach. The RV enroute camp site lies inland beside the highway. Continue down coast along the tideline. Across the highway on Warner Avenue around 4⅞ miles sits the Bolsa Chica Ecological Reserve Interpretive Center, worth a visit. Farther down the beach at 5¾ miles, you pass the parking lot for Bolsa Chica State Beach. Locals still call this Tin Can Beach because in the 1960s millions of cans littered the sand here. Now parking for thousands of cars and conveniently located restrooms and showers line the beach, attesting to its popularity.

Continuing down Bolsa Chica Beach, you reach Blufftop Park in the city of Huntington Beach at 7½ miles. Either walk the paved path atop the 30-foot bluff or continue on the beach. If you walk the beach at higher tides, farther along riprap on the beach may force you onto the bluffs. This long stretch of beach takes you into the heart of what was called Surf City in the 1960s. It's where the rock band the Beach Boys gained fame and the surfing culture really blossomed. Surfing still reigns as king and queen here. The Huntington Beach International Surfing Museum documents the history. You'll probably find a horde of people, especially in the summer, plopped on towels or taking the waves as you end your hike at the Huntington Beach Pier at 9¾ miles.

SUGGESTED ROUND TRIPS AND LOOPS: The Bolsa Chica Ecological Reserve Interpretive Center on Warner Avenue a block off Pacific Coast Highway offers a parking lot and trailhead for the reserve. Another trail starts across the highway from the main entrance to Bolsa Chica State Beach. You can walk several miles of trail exploring this significant remnant of a vast marine estuary. Read how activists saved this wetlands in the adjacent feature article *The Coastal Wetlands of California*.

Coastal Wetlands – continued

against the Coastal Act. Over the years such projects as a nuclear powered desalinization plant, an international airport, and a marina with thousands of homes were proposed. In 1996 the Coastal Commission approved 900 houses on 180 acres of wetlands and 2,500 units on the mesa in spite of the Coastal Act and staff recommendations. Citizen groups sued, giving state and local agencies time to come up with a plan to purchase the area from the Koll Real Estate Group. In 1997 the Ports of Los Angeles and Long Beach agreed to provide almost $68 million in funding to buy 880 acres of wetlands as mitigation for port development. Plans call for eventual restoration of the entire remaining wetlands. As of this writing the fate of the remaining uplands is undecided.

Wetlands endure as a prized development commodity on the southern coast. Expanding population, pressure to develop, and increased pollution from inland sources could spell the end of the southern California coastal ecosystems and the abundant life they contain. Local, state and federal agencies must begin comprehensive, coordinated planning to permanently end development in wetlands, end damage from inland sources, and seriously start the critical process of reclamation and restoration.

SECTION 2
Huntington Beach Pier to Balboa Pier

DISTANCE: 8 miles (12.9 kilometers).

OPEN TO: Hikers.

SURFACE: Beach.

ACCESS POINT: Huntington Beach Pier.

HOW TO GET THERE: From the San Diego Freeway (I-405) take Beach Blvd. south for 5.8 miles to Pacific Coast Highway (Highway I), then turn left and drive one mile to the pier at the end of Main Street.

OTHER ACCESS: Anywhere along the route.

DIFFICULTY: Easy.

ELEVATION GAIN/LOSS: Negligible.

FURTHER INFORMATION: Huntington State Beach (714)536-1454, Huntington City Beach (714)536-5281. For Newport Beach Municipal Beach and Balboa Beach, call the Newport Beach Marine Department (949)644-3044.

FACILITIES: Restrooms, water, picnic tables and parking in Huntington Beach and Newport Beach.

HOSTELS: Colonial Inn Hostel (714)536-3315 is in Huntington Beach four blocks from the beach.

CAMPGROUNDS: Bolsa Chica State Beach and Huntington City Beach (winter months only) offer camping for self-contained RVs.

LODGING: The area has many choices of accommodations.

Huntington Beach, a.k.a. Surf City, for years the unofficial capital of surfing, oozed a funky atmosphere and definite ambiance of laid back cool before cool was even cool. But all has changed as trends dictate that Huntington Beach tear out the old and replace it with big hotels, malls and attitude aimed at collecting tourists dollars. Yet the beach, the surfers and the sun worshippers remain.

This day's walk, the ultimate southern California beach walk, is best done in shorts or swim suit and sandals. The route follows a wide sandy beach, except for a short detour, and takes you past one of the premier suntanning, strolling, strutting, swimming and surfing playgrounds in the country. Massive numbers of sun worshipping beach rats flock to these beaches in the summer to escape the inland heat and do their thing.

From the Huntington Beach Pier stroll down wide Huntington City Beach past the prone bodies, strutting bodies, frisbee throwers, volleyball and football games of the beach culture crowds. At one mile where you pass the end of Beach Blvd., City Beach ends and you continue along the same strand, from here south called Huntington State Beach. Alternately you can follow the paved multi-use

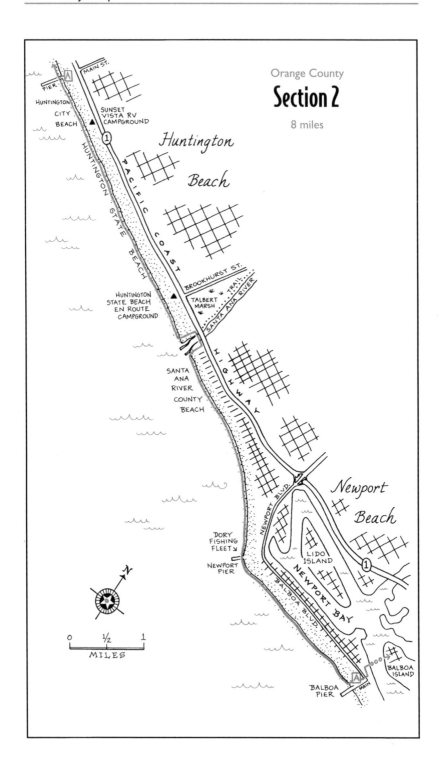

Orange County

Section 2

8 miles

trail that runs along the top of the beach for the next two miles. The level residential expanse inland has channels connecting with the Santa Ana River ahead.

At 3½ miles the beach ends at the river mouth. Turn inland to take a brief detour across the highway bridge over the Santa Ana River. Beyond the bridge CCT returns to the tideline of the beach, here called Santa Ana River County Beach. The River Trail starts here, ending in Yorba Linda 20 miles inland. Walk down coast along the beach, with the pricey houses of Newport Beach soon lining the top of the strand. As a break from the beach, you can instead walk Ocean Front promenade, which starts after the river crossing and runs the entire 5½-mile length of the Newport Peninsula almost to the Newport Harbor mouth. If you walk the promenade, stay alert for bicyclists and inline skaters.

Whether by beach or Ocean Walk, you reach the Newport Beach Pier at 6⅛ miles. The town of Newport Beach surrounds Newport Harbor, the second largest recreational marina in the country with 10,000 berths, and also lays claim to the 6-mile-long sandspit fronting the ocean. This area retains some of the funky beach town flavor that's been lost in neighboring Huntington Beach. It's obvious beach lovers and surfers reign here. The Dory Fleet, unique to the California coast, sits next to Newport Pier. Fishermen have launched from the beach in open wooden boats continuously since 1891. They leave in the wee hours of the morning, returning later to sell fresh fish to tourists and locals alike from stalls right on the beach.

After a stroll on the pier or around the town, continue on the beach, which becomes very broad beyond the pier, passing yet more sun-fried bodies as Newport Beach gives way to Balboa Beach. Beyond 7¾ miles you pass the Balboa Pier parking lot, then reach the Balboa Pier at 8 miles, section's end. After this long beach walk, you may be ready for refreshment at one of the local watering holes.

SUGGESTED ROUND TRIPS AND LOOPS: Walk the beach between the piers, then return on Ocean Front promenade for a 3¾-mile loop. From Balboa Pier walk the beach or the Promenade south to The Wedge at West Jetty View Park, a famous spot where at times the ocean swells form up against the jetty, creating giant 20-foot waves. Daredevil body surfers risk it all to ride waves that crash, or wedge, into the jagged jetty rocks before reaching the beach.

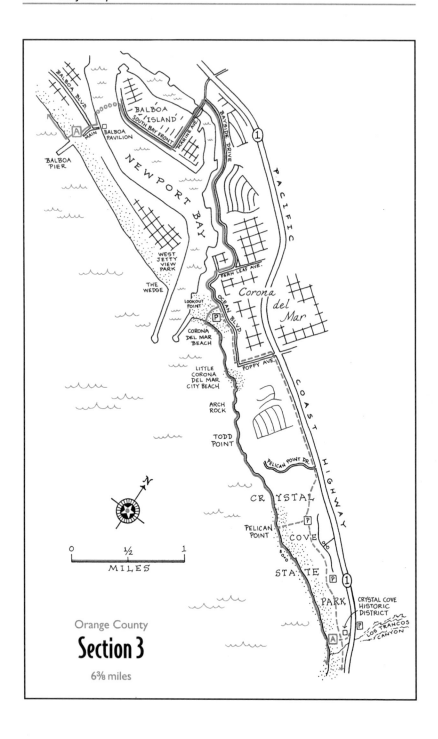

BALBOA BLVD.

BALBOA ISLAND

SOUTH BAY FRONT

BALBOA PAVILION

BALBOA PIER

MARINE AVE.

BAYSIDE DRIVE

1

PACIFIC

NEWPORT BAY

WEST JETTY VIEW PARK

THE WEDGE

FERN LEAF AVE.

Corona del Mar

LOOKOUT POINT

OCEAN BLVD.

CORONA DEL MAR BEACH

LITTLE CORONA DEL MAR CITY BEACH

POPPY AVE.

ARCH ROCK

TODD POINT

COAST HIGHWAY

PELICAN POINT DR.

CRYSTAL

PELICAN POINT

COVE

STATE

PARK

1

CRYSTAL COVE HISTORIC DISTRICT

LOS TRANCOS CANYON

N

0   ½   1

MILES

Orange County

Section 3

6⅜ miles

SECTION 3
Balboa Pier to Crystal Cove State Park Historic District

DISTANCE: 6⅜ miles for tidal route. Add ⅝ mile for inland route (10.3 + 1.0 kilometers).

OPEN TO: Hikers. Bicyclists on streets.

SURFACE: Beach, trail, sidewalk.

ACCESS POINT: Balboa Pier.

HOW TO GET THERE: From Pacific Coast Highway (Highway 1) take Newport Blvd. or Balboa Blvd. south onto the Newport Peninsula. If you take Newport Blvd., after it merges with Balboa Blvd., continue to Main Street. The pier is one block south of the corner of Balboa Blvd. and Main Street.

OTHER ACCESS: Much of the route is accessible.

DIFFICULTY: Easy.

ELEVATION GAIN/LOSS: 90 feet+/90 feet-. Inland route: 130 feet+/140 feet-.

FURTHER INFORMATION: For Balboa Beach and Corona del Mar State Beach, call the Newport Beach Marine Department (949)644-3044. For Crystal Cove State Park, call Orange Cove District, California State Parks (949)494-3539.

FACILITIES: Balboa Beach has restrooms, water, picnic tables and parking near the pier, with urban amenities abundant on the Newport Beach portion of the walk. Crystal Cove State Park has several restrooms on the bluff above the beach and at the Los Trancos parking lot across the highway from the Crystal Cove Historic District.

CAMPGROUNDS: Crystal Cove State Park's El Moro unit 4 miles inland has 32 walk-in campsites.

HOSTEL: Colonial Inn Hostel (714)536-3315 is in Huntington Beach on Section 2.

LODGING: Newport Beach and Laguna Beach have many hotels and motels. Try the affordable Newport Channel Inn across Highway 1 from the beach or the deluxe Portofino Beach Hotel.

This section offers one of the more varied hikes in Orange County. It takes you from the beach culture ambiance of Balboa, past a Victorian pavilion circa 1906, on a short ferry boat ride, through exclusive Balboa Island, and into Corona Del Mar (Crown of the Sea) before hitting the most pristine and well-preserved piece of the Orange County coast at Crystal Cove State Park, tucked in the folds of the convoluted San Joaquin Hills which rise from the coastal plain from Corona del Mar south to around Dana Point. This park's 3½-mile shoreline preserves some treasures: secluded beaches, fragrant coastal sage fields, and a nostalgic collection of rickety beach cottages built in the late 1920s and early 1930s.

Starting at the Balboa Pier, walk inland one block along Main Street past tourist oriented businesses to the Victorian-era Balboa Pavilion on Newport Bay at the end of the street. The passing of the big band era marked the end of the pavilion's

Crystal Cove State Park.

heyday, but a number of businesses flourish here including the Catalina ferry, a restaurant and a harbor cruise service. Turn left on the waterfront walkway past a small amusement park to reach the Balboa Ferry, two blocks down at the end of Palm Street. The quaint ferry takes a few minutes to cross to Balboa Island, remarkably still costing only 50 cents for pedestrians to ride.

Once the ferry drops you on the island, you have a choice of routes. The Bay Front Walkway circles the island, allowing you to go left or right for a scenic route ending at the Marine Avenue bridge. For the most direct route, take the Bay Front walkway to the right, coming to Marine Avenue at 1⅛ miles. While you can continue on the walkway around to the bridge, our described route turns left on the Marine Avenue sidewalk to pass tourist stores. You can buy a Balboa Island T-shirt, a sea shell pendant to go with it, then an ice cream cone to dribble on your new shirt in the hot summer sun.

When Marine Avenue comes to the bridge at 1⅜ miles, cross it. You immediately turn right on Bayside Drive and walk its sidewalk, then some narrow shoulder where the street jogs left up the hill. After Bayside turns inland, turn right on Fernleaf Avenue at 3 miles and follow it two blocks to Ocean Blvd. Turn left and follow Ocean a few blocks to Lookout Point, a little grassy park with benches at 3½ miles. The park overlooks the Newport Harbor entrance and Corona Del Mar Beach.

Here you must decide between the tidal and inland routes. To take the tidal route, passable only at lower tides, walk south a short distance to the entrance to Corona del Mar Beach. Walk down the entrance drive and head south when you get to the beach. Soon you scramble across rocks in the tidal zone to pass Arch Rock. Continue along the tideline rounding Todd Point to reach sandy beach at Crystal Cove State Park around 5 miles. Look for the trail coming down to the beach from the bluff before Pelican Point at 5⅛ miles. The two routes rejoin here.

To take the inland route, continue along Ocean Blvd. to its end, then turn left and follow Poppy Avenue to Pacific Coast Highway. Turn right and walk the bike path along the shoulder. Just past Pelican Point Drive, veer right on the paved path at 5⅛ mile and descend into Crystal Cove State Park. It drops gently toward the beach through thick fragrant coastal sage and hits the sand near Pelican Point at 5⅜ miles. This beautiful area of thick and fragrant coastal sage on the restored bluffs and white clean beach represents the Laguna coast before rampant growth overwhelmed the natural features.

The CCT continues along the tideline of the beach. If you took the inland route, add ½ mile to the distances below. Round sandy Pelican Point at 5½ miles, then continue down the delightful beach. You reach the dilapidated cottages at Crystal Cove, this section's end, at 6⅜ miles. The State Parks department owns the cottages. They recently planned a large hotel here, but local resistance to the hotel convinced them to restore the cottages instead and make them vacation rentals.

SUGGESTED ROUND TRIPS AND LOOPS: From Balboa Pier walk over to the ferry and take it to Balboa Island. For a look at the harbor area with its luxury leisure boats, walk around the Island on the Bay Front Walkway and return via the ferry for a 4-mile loop.

To experience the beauty of Crystal Cove State Park and the unique beach cottages, park at the Pelican Point parking lot and walk the beach to Reef Point (on the next section). Return via the paved blufftop trail for a 4½ mile loop.

SECTION 4
Crystal Cove State Park Historic District to Laguna Beach Main Beach

DISTANCE: 5¼ miles (8.5 kilometers).

OPEN TO: Hikers. Bicyclists on most.

SURFACE: Beach, sidewalk.

ACCESS POINT: Crystal Cove Beach Cottages.

HOW TO GET THERE: Drive the Pacific Coast Highway (Highway 1) to Crystal Cove State Park's Los Trancos parking lot, about halfway between Newport Beach and Laguna Beach. Walk through the tunnel to the cottages and the beach where the CCT runs along the tideline.

OTHER ACCESS: Reef Point, Crescent Bay Point Park, Heisler Park.

DIFFICULTY: Moderate.

ELEVATION GAIN/LOSS: 90 feet+/90 feet-.

CAUTIONS: The tidal rocks are slippery.

FURTHER INFORMATION: Crystal Cove State Park (949)494-3539. For all the Laguna Beach area beaches, call the South Beaches Operation Office of the Orange County Harbors, Beaches, and Parks (949)661-7013.

FACILITIES: Restrooms and water at all Crystal Cove State Park parking lots. Crescent Bay Point Park, Heisler Park and the Main Beach have water, restrooms and picnic tables.

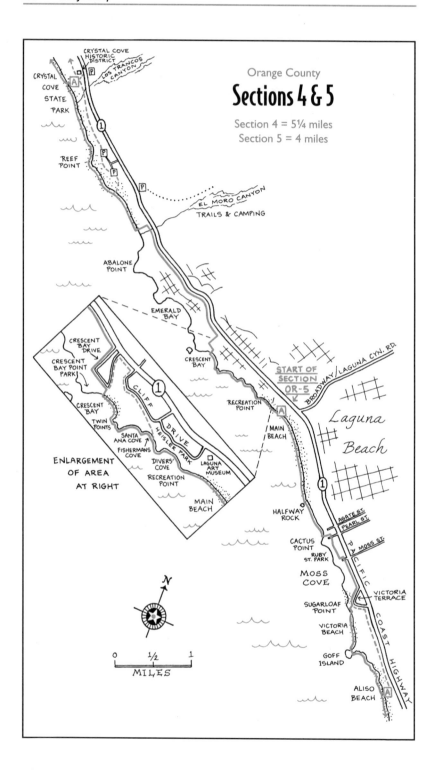

CRYSTAL COVE
HISTORIC
DISTRICT

LOS TRANCOS CANYON

CRYSTAL
COVE
STATE
PARK

REEF
POINT

EL MORO CANYON
TRAILS & CAMPING

ABALONE
POINT

Orange County
Sections 4 & 5
Section 4 = 5¼ miles
Section 5 = 4 miles

EMERALD
BAY

CRESCENT
BAY
DRIVE

CRESCENT
BAY POINT
PARK

CRESCENT
BAY

CRESCENT
BAY
TWIN
POINTS

SANTA
ANA COVE
FISHERMANS
COVE

DIVERS'
COVE

RECREATION
POINT

MAIN
BEACH

ENLARGEMENT
OF AREA
AT RIGHT

CLIFF DRIVE

HEISLER PARK

LAGUNA
ART
MUSEUM

RECREATION
POINT

START OF
SECTION
OR-5

BROADWAY/LAGUNA CYN. RD.

MAIN
BEACH

Laguna
Beach

HALFWAY
ROCK

AGATE ST.
PEARL ST.

MOSS ST.

CACTUS
POINT
RUBY
ST. PARK

MOSS
COVE

VICTORIA
TERRACE

SUGARLOAF
POINT

VICTORIA
BEACH

PACIFIC COAST HIGHWAY

GOFF
ISLAND

ALISO
BEACH

N

0   ½   1
MILES

CAMPGROUNDS: Crystal Cove State Park's El Moro unit 4 miles inland has 32 walk-in campsites.

LODGING: Laguna Beach has abundant choices.

Despite the intense development of the Laguna Beach shoreline, this section takes you to some gorgeous hidden rocky coves with the best tidepooling and snorkeling in southern California. The rocky coves are tucked along the edge of the rugged San Joaquin Hills which rise above the shoreline from Corona del Mar south, rising as much as 1164 feet at Signal Peak at the head of Los Trancos Canyon. After leaving the natural beauty of Crystal Cove State Park, the route passes by an exclusive locked gate enclave, then drops to explore the intertidal zone.

From the Crystal Cove cottages, head south on the beach, passing a series of reefs before rounding Reef Point. After another pleasant stretch along Morro Beach, you leave the beach at 1¾ miles, just before the creek at the mouth of El Moro Canyon where a small trailer park sits perched on a flat spot wedged between the surf and the highway. Take the asphalt road up through the trailers to Pacific Coast Highway and turn right. The route follows on the bike lane beside the highway, bypassing an exclusive locked gate enclave perched on the bluffs above a rocky shore.

Turn right on Crescent Bay Drive at 3¼ miles and follow it to Crescent Bay Point Park at 3⅜ miles. This formal little park, a favorite for plein air painters, provides a scenic rest spot. To get to Crescent Bay Beach south of the point, continue on Crescent Bay Drive. As it begins to curve back toward the highway in one block, take the short deadend street angling downhill. Descend along Circle Drive, then find the stairs to the right descending to North Crescent Bay Beach.

If the tide is in and you can't get around the rocky points, return to Crescent Bay Drive and follow it to Highway 1. Turn right and in one block go right again on Cliff Drive. Take Cliff Drive to the north entrance to Heisler Park. Walk the length of the park and at its south end take the stairs to Main Beach and end your hike amidst volleyball games and frisbee throwers at 5¼ miles.

If you tackle the tidal route, you won't be disappointed. This area features some of the finest tidepooling and snorkeling in southern California. Walk Crescent Bay Beach south to 3¾ miles, then round Twin Points to follow the tideline along the pocket beaches of Santa Ana Cove, then Fisherman's Cove around 4¼ miles. From Fisherman's Cove our route climbs the steps up to Heisler Park. If the tide is low enough you can instead stay on the rocks and round Recreation Point to reach Main Beach. If you climb to the park, you will find a formal setting with grass, gardens, a gazebo, benches, tables and great views. Walk down coast through the park and take the steps down to the beach around 4⅝ miles. Turn left and walk the beach to end your hike amid the bustle of Main Beach and downtown Laguna Beach at 5¼ miles.

SUGGESTED ROUND TRIPS AND LOOPS: At low tide a scramble along the rocks north of Main Beach reward you with good tidepooling. It's 3 miles round trip to Crescent Bay.

> HOW TO IMPROVE THE CCT HERE: Access to the Emerald Bay area is blocked by a locked gate community. To get the route off the busy highway, the owners behind the gates would have to be persuaded to allow public access, or the Coastal Commission would have to find a way to enforce Article 10 of the State Constitution, guaranteeing the public access to the coastline.

SECTION 5
Laguna Beach Main Beach to Aliso Beach

DISTANCE: 4 miles (6.4 kilometers).

OPEN TO: Hikers. Bicyclists on streets.

SURFACE: Beach, sidewalk.

ACCESS POINT: Main Beach in Laguna Beach.

HOW TO GET THERE: Drive Pacific Coast Highway to downtown Laguna Beach. Main Beach is adjacent to the middle of town at the end of Laguna Canyon Road/Broadway.

OTHER ACCESS: Between Main Beach and Aliso Beach, 16 paths/stairs descend to pocket beaches and rocky coves at these street ends: Cleo St., St. Ann's St., Thalia St., Anita St., Oak St., Brooks St., Cress St., Mountain Rd., Bluebird Canyon Rd., Agate St., Pearl St., Diamond St., Moss St., Sunset Terrace, Dumond Dr., 1900 block, Ocean Way.

DIFFICULTY: Easy.

ELEVATION GAIN/LOSS: 80 feet+/80 feet-.

CAUTIONS: Tidal route impassable at high tide. Beaches close at 10 pm.

FURTHER INFORMATION: For Laguna Beach beaches, call the South Beaches Operation Office of Orange County Harbors, Beaches and Parks (949)661-7013, for Doheny State Beach, call (949)496-6171.

FACILITIES: Water, restrooms, and picnic tables at Laguna Beach Main Beach and Aliso Beach.

CAMPGROUNDS: Just east of Dana Point at the start of Section 7, Doheny State Beach has 120 sites for tents and RVs.

LODGING: Laguna Beach and Dana Point have abundant shelter choices, mostly on the high end like the deluxe Aliso Creek Inn, the 114-year-old Hotel Laguna and the Surf and Sand Hotel in Laguna Beach or the Marriott and Ritz-Carlton in Dana Point. South Laguna has several motels at moderate rates.

MAP: See page 296.

Laguna Beach, first and foremost an art town, shelters more than 90 art galleries and hosts three summer art festivals including the world renowned Pageant of the

At low tide this tunnel connects Victoria Beach and Aliiso Beach.

Masters. This event uses live actors and locals to painstakingly recreate the world's great paintings. Laguna Beach separates itself from the rest of the county not only by its artsy and liberal leaning but also by the rugged Laguna Hills, part of the larger San Joaquin Hills. Much of the Laguna Hills is now protected parklands thanks in large part to the efforts of the Laguna Canyon Foundation, which led the way to save the hills from intense development.

Not far from the beginning of this hike, the art scene bustles with all the galleries along the Pacific Coast Highway and the Laguna Art Museum just inland from Heisler Park. Even along the town's downtown shoreline at Main Beach you'll find an art-deco chess table of tile mosaic and artists sketching local scenes as well as the more typical volleyball and basketball courts and playgrounds.

After sampling the local art product, head south along the tideline of busy Main Beach passing hotels and condos perched on the low bluff. As you round Cheneys Point beyond ⅜ mile, the bluffs rise to 40 feet. Continue along the beach around an unnamed point beyond ¾ mile and walk Brooks Beach past Halfway Rock offshore.

Before Cactus Point at 1½ miles, leave the beach and climb the stairs to Agate or Pearl Street. Turn right on Ocean Way and walk it south to bypass several no-pass points. You can take a side trip to visit Woods Cove at the end of Diamond Street and Moss Point and Moss Beach at the end of Moss Street before returning to the route.

When Ocean Way ends at Moss Street, turn left and walk Moss up to Pacific Coast Highway at 2 miles. Turn right and follow the highway's sidewalk to 2⅜ miles, then turn right and walk down Victoria Terrace Drive. In the 2600 block of Victoria Terrace Drive near the corner of Sunset Terrace, take the stairs wedged between houses (you may need to look closely to spot them) and descend to attractive, broad and quiet Victoria Beach at 2⅝ miles.

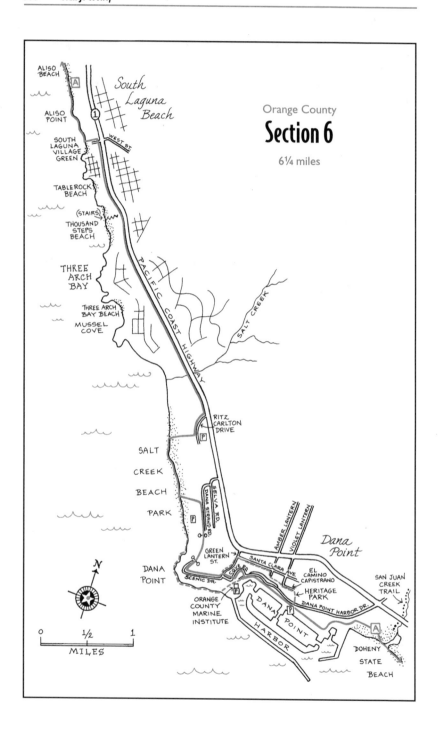

Orange County
Section 6
6¼ miles

From here to Aliso Beach you stay on the tideline unless the tide is high. For this scenic tidal route, walk down beautiful Victoria Beach, marred somewhat at the far end by an unattractive apartment building squatting on a large seawall. Make your way in front of the seawall to reach Goff Island at 3⅛ miles.

The land above Goff Island is in the process of hotel and resort development. The plans include a Laguna Beach city park and a public beach. An abandoned road descends from the present mobile home park atop the bluff to end on a large concrete slab marring the shore-attached island where the remains of a small boat landing sit unused. Cross the abandoned road and follow the rugged shoreline along a scenic small cove and around a point. You come to a natural tunnel in the shoreline rocks with Aliso Beach framed in the distance. Walk through the tunnel and down the sandy beach to Aliso Beach and past the lagoon at the mouth of Aliso Creek. This section ends where the pier once was at 4 miles, near the parking lot at the top of the beach beside Pacific Coast Highway.

ALTERNATE ROUTE: If the seawall at the end of Victoria Beach or the shore south of Goff Island is flooded at high tide, you can either wait out the tide or return to Victoria Terrace Drive, follow it to Pacific Coast Highway, turn right and walk the sidewalk to Aliso Beach.

SUGGESTED ROUND TRIPS & LOOPS: From Main Beach walk the tideline south to Cactus Point and return, 3 miles round trip. From Aliso Beach you can walk the shore north to Victoria Beach unless it's high tide, about 2¾ miles round trip.

SECTION 6
Aliso Beach to Doheny State Beach

DISTANCE: 6¼ miles (10.1 kilometers).

OPEN TO: Hikers. Bicyclists on streets.

SURFACE: Beach, sidewalk.

ACCESS POINT: Aliso Beach County Park.

HOW TO GET THERE: Drive Highway 1 (Pacific Coast Highway) south from downtown Laguna Beach for 3.5 miles to Aliso Beach parking lot across from Aliso Creek Inn.

OTHER ACCESS: Salt Creek Beach Park, Dana Point Harbor.

DIFFICULTY: Easy.

ELEVATION GAIN/LOSS: 340 feet+/340 feet-.

CAUTIONS: Stay out of Aliso Creek which is usually posted for sewage contamination. The route on the rocks around Dana Point is slippery at all times and impassable at higher tides. Use caution if you walk Cove Road, narrow with no shoulders.

FURTHER INFORMATION: For Aliso Beach County Park and Salt Creek Beach Park, call the south Beaches Operation Office of the Orange County Harbors, Beaches and Parks

Dana Point, Then and Now

In 1835 the trading brig Pilgrim sailed around Cape Horn in search of Spanish cowhides for the Boston shoe industry. The Pilgrim put in at what was then known as San Juan to trade with the Spanish mission, San Juan Capistrano. During the 1830s and 1840s, cowhide trading became such big business that the hides were called "California banknotes." Nineteen-year-old Richard Henry Dana, out for adventure and writing material, described a California coast still untouched by the westward movement and lightly settled.

In his book Two Years Before the Mast, he described Dana Point and the cove, "It is the only romantic spot in California. The country here for several miles is high table land, running boldly to the shore, and breaking off in a steep hill, at the foot of which the waters of the Pacific are constantly dashing. For several miles the water washes the very base of the hill, or breaks upon ledges and fragments of rocks which run out into the sea. Just where we landed was a small cove, or bight, which gave us, at high tide, a few square feet of sand-beach between the sea and the bottom of the hill. This was our only landing place. Directly before us, rose the perpendicular height of four or five hundred feet."

Today Dana would hardly recognize his namesake place. The dashing waters have disappeared. Any romantic visions Dana had of the wild and rugged shoreline are replaced by a large marina, extensive fill, and a breakwater that calmed the dashing waters and destroyed a great surfing break. The marina offers extensive boating facilities, fishing from the pier or breakwater, picnicking, swimming and a boardwalk of businesses and restaurants.

The small bustling community of Dana Point sits atop the bluffs overlooking the harbor. Colorful street names such as Green Lantern and Silver Lantern were created by the first developer in 1926.

Sydney Woodruff wanted to dress up his ambitious plans for homes, playing fields and a harbor by lighting the streets with different colors, but his plans were halted by the depression. Dana Point Harbor, built in 1971, finally spurred the building boom.

What remains of the natural landscape lies outside the breakwater on the rocky shoreline at the base of the point and on the headlands above. The shore and offshore rocks are protected by the Dana Point Marine Life Refuge. The tideline supports a variety of algae and invertebrates. Nearshore waters contain the colorful garabaldi, lobster, kelp bass and mackerel.

The Orange County Marine Institute, located at the harbor, conducts a variety of award-winning educational programs for children and adults including classroom and lab programs, lecture series, wildlife cruises, snorkeling trips, whale watching, summer sea camps, and classroom field trips. Much of this activity takes place aboard the Pilgrim, a replica of the brig that brought Dana around the Horn, and the 70-foot research vessel Sea Explorer.

The undeveloped Dana Point Headlands overlooking the harbor and the sea has for years been the site of controversial development proposals. The 120 undeveloped acres, one of three large parcels left on the Orange County coast, contains some of the last coastal sage scrub and open space in the intensely developed area. Opponents to city approvals for hotels and luxury homes overturned the plans by passing a ballot initiative. The owners, Times-Mirror Inc., sued the city over the overturned project. They are proposing 294 homes and a 100-200 room hotel. Activists and environmentalists propose no more than 90 homes, a 100-150 room hotel and an 84-acre natural park. The battle continues in court and at city council meetings over the fate of this nearly last piece of natural coastal land in Orange County.

(949)661-7013, for Doheny State Beach, call (949)496-6171.

FACILITIES: Water, picnic tables, restrooms and parking at Aliso Beach and Doheny State Beach.

CAMPGROUNDS: Just east of Dana Point, Doheny State Beach has 120 sites for tents and RVs.

HOSTEL: San Clemente Hostel (949)492-2848 is three blocks from the beach at end of Section 7.

LODGING: Dana Point has several shelter choices, mostly on the high end like the deluxe Marriott and Ritz-Carlton. The moderately priced Best Western Marina Inn is at Dana Point Harbor. South Laguna has several motels at moderate rates.

Aliso Beach County Park offers a pleasant byway along the Pacific Coast Highway, with all the accoutrements for a fine family outing. The only thing missing is the Aliso Pier, destroyed by storm surf in 1999. The steep beach has large powerful waves popular with board and bodysurfers alike. Families also favor Aliso Beach for its easy accessibility, playground, picnic tables with fire pits, good fishing and concession stands.

From the parking lot at the top of Aliso Beach, walk down to the tideline, turn left and head south. After you round rocky Aliso Point before ¼ mile, watch along the top of the beach for public stairs leading up to West Street. It's the second public stairway, with the first one climbing alongside a condominium 200 feet north of West Street. Leave the beach around ⅜ miles and ascend the West Street stairs to the end of West Street at ⅝ mile. Unfortunately the shoreline ahead is impassable to through foot traffic for the next two miles, first with several pocket beaches guarded by promontories extending into deep water, then by a locked gate housing tract on the bluffs that blocks access along the shoreline.

Walk West Street up to Highway 1 and turn right. Walk the sidewalks along busy Pacific Coast Highway through South Laguna. CCT follows the highway all the way to Ritz-Carlton Drive at 2⅞ miles, but it does pass two beach access paths and stairways where you can descend to the pocket beaches if you want to see what you're missing. The first coastal access descends stairs from Table Rock Drive off Bluff Drive two blocks south of West Street to Tablerock Beach. Continuing along the Coast Highway, at 1⅛ miles you pass a second beach access path at Ninth Avenue. The path called 1000 Steps (actually 219 steps) descends to spectacular 1000 Steps Beach 150 feet below Highway 1, where steep cliffs and offshore rocks frame the isolated cove. Continue along the highway's sidewalk overlooking the gated community between the highway and spectacular Three Arch Bay and Mussel Cove along the shore. You pass Crown Valley Parkway around 2⅛ miles, cross Salt Creek at 2⅝ miles, then come to Ritz-Carlton Drive at 2⅞ miles.

Turn right and walk down Ritz-Carlton Drive to the Salt Creek Beach parking lot. From the west side of the lot, follow the paved path down through Bluff Park to Salt Creek Beach. Walk down to the tideline and turn left. Salt Creek Beach is a 1¾-mile-long, wide sandy gem, framed by Dana Point on the south end. Walk the

The view from Dana Point.

beach south, rounding an unnamed point at 3¼ miles and continuing to the next public stairway at 3⅝ miles, the beginning of the inland route. At very low tides, you can walk around Dana Point on the rocks, described in Alternate Route A.

For the high tide route, walk up the long flight of stairs past an abandoned mobile home park on the right to the parking lot and park picnic area. Walk south through the park to its end, where adjacent Dana Strand Road comes to a vehicle barrier at 4⅛ miles. Walk around the barrier onto an overgrown path, following an old road lined with fencing on both sides that's well posted with "NO TRESPASSING" signs. Follow this road across Dana Point, the last undeveloped and unprotected natural land along the Orange County coast, loaded with beautiful coastal sage scrub and cactus. Local residents steadfastly oppose plans to build high-end houses and a resort on the point, preferring to keep the point in open space. See the adjacent feature article for more of this story.

The path descends to meet the end of Scenic Drive not far from the tip of Dana Point. Walk Scenic past the few houses that have been built here. At 4⅝ miles you come to Cove Road. Our main route turns right to descend narrow Cove Road. See Alternate Route B for a different route along the bluffs.

If you walk narrow Cove Road angling steeply down the cliff, do so with extreme caution. It ends at Dana Point Harbor Drive at 5 miles. For a side trip to the Orange County Marine Institute, turn right. The Institute serves thousands of students every year, conducting classes on marine conservation, ecology and history. The brig *Pilgrim* docks here, a full-size replica of the sailing ship Richard Henry Dana crewed on in 1835 that serves as a teaching tool. The original *Pilgrim* sailed from Boston around the Cape Horn in search of cow hides from the Spaniards for the Boston shoe industry. When the ship anchored in Dana Cove, Dana described the cove in his classic book *Two Years Before the Mast* as ". . . the only romantic spot in California." Now the cove is totally filled by the man-made Dana Point Harbor, created with jetties and massive landfill and jammed with luxury boats and tourist businesses. Dana would hardly recognize it.

From Dana Point Harbor Drive, you can either walk the sidewalk or meander along the harbor past the boats, restaurants and shops. At the south end of the harbor a big parking area for boat trailers sits along a jetty bordering Doheny State Beach. Walk through the parking lot, climb down the low rock jetty and onto the sand. Adjacent to the wide beach and gentle surf excellent for small children, you'll find that Doheny State Beach offers a grassy palm tree studded picnic area and a visitor center at the entrance station on the other side of the picnic grounds. This section ends here on the beach at 6¼ miles.

ALTERNATE ROUTE A: If the tide is low enough, you can venture around Dana Point on the tidal rocks. Be aware that they are very slippery, requiring careful rock hopping. Avoid walking on the delicate tidal life inhabiting the rocks. The distance from the south stairs at Salt Creek Beach to Dana Cove Park next to the Marine Institute is 1⅜ miles, 1⅝ miles to Cove Drive and Dana Point Harbor Drive.

ALTERNATE ROUTE B: To avoid narrow Cove Road and get great views from the bluff, continue on Scenic Drive which becomes Green Lantern Street. Turn right on Santa Clara Avenue. After a short block, detour down Blue Lantern Street to visit the gazebo overlooking the harbor. Then continue along Santa Clara a few blocks and turn right on Amber Lantern Street. At its end, turn left on the boardwalk clinging to the cliff in front of the buildings. This block-long path yields up more great views. Where the path ends, continue on El Camino Capistrano a long block to enter Heritage Park and follow the path curving downhill to the harbor's midpoint. Cross Dana Point Harbor Drive, turn left and walk past the harbor to Doheny State Beach and section's end .

SUGGESTED ROUND TRIPS AND LOOPS: Salt Creek Beach Park is worth a visit by itself. A walk the length of the beach and back is 3½ miles round trip. The beach also affords a chance to explore the tidal zone at Dana Point. If the tide is out, you can make it all the way around to the Marine Institute.

HOW TO IMPROVE THE CCT HERE: At press time, development issues remain unresolved on Dana Point. It's the only unprotected coastal land in Orange County with native coastal sage and cactus. Preserving the land with habitat intact and building trails on the point sensitive to the ecosystem would protect it and allow access.

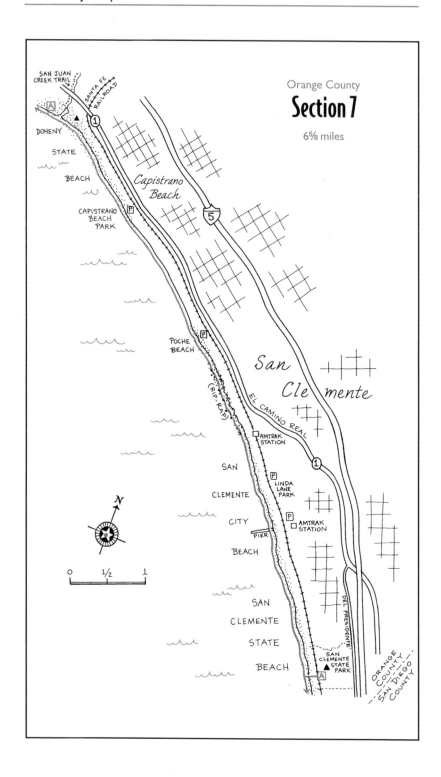

Orange County
Section 7
6⅝ miles

SECTION 7
Doheny State Beach to San Clemente State Beach

DISTANCE: 6⅝ miles (10.7 kilometers).

OPEN TO: Hikers.

SURFACE: Beach.

ACCESS POINT: Doheny State Beach.

HOW TO GET THERE: From Interstate 5 take the Highway 1 exit to Dana Point. Go north about 1.5 miles, turn left on Dana Point Harbor Drive, then immediately turn left into the Doheny State Beach entrance.

OTHER ACCESS: Capistrano Beach, Poche Beach, Linda Lane Park, San Clemente City Beach.

DIFFICULTY: Easy.

ELEVATION GAIN/LOSS: Negligible.

CAUTIONS: The busy coastal railroad tracks parallel the beach so use caution when crossing. Riprapped beaches may be flooded at higher tides.

FURTHER INFORMATION: Doheny State Beach (949)496-6171, for Poche Beach and Capistrano Beach call the South Beaches Operations Office of Orange County Harbors, Beaches and Parks (949)661-7013, for San Clemente City Beach call the San Clemente Department of Marine Safety (949)361-8219, for San Clemente State Beach call Orange Coast District, California State Parks (949)492-0802.

FACILITIES: Picnic tables, water, restrooms, parking at Doheny State Beach, San Clemente Pier and San Clemente State Beach.

HOSTEL: San Clemente Hostel (949)492-2848 is three blocks from the beach and the Amtrak station.

CAMPGROUNDS: Doheny State Beach has 120 sites and San Clemente State Beach has 157 sites, with both campgrounds having hot showers.

LODGING: Accommodations abound throughout the region.

Doheny State Beach was established in 1931 when this area was still rural. For years coming to Doheny was a trip to a wilder place than it is today. Now urban growth crowds both Doheny and San Clemente state beaches, detracting from the sense of open space a park should have. Still, both parks offer camping and a fine beach experience. Between the two state beaches, the CCT mostly follows the beach with a few high-tide detours. This hike and Orange County's Coastal Trail end at San Clemente State Beach about a mile before the San Diego County line.

Before questing forth on this great beach walk, be sure to check out the Visitor Center inland across the wide expanse of lawn near the entrance station. The harbor jetty calms the surf along the beach here, making it a good place for family swimming or novice board surfers. Much of the route is especially subject to ero-

Can the Last Wild Places Be Saved?

No one doubts that the car is king in America, and nowhere is it more greatly glorified than in southern California. There the ugly sibling of the car, unfettered urban and suburban sprawl–also held in high regard–grows cancerously into the fragile open spaces of valley and hill throughout the region. The octopus offspring of this tragic pairing is a network of nature-eating, inefficient freeways and toll roads still being proposed and built, flying in the face of common sense and good planning.

Many onerous proposals in southern California–development in the Ballona and Bolsa Chica wetlands, luxury homes and golf courses on the Palos Verdes Peninsula coast, resorts and more fancy homes at Dana Point–eat away at the remaining wild and scenic land, generating more population, cars and roads. One of the more incredibly stupid and destructive proposals now under consideration calls for a 16-mile toll road through the last wild land in southern Orange County. The Transportation Corridor Agency, already responsible for a toll road slicing the Laguna Hills open space into fragments, says it is needed to relieve traffic on the 8-lane San Diego Freeway. They warn of gridlock by the addition of 575,000 new residents by 2020, increasing traffic by 64%. The proposed route crosses a relatively wild 90-square-mile basin. It would devastate woodlands, creeks, rocky hills, and the habitat of thousands of animals, including seven endangered species. As the proposed route approaches the coast, it crosses lengthwise through 3126-acre San Onofre State Park and along San Mateo Creek, the last totally wild creek in southern California. It would connect to the San Diego Freeway at the mouth of San Mateo Creek near the famous "Trestles" surfing spot.

Citizens concerned about the destructiveness of the proposal are fighting back. Friends of the Foothills, with $50,000 in seed money from the Sierra Club, formed a coalition of 11 activist groups to counter the public relations campaign being waged by the Transportation Agency. Environmentalists make several compelling arguments including the reality that more roads do not relieve gridlock for long without growth controls. If the freeway goes in, it opens the door to mammoth development in the area, defeating the traffic relief with more cars. Endangered species play a major role in the fate of the project. The San Mateo Creek watershed hosts the endangered tidewater gobi, southwestern arroyo toad, southwestern flycatcher and least Bell's vireo. The developers' own report suggests that the habitat for these species would be radically altered or destroyed, while at the same time claiming that mitigation would relieve some of the impacts.

A recent discovery threatens the future of the toll road. The native steelhead trout was thought to have been totally eradicated south of Malibu Creek in the Santa Monica Mountains 76 miles north until a student fishing in San Mateo Creek caught a fish looking suspiciously like a steelhead. Conclusive genetic evidence identified the small population as steelhead. The National Marine Fisheries Service, charged with protecting critical habitat including that for steelhead, could include San Mateo Creek in special management requirements.

The battle for nature is far from over. Toll road officials, veterans of two other projects through wild areas in Orange County, have overpowered all resistance and obstacles to building toll roads before. If they win, expect the road to be completed by 2003, opening up 35,000 acres for development. If they lose, chances are that large portions of the region can be placed in wildlife reserves, keeping a few wild places for the health of Orange County and the planet.

sion on the beach and bluffs, with subsequent damage to real estate because poor planning allowed building in hazardous areas.

From the parking lot, walk down to the tideline of the nearby beach of white sand.Our CCT route proceeds down the beach to San Juan Creek at ¼ mile. If it's too deep to cross, walk inland briefly to the main park road, cross the creek and return to the beach through the campground. San Juan Creek features a bike path running inland on the levee to the town of San Juan Capistrano.

CCT continues along the sandy beach. Beyond one mile you leave Doheny Beach for Capistrano Beach, essentially the same broad white strand with palisades rising 140 feet tall beyond the train tracks and El Camino Real, which run along the top of the beach. From 1⅜ miles a solid row of houses line the top of the beach. When you reach a gap in the houses around 2⅞ miles, you've reached Poche Beach. Walk its tideline south to the park's end around 3¼ miles.

About ⅛ mile further a trailer park sits atop riprap and fill dumped right on the beach, making passage difficult at high tide. If the tide is low enough, walk the tideline of the beach along the base of the riprap. If you can't get past, then carefully cross the train tracks, walk south along El Camino Real, and return to the beach at the other end of the trailer park around 4 miles. Soon you come to a small park beside the Ole Hanson Beach Club, then pass the only Amtrak station (Capistrano Beach) where you can depart the train directly onto the beach.

Continue along the tideline of what's now called San Clemente City Beach, an ample beach of mostly brown sand. After another good stretch of beach at the base of eroded bluffs, you reach Linda Lane Park at 4½ miles followed by popular San Clemente Pier at 5 miles. The pier offers a good place to take a rest and check out the local scene before continuing. San Clemente retains some sense of an older California.

Beyond the pier the beach stretches wide and white for another 1⅝ miles to San Clemente State Beach. Walk the tideline south. You can tell you have arrived at the state park around 6¼ miles because development on the bluff abruptly ends at the park's border. The soft, highly erodible sandstone cliffs and native vegetation are picturesque, suggesting what the region looked like before development. The railroad tracks shored up by riprap at the base of the cliffs blight the scene. Continue along the wild beach, watching for the lifeguard station on the bluff and a tunnel under the tracks that mark the path at section's end. You find the path up the bluffs at 6⅝ miles. The wide path ends in ⅜ mile at the day-use area on top of the cliffs, while the CCT continues along the beach, described in San Diego Section 1.

SUGGESTED ROUND TRIPS AND LOOPS: From San Clemente State Beach, walk down to the San Diego County line at San Mateo Point and return, 2¼ miles round trip. Before the point a small white building sits on the low bluff. This gazebo of Nixon's Western Whitehouse is purported to be Nixon's retreat from Pat's insistence that he not smoke cigars in the main house.

San Diego County

I N CONTRAST TO DEL NORTE COUNTY at the CCT's north end, with sparse population, temperate rain forests and a cool climate, California's southernmost county, San Diego, offers a pleasant, dry desert climate and warm ocean currents, attracting millions of people to live and visit there. The 76-mile coast has miles of beaches, nine major coastal wetlands and two bays, a stand of Torrey pines found at only one other place, isolated beaches beneath spectacular eroding cliffs, and the country's biggest aquatic park. The CCT runs along the downtown San Diego waterfront, one of only two major downtowns so near the trail.

All this sand and sun brings people out en masse to use the coast for every imaginable outdoor endeavor. Favorites include walking, jogging, bird and whale watching, beach strolling, surfing, snorkeling, volleyball, frisbee throwing, hang-gliding, tanning, bike riding, swimming, fishing, sea kayaking, sailing, sand castle building, kite flying and the romantic pastime of sunset watching. San Diego County boasts perhaps the most diverse natural landscapes in the country—a great scenic coastline, the snow covered mountains of Cleveland National Forest and the 600,000-acre desert playground of Anza-Borrego State Park. Manmade attractions also abound—the San Diego Wild Animal Park, Balboa Park, San Diego Zoo, Old Town San Diego, Cabrillo National Monument, and the Gaslamp Quarter attract millions of visitors yearly.

Such rich and diverse recreation choices in year-round good weather generate public demand for extensive facilities. Projects in the works include a Coastal Rail Trail from San Diego to Oceanside, the San Dieguito River Parkway connecting the CCT with the mountains 50 miles inland, serious attempts to save the remaining biologically rich coastal wetlands and coastal sage scrub, and sand replenishment to restore beaches long denuded because of human intervention in natural processes.

The San Diego CCT begins on the remote, quiet undeveloped beaches of San Onofre State Beach, then crosses Camp Pendleton Marine Base on a bike path before hitting the first town at Oceanside. From Oceanside to Point Loma the route follows low-tide beaches. When tides are unfavorable, the inland route passes through small towns on streets and Old Pacific Coast Highway.* The Coastal Trail continues past several coastal wetlands, wondrously scenic Torrey Pines State Reserve, and along Sunset Cliffs with the best sunset viewing anywhere. The route crosses the neck of Point Loma to reach San Diego Bay, then runs along the vibrant waterfront of downtown San Diego. After a ferry ride to Coronado and a walk through town, CCT hits the beach at the Hotel del Coronado where the Coastal Trail's final miles trace the tideline of the beach all the way to the Mexican border at Tijuana.

If you hiked the California Coastal Trail from the Oregon border to the Mexican border, you didn't find fame, but you're among the few who have been chilled by wind and fog at Pelican Bay State Beach and warmed by desert sun at Border Field State Park, all on the same 1200-mile walk. In between you've experienced the splendors and variety of one of the premier coastlines on the planet and you can proudly say, "I walked the California Coastal Trail from border to border."

---

*Old Pacific Coast Highway, also known as PCH, changes names in different towns.

SECTION 1
San Clemente State Beach to San Onofre State Beach

DISTANCE: 6⅞ miles (CCT), plus ⅜ mile from San Clemente State Beach parking lot (11.1 + .6 kilometers).

OPEN TO: Hikers. Bicyclists on bike path.

SURFACE: Beach.

ACCESS POINT: San Clemente State Beach.

HOW TO GET THERE: From Interstate 5 (San Diego Freeway), southbound traffic takes the Calafia exit. Northbound traffic takes the Cristianitos Road exit, goes left, then right on del Presidente to Avenida Calafia. The entrance to San Clemente State Beach is on Avenida Calafia one block from Del Presidente.

DIFFICULTY: Easy.

ELEVATION GAIN/LOSS: 140 feet+.

FURTHER INFORMATION: For San Clemente State Beach and San Onofre State Beach call (949)492-0802.

FACILITIES: Water, restrooms, picnic tables and parking at San Clemente State Beach. Parking and chemical toilets at San Onofre State Beach.

CAMPGROUNDS: San Clemente State Beach has 157 campsites and hot showers. San Onofre State Beach has 221 sites in Bluffs Campground and 162 sites and hot showers at San Mateo Campground 1.5 miles inland on Cristianitos Road.

HOSTEL: San Clemente Hostel (949)492-2848 is three blocks from the beach and Amtrak station.

LODGING: San Clemente has a variety of possibilities.

One of the best beach walks and some of the least disturbed coastal bluffs left in southern California highlight this first San Diego County section. Only the presence of the San Onofre Nuclear Power Plant perched on the shoreline mars the primitive and picturesque scene. While the section starts at San Clemente State Beach in Orange County, it passes into San Diego County after only 1⅜ miles. Most of the section follows the beaches of San Onofre State Beach, a lightly developed state park unit where the land is leased from the Marine Corps, operators of the immense and rugged 130,000-acre Camp Pendleton Base surrounding San Onofre. A paved bike path runs the length of the section, starting at Avenida del Presidente in San Clemente, crossing to the west side of the highway at Cristianitos Road, then following Basilone Road and the Bluffs Campground road to section's end, where it continues through Camp Pendleton.

From the San Clemente State Beach day-use parking area, take the wide trail down the bluffs about ⅜ mile to the wild and sloping beach. After passing through a tunnel under the train tracks, continue to the tideline, turn left and

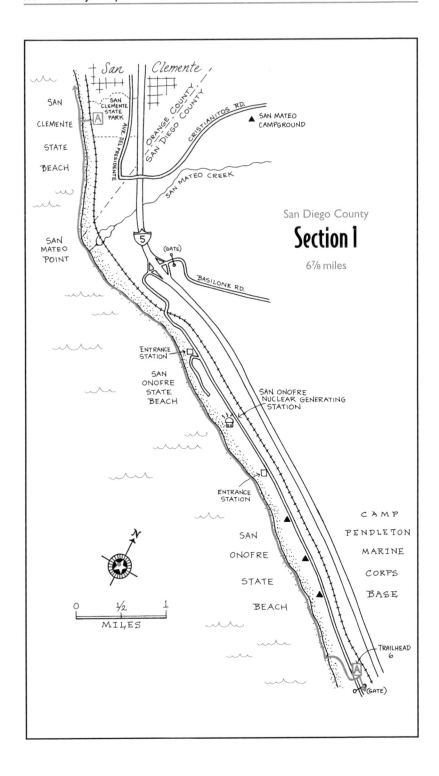

San Diego County
Section 1
6⅞ miles

The eroded bluffs of San Onofre State Beach.

walk down the beach. In the distance palm trees on the horizon mark San Mateo Point. You leave state park land by ⅜ mile, but continue walking down the steeply sloping beach below 60-foot bluffs. Before the point around one mile, notice the small white building standing on its own overlooking the ocean above Cotton's Beach, a prime surfing spot. The building was part of Richard Nixon's Western White House and the location of many cigar-smoke-filled meetings with powerful people.

Continue down the beach to round curving and sandy San Mateo Point around 1⅜ miles, crossing the unmarked boundary into San Diego County. Beyond the point the bluffs end and you pass another famous surfing spot, Trestles, named for the railroad bridge crossing San Mateo Creek. When the Marines controlled the area, they toiled constantly to keep surfers from the outstanding break. Now it's a busy public beach and surfers definitely rule, though they must walk a ways to get here. Wetlands lie inland from the creek's mouth.

Continue along the beach around a sandy, unnamed point at 1¾ miles. You soon pass in front of a private camping area and pass below 80-foot bluffs towering over the train tracks, then reach Surfer's or Surf Beach (part of San Onofre State Beach) with parking and chemical toilets all along Basilone Road at the base of the bluffs. You pass a small lagoon above the mouth of San Onofre Creek before 2⅜ miles. Continue along the seaward curving beach. About midway along Surfer's Beach around 3 miles you pass a small monument inscribed "The Point" with a surfboard mounted atop a flagpole.

At the end of the beach at 3⅞ miles you reach the imposing structure of the San Onofre Nuclear Power Plant. Pass directly in front of it on a walkway built atop the seawall protecting the plant from the ocean. Past this affront to the senses and to a continuous beach, you return to beach at the base of fantastically

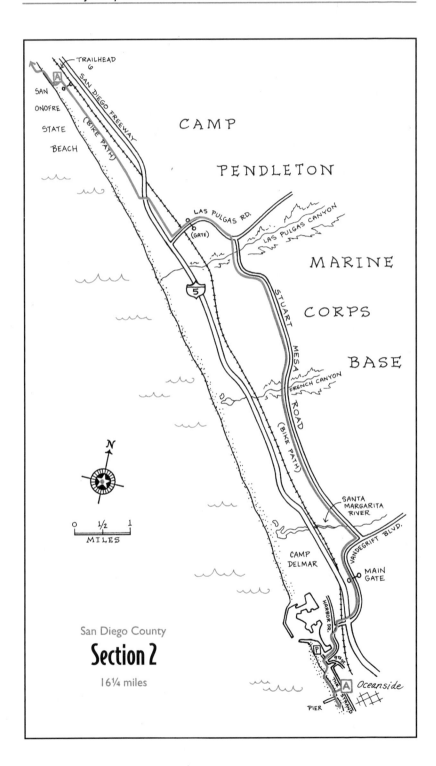

San Diego County
Section 2
16¼ miles

eroded sedimentary bluffs with beautiful coastal sage scrub on top and clinging to the cliff. This is one of the best remote beaches in California, a prime example of what southern California looked like before the human tide enveloped much of the land.

Continue down this beach at the base of 60-foot bluffs. The railroad and the San Diego Freeway both run along the marine terrace atop the bluffs and below the towering hills of Camp Pendleton. By 4⅝ miles the San Onofre Bluffs Campground entrance lies hidden atop the bluff on the old Pacific Coast Highway. As you continue down the beach, the bluffs rise 140 feet in places. Beyond the mouth of a seasonal creek at 5 miles, the first campsites perch atop the bluff. Continue down the beach passing another creek flowing from a deep canyon at 5¾ miles and plenty more campsites on the bluff. San Onofre Mountain rises 1725 feet above the tideline only two miles from the surf.

At 6⅜ miles, watch for the wide path sloping up the bluff at Lifeguard Station 5. The path leads through coastal sage to the top of the bluffs and the parking lot at the end of the San Onofre State Beach access road at 6⅞ miles. A locked gate beyond the end of the road marks Camp Pendleton.

SUGGESTED ROUND TRIPS AND LOOPS: Start from either end of this section and walk the beach to experience its secluded beaches and fine scenery. A complete round trip totals almost 14 miles, but of course you can turn back wherever you want.

SECTION 2
San Onofre State Beach to Oceanside Pier

DISTANCE: 16¼ miles (26.1 kilometers).

OPEN TO: Hikers, bicyclists.

SURFACE: Paved bike path.

ACCESS POINT: San Onofre State Beach.

HOW TO GET THERE: From Interstate 5 (San Diego Freeway) take the Basilone Road exit for San Onofre State Beach. Follow the main road through the park south for 6 miles to Trailhead 6 just before the end of the road.

DIFFICULTY: Moderate.

ELEVATION GAIN/LOSS: 180 feet+/320 feet-.

CAUTIONS: Rattlesnakes find Camp Pendleton a good habitat. Take ample water for the long walk, especially in summer. Almost the entire route is on pavement. Helmets required on base for bike riders.

FURTHER INFORMATION: For San Clemente State Beach and San Onofre State Beach call (949)492-0802. Camp Pendleton Public Affairs (760)725-5011.

FACILITIES: San Onofre State Beach has restrooms, water and parking. Oceanside has all the urban amenities.

CAMPGROUNDS: San Clemente State Beach has 157 campsites and hot showers. San

Onofre State Beach has 221 sites in Bluffs Campground and 162 sites and hot showers at San Mateo Campground 1.5 miles inland on Cristianitos Road.

HOSTEL: San Clemente Hostel (949)492-2848, two sections north, is three blocks from the beach and the Amtrak station.

LODGING: Nearest lodging is in San Clemente and Oceanside.

Walking the beach on Camp Pendleton, a Marine Corps base, is highly restricted because of continual training exercises along the coastal bluffs and beaches and in the vast open spaces of the 130,000-acre base. However, riding or walking the bike path is routine. Whether you enter from the south through the main gate or from the north where the route passes a gate on Las Pulgas Road, the guard will ask you for a driver's license, vehicle registration and proof of auto insurance, even if you are on foot or bicycle, to be considered for access to the base. Helmets are required for bike riders.

The bike path starts at the end of Avenida del Presidente not far south of San Clemente State Beach near the Orange/San Diego County line. The path follows park roads through San Onofre State Beach, passing the San Onofre Nuclear Generating Station before reaching the long stretch of roadside campsites at Bluffs Campground. This CCT section starts at the south end of that campground.

This section begins at San Onofre State Beach's Trailhead 6 where the CCT route leaves the beach and joins the bike path. If you are walking, take note that much of the route is on a bike lane along roads. The bike path enters Camp Pendleton just past Trailhead 6 at a vehicle barrier. The path continues on the pavement of old Highway 101 beside the railroad tracks, following the blufftop through coastal sage scrub. At 2 miles you pass the creek flowing from the mouth of Horno Canyon in the steep hills just north. Before 2⅞ miles the train tracks pass under the nearby freeway.

At 3¾ miles your path also passes under the freeway, then parallels it on the inland side with the tracks again on your left. You reach Las Pulgas Road at 5 miles where you turn left and follow it past an entry gate. At 5⅜ miles you follow the bike path as it turns right on Stuart Mesa Road, dipping across Las Pulgas Canyon around 6 miles and passing leased farmland and military installations. You may see maneuvers involving troops, tanks and helicopters. You follow this long road across the gently rolling marine terrace, dropping back toward the freeway around 8 miles and crossing French Canyon, then more or less paralleling the freeway and the train tracks to around 9⅛ miles. After crossing Cockleburr Canyon at 10 miles, you follow Stuart Mesa Road over a rise, then descend along Newton Canyon on your left. After crossing the creek from Newton Canyon you dip across the Santa Margarita River at 11¾ miles where you're less than ten feet above sea level. Climb slightly to the road's end at 12¼ miles.

Turn right and follow busy Vandegrift Blvd. to Camp Pendleton's Main Gate at 14 miles, then continue along the road to cross Interstate 5. Turn left at the intersection just past the freeway to descend the hill to Harbor Drive South at 15⅛ miles. Just past the intersection you can walk along the walkway past the marina and dockside businesses. At the beach at the end of the marina, follow the road as it swings south and crosses the San Luis Rey River. Turn right on Ninth Street for a short block. When you reach The Strand you can either turn left and walk that concrete walkway ½ mile to the pier, or step out onto the beach and follow the tideline to the Oceanside Pier at 16¼ miles.

SUGGESTED ROUND TRIPS & LOOPS: Although the beach is restricted, Camp Pendleton does allow civilians to drive on the base and tour some of the historic and natural features during daylight hours. At the main gate produce a driver's license, vehicle registration and proof of insurance and request a one-day pass. With the pass you'll get a self-guided driving map to the sites. Featured are a museum of tracked landing vehicles (closed Monday), historic sites including an adobe building from the Spanish mission period, and several natural sites including Rattlesnake Canyon.

HOW TO IMPROVE CCT HERE: Open the tideline of Camp Pendleton to public access and the California Coastal Trail.

SECTION 3
Oceanside Pier to South Carlsbad State Beach Campground

DISTANCE: 6½ miles (10.5 kilometers).

OPEN TO: Hikers. Bicyclists on roads.

SURFACE: Beach, streets as alternate route at high tide.

ACCESS POINT: Oceanside Pier.

HOW TO GET THERE: From Interstate 5 in Oceanside, take the Mission Avenue exit. The pier is one short block north of the end of Mission Avenue.

DIFFICULTY: Easy.

ELEVATION GAIN/LOSS: 60 feet+/60 feet-. 110 feet+/ 110 feet- for high tide route.

CAUTIONS: Portions of beaches may be flooded at high tide.

FURTHER INFORMATION: For Oceanside City Beach, call the Oceanside Department of Harbors and Beaches (760)435-4000, Carlsbad State Beach (760)438-3143.

FACILITIES: The Oceanside Pier area has picnic tables, restrooms, water and the usual urban amenities. Buccaneer Park has restrooms, picnic tables, parking and water. South Carlsbad State Beach has water, restrooms, and parking.

CAMPGROUNDS: South Carlsbad State Beach has 222 sites.

LODGING: Oceanside and Carlsbad have ample facilities.

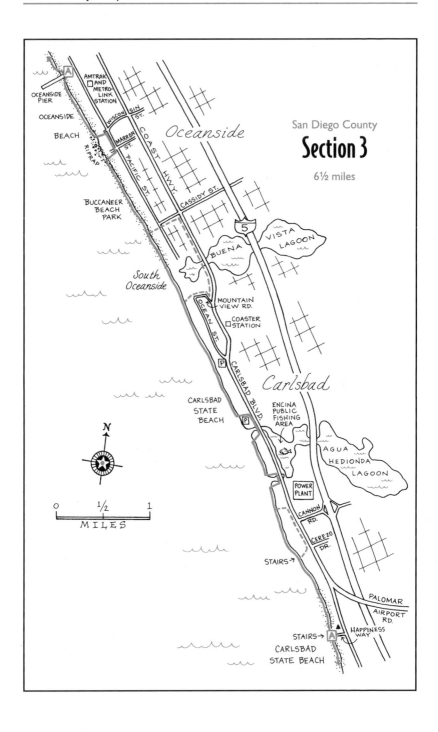

San Diego County
Section 3
6½ miles

OCEANSIDE PIER

OCEANSIDE BEACH

Oceanside

AMTRAK AND METROLINK STATION

WISCONSIN ST.

MARRON ST.

S. COAST HWY.

PACIFIC ST.

RIPRAP

BUCCANEER BEACH PARK

CASSIDY ST.

5

South Oceanside

BUENA

VISTA LAGOON

MOUNTAIN VIEW RD.

COASTER STATION

OCEAN ST.

P

CARLSBAD BLVD.

Carlsbad

CARLSBAD STATE BEACH

ENCINA PUBLIC FISHING AREA

P

AGUA HEDIONDA LAGOON

N

POWER PLANT

0   ½   1
MILES

CANNON RD.

CEREZO DR.

STAIRS →

PALOMAR AIRPORT RD.

STAIRS →

HAPPINESS WAY

CARLSBAD STATE BEACH

From Oceanside Pier all the way to South Carlsbad State Beach, the CCT route follows the beach at low to medium tides with a few short detours. The beach route, blocked at high tide in large part because the bluff has been armored with riprap to protect the houses built right on bluff's edge, also suffers sand starvation due to man-made blocks to natural sand replenishment processes. High tide forces the route on streets part of the time. We describe the low tide route and point out the potential detours along roads.

From the Oceanside Pier walk the tideline of the beach south to the riprap at ¾ mile. You can instead take The Strand, a paved walkway atop the bluff, for a few blocks. From the riprap, turn left and walk up to Wisconsin Street and along it one block. Turn right and follow Pacific Street for two blocks, then turn right on Marron Street to return to the beach at one mile and follow it south.

At 1½ miles you reach Buccaneer Park with restrooms, parking, water and a short path along a small lagoon, Loma Alta Marsh. CCT continues along the tideline, with the beach in this area accessible from the ends of the streets. Farther down the beach before Buena Vista Lagoon, riprap again crowds the beach.

When the beach is flooded, you can take an alternate inland route up Cassidy Street at 2⅛ miles. Add ½ mile to the total distance if you take this route. Walk up Cassidy Street, turn right on Pacific Coast Highway and follow it across the bridge over Buena Vista Lagoon. Take the first right onto Mountain View Drive which soon becomes Ocean Street. In a few blocks where the street turns to parallel the shoreline, return to the beach on a narrow path.

Our low tide route continues past Cassidy Street on the cobble beach, passing along the ocean side of Buena Vista Lagoon at 2¾ miles. If you get tired of the cobbles, at 2⅞ miles you can take the path up to Ocean Street (mentioned at the end of the alternate route above) and walk Ocean to its end at 3½ miles, where the parking lot at street's end marks the beginning of Carlsbad State Beach. Otherwise continue along the cobblestones of Carlsbad City Beach to Carlsbad State Beach at 3½ miles.

A massive two-tiered concrete seawall with walkways fronts the cobble beach at this northernmost of several units of Carlsbad State Beach. Take either of two walkways or the cobble beach to the other end of the seawall and another parking lot at 4 miles. Take the steps up to the main drag, Carlsbad Blvd. (Highway S21), and follow it across the bridge over Agua Hedionda (stinking water). At the south end of the bridge, you can either return to the beach or continue on the sidewalk. At 4¾ miles the beach ends at an inlet. Cut inland to walk the Carlsbad Blvd. bridge across the inlet, then return to the beach. East of Carlsbad Blvd. a giant power plant looms over the beach. The bluffs, although free from development, remain somewhat battered by the many informal paths from the street to the beach. Beginning at 5⅛ miles, houses line the bluffs.

If the beach is passable, continue down the beach at the base of the 40-foot-tall cliffs. You reach a stairway coming down from the bluff at 5½ miles. You can either take the stairs and proceed along the route described below or continue on the beach.

If the beach is impassable at 5⅛ miles, then walk up to the highway sidewalk, turn right and continue to Cerezo Drive at 5½ miles. Adjacent to Cerezo Drive, take the path across the state park-owned marine terrace down to the bluff edge.

From there you can take the stairs down to the beach or walk the path along the undeveloped blufftop. If you stay on the blufftop, you reach a deep, narrow sandy ravine where you descend to the beach at 6 miles.

From there the CCT follows the enjoyable beach at the base of the eroding bluffs to section's end. Where the highway almost touches the beach, you can walk up to the pedestrian gate at the end of South Carlsbad State Beach campground and walk through the campground to the park entrance. The CCT continues down the beach to this section's end at the third set of stairs coming down

San Diego's Coastal Rail Trail and Coastal Rail Service

A San Diego population dead set on outdoor recreation in the fine desert weather of southern California generates a high level of support for developing new recreational opportunities. The large numbers of bicyclists riding along congested Pacific Coast Highway and other roadways and in parks indicated the need for a bike trail system. A coalition of city and county agencies took on the challenge, planning the ambitious Coastal Rail Trail. The new, as yet incomplete trail parallels the coastal railroad line at a safe distance, in some places separated by a fence or vegetation.

Bicyclists, runners, walkers, rollerbladers and wheelchair users look forward to using the 42-mile trail and greenway from Oceanside to downtown San Diego. Along the way the route passes through the towns of Carlsbad, Encinitas, Leucadia, Cardiff, Solana Beach and Del Mar, crossing coastal wetlands and tracing the coastal bluff. Where the rail line crosses narrow bridges, the trail will follow existing roads. An important element in the plan connects the Coastal Rail Trail to other trails including the Coastal Trail, Bay Shore Bikeway, Mission Bay Park, Route 56 Trail, San Dieguito River Park Trail, Batiquitos Lagoon, Route 76 Trail and the San Luis Rey Bike Path, all either planned or in use.

Predictions tell us to expect seven million recreational users annually, saving over 500,000 vehicle trips. Because the rail trail passes through the heavily developed coastal zone, it serves as a commuter trail,

especially useful in the year-round mild weather. Estimates predict 22,500 commuters daily, eliminating even more vehicles from the burdened road system.

Many miles of the Rail Trail already exist, but much remains to be done. Problems to solve include routing on streets in some areas, dealing with narrow rail right-of-ways in several locations, and finding funding of at least $25 million. The CCT route described in this book both serves as an alternative to the Rail Trail and combines nicely with already opened sections of the Rail Trail to form loop trips and better explore the great territory. San Diegans expect a rich walking and cycling experience on the extensive trail system upon the completion of the Rail Trail and its connecting trails.

The Coast Express rail passenger service, with 11 daily trips in each direction between San Diego and Los Angeles, further enhances the choices for hikers, cyclists and all users of the Rail Trail and the CCT. With train stations at San Diego, Old Town San Diego, Sorrento Valley, Solana Beach, Encinitas, Carlsbad and Oceanside, users of both trails can catch any of the daily Coast Express or Coaster runs for a shuttle since they all stop at every station. Choose a train station to start from, then walk, ride or skate north or south to the station of your choice and catch the next train back to your starting point. Along the way you'll be able to explore the towns, wetlands and beaches of the San Diego coast.

from the campground at 6½ miles. The campground entrance station is adjacent to the top of the stairs.

SUGGESTED ROUND TRIPS & LOOPS: From Oceanside Pier walk the beach south or from Carlsbad Beach at Tamarack Avenue, walk it north for up to 4 miles, up to 8 miles round trip. From South Carlsbad State Beach campground, walk the beach north at low tide for up to 1½ miles, up to 3 miles round trip.

SECTION 4
South Carlsbad State Beach Campground to San Elijo State Beach

DISTANCE: 7 miles (11.3 kilometers).

OPEN TO: Hikers. Bicyclists on streets.

SURFACE: Beach, sidewalks.

ACCESS POINT: South Carlsbad State Beach Campground.

HOW TO GET THERE: Take the Palomar Airport Road/Carlsbad Blvd. exit off Interstate 5 and head west then south about .5 mile to the clearly signed Carlsbad State Beach entrance. You can also take the Poinsettia Lane exit of Interstate 5, go .75 mile west to Carlsbad Blvd. then go north one mile to the entrance.

OTHER ACCESS: Ponto Beach, Grandview Beach, Beacon's Beach, Stone Steps Beach, Moonlight Beach, Swami's Park.

DIFFICULTY: Easy.

ELEVATION GAIN/LOSS: Negligible.

CAUTIONS: Many of the beaches are flooded at high tide. Use caution on slippery tidal rocks and cobbles.

FURTHER INFORMATION: South Carlsbad State Beach and Ponto Beach (760)438-3143, for Beacon's Beach, Stone Steps Beach, Moonlight Beach, Swami's Park, call Encinitas Community Services (760)633-2880.

FACILITIES: Restrooms, water, picnic tables at both ends and several points along route.

CAMPGROUNDS: South Carlsbad State Beach Campground has 222 sites. San Elijo State Beach has 171 sites.

LODGING: Carlsbad, Leucadia, Encinitas and Cardiff-by-the-Sea have a variety of facilities.

Depending on your timing, this can be a pleasant excursion on beaches at the base of sandstone cliffs, or an urban walk along streets, or a combination of both. The beach floods at high tide in part because of human intervention in natural processes. A combination of two factors–the Oceanside Marina to the north

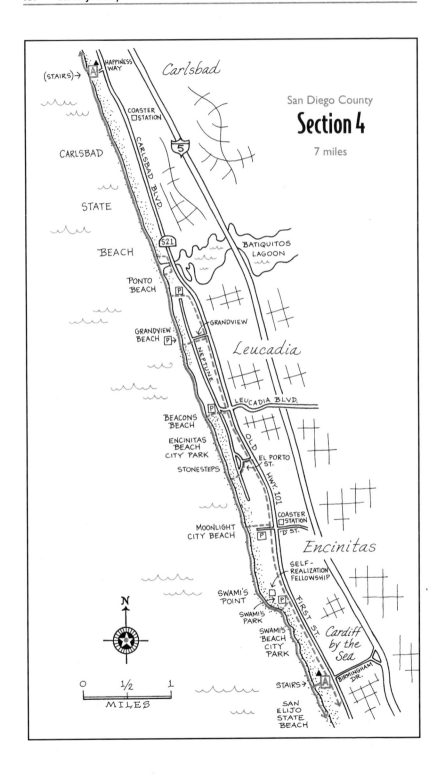

blocking the natural flow of sand, and seawalls built on the beach creating a scouring effect–rob the beach of sand and the public of their right of access. However, low tide allows access to the beach for the entire route. You have several chances to exit the beach and return. Part of the high tide route takes you on Old Highway 101 through Leucadia. It still retains some funky charm from the time this was the main route on the coast, being displaced by Interstate 5 in the 1960s.

Our route starts at Carlsbad State Beach at the bottom of the stairs that descend from near the campground entrance station. (You can instead walk through the campground and hit the beach at the south end). Walk south along the tideline of the beach. At first the beach is tucked at the base of 40-foot-tall bluffs, but by ⅛ miles where you cross the creek flowing from Canyon de las Encinas you can see and hear busy Carlson Blvd. along the top of the campground above the beach. By ¼ mile the beach loses most of the traffic noise as you walk the tideline beneath 60-foot bluffs. Pass the end of the campground by one mile and continue along the beach. The bluffs are lower beyond 1¼ miles, about 40 feet, then drop to only 20 feet by 2 miles where you approach Batiquitos Lagoon.

You reach the mouth of Batiquitos Lagoon beyond 2⅛ miles. When there's a sandbar closing the mouth, simply follow it across. If the mouth is open or deep, you must take the nearby highway bridge across it and return to the beach. Beyond the lagoon the bluffs again rise to 60 feet. Continue along Ponto Beach at the base of these sedimentary cliffs. Around 3 miles it becomes Grandview Beach. Continue along the tideline, passing a palm-lined stairway from the main parking area at 3⅛ miles. By 3½ miles the bluffs on your left rise 80 feet.

The beach changes names again before 4 miles, then six more times in the 3 miles ahead. Continue along narrow Beacon's Beach where stairs descend from the small park above. By 4¼ miles you continue along Encinitas Beach, then it becomes Stone Steps Beach around 4⅝ miles where you pass a lifeguard tower and a stone stairway of 97 steps. Continue along the shore to Moonlight Beach around 5 miles. This popular broad beach, recently replenished with sand, has serious volleyball action and a fast food stand. If the tide is high or rising, you can't make it around Swami's Point ahead. The detour takes D Street to Old Highway 101/First Street, following the latter to San Elijo State Beach at section's end.

If the tide is low enough, continue along the beach, passing the small coves of Boneyard Beach at the base of 100-foot cliffs from 5⅜ miles. At 5⅝ miles you begin to round Swami's Point, only passable at lower tides. The point gets its name from the Self Realization Fellowship Retreat and Hermitage on the point. Built in 1936 for spiritual teacher Paramahansa Yogananda, the center houses monastics at the Hermitage. They care for the grounds and conduct classes and retreats on the teachings of Paramahansaji. The peaceful, magnificent Meditation Gardens, open to the public, contain the steps to the Golden Lotus temple which slipped off the cliff in 1942 due to erosion. Riprap at the base of the cliffs now protects the grounds from further damage.

As you round the point, walking on slippery rocks at times, watch for embedded shell fossils. Pass a large private stairway from the center above. At 6⅛ miles you reach Swami's Beach and the stairs to public Swami's Park on the bluff. You can climb the steps and proceed on the sidewalk to the San Elijo campground gate or follow the CCT along the narrow path at the top edge of the steep cobble

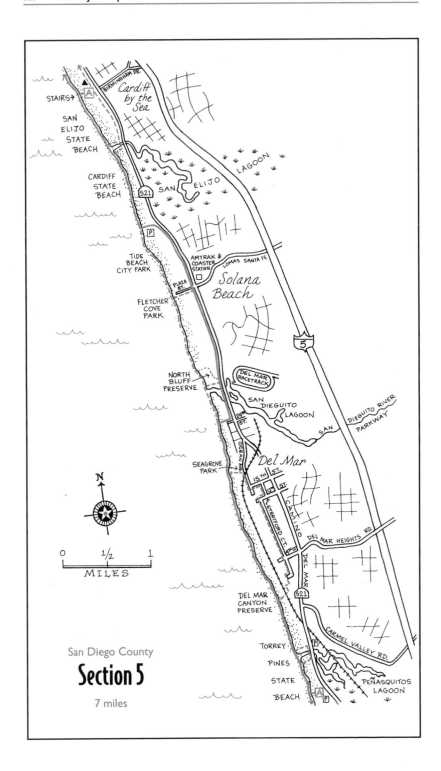

STAIRS→

SAN
ELIJO
STATE
BEACH

CARDIFF
STATE
BEACH

BIRMINGHAM DR.

Cardiff
by the
Sea

S21

SAN ELIJO LAGOON

TIDE
BEACH
CITY PARK

P

AMTRAK &
COASTER
STATION

PLAZA
ST.

LOMAS SANTA FE

Solana
Beach

FLETCHER
COVE
PARK

NORTH
BLUFF
PRESERVE

DEL MAR
RACETRACK

5

SAN
DIEGUITO
LAGOON

SEAGROVE
PARK

29TH ST.

OCEAN AVE.

Del Mar

15TH ST.

9TH ST.

SAN DIEGUITO RIVER PARKWAY

N. STRATFORD CT.

CAMINO DEL MAR

DEL MAR HEIGHTS RD.

S21

N

0   1/2   1
MILES

DEL MAR
CANYON
PRESERVE

CARMEL VALLEY RD.

TORREY

PINES

STATE

BEACH

P

PEÑASQUITOS
LAGOON

A
P

San Diego County

Section 5

7 miles

beach. By 6⅝ miles you continue along San Elijo Sate Beach, soon encountering sand again. This section ends at the stairway at 7 miles. Near the top of the stairs you'll find the entrance station to San Elijo State Beach campground.

ALTERNATE ROUTE: If the tide is high, follow Old Highway 101 the entire way (also called Carlson Blvd. and First Street) , or you may be able to make your way on and off portions using the various beach accesses depending on tide conditions. Along the way you'll pass the part of Leucadia that feels like the 1950s. Visit Moonlight Beach at the end of B Street. Also visit the wonderful Meditation Gardens at the Self Realization Hermitage (locally known as Swami's).

SUGGESTED ROUND TRIPS & LOOPS: From South Carlsbad State Beach Campground, walk down the beach to Batiquitos Lagoon and return, 4¼ miles round trip. During a receding or low tide, walk south from Ponto Beach as far as time and tides allow, leaving low tide enough for the return trip–if you go all the way to Boneyard Beach, its about 6 miles round trip. Or walk the beach north from the San Elijo Campground as far as Swami's Park and return, 1¾ miles round trip.

SECTION 5
San Elijo State Beach to Torrey Pines State Beach

DISTANCE: 7 miles (11.3 kilometers).

OPEN TO: Hikers. Bicyclists on streets.

SURFACE: Beach, trail, sidewalk.

ACCESS POINT: San Elijo State Beach campground.

HOW TO GET THERE: Take the Birmingham Drive exit from Interstate 5 at Cardiff-by-the-Sea south of Encinitas. Drive Birmingham west to its end at Old Highway 101 where San Elijo State Beach campground is directly west.

OTHER ACCESS: Cardiff State Beach, Tide Beach Park, Fletcher Cove Park, Stairs at end of Sea Scape Surf and Del Mar Shores Terrace, Del Mar Bluffs City Park, Del Mar City Beach and Torrey Pines State Beach.

DIFFICULTY: Easy.

ELEVATION GAIN/LOSS: Negligible.

CAUTIONS: Parts of the beach route are impassable at higher tides. Cardiff State Beach closes at sunset.

FURTHER INFORMATION: For San Elijo State Beach and Cardiff State Beach call District HQ (858)642-4200, for Tide Beach Park, Fletcher Cove Park and Seascape Shores call Solana Beach Department of Marine Safety (858)755-1569, Del Mar City Beach (858)755-1524, Torrey Pines State Beach (858)755-2063.

FACILITIES: Water, restrooms, picnic tables and parking at both ends and Seagrove Park.

CAMPGROUNDS: San Elijo State Beach has 171 sites and hot showers. Reserve early.

LODGING: Cardiff-by-the-Sea, Solana Beach and Del Mar have several choices.

This section of the CCT offers a real variety of landscapes and attractions. It passes three of the nine major coastal wetlands in San Diego County, some attractive beaches and beach towns. Nearby sits a race track built by film stars Bing Crosby and Pat O'Brien and attended by Hollywood's finest. It also crosses paths with a proposed greenway leading to a mountain range 55 miles inland. San Elijo Lagoon offers excellent bird watching.

At the base of the wooden stairs from San Elijo State Beach Campground, turn left and hike south on the rocky beach. If the tide is in, or you want to avoid walking on the rocks, then walk south through the campground to reach the outlet of San Elijo Lagoon. Either way the bluffs end and you meet the outlet channel at ⅜ mile. If the lagoon mouth is open and flowing, use the sidewalk of the highway bridge, then turn right and return to the beach (adds ⅛ mile).

Beyond the lagoon you follow Cardiff State Beach, another rocky strand. The large wetlands lie to the east beyond the highway. At ¾ mile a building atop riprap blocks the beach so you may need to walk on the sidewalk around the building. Since the sloped, cobble beach presents quite difficult walking, consider following the sidewalk of the nearby highway for an easier path.

You reach the Cardiff State Beach parking lot at 1⅜ miles. In 1998 and 1999 storms carried away the once large sandy beach and severely damaged part of the lot and the concrete walkway overlooking the beach. At press time it looked like a disaster area.

Beyond the parking lot you can walk the narrow beach at the base of eroding yellow cliffs if the tide is low enough. Our described route follows the road's sidewalks. At the end of the lot, take the sandy path up to the highway. Upon reaching Plaza Street at 2¼ miles, you can turn right for a side trip to the beach at Fletcher Cove Park, also hit hard by '98 storms, but since replenished with sand from Yuma, Arizona. The described route continues on the road.

At 3¼ miles Old Highway 101 descends to San Dieguito Lagoon. The mouth of the San Dieguito River lies westward. The vital San Dieguito wetlands, although severely damaged, hold promise for restoration. Part of the damage done before the importance of wetlands was widely understood happened when the Del Mar Racetrack was built in 1937 on the lagoon. Today an ambitious plan calls for restoration of the lagoon and the river with creation of a 60,000-acre greenway featuring a 55-mile long trail all the way from the lagoon's mouth (and the CCT) to the 4000-foot Volcan Mountains near the town of Julien.

If the mouth of San Dieguito Lagoon is closed then walk down to the beach before the bridge. Otherwise cross the highway bridge, then return to the beach along the lagoon to its mouth, or cut down 29th Street a block down the road. Follow the wide sandy beach south, picking up bluffs at 4½ miles. At 4⅝ miles you come to the town of Del Mar's main beach at Seagrove Park, tucked at the base of 60-foot-tall bluffs. You can take a side trip a few blocks inland on 15th Street to visit trendy downtown Del Mar.

Hikers navigate Flat Rock at Torrey Pines State Beach.

CCT continues down the beach as the bluffs become higher. The steep sandstone bluffs rise 100 feet by 5⅝ miles where you're officially on Torrey Pines State Beach. In the event the beach is flooded at high tide, many locals use the path beside the nearby railroad tracks. Be advised that the tracks are marked "no trespassing" and are patrolled. The third option is to walk up 15th Street and make a right on Stratford Court. At the end of the street you'll find a series of informal paths down to the beach.

Whichever way you go, you reach the mouth of Peñasquitos Lagoon at 6⅜ miles. Use the highway bridge if the mouth is impassable, then return to the beach. The hike ends at 7 miles at the big parking lot for Torrey Pines State Beach where the road passes the parking lot entrance station before heading up the hill to Torrey Pines State Reserve.

SUGGESTED ROUND TRIPS AND LOOPS: Pick a good low-tide day to explore different parts of this route. You will be rewarded with relatively uncrowded beaches and interesting geology along the eroding bluffs as well as many examples of destructive seawalls. Start at Seagrove Park at Del Mar and walk to Torrey Pines State Beach for a 5-mile round trip. You can also start at Cardiff State Beach and walk to Seagrove Park, 6½ miles round trip.

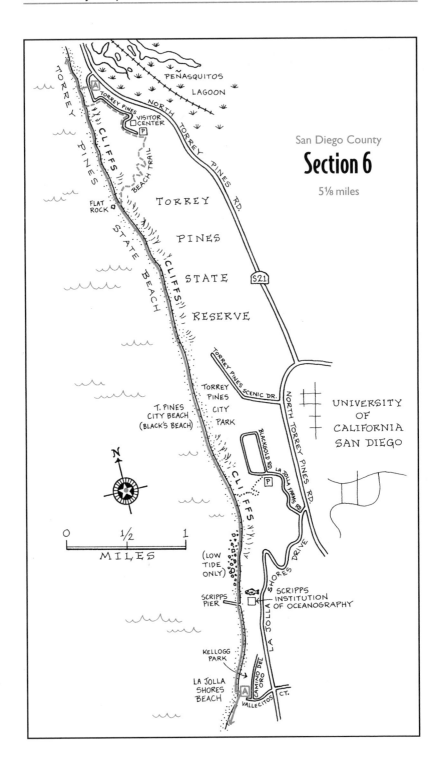

San Diego County
Section 6
5⅛ miles

PEÑASQUITOS LAGOON

TORREY PINES

NORTH TORREY PINES RD.

A

TORREY PINES VISITOR CENTER
P

BEACH TRAIL

FLAT ROCK

TORREY

PINES

STATE

CLIFFS

STATE BEACH

CLIFFS

RESERVE

S21

TORREY PINES SCENIC DR.

NORTH TORREY PINES RD.

UNIVERSITY OF CALIFORNIA SAN DIEGO

TORREY PINES CITY PARK

T. PINES CITY BEACH (BLACK'S BEACH)

N

BLACKGOLD RD.

LA JOLLA FARMS RD.

P

CLIFFS

O   ½   1
MILES

(LOW TIDE ONLY)

LA JOLLA SHORES DRIVE

SCRIPPS PIER

SCRIPPS INSTITUTION OF OCEANOGRAPHY

KELLOGG PARK

LA JOLLA SHORES BEACH

A

CAMINO DEL ORO

VALLECITOS CT.

SECTION 6
Torrey Pines State Beach to La Jolla Shores Beach

DISTANCE: 5⅛ miles for CCT, 6⅛ miles for the upland alternate route (8.2, 9.9 kilometers).

OPEN TO: Hikers.

SURFACE: Beach.

ACCESS POINT: Torrey Pines State Beach parking lot.

HOW TO GET THERE: From Interstate 5, take the Del Mar Heights Road exit or the Carmel Valley Road exit. Turn left on Camino Del Mar and follow it to the large parking lot for Torrey Pines State Beach on the beach side of the road.

OTHER ACCESS: Beach Trail from Torrey Pines State Reserve, Blackgold Road trail, Scripps Beach and Pier.

DIFFICULTY: Easy. Moderate for the Torrey Pines State Reserve route.

ELEVATION GAIN/LOSS: None for Beach Route. Torrey Pines Route: 340 feet+/ 340 feet-.

CAUTIONS: This route must be done at low tide. Make sure you don't get trapped by rising tides. Torrey Pines State Beach parking lot closes at sunset. No dogs allowed. Food is not allowed in Torrey Pines State Reserve.

FURTHER INFORMATION: Torrey Pines State Reserve and Torrey Pines State Beach (858)755-2063, Torrey Pines Association, PO Box 150, La Jolla CA 92037, for La Jolla Shores Beach, call the San Diego Coastline Parks Division (619)221-8900, Scripps Aquarium (858)534-3474.

FACILITIES: Water, restrooms, picnic tables at Torrey Pines State Beach and La Jolla Shores Beach.

CAMPGROUNDS: San Elijo State Beach at the start of Section 5 has 171 sites and hot showers. Reserve early.

HOSTELS: San Diego has two hostels, Point Loma (619)223-4778 and Downtown (619)525-1531.

LODGING: La Jolla has abundant accommodations mostly on the high end, with La Jolla Cove Suites and the Radisson Hotel the most affordable choices. Or try the Crystal Pier Motel in Pacific Beach at the end of Section 7.

This section visits some of the most dramatic scenery anywhere on the California Coast, with great geology and fossils, plant diversity and tranquility and relative solitude within sight of a city of a million people. You walk a remote beach at the base of spectacular, eroding 300-foot sandstone cliffs cut by deep ravines. The high route takes you through Torrey Pines State Reserve. If you take the beach route, find time to come back and explore this reserve, one of the jewels of the state park system. See the adjacent feature article for the story of the rare Torrey pines.

This walk can be done at low tide only. Time the start of your walk to coincide with an ebbing (retreating) tide. Then if you need to wait for the tide to recede as you walk the beach below the cliffs, you know that the tide is moving

Unique Torrey Pines State Reserve

The Torrey pine reigns among the rarest of the rare plants on the California shore. Before the last ice age over 11,000 years ago, Torrey pine forests covered large areas of southern California. Then changing climatic conditions reduced the stands to one of the world's smallest native distributions of any tree. A few thousand Torrey pines grow scattered between La Jolla and Del Mar and a small stand survives on Santa Rosa Island in the sea 170 miles northwest. Most of the trees are protected in the State Parks system's 2000-acre Torrey Pines State Reserve.

The pines gained recognition as rare in 1850, California's first year of statehood, when Dr. C.C. Parry, a botanist with the U.S. government, noticed the trees and named them after his botany professor, Dr. John Torrey. Torrey never saw the trees named after him. Years later Parry returned and urged the city of San Diego to preserve the species against the human depredations of cattle grazing, firewood cutting and road building. Finally in 1899, the city designated 369 acres for a public park. Ellen Browning Scripps purchased and donated more land, and in 1924 the city added an additional 1000 acres. In 1950 the Torrey Pines Association formed to work toward full protection for the pines and the surrounding habitat. In 1959 the city gave the park to the California State Parks Reserve system.

Torrey Pines State Reserve offers much more than its rare pines, containing some of the most dramatic and diverse terrain on the California coast. It remains much as it did when the Kumeyyaay people lived here, before settlers came and transformed San Diego's coastal terraces and hills with urban sprawl. The highly erodable sandstone geology of the hills creates fantastic erosional formations. Peñasquitos Lagoon remains one of the more healthy on the south coast, and the 5-mile-long beach fronting the reserve offers solitude and quiet at the base of spectacular 300-foot cliffs. Diverse, rich plant communities covering the land include coastal strand, coastal scrub, chaparral, Torrey pine woodland, salt marsh, freshwater marsh and riparian. More than 430 species of flora and fauna live within Torrey Pines State Reserve, including 144 birds, 110 invertebrates, 85 plants, 39 mammals, 28 reptiles, 23 fishes and 7 amphibians.

The Reserve restricts some activities in order to protect the habitat. No food is allowed. You can walk the 8 miles of maintained trails, visit and hike the beach, and tour the Visitor Center and Museum. That classic adobe structure, built in 1923 and styled after Hopi Indian houses, commands views of the surrounding terrain. Both locals and tourists come for docent-led walks, hiking, school tours, photography, painting, running, surfing, bird watching, plant identification, and to simply wonder at the magnificence of the natural world maintained here.

The area still suffers the threat of urban encroachment. Surrounding development cuts off wildlife corridors and creates erosion and pollution which damages the lagoon. The pines themselves are weakened by a small gene pool, allowing disease to attack the trees. Three groups aid State Parks in preserving the well-being of the park. Torrey Pines Association, Torrey Pines Docent Society, and the Torrey Pines Wildlife Association concern themselves with park expansion, public education, and wildlife protection. To find out more about the Reserve and these groups, visit the Torrey Pines State Reserve web site at www.torreypine.org/tpnathis.htm.

favorably. The route follows a mostly sandy beach with a few rocky tidepool areas, encountering piles of sandstone talus, huge boulders and big sheets of smooth rock.

From the parking area head south on the beach with the cliffs rising to 300 feet on your left by ¼ mile. The fantastically eroded light brown and yellow cliffs are dotted with Torrey pines and chaparral. Pass small deep canyons in the cliffs at ⅜ mile and ½ mile. By ⅞ mile you pass the deepest canyon yet. Beyond it at one mile you reach Flat Rock offshore and the lower end of the Beach Trail that descends from Torrey Pines State Reserve above, offering an escape route in case you misjudged the tide. You'll find excellent tidepools around Flat Rock.

At all but the lowest tides you may have to wade around the rocky point near Flat Rock to reach the beach beyond. Once you pass the point you can enjoy a long sandy walk in the relative solitude of lightly used Black's Beach. As you move south, you will encounter more people who reach the beach from the south end, either from Scripps Pier or via steep trails down the bluffs. You round another point at 1½ miles to pass another deep canyon around 1¾ miles. Continue down the sandy tideline past the deep canyon at 2⅜ miles to another canyon at 2⅞ miles where a steep stairway descends from the old glider landing strip at Torrey Pines City Park.

Black's Beach marks the scene of a battle between nude sun worshippers and more puritanical voters who outlawed nudity on this beach in 1977. It's been a standoff ever since, with nudity in serene surroundings being the norm in defiance of uptight rules against nudity. The wide beach allows room for everyone to follow their own peaceful pursuits whether in the buff or dressed for hiking. The northern end of the sometimes nude beach is favored by men, with the middle portion between 2 and 3 miles generally considered co-ed and the portion south of the stairway at 2⅞ miles generally favored by surfers and graced with the largest and best waves.Hang gliders grace the sky above, launching from the blufftop and riding on the thermal updrafts. As far as we know, nude hang gliding has not been outlawed.

Continue down the sandy beach at the base of the towering golden cliffs, passing beneath the 326-foot summit of the palisades. Black's Beach narrows as you near its southern end, marked by the paved service road and access/escape trail that winds down from Blackgold Road at 3⅝ miles.

Beyond Black's Beach the sand narrows even more. Soon the beach becomes slippery with tidal rocks. A steep tramway drops from the bluff 200 feet above to an out-of-place beach house perched atop a concrete column on the sand. The Scripps Pier comes into view as you scramble on rocks to reach the point, then return to sand, rounding the point at 4 miles. It may take a low tide to pass.

The world famous Scripps Institution of Oceanography sits on the low bluff near the pier ahead. Walk toward it on the sandy beach or, if the tide is low enough, along the edge of the extensive tidepools beside the shore. Pass the pier at 4⅜ miles. After a final stroll down the wide, gently sloping strand of La Jolla Shores Beach, this section ends at 5⅛ miles at grassy Kellogg Park, marked by tall palm trees at the head of the gentle curve of La Jolla Bay.

ALTERNATE ROUTE: From the parking lot at the access point, walk up the winding en-

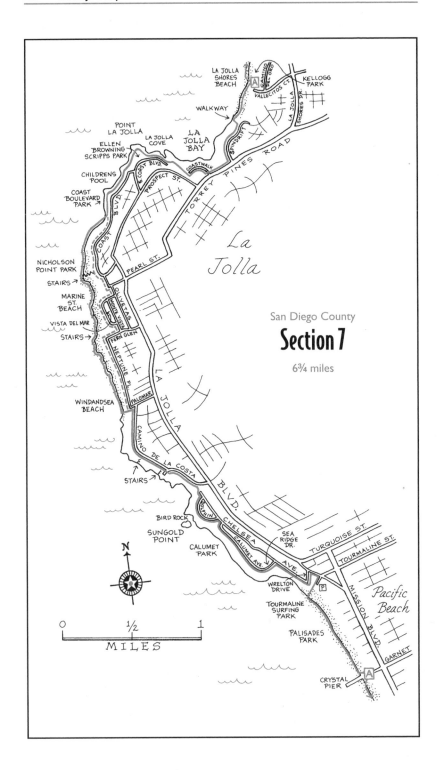

LA JOLLA SHORES BEACH

KELLOGG PARK

VALLECITOS CT.

WALKWAY

POINT LA JOLLA

LA JOLLA COVE

ELLEN BROWNING SCRIPPS PARK

LA JOLLA BAY

SPINDRIFT

TORREY PINES ROAD

COASTWALK

CHILDRENS POOL

PROSPECT ST.

S. COAST BLVD.

COAST BOULEVARD PARK

COAST BLVD.

PEARL ST.

La Jolla

NICHOLSON POINT PARK

STAIRS →

MARINE ST. BEACH

OLIVETAS

MONTE VISTA

VISTA DEL MAR

STAIRS →

FERN GLEN

NEPTUNE PL.

San Diego County

Section 7

6¾ miles

WINDANDSEA BEACH

PALOMAR

LA JOLLA BLVD.

CAMINO DE LA COSTA

STAIRS →

BIRD ROCK

SUNGOLD POINT

CALUMET PARK

DOLPHIN

CHELSEA

CALUMET AVE.

AVE.

SEA RIDGE DR.

TURQUOISE ST.

TOURMALINE ST.

WRELTON DRIVE

P

MISSION BLVD.

Pacific Beach

TOURMALINE SURFING PARK

PALISADES PARK

GARNET

CRYSTAL PIER

N

0   ½   1

M I L E S

trance road, ascending the bluffs into Torrey Pines State Reserve. Local lore has it that when this was the coastal road in the 1920s, the cars would back up the slope because the steepness was too much for their forward gearing. You reach the attractive adobe building housing the Visitor Center at ⅞ mile where docents and park rangers gladly share knowledge of the Reserve. The little museum within covers much of the natural and human history of Torrey pines. Across the street and behind the restrooms, find the Beach Trail which drops down through dense chaparral and the eroded terrain yielding grand views on the way to Flat Rock around 2 miles. Use caution descending the last few hundred feet of narrow and slippery path. From Flat Rock, continue on the beach as described above.

SUGGESTED ROUND TRIPS AND LOOPS: From the Torrey Pines State Beach parking lot, take the road into the park to the Visitor Center, descend to the beach on the Beach Trail, and return to the parking lot for a stunning 3-mile loop. Take a side trip on one of several loops in the Reserve, the Parry Grove Trail and the Guy Fleming Trail, to visit the main groves of pines and add 1¼ miles to your hike.

SECTION 7
La Jolla Shores Beach to Crystal Pier, Pacific Beach

DISTANCE: 6¾ miles (10.9 kilometers).

OPEN TO: Hikers. Bicyclists on streets.

SURFACE: Beach, trail, rocky tideline, sidewalk.

ACCESS POINT: La Jolla Shores Beach.

HOW TO GET THERE: From Interstate 5, take the Ardath Road exit and head toward La Jolla. In about 1.4 miles turn right on La Jolla Shores Drive, then go left on Vallecitos Court and drive to its end at Kellogg Park.

OTHER ACCESS: Much of the route is on streets. Stairs or paths lead to the shore at Ellen Scripps Park, Coast Boulevard Park, Nicholson Point Park, Marine Street Beach, end of Fern Street, Windansea Beach, several along Camino de la Costa, Bird Rock Avenue, end of Linda Way, and end of Chelsea Place.

DIFFICULTY: Easy.

ELEVATION GAIN/LOSS: 200 feet+/200 feet-.

CAUTIONS: Use caution on tidal rocks and don't get trapped by rising tides.

FURTHER INFORMATION: For the beaches along this route, call the San Diego Coastline Parks Division (619)221-8900.

FACILITIES: Water, restrooms, picnic tables and parking at La Jolla Shores Beach. Picnic tables, restrooms and water at Scripps Park and Tourmaline Surfing Park. Urban amenities in Pacific Beach.

CAMPGROUNDS: San Elijo State Beach at the start of Section 5 is the nearest, with 171 sites and hot showers. Reserve early.

HOSTELS: San Diego has two hostels, Point Loma (619)223-4778 and Downtown (619)525-1531.

LODGING: La Jolla has abundant accommodations mostly on the high end, with La Jolla Cove Suites and the Radisson Hotel the most affordable choices. Or try the Crystal Pier Motel in Pacific Beach at the end of this section.

This CCT route winds through the upscale, intensely developed La Jolla area. La Jolla, Spanish for "the jewel," resembles Palos Verdes Peninsula in Los Angeles in that it is part of a large urban area yet separated by both geography and affluence. La Jolla sits on a peninsula full of upscale houses approachable mostly on winding roads through the hills. The section starts and ends on beaches but mostly follows streets in between, with one stretch along a rugged shore and a visit to engaging Point La Jolla, which offers striking views of the rocky shoreline.

Start on broad La Jolla Shores Beach and walk south along the tideline down past the private La Jolla Beach and Tennis Club. Near the end of the beach at ⅜ mile, take the narrow unmarked walkway next to a restaurant up to Spindrift Drive. Turn right on Spindrift Drive and walk its sidewalk to Torrey Pines Road. Turn right and follow Torrey Pines two blocks, then turn right at ¾ mile and follow the little lane called Coast Walk to its end.

At the end of Coast Walk's pavement, take the dirt trail along the bluffs into the La Jolla Ecological Reserve, a 6000-acre reserve protecting the life in the tidal zone and submerged lands from the southern limits of Del Mar to Goldfish Point. It is illegal to disturb the wildlife in this area. The path yields stunning views of the wind- and sea-shaped cliffs of La Jolla Bay. The cliffs contain the seven wave-carved La Jolla Caves. After rounding a cove, the path heads northwest toward Goldfish Point. The path ends before 1¼ miles at a park on Coast Blvd. A stairway here leads down to the bluffs at Goldfish Point, from where you can climb down the rocks to tidepools.

Turn right and walk the sidewalk of Coast Blvd. following the blufftop around the point above coves and beaches tucked in folded, convoluted sandstone bluffs. You come to bustling Ellen Browning Scripps Park at Point La Jolla beyond 1⅝ miles. Tourists take in the sights here while vendors sell jewelry and T-shirts from sidewalk tables. Follow the park path along the cliff edge beneath palms and wind-shaped Monterey cypresses. You pass La Jolla Cove and a path down to its popular, sheltered beach, then pass side trails to Boomer Beach and Shell Beach. Just beyond Scripps Park you pass a stairway to Children's Pool Beach, a fine beach partly shielded by a breakwater. The beach is popular with families and often has sea lions residing on it.

Continue along the walkway above Seal Rock Point, then pick up the sidewalk along Coast Blvd. When you reach the narrow blufftop strip of Coast Boulevard Park at 2⅛ miles, you have a choice of routes. At lower tides CCT descends a path north of Cuvier Street to follow the scenic shoreline. See below for the street route.

The shoreline route makes its way over riprap, around rocky outcrops, and along the sandy cove of Nicholson Point Park to reach Marine Street Beach at 2¾ miles. Continue along this wide beach to its far end where stairs descend from Fern Street. Follow the shore over more rocks and around a small point to reach Windansea Beach around 3¼ miles, legendary as the beach in Tom Wolfe's first book, *The Pump House Gang.* Continue along the sandy beach of La Jolla Strand Park to its end where stairs ascend to Palomar Avenue at 3⅝ miles. The shore just down coast angles out to another unnamed point. While you can't walk the shore to the point, you can easily scramble over a low slickrock formation to reach a small sandy beach called Hermosa Terrace Park. From there you must climb a paved path to the end of Winamar Avenue on Camino de la Costa at 3¾ miles.

If the tide blocks walking the ocean's edge as described above, then continue on the Coast Blvd. sidewalk to Pearl Street. Turn left, then immediately go right on Olivetas Avenue for one block. Turn right on Marine Street and walk to its end where you will find access to its namesake beach. Turn left on Vista Del Mar along the bluff edge, then go right on Monte Vista to its end at Fern Glen. Turn right and walk Fern Glen to its end where there is access to Windansea Beach. The high tide route turns left on Neptune Place and follows it to the end where you go left on Palomar Avenue almost to its end opposite another path to Windansea Beach. A half block before the end of Palomar, turn left on Camino de la Costa. As you follow it south, in one block you pass the end of Winamar Avenue where the main route climbs from the beach.

The CCT continues down Camino de la Costa, rounding the unnamed point around 4 miles, then meeting stairs to the rocky shoreline at both Cortez Place and MiraMonte Place where de la Costa jogs left. At 4⅝ miles turn right and walk through tiny La Jolla Hermosa Park to Chelsea Avenue, walk Chelsea briefly, then go right to follow curving Dolphin Place. Here you'll find a small overlook park, and soon afterward stairs to the rocky beach at Sun Gold Point that descend from the end of short Bird Rock Avenue.

At the end of Dolphin Place, turn right on Chelsea Avenue, then immediately go right on Forward Street, then left on Calumet Avenue. Soon you reach Calumet Park overlooking the rocky shoreline. Follow Calumet Avenue out to Chelsea Avenue and turn right. When Chelsea ends at Wrelton Drive, turn left, then go right on La Jolla Blvd. for one block.

Turn right onto Tourmaline Street and walk through the parking lot for Tourmaline Surfing Park at 6 miles to return to the beach. Turn left at the tideline and walk the beach south beside descending bluffs, enjoying the sea air free of exhaust fumes. Head for historic Crystal Pier in the distance, passing through Palisades Park and into Pacific Beach Park to reach the pier and section's end at 6¾ miles.

SUGGESTED ROUND TRIPS AND LOOPS: Pick a low-tide day and make the shoreline walk from Point La Jolla to Windansea Beach and back for interesting geology and great scenery, 4 miles round trip. If the tides are just right you can continue from Windansea down to La Jolla Strand or Hermosa Terrace Park, adding another ¼ mile round trip. You can also make that 3¾-mile walk one way and ride the #34 bus back to the start.

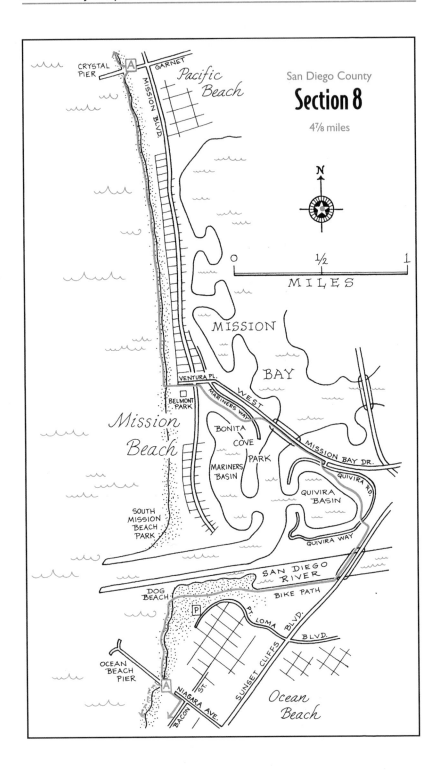

CRYSTAL PIER

GARNET

Pacific Beach

MISSION BLVD.

San Diego County

Section 8

4⅞ miles

N

½   1

0

MILES

MISSION

BAY

WEST

VENTURA PL.

MARINERS WAY

BELMONT PARK

Mission Beach

BONITA COVE

PARK

MISSION BAY DR.

MARINERS BASIN

QUIVIRA RD.

QUIVIRA BASIN

SOUTH MISSION BEACH PARK

QUIVIRA WAY

SAN DIEGO RIVER

DOG BEACH

BIKE PATH

P

PT. LOMA BLVD.

SUNSET CLIFFS BLVD.

OCEAN BEACH PIER

NIAGARA AVE.

BACON ST.

Ocean Beach

SECTION 8
Crystal Pier, Pacific Beach, to Ocean Beach Pier

DISTANCE: 4⅞ miles (7.8 kilometers).

OPEN TO: Hikers. Bicyclists on bike paths and streets.

SURFACE: Beach, sidewalk, bike path.

ACCESS POINT: Crystal Pier in Pacific Beach.

HOW TO GET THERE: Exit Interstate 5 at Garnet Street and head west to Pacific Beach where Garnet Street ends at the pier.

OTHER ACCESS: Mission Bay, Ocean Beach Athletic Area, Dog Beach.

DIFFICULTY: Easy.

ELEVATION GAIN/LOSS: Negligible.

FURTHER INFORMATION: For Pacific Beach, Mission Beach, Mission Bay Park and Ocean Beach, contact the San Diego Coastline Parks Division (619)221-8900.

FACILITIES: Pacific Beach Park has restrooms, water, picnic tables and parking, with urban amenities nearby and along much of route.

CAMPGROUNDS: Private, expensive campgrounds at De Anza Harbor Resort (RVs only) and Campland on the Bay (RV and tent spaces).

HOSTELS: San Diego has two hostels, Point Loma (619)223-4778 and Downtown (619)525-1531.

LODGING: Abundant everywhere, including right beside the CCT where Crystal Pier Motel offers budget rooms and nearby Pacific Terrace Inn offers luxury.

This short section of the CCT starts and ends on a beach and passes through the largest aquatic park on the west coast, 4600-acre Mission Bay Park with 27 miles of shoreline, 11 marinas, six hotels and two campgrounds. This huge park's amenities cover every kind of water sport from swimming and boating to water skiing and windsurfing, with park facilities ranging from picnicking to horseshoes and softball.

The glorious recreational opportunities of Mission Bay Park came with a price. The Spaniards found a deep water embayment and called it False Bay because sailing ship captains occasionally confused it with San Diego Bay on the other side of Point Loma. The San Diego River flowed into San Diego Bay, making Point Loma almost an island at high tide. After California statehood in 1849, the Army Corps of Engineers rerouted the river to empty into False Bay. The Corps then filled the old river mouth, allowing port facilities construction. The new river filled in False Bay with sediments and within 50 years it was a shallow marsh. In the 1940s the Corps began to dredge the bay and in following years the City of San Diego developed the Mission Bay facilities.

This section starts at the quaint Crystal Pier at Pacific Beach Park where a row of cottages line both sides of the pier. The motel built in 1927 offers moderately priced rooms. Occupants have been known to fish from the windows. Looking north from the pier offers an end-on look at the dramatic convoluted cliffs of La Jolla, while the view south surveys a nearly flat, extremely watery world.

From the pier walk south on the popular beach usually crowded with towel rats and a multitude of surfers catching the excellent waves. You can instead choose to walk the Ocean Front Walk in front of the row of beach houses. By ⅝ mile you continue along Mission Beach Park through the aqueous community of Mission Beach.

At 1⅝ miles you want to turn left to head inland at Belmont Park, easily identified by the big white wooden roller coaster not far ahead. Walk up Ventura Place to the left of the roller coaster and old-fashioned merry-go-round and cross busy Bayside Blvd. into Mission Bay Park. Stay to the right of West Mission Bay Drive and walk through the Bonita Cove Park area either on the grass, the concrete walkway or along the sandy shoreline. Cross the top of Mariners Point, then angle northeast to the West Mission Bay Drive bridge and follow the walkway across Mission Bay from 2¼ miles.

After you get off the bridge, turn right on Quivira Road at 2⅝ miles. Where the road promptly splits (the Hyatt Islandia is to the right) you want to head generally southeast. You can walk either the road's sidewalk, through the grassy area, or along the shore of the Quivira Basin marinas. At the east end Quivira Basin where Quivira Road swings right to head southwest, take the bike path on the left up to Sunset Cliffs Blvd. Cross the San Diego River on the Sunset Cliffs Blvd. Bridge around 3¼ miles, then turn right to follow the bike path west along the levee. The path passes athletic fields before coming to Dog Park and Dog Beach where dogs run free at 4⅜ miles. Cross the big expanse of sand to the ocean shoreline, then turn left and follow the tideline of Ocean Beach to the pier and the end of the section at 4⅞ miles.

SUGGESTED LOOPS AND ROUND TRIPS: Mission Bay's paved multi-use trail circles the bay, providing opportunity to explore this vast area on bike or foot.

SECTION 9
Ocean Beach Pier to Downtown San Diego Waterfront

DISTANCE: 10⅛ miles (16.3 kilometers).

OPEN TO: Hikers. Bicyclists on bike paths and streets.

SURFACE: Beach, trail, sidewalk.

ACCESS POINT: Ocean Beach Pier.

HOW TO GET THERE: Exit Interstate 5 onto Interstate 8 heading west toward Ocean Beach. Take Sunset Cliffs Blvd. to Niagara Avenue, turn right and drive to the pier at the end of the street.

OTHER ACCESS: Anywhere along route especially Ocean Beach City Beach, Sunset Cliffs Park, Spanish Landing Park, Embarcadero.

DIFFICULTY: Moderate.

ELEVATION GAIN/LOSS: 420 feet+/420 feet-.

CAUTIONS: Watch for traffic on busy city streets. Use caution if you walk the tidal zone: watch for slippery rocks, sneaker waves and rising tides.

FURTHER INFORMATION: For Ocean Beach and Ocean Beach Park, call the San Diego Coastline Parks Division (619)221-8900, Maritime Museum (*Star of India*) (619)234-9153.

FACILITIES: Ocean Beach Pier has restrooms, water and parking. Urban amenities abound at both ends. Restrooms, water, picnic tables and parking at Spanish Landing Park.

HOSTELS: San Diego has two hostels, Point Loma (619)223-4778 and Downtown (619)525-1531.

LODGING: You'll find many choices of accommodations in the area. Two budget choices close to the access point are Ocean Villa Motel and Ocean Beach Motel.

Trekking from Ocean Beach to the Point Loma area to San Diego's downtown waterfront offers both variety and abundant rewards in this intensely urban area. Features include one of the best sunset viewing areas on the west coast at Sunset Cliffs, scrambles on beaches and eroded bluffs, the busy downtown waterfront with an impressive historic sailing vessel, the *Star of India*, and, on clear days, our first view of Mexico after 1150 miles of trail.

This walk starts at the Ocean Beach Pier, at 2100 feet currently the longest pier on the west coast. For a different perspective on the coast, walk out to the end of the pier and back, ¾ mile round trip. From the pier the CCT then winds its way through residential neighborhoods before returning to the coast along Sunset Cliffs Blvd. The low tide route from the pier bypasses the streets for almost a mile of rocky shoreline before climbing to Sunset Cliffs Blvd. via one of several stairways. After more residential streets, the route follows the urban shoreline of San Diego Bay to the skyscrapers at the bayside heart of downtown.

To do the inland route start at the pier and follow Niagara Avenue uphill for a

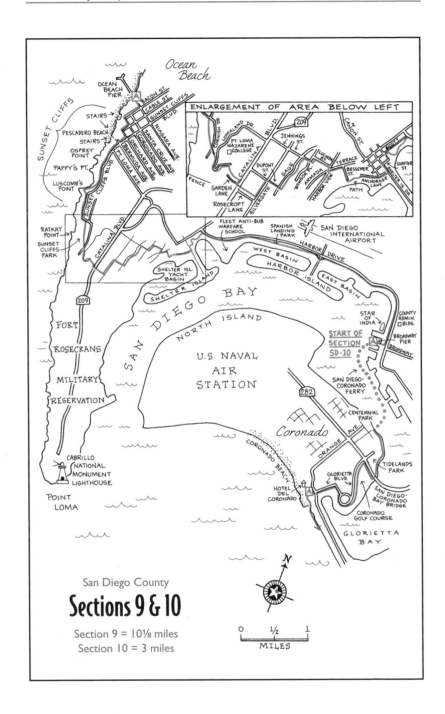

San Diego County
Sections 9 & 10
Section 9 = 10⅛ miles
Section 10 = 3 miles

block, then turn right on Bacon Street for two blocks. Go left on Coronado Avenue, right on Cable Street, then left on Orchard Avenue for one block each before turning right on Sunset Cliffs Blvd., all accomplished in six short blocks. Walk south along the sidewalk of Sunset Cliffs Blvd.

To do the low-tide beach walk, take the concrete path that starts under the pier south for 300 feet, then descend the stairs to the shore and turn left. Some of this route consists of concrete walkway set into seawalls, part is on tidal rock and some on flat tidal rocks imbedded with fossil shells. Follow the shore out around a point and along the rocky coast, coming to the first stairway leading to Santa Cruz Street. Round a small cove at ⅜ mile before heading out to a narrow point, then passing Alligator Rock. Walk down the rocky shore below 40-foot cliffs to the Orchard Street stairs at ⅝ mile. If you continue down Pescadero Beach to the third stairway at Bermuda Street beyond ¾ mile, the cliffs shrink to about 20 feet. Exit the beach, walk up to Sunset Cliffs Blvd. and turn right at ⅞ mile.

The CCT follows Sunset Cliffs Blvd. south, returning to the shoreline at 1⅛ miles. Follow an informal path along the bluff's edge, rounding Osprey Point, then Pappy's Point. This premiere sunset viewing area faces directly west. In a few places you must walk on the road shoulder where erosion has eaten into the bluffs. Round broad Luscomb's Point at 1⅞ miles.

Where Sunset Cliffs Blvd. ends at Ladera Street at 2⅜ miles, you have two options: easy and difficult. Both options take you through undeveloped Sunset Cliffs Park and the Point Loma Nazarene College Campus. Before you decide, consider descending the nearby stairs to a fine cove with a sandy beach and extensive wave-cut reefs. The easy route goes up Ladera Street for a block, turning right on a wide path across from the end of Cordova Street. Take this path to Cornish Drive at 2⅝ miles where you turn right. Follow this campus road past dormitory buildings and athletic fields as it climbs, curving up the hill. In front of the history and political science building, turn right up a short driveway into a parking lot. Head for the trees across the lot where you pick up a dirt path. You reach the deadend of Garden Lane at 3⅛ miles.

The more difficult option from Sunset Cliffs Blvd. at Ladera Street (it takes patience to find your way through this neglected parkland of informal trails and eroding terrain) takes the dirt path at the end of Sunset Cliffs Blvd. that crosses in front of a little house on the bluff. Go about 500 feet, then turn left up the eroded bluff and into the grove of stunted eucalyptus trees not far up the hill. Turn right through the lower end of the grove to a parking lot. At the far corner of the lot angle down towards the shore. You will soon come to a small eroded valley. Turn uphill along the valley's edge and circle around the top. Just past the valley, take the informal trail right down into a ravine and up the other side to a ball field. Walk along the uphill side of the field. At the far end turn right and angle toward the shore. The trail curves above a lone palm tree and heads directly toward a fence. Turn left at the military base fence and follow the steep well worn, informal path up the hill along a ravine on you left, then down into the head of the ravine. The trail follows the base of a cliff, then climbs steeply up an incline for 50 feet. At the top Garden Lane lies 100 feet across a flat area at 3⅜ miles (so the difficult route adds ¼ mile to the total).

From the end of Garden Lane, the CCT follows quiet residential streets over to Point Loma Marina. From Garden Lane jog right on Catalina Blvd. briefly, then

San Diego Bay and downtown from near Point Loma.

go left on Rosecroft Lane, left on Silvergate Avenue, right on Dupont Street, left on Gage Street and right on Jennings Street. Go left on Bangor Place then immediately turn right on Lucinda Street where you have the first view of Mexico twenty miles south, with downtown San Diego and the harbor not far to the east.

At the bottom of Lucinda Street, jog right on Harbor View Place briefly, then make a hard left down Armada Terrace to go right on Bessemer Street. At its end turn left along the shoreline path and come out on Anchorage Lane at 4⅞ miles. Walk Anchorage to its end, turn left on Shelter Island Drive for a block, then go right along Scott Street briefly. You then turn right on Dickens Street into the sports fishing marina. Walk along the dockside businesses, then make your way across a parking lot to Harbor Drive. Turn right and walk the sidewalk past the Navy's anti-sub warfare school and over a bridge. Beyond the bridge turn right into Spanish Landing Park at 6⅜ miles. Walk the shoreline pathway to the main entrance road to the San Diego International Airport across Harbor Drive. Pick up the bike path here and follow it east along the harbor. After the bike path and Harbor Drive turn south along the Embarcadero, you pass several historic ships including the impressive three-masted *Star of India* built in the 1870s. The section ends at 10⅛ miles at the Broadway Pier where you'll find the ferry to Coronado for the next section's adventure.

SUGGESTED ROUND TRIPS AND LOOPS: Drive or walk out to Cabrillo National Monument to visit an historic lighthouse, take in the visitor center and learn about the voyage of Juan Cabrillo in 1542 as he explored the California coast, or walk a trail through healthy stands of coastal sage scrub. The walk from the CCT route to the monument and back is about 6 miles round trip from the corner of Garden Lane and Catalina Blvd. Recent proposals call for a loop trail on Point Loma but for the present you must walk or drive the road out and back. The views are stunning from the high ridge of the point where much of the military reservation preserves the natural environment.

At the end of Bessemer Street, turn right (instead of left as on the route) on the shoreline path. It skirts the bay shore for 1½ miles before ending at a military fence. At one time the path connected to a street, now blocked by a private security fence.

SECTION 10
Downtown San Diego Waterfront to Hotel del Coronado

DISTANCE: 3 miles plus a 15-minute ferry boat ride (4.8 kilometers).

OPEN TO: Hikers, bicyclists.

SURFACE: Paved trail, sidewalk.

ACCESS POINT: Broadway Pier.

HOW TO GET THERE: Broadway Pier is on Harbor Drive at Broadway in downtown San Diego just off Interstate 5.

OTHER ACCESS: Coronado Tidelands Regional Park and all along the street route in Coronado.

DIFFICULTY: Easy.

ELEVATION GAIN/LOSS: Negligible.

CAUTIONS: San Diego-Coronado Bay Bridge allows no pedestrians or bicycles.

FURTHER INFORMATION: San Diego-Coronado Ferry (619)234-4111.

FACILITIES: Urban amenities abound along the route.

HOSTELS: San Diego has two hostels, Point Loma (619)223-4778 and Downtown (619)525-1531.

LODGING: Downtown San Diego and Coronado both offer many choices.

MAP: See page 342.

The land surrounding the natural harbor now called San Diego Bay was the home of the Yuman-language Kumeyaay people for at least a thousand years, perhaps ten thousand or more. The Kumeyaay were prospering in this land of aquatic bounty and mild climate when Juan Cabrillo sailed into the bay in 1542 and stayed for six days, claiming the land he called San Miguel for Spain. Sixty years later Sebastian Vizcaino visited the area and renamed it San Diego.

Though it wasn't until 1769 that the Spaniards finally established a settlement here, San Diego still became California's and the entire west coast's first European town. Still, it remained a rather sleepy village until gold was discovered in the mountains to the east during the late 1800s when San Diego first became a boom town. The railroad arrived soon after and since then the boom has continued almost unabated. In the early 1900s the U.S. Navy discovered the San Diego Bay, building ample facilities and eventually making San Diego the permanent home of the West Coast fleet. For years San Diego was first and foremost a Navy town. Now with a growing population of 1.25 million and military and defense industry downsizing, San Diego has become, though still nominally a Navy town, primarily the center of a vast outdoor playground. People here tend to be outdoors whenever they can, making good use of the city's numerous parks, the county's 76 miles of shoreline and the vast desert and mountain parks to the east.

This short interesting section samples the heart of this vast playground, beginning on the bustling waterfront beside the high-rise downtown and ending at the Hotel del Coronado ("Hotel Del"), the historic and totemic symbol of local tourism. This section's excursion includes a ferry boat ride across busy San Diego Bay, stunning views of downtown San Diego, plenty of tourist oriented shops and the tranquil gardens and sparkling waterfront of affluent Coronado, an "island" that's really a peninsula.

Start out by buying an inexpensive one-way ticket for the ferry that chugs from the Broadway Pier to Coronado every half hour. After the 15 minute crossing, leave the ferry and turn left on the multi-use path along the concrete walkway past boutiques, shops and restaurants. The path reaches the shoreline at ¼ mile, then passes several hotels before reaching Coronado Tidelands Regional Park, a big grassy recreation park with a small beach on San Diego Bay. Follow the multi-use path down coast with views of San Diego Bay. Beyond the park, the path passes under the San Diego-Coronado Bridge at one mile and turns right to follow a fence along the edge of the municipal golf course.

The multi-use path ends at Glorietta Blvd. where the CCT turns left. Either walk along the edge of the golf course on the grass or on the sidewalk across the street. Glorietta curves gently to the left, then makes a sweeping half circle around 2 miles before reaching the municipal tennis courts. Beyond the courts at 2⅝ miles you'll find a bike path with a sign marked "IMPERIAL BEACH." This path follows the entire south end of San Diego Bay.

Our route continues on Glorietta Blvd., crossing busy Silver Strand Blvd. at the crosswalk. Turn right and walk the sidewalk along Silver Strand Blvd. briefly, then turn left into the main vehicle entrance for the Hotel del Coronado where our route ends at 3 miles in front of the grand front entrance of the Hotel Del, bustling with arriving guests, porters and valet parking attendants. The huge hotel, one of the largest wooden structures in the United States, was built in 1888 in grand Victorian style. It remains a premiere west coast hotel, having attracted celebrities, eleven presidents and countless tourists from its inception. You can check out the spiffy grounds, luxurious interiors and the museum in the basement to get a full appreciation of the immensity of the structure.

SUGGESTED ROUND TRIPS AND LOOPS: Take the ferry from San Diego and hike the route described above, tour the Hotel Del, walk up to a mile north on the beach and back, then return to the ferry via Coronado's main street, Orange Avenue, for a 7-mile loop. Another choice from the Hotel del Coronado is to walk the white wide beach north to the fence of the military reservation and back for a 2-mile round trip.

SECTION 11
Hotel del Coronado to Imperial Beach Pier

DISTANCE: 8⅛ miles (13.1 kilometers).

OPEN TO: Hikers. Bicyclists on bike path.

SURFACE: Beach or paved bike path.

ACCESS POINT: Coronado Beach at Hotel del Coronado.

HOW TO GET THERE: Take the San Diego-Coronado Bay Bridge (Highway 75) to Coronado and turn right on Orange Avenue. After Orange Avenue turns south to become Silver Strand Blvd., you can't miss the hotel on the right.

OTHER ACCESS: Silver Strand State Beach.

DIFFICULTY: Easy.

ELEVATION GAIN/LOSS: Negligible.

CAUTIONS: The beach south of Coronado is sometimes closed for military maneuvers.

FURTHER INFORMATION: For Coronado City Beach and Coronado Shores Beach call Coronado Recreation Services (619)522-7342, for Silver Strand State Beach call District HQ (858)642-4200, for Imperial Beach call the Imperial Beach Lifeguard Station (619)595-3954.

FACILITIES: Urban amenities at both ends. Water, restrooms, picnic tables and parking at Silver Strand State Beach.

HOSTELS: San Diego has two hostels, Point Loma (619)223-4778 and Downtown (619)525-1531.

LODGING: Coronado and Imperial Beach have a variety of accommodations.

One long straight beach describes this route from the affluence of Coronado to the working class town of Imperial Beach, the southernmost town on the California coast, just a few miles from the Mexican border. If you are one of the hearty few walking the entire length of the coast, then here on this beach it might dawn on you that you're near the end of your journey after three months of trekking.

After you've looked around the Hotel Del taking in the sights and history of this Victorian spectacle, or checked out the old historic neighborhood in the hotel area, make your way through the hotel grounds out to the wide sandy beach and head south. After passing several huge multi-story condominium buildings on and beside the beach, you reach open beach around ¾ mile. You are on the Pacific shore of the narrow sandspit peninsula that separates San Diego Bay from the open ocean. Here the peninsula is less than ¼ mile wide, with the entire promontory rising less than 20 feet above sea level.

For the next 2⅞ miles ahead the peninsula is held by the U.S. Navy as their Amphibious Training Base. If military training activity from the base facilities

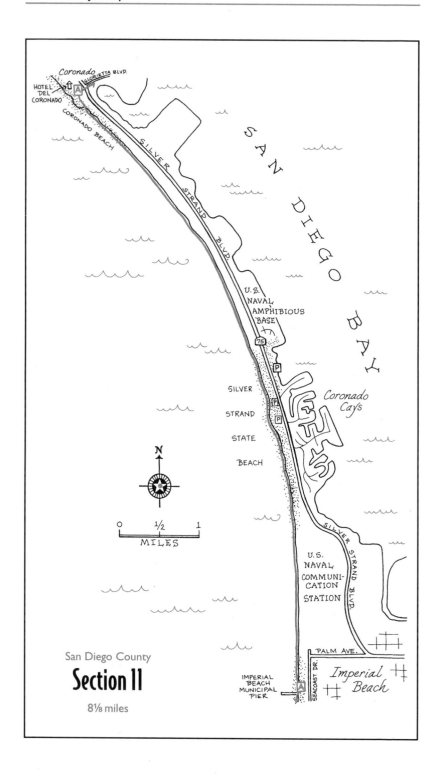

Coronado
GLORIETTA BLVD.
HOTEL DEL CORONADO
CORONADO BEACH
SILVER STRAND BLVD.

SAN DIEGO BAY

U.S. NAVAL AMPHIBIOUS BASE

75

P

Coronado Cays

SILVER

STRAND

STATE

BEACH

P

P

N

0   ½   1
MILES

SILVER STRAND BLVD.

U.S. NAVAL COMMUNICATION STATION

PALM AVE.

IMPERIAL BEACH MUNICIPAL PIER

SEACOAST DR.

Imperial Beach

San Diego County

Section 11

8⅛ miles

behind the low dunes occupies the beach, then return to Hotel Del and take the bike path paralleling Silver Strand Blvd., then pick up the beach again at Silver Strand State Beach. If you can proceed, it's best to stay close to the water on this stretch. Except during training exercises, the beach, little used by any but strollers and runners, seems remote with only the wind and crashing waves for company. Around 3 miles the eastern side of the peninsula has a private housing development, so you may see a few more people on the beach.

You reach Silver Strand State Beach at 3⅝ miles with restrooms and water just ahead. Continue along the tideline of the beach. The long, skinny park facility is popular with sunbathers, swimmers and surfers and also with some of the residents of the Coronado Cays housing development on the peninsula's east shore around 4⅜ miles. You finally leave Silver Strand State Beach at 5⅝ miles.

As you continue along the north end of Imperial Beach, the peninsula broadens, allowing Silver Strand Blvd. to finally veer away from the beach, leaving you with the roaring surf as the main soundtrack. Behind the dunes around 6¾ miles, you can see the huge antennae for a U.S. Naval Communication Station. At 7¼ miles you cross the city limits into quiet Imperial Beach, with houses lining the top of the strand. Continue down the beach to the Imperial Beach Municipal Pier and section's end at 7¾ miles.

SUGGESTED ROUND TRIPS & LOOPS: From either end of the section or from Silver Strand, walk along the beach for as long as you like and return.

SECTION 12
Imperial Beach Pier to Mexican Border, Border Field State Park

DISTANCE: 3½ miles (5.6 kilometers).

OPEN TO: Hikers.

SURFACE: Beach.

ACCESS POINT: Imperial Beach Pier.

HOW TO GET THERE: From Interstate 5 about 9 miles south of San Diego, take the Palm Avenue exit and go 3 miles west. Turn left on Ocean Lane and go .25 mile to the pier.

OTHER ACCESS: South end of Seacoast Street, Border Field State Park.

SOUTH END ACCESS: Exit Interstate 5 south of Imperial Beach and 2 miles north of the border onto Dairy Mart Road and head south. At the end of Dairy Mart in 1.25 miles, turn right and head west on Monument Road for 4 miles to road's end and the parking lot for Border Field State Park.

DIFFICULTY: Easy.

ELEVATION GAIN/LOSS: Negligible.

CAUTIONS: The Tijuana River mouth may be too deep to ford at high tide or high runoff. Also the river is notoriously polluted because it runs through Tijuana, a

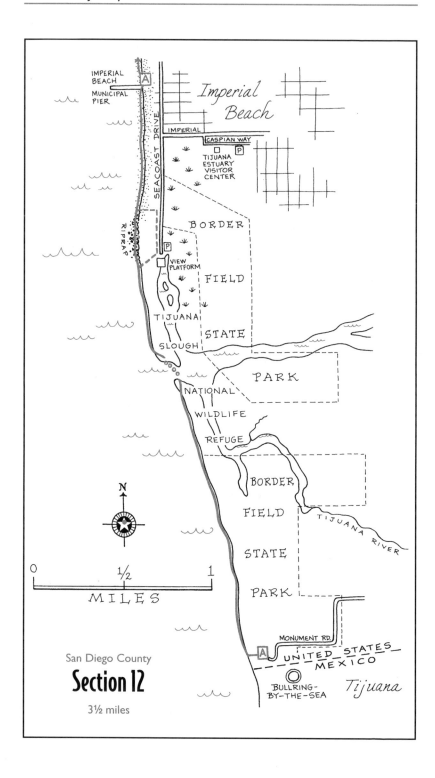

IMPERIAL BEACH
MUNICIPAL PIER

A

SEACOAST DRIVE

Imperial Beach

IMPERIAL

CASPIAN WAY

P

TIJUANA ESTUARY VISITOR CENTER

RIPRAP

P

VIEW PLATFORM

BORDER

FIELD

STATE

TIJUANA

SLOUGH

PARK

NATIONAL

WILDLIFE

REFUGE

BORDER

FIELD

STATE

PARK

TIJUANA RIVER

N

0   ½   1

M I L E S

San Diego County

Section 12

3½ miles

MONUMENT RD.

A

UNITED STATES
MEXICO

BULLRING-
BY-THE-SEA

Tijuana

border town with major sewer problems. Illegal immigration from Mexico remains a dilemma, but a heavy U.S. Border Patrol presence has recently reduced the flow of illegals in this area. The dunes area is closed to protect bird breeding habitat.

FURTHER INFORMATION: For Imperial Beach, call Imperial Beach Lifeguard Station (619)423-8328, for Border Field State Park, call Tijuana Estuary Visitor Center (619)575-3613.

FACILITIES: Imperial Beach has parking, restrooms and water near the pier plus cafes and stores nearby. Border Field State Park has restrooms, picnic tables and parking.

LODGING: Imperial Beach has several motels and hotels.

After the convoluted route through the urban sprawl of San Diego, this last CCT section encounters a windswept natural preserve of wetlands and an estuary backed by rugged desert hills. The natural environment here is blemished yet intact. Sewage and sedimentation severely pollute the 2500-acre Tijuana Marine Estuary. The river waters and the lovely crashing waves on the beach remain much too polluted to swim in. However, efforts by U.S. and Mexican officials in recent years have improved sewage disposal in Tijuana and controlled sedimentation on both sides of the border. Recent plans by the U.S. Immigration Service to rebuild the border fence into a massive structure requiring severe grading would result in further damage to the estuary. The fence also stands as a terrible symbol of the contrast between the Mexican and United States economies. Illegal immigration continues in spite of the "keep out" signaled by the fence.

So far, the beach front part of the working class town of Imperial Beach remains the same as it has for years, relatively uncrowded and distinctly unbusy. Planning is under way, however, for a massive "Pier Plaza Renovation," dubbed Surfhenge by the locals. For now the pier is still the main attraction when the fish are biting. Fisherfolk may catch bonita, mackerel, perch, halibut and a variety of other fish from the pier. Imperial Beach is also popular with surfers, being one of the few San Diego area beaches remaining with no restrictions on surfing.

For a good vantage point from which to survey this last section of the CCT, walk out on the Imperial Beach Pier. Down coast you can see the border fence jutting out into the surf. Behind it looms the Bullring by the Sea, home to the Mexican passion of bullfighting.

Head south from the pier on the wide beach. Beyond ¾ mile you encounter riprap in front of a housing development. You can walk the tideline past the rocks unless the tide is high. At high tide detour up one of the short streets to follow Seacoast Drive south to its end. Seacoast Drive fronts the estuary. At the street's end sits a wildlife viewing platform overlooking Oneonta Slough. From here, the detour returns to the beach. Continue south along the tideline toward the river mouth. Stay off the protected dune habitat.

You reach the mouth of the Tijuana River around 1⅞ miles, which usually requires a challenging crossing. At low tide during the dry season you may be able to wade or walk a sand bar across. If you wade, be advised the water may be

The Fence and the Mexico-U.S. Border

The last three miles of the California Coastal Trail south from the town of Imperial Beach follow the beach adjacent to the Tijuana River National Estuarine Research Reserve (TRNERR). You can't miss the end of the journey at Border Field State Park. A huge fence made out of foot-thick pipes descends from the bluff into the surf, marking the border between Mexico and the United States of America. It denotes an abrupt and unsightly end to a remarkable trail tracing one of the world's great coastlines. Across the border the decrepit buildings of the city of Tijuana fill the landscape. The "Bullring by the Sea" sits just beyond the fence on the coastal bluffs.

The fence defines more than a line on a map or a different set of cultural values. For one, it symbolizes official U.S. policy towards a friendly neighbor, a policy meant to stop illegal immigration by Mexicans seeking employment in the robust American economy. Plans by the U.S Border Patrol to strengthen the fence not only represent the rising zeal to keep out Mexican citizens, but also signal an uncaring attitude towards the sensitive marsh lands and hills inland from the sea along the border.

For many years the border area suffered from a host of problems. Massive illegal immigration created equally huge enforcement problems for the Border Patrol. At the same time, the extensive wetlands along the Tijuana border and the watershed of the Tijuana River suffered severe pollution and erosion problems. The proposed solution to immigration threatens to unravel years of efforts to clean up the watershed while heightening bi-national tensions. Congress authorized the Border Patrol to build a second and bigger fence and even a third one. The new 15-foot-high fence plan, to run 14 miles east from the ocean to the Otay Mesa, includes an all weather road between the fences with sensing devices and lighting. The project threatens newly acquired and existing parkland. Cut and fill of the hills and gullies would create serious erosion problems for the estuary and destroy sensitive habitat. Equally alarming, the law allows for the waiver of any environmental review.

This mammoth project comes in spite of recent doubling of border patrol agents and a sharply declining arrest of immigrants in the zone. Now much immigration occurs inland through Cleveland National Forest. The immigrants create new trails and campsites, and they are jeopardized by rough terrain and cold weather.

None of this sits well with organizations concerned with the health of the TRNERR or with relations with our Mexican neighbors. For sixteen years the Tijuana River Management Agency, made up of ten agencies and organizations from both sides of the border, has spent around $15 million to restore the natural resources and improve access to parklands.

The summer of 1998 saw no engineering plans nor any environmental documents submitted to state or local agencies even though 3½ miles of the eastern portion have already been built by the U.S. Army Corp of Engineers. This in spite of the fact that much of the fence project lies on land designated within the city of San Diego's Multiple Species Conservation Program, TRNERR, and Border Field State Park. The coastal segment of the project comes under the jurisdiction of the Coastal Management Act as managed by the California Coastal Commission. Mexican agencies involved in environmental cleanup and conservation received no notice of the project. Many groups have awakened to the threat to this sensitive landscape and now demand that environmental assessments be made and that other less severe and more humane solutions be found to the problem of immigration.

severely polluted. However, don't let the river stop you less than 2 miles from the border. If the river is too deep to cross near its mouth, you can pack a small one person raft and 200 feet of light rope. If your party consists of more than one person, then tie rope at each end of the raft. The lead person must paddle across while the rope plays out. Then the other hikers pull the raft back while the first person plays out the rope, then the lead person pulls the next person across.

Once you've solved the crossing, make a dash for the border on the wide, pleasant, empty beach. You reach the tall imposing border fence at 3¼ miles. Across the fence you can glimpse the bull ring and part of the immense, sprawling city of Tijuana.

If you are finishing a walk of the entire coast, you may feel the way Coastwalk's Whole Hikers did at the end of their 112-day walk on September 20, 1996, after 1156 miles. With elation we all touched the fence together and stuck our feet through the bars to step on Mexican sand. We were greeted by a Mexican couple who had heard about our arrival and congratulated us on the journey. After the tearful, happy ending, the group retired to the Tijuana Estuary Visitor Center where 70 people celebrated the successful journey with awards, speeches and a delicious Mexican banquet.

When you're ready to leave the beach and bid farewell to the coast, walk east to find the parking lot and restrooms on top of the bluff at 3½ miles. A stone marker here commemorates the establishment of the border in 1849.

SUGGESTED ROUND TRIPS AND LOOPS: Visit the Tijuana Estuary Visitor Center at 301 Caspian Way in Imperial Beach to see displays on wildlife and the estuary. About four miles of trails around the estuary start at the Visitor Center.

Coastwalk Whole Hikers celebrate their arrival at the Mexican border after an exciting long walk.

More About the California Coastal Trail

"California's beautiful coastline serves as a commons for all the people."
—Bill Kortum, Coastwalk founder

The California Constitution guarantees the public's right to access to the state's navigable waters. Courts have ruled that this includes the state's tidelands. In fact, the State of California owns the tidelands and submerged lands seaward of the mean high tideline.

The State Lands Commission has administered the state's tidelands since 1938. They use the average of normal tides over the past 19 years and an analysis of what causes shoreline changes over time to establish the mean high tideline. While this formula is complex, you can safely follow this general rule:

At the least you have the right to walk on the wet beach. Of course where lands are in public ownership you have the right to walk on a much larger area along the coastline.

The California Coastal Trail matches any long distance trail in the country for scenic beauty, for diversity, for the countless features of human and natural history it encounters. The way the California coast unfolds along the CCT rivals the drama offered by any trail — redwoods to cactus on one trail, the Pacific Ocean nearly always in view.

The CCT is a state of mind as well as a physical path through the landscape. Even if you never walk the whole, only parts, you can envision the trail going beyond your last steps of a day hiking. You realize you could keep going, that tomorrow you could head on down the trail to Mexico or up to Oregon, an alluring possibility. Each day would bring new beach, different dunes or bluffs, another river flowing into the ocean, or a new town.

The CCT may be the most diverse trail, and one of the most used trails on the planet. It traverses beaches, bluffs, marine terraces, rocky tidelands and mountains. The CCT encompasses single track and multi-use paths, and traverses sand, pavement, rocks and sidewalks through wilderness and cities. You can walk remote trails and beaches where few tread, or walk southern California beaches visited by millions annually. On given parts of it you will see backpackers, horse riders, bicyclists, runners, wheelchair users, roller skaters and babies in strollers. The trail passes through federal, state, county and city parks, through special districts and military bases and in a few places crosses private land on easements. In some areas the trail is unbroken for many miles and in others it is broken up by the barriers of private property and geological features.

Although the CCT is not yet complete and much of the route is unsigned, Coastwalk and Bored Feet were encouraged by the outpouring of public, media and government support for the 1996 Whole Hike. This support told us the time had come to write the first complete guide to the CCT so that hikers could negotiate the route successfully despite the trail's incomplete status. For hikers to have a complete guide, we've needed to include lengthy sections that can only be walked on road shoulders. The ultimate goal is to have the entire trail as close to the coast as possible on a designated pathway, even if it's a sidewalk through a town.

In the enlightened future of our nation, when hiking, whether in wilderness, through parks or greenways, in cities, towns or villages, is understood as both a physical and spiritual necessity for health and sanity, then these barriers will fall away, and all Americans will understand the fullest and richest meaning of freedom, the freedom to experience fully the gifts of our magnificent planet earth.

Chronology of the California Coastal Trail

1972   California voters pass the citizen's initiative, the Coastal Protection Act, affirming the public's right to access to the coast. One of the manifestations of this right was public discussion of the idea of a California Coastal Trail.

1975   The California Coastal Plan of 1975 identifies the Coastal Trail as part of the public's right to access to our coast. The Plan, drawn up and approved by the California Coastal Commission, includes Policy #145 calling for establishing a Coastal Trail for public access. The legislature approves this as part of the California Resources Code.

1976   The California legislature passes the California Coastal Act which further details the public's right to access to the California coast. The Act also calls for establishing the Coastal Conservancy.

1983   Coastwalk is founded in Sonoma County with the first hike including 70 people on a 60-mile walk from Gualala to Bodega Bay.

1988   About 400 miles of the California Coastal Trail are complete and walkable thanks largely to efforts within the California State Parks Department, the National Park Service and the Coastal Conservancy.

1990   The Coastal Trail includes 730 miles "providing public access and an unmatched experience of the state's natural and urban environments."

1991   Coastwalk's Board of Directors officially states that one of the group's primary goals is to complete the California Coastal Trail.

1992   The Coastal Conservancy and Coastwalk collaborate on a 36-page booklet, *The California Coastal Trail: Missing Links & Completed Segments.*

1994   Coastwalk and the Coastal Conservancy produce a twenty-minute slide-and-sound show, *Dream and Reality: The California Coastal Trail.*

1996   Coastwalk and the Coastal Conservancy sponsor and Coastwalk leads the California Coastal Trail Whole Hike, the first ever group walk of the entire coast from the Oregon border to the Mexican border.

1998   Coastwalk and Bored Feet Press co-publish Volume One of the first complete guide to the California Coastal Trail. This project determines that as of spring 1998, about 980 miles of the California Coastal Trail are essentially complete, following existing trails and beaches or back roads and city sidewalks reasonably safe for walking. The other 215 miles follow highways on provisional routes not recommended but possible to walk.

1999   California Governor Gray Davis nominates the California Coastal Trail as the state's Millennium Legacy Trail, and the federal Department of Transportation officially so designates the CCT.

2000   Coastwalk and Bored Feet Press co-publish Volume Two of the first complete guide to the California Coastal Trail. Coastwalk celebrates the CCT as California's Millennium Legacy Trail and accelerates efforts to complete the trail. Voters pass Proposition 12, approving $2.1 billion for parks, coast and open space, including $5 million for the California Coastal Trail.

Help Complete the California Coastal Trail

Conservation and trails go hand in hand for many hikers. Most people hike both for health and to enjoy nature. To have pleasant places to hike, we must work to protect the environment. California is continually assaulted by development threats. Many elected officials seek office to support growth forces while others run to protect natural values. To support the Coastal Trail and the California environment, ask your candidates and officials these important questions:

Will they *support adequate funding for parks and trails?*
Will they *fight development in sensitive habitats and open space?*
Will they *support acquisition of parks, natural lands and open space?*
Will they *make parks, open space and trails a part of approved growth projects?*

Government cannot do it alone. Hundreds of organizations advocate for parks and recreation users. Support groups that help parks, develop urban parks and greenways, and protect habitat, plants and wildlife.

Other ways you can help complete the CCT:

❏ Tell your friends and co-workers about the CCT or give them this book.

❏ Contact your state legislators and officials and tell them you think it's high time the CCT be completed and clearly signed.

❏ Talk to park rangers and tell them you care about the CCT.

❏ Volunteer for trail building and maintenance projects on the CCT.

❏ Organize some friends and spend a day picking up litter along the CCT.

❏ Support a coastal land trust and tell them you want to see completion of the CCT become one of their priorities.

❏ Become aware of and involved in coastal issues that threaten the natural splendor of California's coast.

❏ Contact your congressional representatives and tell them you want California's coastal military bases to allow the CCT along their shorelines. Whenever such bases are decommissioned, work to insure that the new land use includes a route for the CCT.

❏ Sign up for a Coastwalk along the CCT. Coastwalk leads CCT hikes every summer in each of California's fifteen coastal counties.

❏ Take a friend on a hike along the California Coastal Trail.

To support completion of the CCT or get information on trail and conservation groups, contact Coastwalk at 1-800-550-6854 or on the web at www. coastwalk.org/coastwalk.

Through-Hiking the CCT

If you're contemplating a long distance hike along the California Coastal Trail, you need to consider many things and do a lot of planning to prepare for your trip. If you plan to hike the entire CCT in one continuous trek, your planning and preparations must be particularly detailed. Coastwalk's 1996 "Whole Hike" took 96 hiking days plus 16 rest days to cover the entire 1194 miles. That amounts to an average of 12.4 miles per hiking day. That would be "The Journey of a Lifetime" for all but the most experienced long distance hiker.

The CCT covers many different kinds of terrain and passes through extremely remote, rugged terrain as well as urban landscapes. Different sections require extremely different levels of hiking ability. If you plan to hike the entire CCT, you need to start training unless you're already extremely fit.

You can conduct a long distance hike several ways. The most difficult is backpacking the entire trail. Perhaps the easiest would be to use lodgings along the way and eat out daily, but you'll find no lodgings for spans of 24 to 50 miles along the Lost Coast, at Point Reyes and Big Sur, so you'd need another way to cover those miles. If you plan your hike around lodgings, you'll need advance reservations for most places during summer. The lodging/cafe option requires a healthy budget.

However you do your long distance trek, here are some suggestions on possible ways to go, followed by some essentials to consider.

Some Options

Use a support vehicle: Vans shuttled the 1996 Whole Hike group to the nearest campsite or hostel, returning them to the CCT the next day to resume the walk. A solo hiker or small group might find a friend to be driver, cook and/or errand runner. A larger group could use a van, hiring someone to provide support. People using a support vehicle will still need to backpack the Lost Coast and Point Reyes.

Backpack: The freedom of backpacking means you don't have to rely on any vehicle support, but the downside is carrying extra weight. Also, official campsites may not be available when you need them. In that situation, the options are

staying in lodging or quietly finding a hidden spot to sleep.
Hybrid Plan: Combine various options into your own plan. Backpack areas requiring it and those with good camping. Use van support/lodgings elsewhere. **A fourth option:** Do as much of the trail as time permits each year. This book serves as a handy way to keep track of progress over the years.

Essentials

Being prepared is fundamental for any long distance hiking trip. We'll mention some of the most important essentials. Keep in mind, however, that entire books have been written on the logistics of such trips. For longer treks you should consult one. Several good books discuss planning through-hikes on the Pacific Crest and Appalachian trails. These aren't guidebooks, but books on how to make a long distance trek. Most of their planning information will be useful.

Get in shape before you start. While this isn't a mountain expedition, be prepared to hike some long days and rugged terrain. Parts of the CCT cross slippery tidal rocks and climb and descend steep hills. Walk every day starting several months before departure, and increase distances gradually.

Have the right gear, not just a lot. Boots must be comfortable but not necessarily expensive. I wore out two pairs of $30 light hiking boots from Oregon to Mexico. Boots with good ankle support will pay off on rougher sections. Good socks such as the new long wearing, comfortable socks of blended fibers are essential. Carry sandals for wading streams. Comfortable camp shoes are invaluable for resting boot-weary feet. Carry a fluorescent vest for times you must road walk.

Bring clothes to dress in layers to adjust for temperature and weather changes. See Preparing for Your Hikes on page 20. Bring two pairs of quick-drying long pants so you can switch when a pair gets wet.

Carry a first aid kit including any personal medicines you may need. Include an ample supply of moleskin to protect against blisters.

A comfortable pack is essential. Even with a support vehicle you'll need a sturdy day pack roomy enough for day gear and lunch. If you're backpacking and camping the entire way, you'll need an expedition pack for treks over 100 miles. If your backpack is only for sections requiring backpacking, a mid-size pack roomy enough for five-day trips is sufficient. Packs come in many sizes, shapes, and suspension systems, but don't skimp if you'll be carrying it many miles. Before your trek, be sure to hike a ten- or twelve-mile day or two with your pack loaded with the full weight you plan to carry.

Depending on the nature of your trek, you may want a sleeping bag, sleeping pad, lightweight backpacking stove, cookware, eating utensils, good light tent, ground cloth, clothesline, and numerous other items. In addition to this section, be sure to consult the list on page 20.

When you're on your long distance trek, pay close attention to the weather and to ocean conditions. Don't get caught by a "sleeper wave."

Plan boat crossings in advance or plan on adding miles to walk around river mouths, bays and harbors.

On longer treks, always have a tentative plan of what you can reasonably hike during the next two or three days, including where you'll spend the night. In the busy summer season, call ahead if you think a reservation might be needed.

Further Reading

(o.p.) denotes out of print

Adams, Rick and Louise McCorkle, *The California Highway 1 Book*, Ballantine Books, New York, 1985. (o.p.)

Berrill, N.J. and Jacquelyn Berrill, *1001 Questions Answered About the Seashore*, Dover Publications, New York, 1976.

Big Sur Land Trust, *Monterey Bay State Seashore, a Study for the Preservation of the Monterey Bay Dunes*, Big Sur Land Trust, Carmel, California, 1992. (o.p.)

California Coastal Commission, *California Coastal Access Guide*, Fifth edition, University of California Press, Berkeley, 1997.

California Coastal Commission, *California Coastal Resource Guide*, University of California Press, Berkeley, 1987. (o.p.)

California, A Guide to the Golden State, Federal Writers Project Staff, State of California, American Guide Series, Somerset Publishers, Santa Barbara, 1980, reprint of 1939 edition.

California Escapes, Handbook to California State Parks, American Park Network, San Francisco, 1997. (o.p.)

Chase, J. Smeaton, *California Coast Trails: A Horseback Adventure from Mexico to Oregon*, Tioga Publishing, Palo Alto, California, 1987, reprint of 1913 edition. (o.p.)

Citizen's Guide to Plastics in the Ocean: More Than a Litter Problem, Fourth edition, Center for Marine Conservation, Washington, D.C., 1994. (o.p.)

Comprehensive Management and Use Plan, de Anza National Historic Trail, 1996.

Denninger, Melanie, "Bolsa Chica Quandary," *California Coast & Ocean*, Volume 12, No. 4, (Winter 1996–1997).

Donley, Michael W., and others, *Atlas of California*, Pacific Book Center, Culver City, California, 1979. (o.p.)

Explore, a series of pamphlets for the Year of the Coast, U.S. Army Corps of Engineers, San Francisco, 1980. (o.p.)

Gales, Donald Moore, *Wildflowers, Weeds, Wildlife and Weather*, Third edition, FoldaRoll Press, Palos Verdes Peninsula, California, 1988. (o.p.)

Gordon, Burton L., *Monterey Bay Area: Natural History and Cultural Imprints*, Third edition, Otter Books, Santa Cruz, California, 1996.

Griggs, Gary, and Lauret Savoy, *Living with the California Coast*, Duke University Press, Durham, North Carolina, 1985. (o.p.)

Gudde, Erwin G., *California Place Names*, Fourth edition, University of California Press, Berkeley, 1998.

Gustaitis, Rasa, "California's Vanishing Beaches," *California Coast & Ocean*, Volume 12, No. 1, (Spring 1996).

Hedgepeth, Joel, *Introduction to Seashore Life of the San Francisco Bay Region and the Coast of Northern California*, Fourth edition, University of California Press, Berkeley, 1970.

Heizer, R.F., and M.A. Whipple, editors, *The California Indians: A Source Book*, Second edition, University of California Press, Berkeley, 1971.

Hewitt, Lonnie and Barbara Moore, *Walking San Diego*, Mountaineers Books, Seattle, 1989.

Iacopi, Robert. *Earthquake Country*, Fourth edition, Fisher Books, Tucson, Arizona, 1996.

Jackson, Ruth. *Combing the Coast: Highway 1 from San Francisco to San Luis Obispo*, Chronicle Books, San Francisco, 1985. (o.p.)

Jaconette, Lucinda, *Monterey Bay and Beyond: The Best of California's Central Coast from Santa Cruz to San Simeon*, Chronicle Books, San Francisco, 1994.

Jorgen, Randolph, *Mountains to Ocean, A Guide to the Santa Monica Mountains National Recreation Area*, Southwest Parks and Monuments Association, Tucson, Arizona, 1995

Kroeber, A. L., *Handbook of the Indians of California*, Dover Publications, New York, 1976, reprint of 1925 edition.

Margolin, Malcolm, *The Ohlone Way: Indian Life in the San Francisco-Monterey Bay Area*, Heyday Books, Berkeley, 1978.

McAuley, Milt, *Guide to the Backbone Trail: Santa Monica Mountains*, Canyon Publishing Company, Canoga Park, California, 1990.

McAuley, Milt, *Hiking Trails of the Santa Monica Mountains*, Sixth edition, Canyon Publishing Company, Canoga Park, California, 1991.

McConnaughey, Bayard H. and Evelyn, *Pacific Coast* (Audubon Society Nature Guide Series), Alfred A. Knopf, New York, 1985.

McKinney, John, *Walking the California Coast, One Hundred Adventures Along the West Coast*, HarperCollins, New York, 1994.

Nelson, Sharlene and Ted Nelson, *Umbrella Guide to California Lighthouses*, Epicenter Press, Kenmore, Washington, 1993.

Neuwirth, Donald B., and John J. Osborn Jr., *The California Coast: A Traveler's Companion*, Countryman Press, Woodstock, Vermont, 1998.

Nisbet, Briggs, *The California Coastal Trail: Missing Links & Completed Segments: An Inventory*, California State Coastal Conservancy and Coastwalk, Oakland, 1992. (o.p.)

Peterson, Roger Tory, *Field Guide to Western Birds* (Peterson Field Guide Series), Third edition, Houghton Mifflin, Boston, 1990.

Philipp, Cathy, *On the Trail: Malibu to Santa Barbara*, Cathy Philipp Publishing, Thousand Oaks, California, 1997.

Pocket Guide to California's Public Piers, California Coastal Conservancy, Oakland, 1993. (o.p.)

Puterbaugh, Parke, & Alan Bisbort, *California Beaches,* Second edition, Foghorn Press, Santa Rosa, California, 1999.

Schaffer, Jeffrey P., *Hiking the Big Sur Country: The Ventana Wilderness*, Wilderness Press, Berkeley, 1988.

Stienstra, Tom, *California Camping*, Eleventh edition, Foghorn Press, Santa Rosa, California, 1999.

Wuerthner, George, *California's Wilderness Areas: Volume One: Mountains and Coastal Ranges*, Westcliffe Publishers, Englewood, Colorado, 1997.

Yonay, Ehud, "The Politics of Big Sur," in *The Best of California*, Capra Press, Santa Barbara, 1986.

Acknowledgments

We offer a robust and heartfelt thank you to the hundreds of people who helped create this book. In particular we wish to thank Donna Bettencourt for her meticulous and at times seemingly unending job of editing, Elizabeth Petersen for her elegant design and precise production, Marsha Mello for her beautiful, detailed maps of the California coast, and the Coastwalk Board of Directors of 1996 through 2000 for their enthusiastic support and funding for the project.

The Whole Hikers of 1996 spent 16 weeks together exploring the glories of the California coast and persevering through long days on the trail, too many miles of highway, personality clashes, blisters, aches and pains, yet made it to the border in spite of everything. Without their efforts, we would not have undertaken this immense project. The Whole Hikers were Beverly Backstrom, Marilyn Goeller, Barbara Johnson, Fay Kelley, Al LePage and Richard Nichols. Two other Whole Hikers, Bob Cowell and Dinesh Desai, completed the San Francisco to Mexico portion with the group in 1996, after providing the essential service of scouting and pre-hiking the Oregon to San Francisco leg in autumn 1995 so that the 1996 hike could be successful.

Providing essential planning and support so that the Whole Hikers could complete the Whole Hike were Vivian McFarling, Tom McFarling, Emily DeFalla, Tim Reed and Brenda Nichols. The dozens of other individuals who guided, shuttled, fed and housed the hikers are too numerous to mention here, but we thank them heartily.

Many thanks to the people who reviewed chapters for accuracy and made valuable suggestions: Dan Stefanisko, Steven Dean, John Magee, Jerry Loomis and Arlene Breise for Monterey County, Nancy Graves, Carolyn Pye and Phil Teseri for San Luis Obispo County, Jane Freeburg, Mark Schlenz and Bill Denneen for Santa Barbara County, Tom Maxwell and Burt Elliot for Ventura County, Sunshine, Don Nierlich and Pat Garrow for Los Angeles County, Diane Savage and Mel Savage for Orange County, Steve Kononenko for San Diego County, and Milt McAuley and the Santa Monica Mountains National Recreation Area staff for the Backbone Trail.

People who hiked and helped research parts of the route include Lee Otter for Pebble Beach, John Magee for Garrapata State Park, Garret Tollkuhn and Ken Stanton for the Big Sur high route, Bill Denneen for Point Sal, Jim Blakely for Santa Barbara County, Brenda Nichols for Los Angeles and Bob Jones for Laguna Beach. Others who provided invaluable information include Jan Feldman, Barbara Woyt, Brian Hatfield of California Department of Fish & Game, Becky Siemen of Cayucos Land Conservancy and Pamela Iguchi of Trust for Public Land.

We thank all the people of the California State Parks Department who have kept open and maintained more than 60 coastal parks and beaches in the face of daunting budget cuts. Thanks also to all the other agencies, organizations, individuals and government entities that have worked so hard to create the California Coastal Trail.

With special thanks to Mary Nichols and Peter Douglas for providing their eloquent forewords, and to Liz Petersen, Eden Lorentzen, and Brenda Nichols for putting up with our near total immersion in this project.

Photograph Credits

PAGE	DESCRIPTION	SOURCE
13	Pecho Coast Trail	Bob Lorentzen
21	South end of Big Sur from Buckeye Trail	Richard Nichols
42	Frank L. Wright house at Carmel Beach	Richard Nichols
55	Garrapata cliffs	Richard Nichols
74	Glade, Marble Ranch, Coast Ridge Road	Bob Lorentzen
81	Cone Peak from Vicente Flat Trail	Bob Lorentzen
90	Pacific Valley Headlands	Richard Nichols
97	Point San Luis Lighthouse from Pecho Trail	Bob Lorentzen
112	On the way to San Simeon Point	Richard Nichols
131	Near Islay Point, Montana de Oro State Park	Bob Lorentzen
142	Pismo Beach from Shell Beach	Bob Lorentzen
151	Cliffs east of East Beach, Santa Barbara	Bob Lorentzen
155	The way onto Mussel Rock dune	Bob Lorentzen
156	CCT descends steep gully to Paradise Beach	Richard Nichols
172	South toward Point Conception	Bob Lorentzen
187	South toward Coal Oil Point	Bob Lorentzen
200	Chumash tar seep at Carpinteria State Beach	Bob Lorentzen
205	CCT near Point Mugu	Richard Nichols
209	Rincon Point	Richard Nichols
231	On Santa Monica Mountains Backbone Trail	Richard Nichols
235	Beach at Ventura-Los Angeles County Line	Richard Nichols
237	Dume Cove & S.M. Mtns. from Point Dume	Richard Nichols
244	Zuma Beach from Point Dume	Richard Nichols
256	Sta. Monica Pier & State Beach	Richard Nichols
268	Portuguese Bend Cove from Halfway Point	Richard Nichols
275	Palos Verdes land in turmoil st Sunken City	Richard Nichols
283	Huntington State Beach bluff trail	Diana Savage
294	Crystal Cove State Park	Diana Savage
299	Tunnel between Victoria and Aliso beaches	Richard Nichols
304	View from Dana Point	Richard Nichols
311	Imperial Beach Pier	Richard Nichols
315	San Onofre State Beach	Richard Nichols
329	Flat Rock, Torrey Pines State Beach	Richard Nichols
344	San Diego Bay & downtown	Richard Nichols
353	Whole Hikers celebrate "1150 miles"	Richard Nichols

COVER PHOTOS:

front, top	CCT ascends Point Sal	Bob Lorentzen
front, center	Toward Santa Barbara's Butterfly Beach	Bob Lorentzen
front, bottom	Bixby Bridge, Big Sur	Richard Nichols
back, top	R.H. Meyer State Beach, L.A. County	Richard Nichols
back, bottom	California Coastal sunrise	Richard Nichols

Index

About Coastwalk

In 1982 Bill and Lucy Kortum had an idea—walk the entire Sonoma County coast with 1000 people to emphasize the public's right to access and enjoyment of the California coastline. In 1983 that idea was implemented in a more manageable form by Tom and Vivian McFarling who organized a one-time seven day walk with 70 people. The group walked the 60 miles from Gualala to Bodega Bay in a joyous celebration of the wonder and beauty of the Sonoma coast, also demonstrating that not all the coast was open to the public in spite of Article 10 of the California Constitution guaranteeing public access. Susan Swartz of the Santa Rosa Press Democrat came along and phoned in daily reports which the newspaper published with ample graphics and photos.

This "one time" event remains with us seventeen years later. Everyone had so much fun that it's been repeated every year since. Original Coastwalker Jon Toste exported the idea to Marin County in 1985. In that same year Coastwalk gained non-profit status. By 1991 a paid part-time director was added. In 1994 Coastwalk fulfilled a long held dream to conduct walks in all 15 of California's coastal counties. The Kortums' original idea of 1000 walkers has multiplied as Coastwalk has led thousands along the coast. In 1996 Coastwalk realized yet another dream by conducting the first ever group walk of the entire coastline from the Oregon border to the Mexican border. During that walk the authors first realized that this book needed to be written.

Our "flagship" events, the annual summer walks in each of the fifteen coastal counties, are kept affordable, interesting and fun because of a large group of dedicated, talented and exceptional volunteers. They help for many reasons, but two stand out. First, they derive great pleasure in sharing our beautiful coast with fellow walkers. Second, they believe in Coastwalk's goal of completing the California Coastal Trail and protecting the coastal environment.

We still have much work to do to complete the CCT. Yet our yearly Coastwalks, the 1996 Whole Hike and our continuing and persistent advocacy have had an impact. The Coastal Conservancy has made the CCT a priority while the Coastal Commission lists the CCT as one of its three top priorities in its "Coastal Access Action Plan." In March 2000 a parks bond act for $2.1 billion that includes $5 million in funding for the CCT was overwhelmingly approved by California voters. This funding will substantially increase efforts toward completing the CCT.

To continue our work we depend on the support and participation of the public. We invite you to learn more about Coastwalk. We'd also like to hear about any long distance hikes along the California Coastal Trail, or other experiences you've had along the CCT.

Please write or call us at:

Coastwalk, 1389 Cooper Road, Sebastopol CA 95472.

1-800-550-6854: Call us and leave your name and address for our free brochure of hikes.

Contact us via email at: coastwalk@sonic.net. Our Web page is: www.coastwalk.org/coastwalk. Also check out www.californiacoastaltrail.org.